TOWARDS A SCIENCE OF STATES:
THEIR EVOLUTION AND PROPERTIES

Erik Moberg
www.mobergpublications.se

TABLE OF CONTENTS

Preface to the earlier Amazon e-book

This book is an updated translation of a Swedish book which, entitled "Statsvetenskap", was published in the spring of 2011. The explanation of this Swedish title, as well other material of a kind usually presented in a book's preface, is, however, in this book to a large extent rather displayed in the main text, particularly at the end of chapter 1. Here I can therefore be quite short.

First a technical detail. When indicating years I have used a minus sign rather than the conventional abbreviations BC or B.C. And when there is no risk of misunderstanding I have just omitted the minus sign.

Then, and since this is a translation of a Swedish book, I will once again express my gratitude to those who read and criticized drafts in that context. I will first mention Mikael Gilljam and then, in alphabetical order, Örjan Berner, Eskil Block (1932–2013), Benny Carlson, Karl-Axel Edin, Sören Holmberg, Bengt K Å Johansson, Axel Moberg, Carl-Axel Olsson (1941–2013), Per Strangert and Carl-Johan Westholm. Many thanks for all your contributions!

When working with this English translation I have also had the benefit of support as well as critical comments. In particular I want to mention Mark N. Franklin. He has read the whole manuscript and made many most valuable suggestions for improvements. Thanks Mark for all of that! I also want to thank Andreas Bågenholm for valuable criticism and Reinhold Fahlbeck for persistent and encouraging support.

For the work with this English version of the book I also got a generous grant from Jan Wallander's and Tom Hedelius' Foundation. This helped me a lot and I hereby express my gratitude!

But in spite of all help, and all efforts, there certainly remain faults in the book and it certainly has its shortcomings of various kinds. For these deficiencies I am myself, of course, the only one responsible.

Lövestad, February 22, 2014

Erik Moberg

PREFACE TO THIS CREATESPACE BOOK

In all essentials this book is just a printed version of the earlier e-book. However, since it is published somewhat later, and since we are living in a dynamic world, it has been possible, and also appropriate, to update it in some respects. This relates particularly to the Appendix, but also to some passages about the consequences of the Arab spring in the main text.

Lövestad, January 4, 2015

Erik Moberg

1

THE STATE AS AN INSTITUTION, AND AS AN OBJECT OF STUDY

THE STATE AND THE MONOPOLY OF VIOLENCE

Of all institutions created by man, the state is the most important. The state is a necessary condition for a good and civilized human life. Almost all important human cultural achievements have taken place within states, and all lasting economic growth and development have occurred in states. All other more developed human institutions such as commercial enterprises, public administrations and organizations of various kinds also depend on the state as a prerequisite. Among all institutions the state, therefore, is the principal one.

But all of this holds only for the good state. For even if the state is a necessary condition for human civilization it is by no means a sufficient one. State-power, for certain, is not necessarily good. It is only with the resources of a state, or of a disintegrating former state, that really large scale persecution of human beings, and really widespread brutal cruelty, can be carried out. And that kind of use of power is not only exemplified by the totalitarian regimes of the twentieth century but also, for instance, by ancient Assyria, Chinese Chin (about year −200) and the state of the American Aztecs. States, thus, can be good, but they can also be bad or evil, and they can, obviously, have properties somewhere in between these extremes. World history is full of examples of states of all of these kinds.

But, then, what makes a state a state? What are the defining properties of a state? Certainly the definition, to some extent, has to be vague, but still it seems reasonable that a societal entity, in order to be called a state, should have a certain stability over time, and also have a core geographic area, which it continuously controls, even if the borders otherwise, due to war for instance, may change to some extent. In addition to these properties there is however one more, which in fact is the most important, namely that a state—within its geographical area—

has a monopoly of the use of violence against human beings which is, on the whole, upheld and respected. The most prominent spokesman for this idea about the state is the German social scientist Max Weber (1864–1920) who held that "a state is a human community that (successfully) claims the *monopoly of the legitimate use of physical force* within a given territory".[1] Consequently it is common to talk about the monopoly of violence of a state. All states—good as well as bad or evil ones—have a police force of some kind. This force, with its disposal of weapons, prisons, and so forth, is the most important instrument for exercising the monopoly of violence.

The importance of the monopoly of violence is directly related to the fact that states represent wealth. The permanence over time and the geographical core area I have talked about stand for stability and thereby also for possibilities for development. It becomes possible for human beings to settle, and to cooperate with each other in various ways, and in so doing to become more productive than, for instance, in a nomadic life. But this also entails problems. The concentration of wealth may easily become a temptation for thieves and robbers of various kinds. Individuals living within the society may be tempted to steal from their neighbors. And the prosperous society in its entirety may be an attractive object for attacks and plunder-raids from outside. Threats like these must be warded off if the advantages of permanent residence and cooperation are to materialize, and this requires effective means of violence. It must be possible to stop and disarm gangsters and thieves within the society, and to ward off armed attacks from outside. If there are means of violence for these tasks, then there is also something which may be called a state. The state provides, by means of its monopoly of violence, the stable structure within which people—more or less freely and constructively—can cooperate with each other.

Thus, concerning violence, monopoly or lack of competition is a necessary condition for a good human life. This is worth noticing since monopoly in most other circumstances, at least from a liberal point of view, hardly is desired. In economic markets, for instance, competition is considered beneficial and monopoly harmful. But for the use of violence

---

[1] Weber, p. 78, Weber's italics. The text is included in a speech, Politics as a Vocation, originally given at Munich University in 1918. The source is also available at the Internet.

this is not so. Rather, if the monopoly of violence is not maintained, we will get a chaotic or anarchistic situation, or, in other words, a stateless situation.

It was a situation of this kind that the Englishman Thomas Hobbes (1588–1679) described in his book "Leviathan". According to Hobbes the anarchy could however be avoided if an absolute sovereign was given the power to prevent human beings from fighting each other, and this sovereign was Leviathan—so called by Hobbes with a sea monster in the Old Testament as a model. Using Weber's and our terminology Leviathan, by exercising the necessary monopoly of violence, created order and peace. But stateless and anarchistic situations do not only belong to the world of philosophy and myths. During the passage of world history there have been, at different times and in different places, countless situations of this kind. And they have not disappeared. A contemporary (2014) example—but certainly not the only one—is Africa's Somalia.[2]

A monopoly of violence thus can be used to preserve law and order for the benefit of the inhabitants, and for hindering attacks from outside. But it is not only the case that the monopoly can be used for these purposes. The monopoly itself may also be the object of threats of various kinds. A monopoly of violence is, after all, something utterly powerful, and various kinds of actors may therefore try to challenge it for their own purposes, or even to take hold of it. As long as states have existed there have also been coups directed against the leaderships of these states, as well as efforts to establish new and competing centers of power. Examples from later times are the Sicilian mafia and criminal motorcycle gangs. But monopolies of violence also face other kinds of risks. They may weaken or degenerate in various ways without this being the result of conscious acts directed against the monopoly. A bureaucracy may, for instance, become swollen and ineffective, and this and similar processes may lead to the fall of states.

A different kind of problem is related to the internal laws that are to be upheld. The nature of these laws is by no means given, and they may vary considerably from state to state. The degree to which they affect the personal lives of ordinary people may for instance differ. Obviously a dictatorship, in this respect, usually goes far beyond the limits implied by

[2] For more examples see table 10 in the Appendix.

democratic and liberal values. But even in a modern welfare state it may be possible for special interests, by perfectly legal and democratic means, to engage the monopoly for their own purposes. And this raises the question whether, in such cases, there is a borderline between the use and misuse of the monopoly, and where, if so, that borderline goes. Obviously different persons, depending on their political opinions, may answer this question differently. Here, however, we are only interested in indicating the connection with the monopoly of violence. In the democratic state the reach of the monopoly of violence is not given—like everything else it has to be determined by democratic means.

Another complication is related to the very concept of monopoly of violence. Even in modern democratic states weapons of different kinds are spread among the citizen and in the US, for example, the relevant laws are quite permissive. This, however, does not necessarily mean that there is no monopoly of violence. Usually there are also rules for how the weapons among the citizens may be used, and as long as these rules are respected, the monopoly of violence is, according to the view adopted here, upheld.

STATES OF DIFFERENT KINDS

A state is thus characterized by its monopoly of violence, but this monopoly can, as I have already indicated, be handled in very different ways. We are therefore interested in classifying states, and the classification should, as every classification, not only be simple but also rich in consequences. Here I will start with the classification which is the most common, and probably also the most established, namely the one between dictatorships, oligarchies and democracies. This classification is also, since it was introduced by Plato (427–347) and Aristotle (384–22), the oldest one.[3] Among democracies I will however also make a distinction between direct and representative democracies, and this distinction is at least as important and sharp as those between the other types of states. But Plato and Aristotle obviously could not know about this distinction since the representative democracy began its development about two thousand years after their time. Hence the absence of the distinction

---

[3] Bogdanor, title words "Aristotle" and "Plato".

in their classification—when they were active there was only one type of democracy, the direct one.

I will thus deal with four main types of states. In a dictatorship it is one single person, or possibly a small group of collaborating persons, who controls the monopoly of violence. In an oligarchy this control is instead in the hands of a larger group of people—for instance some leading or dominating families—but still only a very small fraction of the total population. In democracies, finally, the whole adult population takes part, at least in principle, in state decision-making, although in different ways in the two cases. In a direct democracy the population itself comes together—for instance in some open place—in order to discuss common problems and take the relevant decisions. Obviously—in this case—the population must not be too big. In a representative democracy the decision-making is rather left to elected representatives who meet in some kind of assembly. Sweden has, for instance, its parliament with one chamber or house, in Swedish called the "Riksdag", and in the US there is the Congress with its two chambers, the Senate and the House of Representatives.

Clearly this classification of states is simple, but its richness in consequences is perhaps less obvious. Its being so is however due to the fact that the degree to which a state is governed by rules depends on whether it is a dictatorship, an oligarchy, a direct democracy or a representative democracy. In particular the rules for succession are interesting in this context, even if the rules for governing in general also are important. In dictatorships these rules, to the extent that they exist at all, are casual and hardly compelling. In representative democracies, on the contrary, they are detailed, exact, compelling and, on the whole, respected. In oligarchies and direct democracies the rules, and the respect for them, have usually been somewhere in between these extremes.

States of the four kinds mentioned are the subject of this book. How are they created? How and why do they fall? Which properties do the different kinds of states have? Why are some considered good, and some bad—and by whom are they considered good or bad? What are the mechanisms behind the varying outcomes? In what follows each of the types of states will get its own chapter, and there I will deal with the questions above in more detail.[4] But even so it may be appropriate to anticipate, here, the following discussion with a few words.

To begin with, dictatorship has been, throughout the history of the world, by far the most common type of state. It is relatively easy to explain the emergence of a dictatorship, and dictatorships have also appeared in all times, within widely different geographical areas, and completely independent of each other. The dictatorship can therefore be considered the most natural, or the most primordial, kind of state, which obviously, however, does not mean that it is the best. Going then to the representative democracy it is, in all the respects mentioned, strikingly different. It is difficult to explain its appearance—why this is difficult will be made clear in what follows—and it is in fact remarkable that it has happened at all. But it did happen in a unique sequence of events—a series of unlikely incidents—very late in the history of states. And the result, the fantastic result one must say, then spread to more and more states by means of, basically, copying processes. Thus, the first prototype, having become a reality through a happy chance, was a prerequisite for the present spread of representative democracies all over the world. Continuing then with direct democracy it has never, at least as far as is now known, been particularly frequent, and, furthermore, it has disappeared since long. Roughly the same is true for oligarchies, at least for the historical past. But perhaps new oligarchies may appear in the future. Direct democracies of the old kind will however, in all likelihood, never appear again, even if new varieties not should be ruled out. Here, as well as in other areas, modern information technology may give rise to surprises.

POLITCAL SCIENCE OR "STAATSWISSENSCHAFT"

Thus, and obviously, the state is an important object of study, but *where* is this object to be studied, and *how* should it be studied? To answer the first question I have to start with a terminological clarification, namely about the name of the relevant academic discipline.

The problem is that the discipline within which states and politics are studied happens to have two different names. In English-speaking countries the discipline is usually called "political science", and the same

---

[4] In the Appendix about the present states in the world states with properties between representative democracies and dictatorships will however also be dealt with.

is true for some other countries. In France, for instance, the discipline is called "science politique". But there is also another name, which translated into English means "the science of the state". Thus, in Germany the discipline is called "Staatswissenschaft", and in Sweden, my own country, the discipline is correspondingly called "statsvetenskap". For this reason, and since this book is about states, it was straightforward to give the original Swedish version of it the title "Statsvetenskap". To give this version of the book, the English one, the title "Political science", the common translation of "statsvetenskap", would, however, be just strange. And this is the reason why this English version of the book is entitled, somewhat more long-windedly, "Towards a Science of States: their Evolution and Properties".

After this clarification it should now be obvious that the state should be studied within the discipline of political science. Still this is done only to a rather limited extent, and when it is done, it is done rather unsystematically. Political science, as now practiced at universities, is, as a matter of fact, an utterly disintegrated discipline. A clear sign of this is that the discipline lacks standard text books. And by this I do not mean that there are not any books which students have to read and be examined on in order to advance within the discipline, but that these books can vary very considerably from university to university. There are not, as in many other disciplines, any books which present something which may be called the core of the discipline. A political scientist does not have to know anything about the state as an institution, as it has been described above, and can still advance considerably within the discipline. He, or she, may for example specialize on measuring opinions, on gender issues, on mass media, on a particular period of a certain country's politics, on interest organizations, or on something else which has as much, or as little, to do with the state and the state's monopoly of violence.

The reason for this situation has to do, I think, with the answer to the second question, the one about *how* the state should be studied. It seems obvious that the study of something, in its varying appearances, as shifting and multifaceted as the state requires some kind of theory— without that the issues easily become insurmountable and unmanageable. To some extent it will be necessary to abstract in order to get rid of details without importance, and in order to make visible the dominant patterns. In other words one has to be somewhat practical and, as the saying goes, "there is nothing more practical than a good theory".[5] But political science is, and has by tradition been, a discipline to a large extent without theory. The well-known political scientist William Riker (1921–93) once wrote about this as follows:[6]

> "In most scientific disciplines, the word 'theory' refers to a set of deductively related sentences that together describe the portion of the world studied with a particular discipline."

And after that he continued:

> "[I]n this paper I intend to use the word 'theory' as it is used in other sciences. Given our tradition, this is rather difficult because, until recently, there has been no set of sentences about politics to which "theory" could be applied with ... justification. Beginning, however, with the publication of Duncan Black's essay, 'On the Rationale of Group Decision Making' there has existed a deductive and testable theory about political events."

The essential part of Black's essay, to which Riker attached so much importance, was the so called median voter theorem, about which I will write more in chapter 10. Here and now it is Riker's contention that political science had almost no theory at all that is important. Basically I think he was right, even if he disregarded some political scientists earlier in history. Had he forgotten, one may ask, theorists such as Niccolò Machiavelli (1469–1527), John Locke (1632–1704) and Charles-Louis de Secondat Montesquieu (1689–1755)? For certainly these men, whom we will become acquainted with in what follows, to a considerable extent dealt with theory in Riker's sense, as well as Plato, Aristotle and Hobbes whom we have already met. But concerning political science, as practiced at universities in Riker's own time, his comment was, nevertheless, appropriate. And even if a considerable theoretical development has occurred after the presentation of the median voter theorem—to a large extent inspired by that theorem—the political science departments have, on the whole, not been affected by this. To a large extent this development belongs to the so-called public choice-theory, which has never, really, been

---

[5] The saying is sometimes attributed to the Scottish physicist James Clerk Maxwell (1831–79), sometimes to the German-American psychologist Kurt Lewin (1890–1947).
[6] Riker (1983), p. 47.

accepted by main stream political scientists. And this theory, anyway, only deals with rather small parts of political reality.

It thus seems as if the fragmentation of political science, the discipline's lack of core, and thereby its lack of standard text books, are closely related to its lack of theory. There is no widely accepted theory that holds the discipline together, or even parts of the discipline. This being so is part of the inspiration for this book. It all started when I became interested in representative democracies' ways of functioning, which led to a theory which will be presented in chapter 10. When developing this theory I also wrote a textbook on public choice-theory, and in connection with that I came to know the American social scientist Mancur Olson (1932–98). Thereby I became familiar with his idea about a second invisible hand, which may lie behind the creation of primitive, stationary monopolies of violence. About this I will write much more in chapter 3. Here it is enough to say that the idea is an important and interesting point of departure for theories about states, and that is how I will use it here.

This book thus contains a draft or a plan for a comprehensive theory about states, and at the same time it aims at being an elementary text book in political science. This dual ambition, as should be obvious from what I have written, is based on my contention that the two things are closely related and dependent on each other. But the ambition is also far-reaching and thereby impossible to realize fully in a first book such as this one. The book has, and to a considerable extent must have, the character of a sketch. But I hope that this sketch, with its unavoidable deficiencies, still will prove interesting and thought provoking, and, hopefully, also may serve as an inspiration to further works of various kinds. Political science—when including the science about states—is a critically important discipline.

2

STATES DURING 5000 YEARS

HUMAN BEINGS BEFORE THE FIRST STATES

The first known states appeared about 5000 years ago, but even if this time is now remote, it nevertheless belongs to man's very recent history. Human beings of the kind we know—*Homo sapiens*—have, according to what is known today, existed for about 150 000 years.[7] Even this period of human existence is however short in a larger context. During about the last three million years[8]—which themselves, in a geological perspective, belong to the very latest history of the earth—cold periods, the last ones about 100 000 years long,[9] have interchanged with much shorter, warmer periods, usually about ten to twenty thousand years long.[10] During the long and cool periods, the so-called ice-ages or glacials, large parts of the continents of the northern hemisphere were covered by ice, whereas this ice to a large extent withdraw or disappeared during the intervening warmer and shorter inter-glacials. Just now we are living in such a warm period, which started about 15 000 years ago[11], and the warm period preceding that one began about 130 000 years ago[12]. This means that the first human beings appeared on earth during a cold period and that we are now living in the second inter-glacial after this appearance. And after the beginning of this second warm period about 10 000 years passed until the first states appeared. But how did human beings live before that? How did they spend their lives during the multi-millennial period from their arrival on earth to the appearance of the first states?

Let us first make clear that the geographical outline of the earth, and I am here thinking about the extension of continents and oceans, during man's time on earth has been basically the same as today. The time

---

[7] Macdougall, pp. 193, 203; Oppenheimer, p. 16.
[8] Macdougall, p. 8.
[9] Plimer, p. 240.
[10] Macdougall, p. 8.
[11] Plimer, p. 236.
[12] Plimer, p. 240.

scale of continental drift is totally different from that of human history. Still, since so much water was bound in ice during the cold periods, the sea level was then much lower than today—probably around 120 meters lower.[13] And therefore there were land bridges in some places where there are now sea straits between islands or continents.

According to the evidence available today man, like other animal species, appeared in one single place, and this place, for man, was somewhere in Africa. Human beings thus have a common origin; they did not appear at different places on earth independently of each other. And, as we have seen, they appeared during a glacial period. During that period African climate was not very good for human beings but matters improved when the warmer inter-glacial materialized. When this inter-glacial turned into a new glacial life became however much more difficult again—a more arid climate turned forests into grasslands penetrated by cold winds.[14] But at the same time land bridges arose and migration became possible. And humans did migrate. More than 70 000 years ago some of them moved from Africa to the southern part of the Arabian Peninsula and from there further in various directions.[15] They thus reached Australia about 65 000 years ago, Europe about 50 000 years ago and, after having crossed what is now the Bering Strait about 20 000 years ago they reached the southern part of North America about 15 000 years ago and South America about 12 000 years ago.[16]

There were thus human beings on all continents long before the time for the appearance of the first states about 5000 years ago. But even if there were no real states during this time people, nevertheless, and gradually, formed tribes and tribal societies. From the beginning a tribe may have consisted of people living close to each other, for example because they belonged to the same family, or, simply, because they had just happened to be in the same area and met there. Then some of these tribes may have grown and acquired more and more members, and bigger tribes like that are sometimes called peoples. For the purposes of this book the distinction between "tribe" and "people" is, however, without significance.[17]

---

[13] Macdougall, pp. 62-3.
[14] Macdougall, p. 194; Oppenheimer, pp. 78, 80; Plimer, pp. 188, 204, 207.
[15] Oppenheimer, p. 88.
[16] Macdougall, pp. 204, 206; Oppenheimer, p. xxii.

But still, and obviously, the tribes were different, for instance with respect to their way of living, their technical knowledge, their religious views, and so forth. Of great importance, in particular, was that they maintained themselves in different ways. Concerning this there are, in particular, two kinds of people that are of interest here. I will call them the peoples of the steppes, and the peoples of the river valleys.

On the steppes to the north of the Black Sea and the Caspian Sea, from the Danube in the west to Mongolia in the east, there lived people who were destined to be of utmost historical importance. Originally they were nomads, hunters, fishermen and gatherers, but gradually some of them turned to cattle breeding, and thereby to a more settled life. This made possible a different and richer life, even if one fundamental precondition, namely the crucial dependence on animals, remained the same. The grass on the steppes could be grazed by the animals but was unsuitable for human food, and it was also difficult or impossible to grow useful vegetables, such as grain, on the dry steppes. The steppe peoples therefore, to a large extent, lived by and on animals. From the animals they got not only food but also hides, wool, traction power, and so forth. The great historical importance of these steppe peoples is directly related to this utilization of animals.[18]

In the previous chapter I wrote that practically all important human cultural achievements have occurred within the framework of states, and that formulation thus gave a certain room for exceptions. Some of these exceptions materialized among the steppe peoples I am writing about here. They took two of the most important development steps in the history of man, namely the domestication of the horse, and the invention and development of the spoked wheel. Obviously these accomplishments were of great importance in many ways, but in this book the military applications are of particular weight. The steppe peoples' military technique would prove to be of utmost importance for the rise and fall of states, and that is what we are interested in here. More about the horse, and about the wheel, therefore follows in chapter 4. In order to put this issue in a somewhat broader perspective it should however be mentioned, even if this book is not about history of languages, that the peoples

---

[17] For a discussion of these problems see Rollason, pp. 37-58.
[18] Anthony, pp. 123-38.

mentioned were the first Indo-Europeans. It was their military skill which made their particular language the origin of that very great and widely spread family of languages, which we today call the Indo-European one.

Then we turn to the peoples of the river valleys. Very early people came together in fertile areas around rivers such as the Euphrates and the Tigris in Mesopotamia (roughly today's Iraq), the Nile in Egypt, the Indus and the Ganges in India and the Yellow River in China. These peoples may have formed tribes in the same way as the peoples of the steppes, but their way of life was different. Whereas life on the steppes was based on animals, the peoples of the river valleys, rather, grew vegetables of various kinds, and in particular grains such as millet, wheat, corn and rice. And the transition from using nature's plants to systematic farming was, in the same way as the domestication of the horse and the development of the wheel, a very important development in man's history.

It is hardly surprising that the peoples who had adopted this life-style also formed the first states. These peoples were almost necessarily settled, not as the steppe peoples sometimes settled, sometimes roaming. This entailed development possibilities, but also vulnerability. The protection inherent in mobility was not available. The farmers' successively richer and richer societies could easily be attacked, conquered and plundered from outside. And even if life essentially was based on vegetables there could, within these societies, also be easily stolen, valuable animals of various kinds. A military defense was therefore necessary, and when such a defense began emerging, the tribal society was on its way to become a state.

But even after states had begun to appear tribes would continue to be of great importance for a long time. Certainly there existed states here and there, but still the main part of the populated area of the earth was stateless. Tribes, or peoples, who had not formed any states so far continued to play important roles in different ways. Some of them created, in due time, their own states. But it also happened that tribes, by constituting a threat against their surroundings, stimulated other tribes to create states, which otherwise, perhaps, would not have appeared. And in still other situations tribes successfully defeated already established states. In what follows we will see many examples of all of this.

SOME IMPORTANT STATES IN THE HISTORY OF THE WORLD—A QUICK SURVEY

In figure 1 some of the states in world history are shown. Along the horizontal axis is shown the time of existence for the state concerned, and along the vertical axis the longitude for the capital of the state. The figure is by no means all-inclusive—there are lots of states which are not there—I have only included those which in one way or another are of interest for the discussion in this book. The intention is to make it possible for the reader to place the states I am going to write about—in this chapter and the following ones—in their historical context. Before starting to deal with the individual states in this way I shall however raise a few questions related to the general overview given by the figure.

For a start, which were the very first states? This question is not easily answered. To some extent this is so since the state concept itself, in spite of the efforts in the introductory chapter to give it some precision, nevertheless is vague, and to some extent since the archaeological remains from the distant times we are dealing with are scarce and difficult to interpret. The first states about which our knowledge is reasonably good appeared, however, about 5000 years ago in the fertile river areas of Mesopotamia and Egypt. At that time, in those areas, written languages had been created, and therefore, in addition to archeological finds there are also written documents.[19] For this reason I consider these states, which anyway were quite early, as the earliest ones.

After these first states many more followed. From the beginning, when the first states appeared, only a very small part of mankind lived within any state at all, and only a very small part of the land surface of the earth was covered by states. But gradually this changed. Finally we have reached the situation of today when practically all human beings live within a state of some kind, and practically all land is covered by states. The world has—using the word in a meaning totally different than the common one—become nationalized.

This nationalization has, however, not gone on haphazardly, but rather followed some more or less obvious lines of development. Take for

---

[19] Finer (1997a), p. 99.

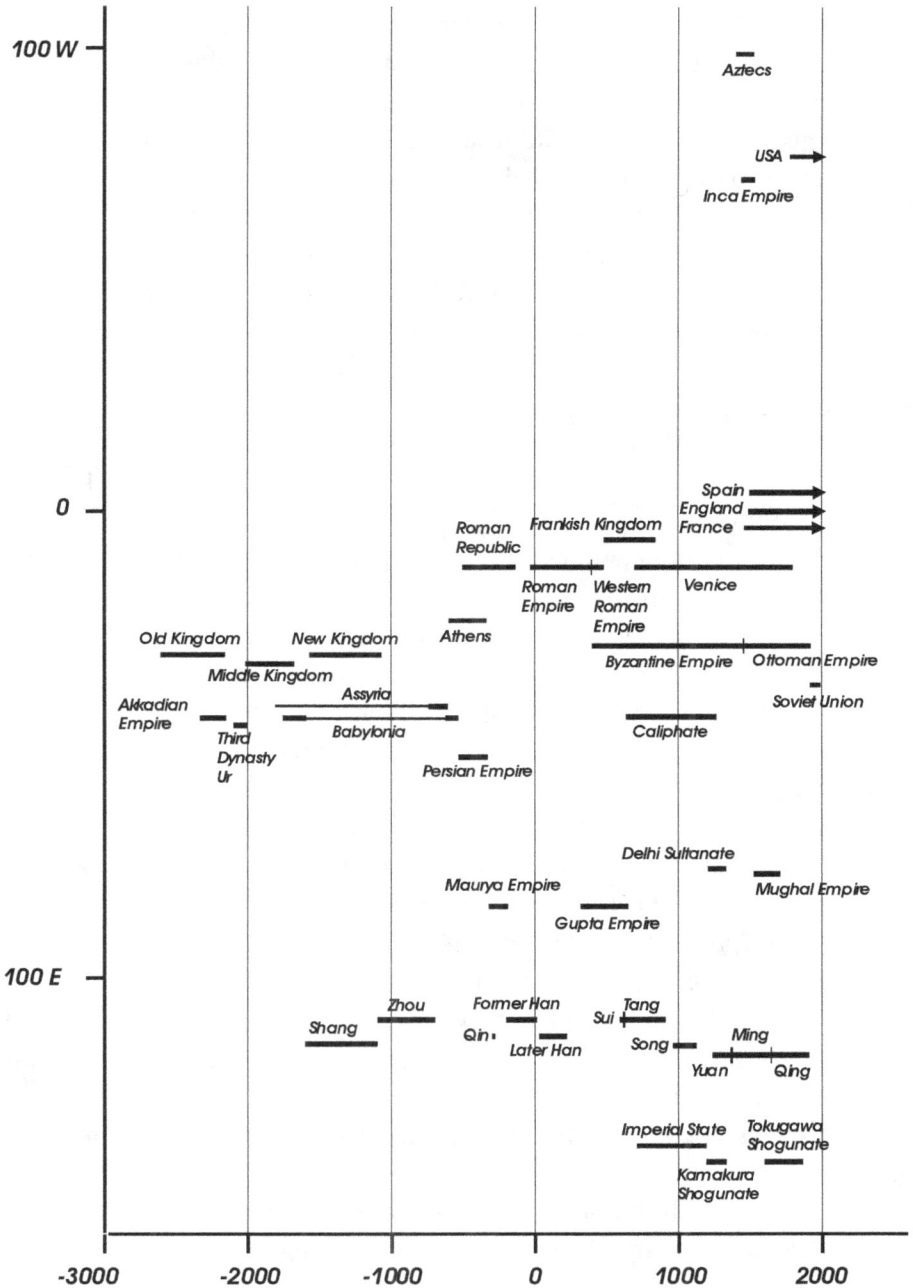

Figure 1: Some important states in the history of the world

instance the Chinese states from Shang to Qing. In this sequence earlier states have to a considerable extent influenced later states, for instance concerning institutional patterns, and there is in that sense a continuity. But at the same time these Chinese states—and I am then still primarily considering their institutional development—have hardly influenced, or become influenced by, other states outside the group, for example Indian or Japanese states. The Chinese states therefore, on the whole, represent a separate *line* of development. And the same is the case with the Indian states, the Japanese states, and the early American states of the Aztecs and the Incas. In spite of some contacts, for example through foreign trade, about which I will write more in chapter 5, these lines of development have, nevertheless, been so relatively isolated from each other that it is not only possible, but also practical, to treat them separately. I will therefore do so.

The development lines just mentioned do, however, include only some of the states in the figure. There remain quite a number of states that belong to a *course* of events which is much broader, and much more complicated, than the "lines" hitherto mentioned. The states belonging to this course of events have to a considerable extent influenced each other—their destinies are linked. In the presentation here I will concentrate on some of the most important of these states—the interesting and significant Phoenician state is, for instance, not included. My description of the course starts with the early states in Egypt and Mesopotamia, continues with the Persian Empire, the Greek city states—among them Athens and Sparta—and the Roman Republic and Empire. After that it goes on with the chaos which followed the collapse of the Western Roman Empire—a chaos out of which grew states of utmost importance. Early among those was Venice, whose merchants developed institutions of fundamental importance for enterprises and commerce. Another important state was England of the seventeenth century. In that country emerged the embryo to the kind of constitution which, much later, was to dominate the world, namely representative democracy. This kind of democracy has very significant advantages, among them that it is the only constitutional type which can, in the long run, accommodate the market institutions for which development Venice had been a pioneer. In the following presentation I will start with this course, which I will call the main-course. After that I will continue with the earlier mentioned "lines", which I will call side-lines.

Before getting into this I shall, however, present another very general survey, namely concerning some important states' areas and populations. These data, which I will refer to now and then in what follows, are presented in table 1.[20] It goes without saying that the figures to a large extent are approximate. It also should be added that the Athenian population figure includes slaves. And that the area for the Roman Empire is the land area—the great Mediterranean Sea, which lay within the Empire, is not included. Finally, the population figures for Chinese Ming represent the growth during the period of the dynasty.

Table 1: Areas and populations of some important states in world history

State	Area, hundreds of thousands of square kilometers	Population, millions
The Old Kingdom (Egypt)	0.4	1
The New Kingdom (Egypt)		4
The Assyrian Empire	16.5	
The Persian Empire	64.8	50
Athens	0.03	0.3
The Roman Empire	41.4	60
Chinese Han	38.9	60
Chinese Tang	100	56
The Frankish Empire	10	
The Caliphate	127	30
Chinese Ming		70-160
The Ottoman Empire	59	30
The Aztecs' state	3.0	
The Mughal Empire	50	100
Chinese Qing (year 1800)	135.9	300
Contemporary USA	98.3	318
Contemporary Russia	170.1	144
Contemporary India	31.7	1241
Contemporary China	95.4	1361

And so I turn to the main course.

---

[20] Most of the historical data are from Finer.

THE MAIN COURSE

THE EGYPTIAN STATES

The first states, as we have seen, may have been those in Mesopotamia, or those in Egypt, and these states were anyway about contemporary. This being so I start with the Egyptian states since they, by their relative simplicity, constitute a better point of departure. When we get to the more complicated conditions in Mesopotamia, it becomes interesting to compare with the Egyptian simplicity.

The Egyptian Kingdom was created about the year 3000 when the king of Lower Egypt—essentially the Nile delta—conquered his neighbor kingdom Upper Egypt—around the Nile valley proper. Not much is however known about the early period of this new kingdom and the traditional separation of Egypt's history into three periods, those of the Old Kingdom, the Middle Kingdom and the New Kingdom, thus starts somewhat later than 3000. According to this separation the Old Kingdom existed from about 2610 to 2160, that is for about 450 years. Then followed what is usually called the first intermediate period, characterized by disintegration and lack of consolidation. After that, from about 2040 to 1650, came the Middle Kingdom which thus existed for about 390 years. And finally, after another intermediate period, the second one, came the New Kingdom, which existed from about 1570 to about 1070, or about 500 years.[21]

The Egyptian states thus had a remarkable stability and became extremely long-lasting. This is obvious already from the dates above, but becomes further underlined if we consider the three kingdoms as a single entity, and furthermore include the long period from 3000 to 2610, preceding the Old Kingdom, which is not unreasonable. In spite of our lack of knowledge of the period before the Old Kingdom, and in spite of the intermediate periods, the way the state was ruled, its culture, and its economy's way of functioning, were essentially the same throughout. The stability was thus extraordinary. Only the Chinese states exhibit, as we will see later on, a similar stability. But, then, what were the reasons for this stability?

---

[21] Walters (1980a), p. 22.

First, the conditions for subsistence were exceptionally good. The areas in the Nile valley were extremely fertile and there was grown, above all, barley and wheat. But even if it was a river land no rain fell within the country itself. Rather, the water came from the yearly recurring rains in the Ethiopian highlands to the south, and extensive irrigation systems which made it possible to use the water more efficiently were gradually built. The regularity of the water supply, from year to year, was also considerable—no sudden new turns of the river, no sudden vast inundations.

But the Nile not only provided excellent conditions for agriculture, it also was a perfect highway for transport. Since the country was narrow the distances from the river to all places within the state were short. It was also easy to cruise along the river—since the winds on the whole came from the north, one could sail upstream and float downstream. And the river was not only used for transporting grain and goods of various kinds, but also for administrative purposes, and for transport of soldiers and military units.[22] The Nile, therefore, was an effective tool for the rulers' control of the country.

In addition to this the geographical conditions provided an effective defense against attacks from outside. The narrow river valley was bordered, on both sides, by vast and, basically, impassable deserts. The only borders which enemies from outside could penetrate were the northeastern one towards Sinai and the southern one towards Nubia (essentially today's Sudan).[23] And these borders were to become of military importance. The first time this happened on a larger scale was in the second intermediate period when the Asiatic tribe Hyksos—a tribe which is not known for anything else—invaded Egypt from the north-east.[24] Somewhat later the New Kingdom itself attacked its neighbors. In this way not only new areas in the south were conquered, but also Sinai and large areas along the eastern Mediterranean coast. Furthermore, extensive military expeditions were carried out far beyond the conquered areas, all the way to the Euphrates for instance.[25]

---

[22] Finer (1997a), pp. 135-6, 155-6.
[23] Mieroop, pp. 112-5.
[24] Chrissanthos, pp. 2-3.
[25] Mieroop, p. 164; Walters (1980a), p. 28.

Such, then, were the external conditions of the Egyptian states. Turning then to the Egyptian society it may first be noticed that it was ruled by a dictator—the pharaoh—who, below him or her, had a centralized bureaucracy. Furthermore there was no monetary system, and hardly any markets. Rather the economy was a centralized storage-redistribution economy, or even a command economy, in which people produced what they were ordered to produce. A large part of the result was taken by the state for its own use, or for storing, in order, perhaps, to be redistributed, to some extent, to the inhabitants later on. In these processes scribes had central and important roles, and they were many and powerful since the written language of hieroglyphs was difficult. Protocols and book keeping were of utmost importance.[26] In addition to the scribes the priests also constituted an important elite. Religion and the ruling of the state were intimately intertwined, or even just different aspects of the same thing. The dictator was not only considered an intermediary to some god, but, at least in some periods, as a god himself. Since the priests served this divine chief of state, the distinction between them and other bureaucrats was not sharp. The populations of the Egyptian kingdoms thus contained a very thin, upper layer consisting of the pharaoh and his court and harem, the priests, the scribes and bureaucrats of other kinds.[27] But how were matters beyond that? What were the conditions for the great remainder of the population?

About this opinions differ. One opinion is that the Egyptian kingdoms were flagrant two-layer societies in which the great mass of the people, living under basically similar conditions, was repressed by the upper, slim, top-layer. Another opinion holds that there was, below the top-layer, a considerable diversification, and that there even existed a vital, independent middle class.[28] One authority, having gone far in stressing the first opinion, is the British historian and political scientist Samuel E. Finer (1915–93).[29] In his monumental work "History of Government" he even makes a comparison with the Soviet Union of Stalin.[30] Although repression and control was sharpened in the New Kingdom the rulers

---

[26] Roberts, pp. 52, 75.
[27] Finer (1997a), p. 183.
[28] Mieroop, p. 105; Wilkinson, p. 137.
[29] Finer (1997a), p. 167-8.
[30] Finer (1997a), p. 194.

had, he holds, from the very beginning, compelled the population, and the whole population, to work for the state.[31] As I will argue later on in chapter 6 this, probably, reflects an underestimation of Stalin's capacity for repression, but still it underlines the contention about the despotism exercised by Egyptian rulers.

On the whole the internal economy thus lacked both money and markets, but this did not stop the Egyptian states from engaging in foreign trade on which they were, in fact, dependent. And this is a kind of situation which we will meet again and again in what follows. Many of the early states were what, with modern terminology, is sometimes called state-trading countries. From Lebanon the Egyptian states imported cedar wood, which was outstandingly suitable for building the ships used on the Nile. And to the south, in Nubia, were deposits of gold, which was sometimes imported, sometimes robbed or stolen.[32]

What comes first to mind when thinking about ancient Egypt is perhaps the pyramids. These, or anyway the biggest ones, were built early, in the beginning of the Old Kingdom. How was this possible, one may ask, and part of the explanation may be that Samuel Finer's contention about Egypt as a fully realized slave society is correct.[33] Also important was however that Egypt hardly had any military problems, and consequently no defense expenditures, and that, therefore, a very large part of the gross national product could be used for building. The pyramids were, however, not only big but also technically impressive.[34] Thus, the technique used for forming the huge blocks of stone, and for transporting them to their final positions in the pyramid, is still to some extent unknown and a matter of ongoing discussion. The geometrical precision, concerning for instance the form and orientation of the base quadrate, and the angels of the sloping sides, is in some cases—for the Cheops Pyramid, for example—remarkable.[35] The Egyptians were also skilful ship builders, but in other respects their technical knowledge was less developed. The military technique necessary for the New Kingdom's

---

[31] Finer (1997a), p. 81. See also Wilkinson, pp. 364-8.
[32] Bard, p. 58; Mierooop, pp. 49-51.
[33] See also Finer (1997a), p. 81.
[34] Brewer & Teeter, pp. 174-88; Finer (1997a), pp. 138-9; Mieroop, p. 76.
[35] Wilkinson, p. 83.

conquests was, for instance, not invented by the Egyptians themselves but taken up from their enemy Hyksos.[36]

The fall of the New Kingdom was caused by both internal disintegration and attacks from outside—a pattern which we will meet again and again in what follows. Among the states that, one after the other, were to conquer the Egyptian lands were Assyria, the Persian Empire and the Roman Empire. Assyria had its core area in Mesopotamia, and therefore it may now be fitting to turn to the states there. But we will start from the beginning and thus get to Assyria only later on. Consequently we go about two thousand years back in time.

THE STATES IN MESOPOTAMIA

"Mesopotamia" is Greek and means "the land between the rivers". The word is thus the name of an area—roughly corresponding to today's Iraq—not of a state. During the times of the first states in this area their external conditions were complex and unstable, or even turbulent, not straightforward and enduring as in Egypt. The contrast is sharp. The development, which will be described in more detail in what follows, starts with the small Sumerian city states, goes on with two short-lived but area-wise very extensive states, the Akkadian Empire and Ur, and finishes with a thousand year struggle between the giants Assyria and Babylonia. Altogether it is a story of about 2500 years.

I will however start with the general social patterns which, to a large extent, were similar to those in Egypt. People in Mesopotamia thus lived, in the same way as people in Egypt, from grains grown by means of irrigation. But even so the water behaved differently in the two areas.[37] In Mesopotamia the rivers suddenly could take completely new courses, and large-scale inundations were quite common. The evaporation of the water also made the meadows gradually more salted, which made it necessary to shift some of the production from wheat to the more salt-permitting barley. Problems like these did not exist in Egypt. But in spite of these differences the patterns of living—characterized by settled dwelling, irrigation, grain growing, and possibly some fishing—were the same in the two river cultures.

---

[36] Wilkinson, p. 204.
[37] Finer (1997a), p. 106; Roberts, p. 49; Roux, pp. 6-7.

Also in other respects the Mesopotamian societies were similar to the Egyptian ones. Thus they were basically money-less, storage-redistribution economies in which scribes who handled the book-keeping—and thus supervised the production, the deliverances to store-houses, the distribution from these to consumers, and so forth—were critically important functionaries.[38] Their written language was however quite different—even if also very difficult—namely cuneiform rather than hieroglyphs.

Furthermore the rulers in Mesopotamia, in about the same way as Egypt's pharaohs, were considered gods, or at least as being of divine origin.[39] And even if the rulers did not build pyramids—one reason being that there was no supply of stone—they, nevertheless, built big pyramid-resembling so called ziggurats of clay and bricks, among which the mythological Tower of Babel is the most well-known.[40] The ziggurats were not, to be sure, graves as the pyramids, but still they were religious manifestations. Religion was important and from this followed that the priests—as in Egypt—constituted an influential and powerful group.

The cultures in the Nile valley and in Mesopotamia were thus quite similar in many ways, but still the social life in the two areas took very different paths. The reason for this, at least to a large extent, seems to be the different conditions for military activities. While the Egyptian states lay protected behind vast deserts, and also had the Nile as an important tool for the rulers' control of the country, Mesopotamia was open and unprotected.[41] East of the large, plain land surrounding the rivers were the wild, high Zagros mountains (in today's Iran), and to the north the Anatolian mountains (in today's Turkey). In these mountainous areas there were people who were the best soldiers of their time, and who descended from the tribes north of the Black Sea and the Caspian Sea mentioned earlier. Even westwards there were serious threats. True, the Syrian deserts were there, but they were not as impregnable as the deserts around Egypt, and hostile Bedouin tribes lived there. So, if the first two Egyptian states, and in particular the first one, had lived peacefully, violence and war were manifest realities from the very begin-

---

[38] Roberts, p. 52.
[39] Finer (1997a), p. 116; Roux, p. 107.
[40] Bertman, pp. 194-8; Derry & Williams, pp. 158-9; Roberts, p. 54.
[41] Bertman, p. 262.

ning in Mesopotamia. This is the great difference between Egypt and Mesopotamia and probably the main reason for the complex and turbulent societal development in the latter area. I will even go as far as to say that the importance of violence for the creation and maintenance of states is demonstrated more clearly in Mesopotamia than probably anywhere else.

For a start—and here I am talking roughly about the year 3000— there appeared in the southern parts of the area some twenty city-states, each one consisting of just a single urban settlement and surrounding agricultural land. These were the so called Sumerian city-states—named after one of the main peoples of Mesopotamia, the Sumerians—among which two of the most prominent were Ur and Uruk.[42] For their defense the cities were surrounded by strong, solid walls, which in some cases even could be double and also equipped with towers.[43] It was this restriction to a single, defended city with its surrounding lands which made these states *city-states*. Egypt, on the contrary, for which serious defense problems appeared only late in its history, was already from the beginning a *country-state*, or a territorial state, that is a state which controlled a large, unified territory.

The Mesopotamian states were however not only threatened from outside, they were also incessantly fighting each other.[44] And then it could happen that some state—if its ruler was a skilful enough warrior, and had resources enough at his disposal—defeated the other ones. If so he could also create a realm which, at least for some time, could be quite extended.

The first successful ruler of this kind was Sargon of Akkad, who created the so called Akkadian Empire.[45] This empire, which existed, approximately, from 2340 to 2150, was thus created when there had been Sumerian city-states for almost seven hundred years. We can also notice that its lifetime just about coincides with the final part of Egypt's Old Kingdom. But even if the empire was not long-lasting, it was, on the other hand, extraordinarily extensive. It included all the plains around the Euphrates and the Tigris, from the Persian Gulf in the south to about the place of the present city of Mosul. Possibly it also extended through Syria to the Mediterranean, although the information about that is vague and

---

[42] Roux, p. 131.
[43] Roux, p. 126.
[44] Roux, p. 138; Finer (1997a), p. 101.
[45] Jacobsen (1980b), pp. 84-9; Roberts, pp. 58-9; Roux, pp. 146-60.

uncertain. But even if only the first area mentioned is taken into account, it was, nevertheless, a very large state in its own contemporary time. It was, for instance, significantly larger than Egypt's Old Kingdom. The exact position of the capital Akkad is not known, even if it certainly was somewhere in the area where the Euphrates and the Tigris flow closest to each other, that is near today's Baghdad, or perhaps even beneath[46] that city.

The empire fell due to a combination of inner instability and attacks from outside, by the nomad tribe Guti from the Zagros Mountains. The Akkadian Empire's life cycle followed, in fact, a pattern which was to be repeated again and again. A prominent expert on ancient Mesopotamia, Georges Roux, has described this pattern as follows:[47]

> "The rise and fall of the Akkadian empire offers a perfect preview of the rise and fall of all subsequent Mesopotamian empires: rapid expansion followed by ceaseless rebellions, palace revolutions, constant wars on the frontiers, and in the end, the *coup de grâce* given by the highlanders: Guti now [Akkadian empire, 2150], Elamites [Third dynasty Ur, 2000], Kassites [Hammurabi's Babylonia, 1595], Medes [Assyria, 612] or Persians [Media, 539] tomorrow."

In the last sentence of the quotation I have, after each of the mountain peoples mentioned, indicated the empire which was given the *coup de grâce* and the year when this happened. The parentheses thus do not belong to the text quoted, but may be helpful later on, when the processes are described in more detail.

Somewhat after the fall of the Akkadian Empire—around 2100—a new big state was created, this time originating from the city-state Ur in the southern part of the area. One usually talks about the Kingdom of Ur, or, referring to the governing family, about the Third Dynasty Ur. This state, which covered about the same area as the Akkadian Empire, was however still more short-lived—it fell about the year 2000, that is after some 100 years. But this short time was to a large extent—as it seems—characterized by peace and order, and extensive building projects of various kinds were undertaken.[48] Big ziggurats were built, a wide-spread network of roads was created, and canals, both for irrigation and tran-

---

[46] Morris, p. 189.
[47] Roux, p. 159.
[48] Roux, pp. 161-75.

sport, were dug. Furthermore, and for the state's protection, a fortified wall of another kind than the former city-walls was built, namely a long, unbroken wall along a possible front sector in the north-east between the Tigris and the Zagros Mountains.[49]

The downfall, when it came, followed the pattern described above.[50] The decisive outer attacks came from two directions—the one from the Elam state in the Zagros Mountains, not mentioned before, and the other from a tribe, the Amorites, in the western deserts. The collapse ended by hostile forces besieging the Ur city. The people inside the walls suffered severely from hunger and finally, possibly hoping for a mild treatment, opened the gates. But their hope proved ill-founded. They were massacred, and the city looted and destroyed.[51]

The Akkadian Empire and the Ur Kingdom thus covered roughly the whole of Mesopotamia, they were relatively short-lived, and the one followed after the other. With the following states, Babylonia and Assyria, this was not so—they were, on the contrary, to a large extent contemporary, in a sense long-lasting, and competitors to each other. Sometimes the one was the biggest and most powerful of the two, sometimes the other. The capital of Babylonia, Babylon, lay in the middle of the Mesopotamian area, roughly in the same place as Akkad, whereas the capital of Assyria—first Ashur and thereafter Nineveh—lay far to the north in the Tigris valley. The life-time for Babylonia can be set from about 1760 to 539, and for Assyria from 1813 to 612. So we are dealing with a period of about a thousand years, even if the life spans of the two states are somewhat dislocated in relation to each other. Assyria appeared somewhat earlier than Babylonia and also disappeared somewhat earlier. But having said this, it should also be said that both states, within their seemingly long life-times, went through very considerable transformations. In fact it even was the case, and that is true for both states, that periodically they were almost, or perhaps even completely, extinguished. So certainly there was no stability. Basically it may therefore be more correct to talk about a number of states with the same name—either the name of Assyria or that of Babylonia—which, with some interruptions, follow each other.

---

[49] Roux, p. 169.
[50] Roux, pp. 175-8.
[51] Jacobsen (1980a), p. 83.

I will start with Assyria. Its total duration, from 1813 to 612, may be divided into two periods, one longer and earlier and one shorter and later. The dividing year is 744. The earlier period thus is more than thousand years long, while the later hardly reached 150 years. Still, the really interesting period is the later one, since that was the time of the great Assyrian Empire. About the earlier period I will therefore just say that it was characterized by almost permanent warfare conducted with varying degrees of success. Sometime the territory was not larger than at most a small core-area around the upper parts of the Tigris, sometimes it was vast and extended.[52]

The later period started when the first of a sequence of skilful warrior kings—Tiglathpileser III (governing 744–27)—took the throne and started building what was to become the world's first real empire.[53] And by real I do not only mean that the state expanded over a very large area but also that, within its borders, peoples, languages and cultures of very different kinds were present. When the empire was at its largest, under the king Ashurbanipal (governing 668–27), it included, in addition to all the plains around the Euphrates and the Tigris, all the way down to the Persian Gulf, the western parts of the Zagros Mountains, the Anatolian mountains and the eastern coastal area of the Mediterranean. Furthermore the Nile delta was taken, and thereby important parts such as the capital Memphis, from the then Egypt. This Egypt, even though ruled by a pharaoh, was however only a pale copy of the once so mighty New Kingdom, which had passed away about 1070, that is a few hundred years earlier.

The purpose of the wars was to some extent, or perhaps even mainly, to take and bring home spoils of various kinds. The Egyptian campaign included, for instance, a raid southwards against the former capital Thebes, where, among many other trophies, two big obelisks, each weighing 38 tons, were stolen and brought home. In due course the results were seen in, among other places, Nineveh. An abundance of war trophies, not only from Thebes but also from Memphis, from Elam's capital Susa, and from still more cities, made Nineveh a shining metropolis. But

---

[52] Finer (1997a), p. 211; Grayson (1980b), pp. 101-8; Morris, pp. 245-8.
[53] Finer (1997a), pp. 210-37.

the Assyrians not only robbed, they also, to the best of their abilities, destroyed what remained in the cities they attacked.[54]

The capital Nineveh thus became more and more splendid. But in
spite of this, one of the kings between Tiglathpileser and Ashurbanipal,
Sargon II, had a completely new capital, Dûr-Sharrukin, built for himself.
There a grandiose royal palace, with more than two hundred rooms, lavishly decorated with lots of frescoes, glazed bricks, sculptures, and so
forth, was erected. And all of this was done in just 10 years. According to
one judgment, which seems reasonable, thousands of prisoners of war
and hundreds of artists and artisans must have been engaged. But only
one year after the inauguration Sargon II was killed in war, and the kings
following him preferred Nineveh.[55]

Now, what kind of state was the Assyrian Empire? First, it was an
extreme, disciplined and skillfully led military power. The most advanced
military techniques of the age were mastered and developed. About this I
will write more in chapter 4. The domestic policy, if it may be called so,
was extreme as well. The governing was centralized and ruthless and included, among other things, large-scale deportations of people.[56] The purpose was to eradicate local patriotism which could ignite revolts. But
even so revolts occurred all the time and the suppression of these was, to
say the least, brutal. The insurgents were flayed alive, impaled, beheaded,
mutilated in various ways, and so forth.[57] Some other, somewhat more
constructive, activities were however also undertaken, even if, in those
cases as well, by the use of force. Thus, for example, large-scale irrigation
projects were carried out.[58] The labor force was taken from the domestic
population—which the king considered his private property and exploited extremely hard—and masses of prisoners of war. And at the same
time very considerable intellectual and scientific activities were also go-

---

[54] Mieroop, pp. 292-3; Roberts, p. 116; Roux, pp. 287-8, 331, 335; Wilkinson, p.
436. The general information about the obelisks is given by, for instance, Roberts
and Roux, but the specified information about the weight I have found only in
Roux. One may however ask how things so heavy could be transported from Thebes to Nineveh.
[55] Grayson (1980b), p. 105; Leick, p. 224; Roberts, p. 116; Roux, p. 315.
[56] Grayson (1980b), p. 105; Roux, p. 307.
[57] Bertman, p. 268.
[58] Roux, p. 323.

ing on. For the preservation of the results of these efforts Sargon II and Ashurbanipal created great libraries.[59]

But the empire was not to last long. The collapse came in 612 when Nineveh fell and was plundered after a siege of three months, and the process leading to that was exactly of the kind described in the quotation from Roux above.[60] The *coup de grâce* was however not only delivered by the Medes from the Zagros Mountains, but also by the arch-rival of a thousand years, Babylonia. About the Medes I will write more in the next section, but before that Babylonia should be dealt with. I start from the beginning, which takes us about a thousand years back.

If Assyria's start was drawn out Babylonia, on the contrary, expanded rapidly and quickly from the very beginning. The first king Hammurabi (governing 1792–50) thus got control over a very large territory. I will tell the story of Babylonia by concentrating on Hammurabi and two other prominent, but much later, kings, namely Nabopolassar (governing 625–05) and his son Nebuchadnezzar II (governing 604–562).

Babylon was, when Hammurabi inherited the state from his father in 1792, a small city-state among others. But Hammurabi, being the skilful warrior he was, in a short time conquered almost all of Mesopotamia and also consolidated the territory's administration. In that way Babylonia, the so far largest and best consolidated state in Mesopotamia, was created (we are now, it should be remembered, about a thousand years before the time of the Assyrian Empire). And in the capital Babylon was built—as a city within the city—an enormous palace with some three hundred rooms for the king and his administration.[61]

Hammurabi is in particular known as law-maker, or even as the first law-maker. This, however, is a truth with some need for modification since he had predecessors, but still he developed the law, put it together, and had it written down. Possibly some would also say that he brutalized the law—the principle "eye for eye, tooth for tooth", emanates for instance from Hammurabi, or was, at least, clearly formulated in his written law.[62] And this was not the only remarkable accomplishment in Babylonia. Thus, and at this time, the Epic of Gilgamesh, often considered as the first great

---

[59] Finer (1997a), p. 213; Kriwaczek, pp. 251-2.
[60] Kriwaczek, p. 255.
[61] Roberts, p. 63; Roux, p. 214.
[62] Bertman, pp. 68-70; Grayson (1980a), p. 91; Roberts, pp. 61-2; Roux, pp. 201-7.

master piece in world literature, was also given the written form in which
it is known today. Gilgamesh was a king in Uruk somewhere around the
year 2500 and the story about him had, before it was written down,
thrived in oral tradition.

After Hammurabi some more kings followed, and then the state
collapsed in 1595, that is about two hundred years after Hammurabi's
ascendance to the throne. In this case the *coup de grâce* was delivered by
the Hittites—a tribe which had established a big and powerful state in
Anatolia to the north—who conquered and looted Babylon. But there
their success ended. They were, in their turn, defeated by another—in the
coulisses awaiting—equestrian tribe from the north, the Kassites, which,
for the time being, took the throne and the state. After that Babylonia's
destiny fluctuated for a long time. Various sovereigns followed after each
other, Babylon was conquered and destroyed anew, and so forth.[63]

But then, about 625, a new period of greatness started with the king
Nabopolassar. It was he who, together with the Medes, crushed the
Assyrian Empire 612 in the way already described and after him his son
Nebuchadnezzar II continued on the same road. In the battle of Kerke-
mish—on the border of today between Syria and Turkey—he defeated, in
605, Egyptian forces which at that time, because Egypt was allied with the
recently fallen Assyria, occupied the area. Thereby a new large empire,
having roughly the same area as Assyria, was created. The whole, eastern
coastal area of the Mediterranean now lay open for the Babylonians, and
they did not hesitate to occupy it as a potential, lucrative source of taxes.
But the peoples concerned revolted and the tax collecting became difficult. In his efforts to suppress the revolts Nebuchadnezzar, among others,
besieged Jerusalem and, after eighteen months, succeeded in taking the
city. After having looted and destroyed it, and demolished the walls, he
took thousands of its inhabitants to Babylon—the Babylonian captivity.[64]
Thus also the Babylonians engaged in large-scale transfers of people in
order to cope with threatening insurrection.

But Nebuchadnezzar also cared about his formerly destroyed capital Babylon and had it rebuilt—using prisoners of course, and among
them the ones from Jerusalem. And the city was not only rebuilt but also

---

[63] Grayson (1980a), pp. 92-4; Roux, pp. 241-52.
[64] Roberts, pp. 114-5; Roux, pp. 377-381; Wilkinson, pp. 441-2.

enlarged and enriched to the extent that the Greek historian Herodotus (485–25), after having visited the city, described it as the most glorious in the world. To be sure Herodotus saw the city about a hundred years after Nebuchadnezzar's time, but later archeological evidence has, on the whole, confirmed his impressions. Inside the city was the Tower of Babel and Nebuchadnezzar's enormous, splendid, private palace where he, the dictator, lived surrounded by his family, his court, and his harem guarded by eunuchs. And around the city there were two parallel, impressive, fortified walls.[65] Possibly there also was, in the city, the so called Hanging Gardens—gardens located on terraces—even if some scholars argue that these gardens, rather, had their place in Nineveh.[66]

Finally, it is important to add that impressive scientific achievements were carried out in Babylonia, in particular within astronomy and mathematics. In this respect Babylonia thus was similar to Assyria. Astrological beliefs gave rise to wide-ranging and exact astronomical observations. Within mathematics both algebra and geometry were cultivated. Babylonians were, for instance, familiar with square roots as well as cube roots, and the square root of 2 was calculated with great precision. A precondition for this was a positional numeral system, such as ours, although their system had six figures rather than our ten. As a matter of fact we have remnants of the Babylonian system in the form of the partition of the circle into 360 degrees and of the hour into 60 minutes. Within geometry the Babylonians were familiar with some of the results with which the Greeks Pythagoras (about –450) and Euclid (about –300) are usually credited.[67]

But also Babylonia was to disappear, and those who brought that about were the Persians who conquered not only Babylonia but also Media, and in addition to that much, much more.

THE PERSIANS, THE GREEKS AND THE ROMANS

The Medes and the Persians were both equestrian peoples having come from the north to the Zagros Mountains. The Medes, who were slightly earlier than the Persians, at first founded their own state, Media, which

---

[65] Grayson (1980a), pp. 99-100; Roux, pp. 389-400.
[66] Leick, p. 243.
[67] Grayson (1980a), pp. 100-1; Roberts, p. 63.

covered much more than the mountainous core areas, and then, together with Babylonia, crushed Assyria. Soon thereafter, in 539, the Medes as well as the Babylonians were defeated by the Persians, and thereby the tremendous expansion of the Persian state started. But this state was not the only interesting one in its own time. The Greek city-states, and among them Athens and Sparta, were more or less simultaneous. And at this time the beginning of what was to become the great Roman states also appeared on the scene. This section is about these states, and I will start with the Persian Empire.

The Persians were skillful, conquering-minded warriors and about 500, when their empire was about forty years old, it had its greatest extension. It was then much bigger than the earlier Assyrian and Babylonian empires and it was, until then, by far the largest empire in history.[68] From the core areas in the Zagros Mountains it went far in all directions. In the west—and beginning from the south—it included the Libyan Desert, Egypt, the whole eastern Mediterranean area, and Turkey including some areas to the west of the Dardanelles and the Bosporus. The northern border, then, and starting from the west, went along the southern coast of the Black Sea, over Caucasus, along the southern coast of the Caspian Sea, and from there almost reached the Aral Sea in order to continue still a bit eastwards. From there the eastern border then went southwards along the Indus River all the way down to the Arabian Sea. The southern border, finally, started with the coast of the Arabian Sea and the eastern coast of the Persian Gulf in order to continue, from there, along the northern edge of the Arabian Peninsula, to Egypt and Libya. The number of inhabitants has been estimated to roughly 50 millions and that population, naturally, was utterly heterogeneous.[69] This empire—although with some territorial losses—remained under shifting conditions until Alexander the Great conquered all of it around 330. The state thus became about 210 years old.

Among the Persian kings the first four are the most interesting for us. First came Cyrus, who defeated the Medes and the Babylonians, and after him, when he had died in battle, followed his son Cambyses, who continued the conquests, in particular by taking hold of Egypt. Then, after

---

[68] Finer (1997a), pp. 287, 289; Roberts, p. 161; Wilkinson, pp. 445-53.
[69] Finer (1997a), p. 287.

the death of Cambyses, a fight of succession between his brother and one of his generals ensued. The general murdered the brother and a great number of his adherents and thereby became the next king, Darius I. He consolidated the empire by improving the road network and by improving the bureaucracy and the tax collecting system—among others he divided the empire into some twenty administrative provinces, the so called satrapies. Susa, on the plains just to the east of the lower course of the Tigris, where the Zagros Mountains start raising, was made capital. Darius, however, also started the wars, ultimately so disastrous, with the Greek city-states, about which I will write more later on. After Darius came his son Xerxes during the reign of whom the Greek wars were finally lost. After that Xerxes essentially devoted himself to perfecting his own, new and grandiose capital Persepolis further southwards in the country. In the time of Xerxes, who was murdered in a harem intrigue in 465, the empire also started crumbling, and the disintegration continued under a number of following kings.[70]

To a large extent the Persian Empire seems to have been rather tolerant towards its inhabitants—at least until the end of Darius' reign.[71] Religious tolerance prevailed and the empire was even the first secular state in the history of the world.[72] There were no priests in the administration.[73] The peoples of the conquered lands, which became satrapies, were allowed to keep their religions, and basically to live as they wanted, as long as they paid their taxes to the central government. And the tolerance was manifested in other ways as well. When Cyrus had taken Babylon he not only abstained from plundering the city, he also liberated the Jews in the Babylonian captivity and even let them rebuild the temple of Jerusalem. The initial conquests, those undertaken by Cyrus and Cambyses, also seem to have been uncomplicated since at least parts of the affected peoples felt oppressed by their own kings and therefore looked upon the Persians as liberators. A tolerance of this kind was hardly a characteristic of the states earlier described here—it appears, on the whole, as something new. Perhaps the rulers realized from the beginning that an empire, as vast and heterogeneous as the Persian was

---

[70] Roberts, p. 212.
[71] Finer (1997a), pp. 297-8, 309; Roberts, p. 163.
[72] Finer (1997a), p. 89.
[73] Finer (1997a), p. 315.

intended to become, could not be kept in order by means of brutal
repression and mass-deportations of people, and that other methods
therefore were needed.[74] In spite of this general tolerance punishments
for alleged, actual crimes could however, as we will see in chapter 6, be
utterly hard and cruel.

What now remains of the story of the Persian Empire are the wars
with the Greek city-states, often called the Persian wars. I will soon come
to them, but first I will introduce these Greek states. Among them were,
for instance, Argos, Athens, Ionia, Corinth, Miletus, Sparta and Thebes
(not to be mixed up with Thebes in Egypt), and they had all been founded
by Greek-speaking tribes who, from the north, had moved towards the
Greek peninsula and the northern and eastern coastal areas of the Aegean
Sea. The states usually consisted of a city with surrounding agricultural
lands and villages, and this pattern depended on topography.[75] The small
cultivable areas were separated by mountains. And, in spite of their common origin and perhaps due to these topographical realities, these small
states never succeeded in uniting. Rather, they were often fighting each
other. But even so, they also had common enemies, above all the Persians.

In what follows I will deal with Athens and to some extent with
Sparta. Before the Persian wars, around 600, Athens went through a
period of transformations of utmost interest. During this time the regime
first changed from oligarchy to dictatorship and from there to direct
democracy. These changes were directly related to the development of
the Greek infantry forces—the so called hoplites—and I will describe
these matters in more detail in chapters 4 and 7.

The Persian wars started when the Persians attacked Athens, by
then a direct democracy, at Marathon on the Attica peninsula in 490. The
Athenian infantry defended their state successfully and won the battle
sensationally. After that, the Persians waited for ten years before attacking again. During that time Darius had died and been succeeded by
Xerxes, and now the battles followed rapidly after each other. First troops
from Sparta lost at the strategically important, narrow pass of Thermo-
pylae north of Attica in 480. This, however, was to remain the only Persian victory. Later in the same year, in the biggest naval battle in ancient

---

[74] Lane Fox, p. 100.
[75] Finer (1997a), p.322; Lane Fox, pp. 28-9.

history, an Athenian and Corinthian fleet defeated the Persian fleet at Salamis at the west coast of Attica. In the year after that, 479, the Persian troops still remaining on the Greek peninsula were crushed by Greek infantry, mainly from Sparta, at Plataea some tens of kilometers to the north-west from Athens. Then, somewhat later in the same year, Athenians and Spartans chased a Persian fleet across the Aegean Sea and defeated it at the battle of Mycale. And thereby all was over.[76]

The Persian wars thus took place during a very short period of time—at first the battle of Marathon and thereafter, after about ten years, the four remaining battles within two years. And all battles, except the last one at Mycale, took place on Greek land or water. This indicates that the wars were Persian wars of aggression, which is compatible with the Persian expansionism in general. But there is also another explanation. Before the outbreak of the wars some Greek settlements on the eastern side of the Aegean Sea had tried to break away from Persia, and when the Persian tried to stop that the Greeks affected had asked Athens, among others, for help. The demand was to some extent responded to, and the Persians' attack at Marathon may have been a retaliation for that. But this could hardly be the whole explanation. If so, why did the Persians not stop after Marathon? Why did they come back ten years later? Was the different personalities of Darius and Xerxes the decisive factor?

For the Persians the losses became a staggering blow from which they never recovered, but for the Greeks, and in particular for Athens, the effect was the opposite. After the wars Athens became the leader of the victors, who formed the Delian League. In this way Athens managed to collect enormous tax incomes, and it was by means of these resources that Athens entered its period of greatness, the classic epoch, or its Golden Age. Before getting to that one it should however be noted that the peace period after the Persian wars became short, scarcely fifty years. The reason was that Athens exploited its central power-position in the Delian League in a way which was increasingly resented not only by the members of the league, but also by the outsider Sparta, which led another league, the Peloponnesian one. This conflict led to the drawn out Peloponnesian war (431–04) in which Athens and Sparta were the main adversaries. Finally Athens was compelled to accept an unfavorable peace.

---

[76] Lane Fox, p. 104.

But the peace during the fifty years before the Peloponnesian war was, nevertheless, long enough to be of decisive importance. Athenian politics at that time was led by Pericles (governing 443–29), who, among other achievements, initiated the building of The Acropolis. During this time intensive artistic activities, and scientific ones, also flourished. Names such as Sophocles (497–06), Socrates (470–399), Aristophanes (circa 445–385), Plato (427–347) and Aristotle (384–22) may be mentioned. In this book Plato, who was active after the Peloponnesian war, is of particular interest. He was the first important political scientist and wrote the great work "The Republic". A main theme was the criticism of Athens' direct democracy, which, according to Plato, led to fragmentation and weakness. His recommendation was rather a less democratic constitution such as Sparta's (which will be described in chapter 8).[77]

The Persian wars thus became, if the expression is permitted, one of the most consequential road choices of world history. Had the Persians won, Athens' stunning, cultural achievements would never have become reality, and Western history would have been very different. But this extraordinarily rich civilization also, of course, came to an end. Soon not only Athens and Sparta, and all other Greek city-states, but the Persian Empire as well would disappear, and the reason was a rapid shift of influence to a couple of extraordinary warriors from Macedonia just to the north of the Greek lands. The first one was Philip of Macedonia (383–36), who occupied large parts of the Greek peninsula.[78] The next one was his son, and by the way also Aristotle's pupil, Alexander the Great (356–23), who, during a ten-year period from his raise to power at the age of 22 until his death, crushed the Persian Empire, continued to the Indus, turned back to Egypt, in order to, at last, go to Babylon where he died—possibly poisoned[79] or possibly of malaria[80]—at the age of 33.[81] All the time he was victorious, and he plundered and destroyed far and wide, for instance in Persepolis. But perhaps Alexander, nevertheless, is most remembered for the cities he created and gave the name Alexandria, among which the one in Egypt is the most well-known. The conquests of Philip

[77] Roberts, pp. 188-211.
[78] Lane Fox, pp. 192-200.
[79] Morris, p. 269.
[80] Roux, p. 413.
[81] Lane Fox, pp. 229-40.

and Alexander were however never consolidated—talking about an empire, which is often done, is therefore misleading. After Alexander's death
different parts of the areas occupied were taken over by his generals. A
state was never created.[82]

That, however, happened in another part of the world. At about the
time of Philip's and Alexander's worst ravaging, something which was
destined to become a formidable, great power—the Roman state—had
already begun to take form. And this state, in the same way as so many
other ones, had its origin in tribal societies and tribal wars. Rome, in the
beginning a common, simple village, was strategically situated at the
mouth of the Tiber.[83] The area's dominating power at that time—Etruria,
the state of the Etruscans—used the river for transports between the
cities to the north (in today's Toscana) and the fertile plains in the southern coastal areas (in today's Campania), and the Romans, therefore, could
exploit the situation by controlling the transports. But for this they had to
be able to control their region militarily. Being skilful warriors they did,
however, not only this. In due time they also conquered Etruria, Latinized
its culture, and went on expanding still more.[84]

According to the tale Rome was founded in 753 and this is probably
roughly correct. It started as a kingdom, but in 509 it was converted to a
republic, or to something which we, with the terminology used here, may
call an oligarchy. This, thus, happened at about the same time as Athens,
and some other Greek city-states, adopted direct democracy. Both transformations—the Greek and the Roman—are of utmost interest for the
issues discussed in this book. In both cases the driving force behind the
change was improvements in the technique of infantry warfare. The
spread of participation in war made unavoidable a spread of power. The
Greek infantry soldiers were the hoplites, with whom we are already
acquainted, and in Rome the new infantry soldiers were called legionaries. Thus, and because of this military development, the first known
states in world history with a widely known and respected system for political decision-making had appeared. More about this follows in subsequent chapters.

---

[82] Chrissanthos, pp. 77-88; Roberts, pp. 214, 219; Roux, pp. 412-3.
[83] Ogilvie (1980a), pp. 245-8.
[84] Finer (1997a), pp. 388-93.

The expansion of the republic continued.[85] About 270 Rome had conquered considerable parts of the Italian peninsula and started to get interested in Sicily, where there were Greek settlements and, more important, areas controlled by Carthage, the great power to the south of the Mediterranean. This led to the so called Punic wars which the Romans finally won, but only after some severe setbacks. The first of these were naval casualties at the coast of Carthage.[86] Then the problems culminated when the Carthaginian general Hannibal, with an army including among other resources elephants, advanced through Spain and southern France, over the Alps, and into northern Italy. There, during the years from 218 to 216, he won four great battles against the Romans. Altogether some 150 000 Roman soldiers, it is estimated, were killed. After the fourth battle the republic's predicament was most precarious. But Hannibal avoided completing his successes by marching towards Rome. The Romans, on their side, also avoided real battles and switched to delaying, attritional warfare. Therefore the decisive battle did not occur until several years later, in 202, when Hannibal was defeated on the North African coast by a Roman army.

That put an end to the mighty Carthaginian state, and after that nothing could stop the Romans any more. In a short time they conquered the whole Mediterranean area and the Mediterranean Sea became a Roman inland sea. As early as some years before 0 the state included the whole coastal area of the Mediterranean, large parts of today's Spain and France, those parts of today's Germany which lay to the west of the Rhine, the whole of today's Greece, most of today's Balkans and large parts of today's Turkey. What was to become included furthermore, during the early part of the Empire—about which more follows below—was Egypt, the remaining parts northwards up to Danube, and England all the way up to the Scottish border.

In its combination of speed and magnitude this expansion has few counterparts—what first comes to mind is perhaps the initial, very fast expansion of the Persian Empire. But in spite of its military triumphs the Roman Republic was unstable, and was therefore followed by the Roman Empire. This meant, with the terminology used here, a transformation

---

[85] Ogilvie (1980b), pp. 248-52.
[86] Morris, p. 270.

from oligarchy to dictatorship. Basically two problems caused the collapse of the Republic—the one social and the other constitutional. The social problem was a gradually more and more unequal distribution of property—the big landowners, usually also successful military officers, became richer and richer, and the great mass of people more and more poor.[87] The constitutional problem, which will be described in more detail in chapter 8, had its ground in the fact that the constitution, gradually, became less and less manageable, and finally unmanageable. One problem was that final, valid decisions could be taken by different authorities and thereby be contradictory, another, which rather was an opposite problem, that many actors, in various roles, were endowed with veto power. The fall of the Republic started when the brothers Tiberius (163–33) and Gaius (153–21) Gracchus, belonging to a well off family, in their roles as Tribunes of the People (see chapter 8) advocated the claims of the poor. After having proposed a law about land redistribution Tiberius was murdered in 133.

The struggle thereby started continued as a civil war which, after numerous entanglements, did not stop until Augustus, in –31, made himself emperor. Before that the civil war had gone through several phases with autonomous generals, and their armies, fighting each other. Above all, Julius Caesar, on his own initiative and without orders from Rome, waged a large-scale war of his own—it lasted for seven years—in today's France. He thereby expanded the Roman area considerably, made himself utterly rich by plundering, and gained his soldiers confidence. These, obviously, appreciated the victories and, furthermore, were allowed to loot the local population, and to treat it with exceptional brutality and cruelty. Thus, in one case, after a battle, 430 000 men, women and children were caught in a trap and all killed.[88] In other situations punishments such as cutting off hands were used. In connection with the activities in France Caesar also made two short expeditions to England, and one, across the Rhine, into Germany. After the years in France he then continued to other parts of the Roman area—for instance to Greece, North Africa and Spain—in order to, in the civil war, fight other generals and their armies. After having succeeded in this he returned to the city of Rome, where he

---

[87] Finer (1997a), p. 424; Roberts, p. 240.
[88] Chrissanthos, pp. 138-46. I do not have any doubts about Caesar's cruelty, but the figure nevertheless seems high. It is however the one given in the source.

made himself dictator in −45 and was murdered in −44. Then a new struggle for power ensued. The ones finally remaining in this fight were Mark Antony (−83− −30) and Augustus (−63−14). The former had for a long time been a close and loyal friend of Caesar, and the latter was Caesar's adopted son. Augustus won the final duel, and after that Antony and his[89], and Caesar's former[90], mistress, the Egyptian queen Cleopatra, committed suicide[91]. In that way Augustus became the first emperor of the Roman state, which thereby, after having been the Roman Republic was converted into the Roman Empire.

The Empire thus was a dictatorship even if it, at least during a long initial period, was a mild one. Much evidence favors the contention, in fact, that it was one of the mildest and most civilized dictatorships ever to have existed. The early period was to a large extent characterized by peace, order and cultural magnificence. Augustus (governing −31−14), after the collapse of the Republic, skillfully consolidated the state, and after him a number of later emperors continued in the same way. Claudius (governing 41−54) was, in spite of his hardly imperial style, and his even laughable behavior, a skillful administrator, who gave, for instance, large population groups Roman citizenship. Hadrian (governing 117−38) did not only build the well-known wall across England at the empire's northern border but also carried through a number of important administrative reforms. Among the good emperors were also Marcus Aurelius (governing 161−80), about whom I will write more in chapter 6. So in spite of the fact that there were, during this time, also cruel, or even bestial, emperors such as Caligula (governing 37−41) and Nero (governing 54−68) it was, nevertheless, and basically, a good time. The expression *Pax Romana*—the Roman peace—designates in particular the time from Augustus to Marcus Aurelius, that is from −31 to 180.[92]

The cultural achievements—material as well as spiritual—during this period also were considerable. The technique for building with concrete was developed by the Romans who thereby made it possible to erect vaults—bridges as well as cupolas—with spans which, until then, had been unthinkable.[93] The result was not only a most impressive road

---

[89] Wilkinson, pp. 497-8.
[90] Wilkinson, pp. 503-5.
[91] Wilkinson. p. 508.
[92] Chrissanthos, pp. 172-3.

network and aqueducts but also a large number of cities all over the empire with a typical Roman style. They all had, in about the same manner, an amphitheatre, baths, markets, colonnades and a kind of big, vault-covered buildings called basilicas. During this time—and in particular during the reign of Augustus—Latin literature also reached a culmination. The poets Virgil (–70– –19), Horace (–65– –8) and Ovid (–43–17) and the historian Tacitus (circa 55–120) may in particular be mentioned.

The *Pax Romana* period ended when the military once again began dominating Roman Politics.[94] Augustus' consolidating efforts, after the civil war between the generals at the end of the Republic, to a large extent amounted to gaining control over the army. The Empire should not expand any further. Never again should a new Caesar get a chance. But even if Augustus succeeded in creating a long period of peace, it finally came to an end. The army, or parts of the army, again gained influence and a long period with professional military officers as dictators followed. Some of these were competent and created order, while civil war characterized the rule of others. At this time the attacks on the Empire from outside also became more serious. For their defense fortified walls were built around several cities. About 270 even the city of Rome, which until then had not had any wall, got one.

Two emperors far into this military period are of particular interest, namely Diocletian and Constantine. Diocletian (governing 284–305) gained power because he was a good warrior and therefore had at least some support from the army. He was, during his reign, almost constantly travelling in the large empire. The city of Rome he visited only once, in 303. Trying to consolidate the state he undertook a series of far-reaching measures. He strengthened the central control over the army, which however, at the same time, was made bigger. Security, which hitherto essentially had been a hard shell around the empire, was enlarged also into its inner parts so as to prevent enemies, who had penetrated the borders, to ravage freely in the interior. Furthermore he empowered the civil administration. But even if these measures were effective they also increased severely the burdens of the tax-paying masses. Diocletian also persecuted intensively the increasing number of Christian inhabitants

---

[93] Derry & Williams, pp. 163-72; Finer (1997a), p. 559; Liebeschuetz, p. 258.
[94] Browning, pp. 260-9.

and ordered their books to be burned. Realizing that the empire was too large to be governed from one centre, by one person, he also appointed a vice emperor, who was to be responsible for the western parts of the empire, and thereby the division of the empire had begun. And in order to make the power shifts easier and more controlled he introduced a system in which, during the reign of the incumbent emperor, potential successors were trained for the task. This, however, did not lead to the intended smooth shifts of power, but rather to destructive power struggles.

During one prolonged and chaotic such struggle—at a certain time seven persons simultaneously laid claim on the throne—Constantine became emperor, and in due time also the only emperor (total ruling period 306–37). Constantine the Great, as he is also called, made himself known for, in particular, two things. The one is that he, after an experience which he considered a vision, became a Christian himself, and thereby also made Christianity an accepted religion. This was the initiation of the process which finally made Christianity the state religion of the Empire.[95] The other is his elevating, in 330, the Greek city Byzantium to a second capital of the Empire.[96] The city was also given the name Constantinople, and the Empire thereafter thus had two capitals, Rome and Constantinople. The position of the latter was of great strategic importance—the city lay on the junction between the land road from the countries east of the Mediterranean to Europe and the sea road from the Mediterranean to the Black Sea.

In 395 the Empire was finally, and definitely, divided into the Western Roman Empire and the Eastern Roman Empire. The borderline may roughly be described as a straight line starting along the Danube—where the river flows through today's Hungary—going southwards between today's Italy and Greece, and then further southwards across the Mediterranean into today's Libya, dividing that country at about the middle. The two empires thus created were to meet very different fates. Western Rome, in which the Latin language dominated, and which also was the state in which the military tradition continued to dominate, collapsed definitely about a hundred years after the partition. To some extent the reason was attacks from the outside—in particular by various

---

[95] Browning, pp. 263-4.
[96] Browning, p. 264.

Germanic tribes—but also a considerable internal disintegration.[97] Eastern Rome, on the contrary, was to survive until as late as 1453, and Constantinople was to become a glorious world metropolis.

THE BYZANTINE EMPIRE AND THE WORLD AROUND IT

The eastern part of the former Roman Empire thus became an independent state in 395, coexisted with the Western Roman Empire for barely a hundred years, and after that continued as the only remaining part of the former empire. From about that time it is also called the Byzantine Empire or just Byzantium. In the beginning its area was large and covered much of the lands around the eastern Mediterranean including today's Turkey, Egypt and the eastern parts of today's Libya. The country was influenced by Greek and even oriental culture, and the main language was Greek. The first emperors, by expansion and modernization, converted Constantinople into a glorious world metropolis often called New Rome. The city became an important center of international commerce. The impressive church of Hagia Sophia was built. Big, effective walls for protecting the city against attacks from its land side were also built at an early stage. Attacks from the sea could be met with so called Greek fire, an incendiary weapon possessed only by Byzantium.[98] And these means of defense were needed since Byzantium had enemies and was continuously engaged in wars. Losses also made the territory successively smaller, but the capital remained unconquered for a long time, and the state thereby kept its identity.

Byzantium's first enemy was a new Persian empire which, using the name of the ruling dynasty, is called the Sassanid Empire. In 619 these Persians conquered Egypt, and since Egypt was a great producer of wheat Byzantium thereby lost a substantial part of its means of subsistence. In 626 the Persians failed however in their effort to conquer Constantinople, and somewhat later, in 650, they, themselves, were beaten by a new, budding empire, the Caliphate.[99]

The Caliphate—so called since the leader of it had the title caliph— was founded by the Arab Muhammad (circa 570–632). During its first

---

[97] For a detailed discussion of the causes of the fall see Rollason, pp. 18-33.
[98] Derry & Williams, p. 268; Lane, p. 40.
[99] Herrin, p. 26; Roberts, pp. 320, 331.

century the expansion was extraordinarily rapid and reached far. For a start the whole Arabic peninsula, Syria, Mesopotamia and the Sassanid's Persia were taken. After that the Arabs turned both eastwards and westwards. Eastwards conquests were made as far away as in today's Afghanistan and Pakistan, and fighting was undertaken still further to the east, perhaps as far away as in China.[100] Westwards was Byzantium, and beyond that Venice and the Frankish Kingdom (which both will be treated in the next section) were beginning to take form. In order to reach these places two routes were, in principle, available, one shorter route to the north of the Mediterranean, which however had to pass Constantinople, and one longer to the south of the sea. In spite of intensive efforts to conquer Constantinople, at first by a series of sieges 673–78, and then by still another siege 717–18, the Arabs however never succeeded in opening the northern route. Finally they therefore took the southern route and went through Egypt, through the rest of North Africa, over Gibraltar into Spain, and a long way into France. There, at last, they were stopped by a Frankish army at the battle of Poitiers in 732.

The first capital of the Caliphate was Damascus, but soon it was moved to Baghdad, which was turned into a splendid metropolis. The city became an important international, commercial gathering place, and also a center of art and science—it became a kind of anti-pole, or competitor, to Constantinople.[101] Here Plato, Aristotle and Euclid were translated into Arabic, and it was in this way that this literature, after having been further translated from Arabic to Latin, reached Europe.[102] The Arabs also adopted a numeral system developed by the Indians, namely the system which is the decimal system of today. In contrast to the Babylonians, whose system I have already written about, the Indians, however, used ten figures, including the important zero. It is because of this intermediate landing of the decimal system in the Caliphate that we today talk about Arabic numerals—numerals which for all mathematics are superior to the clumsy Roman ones. The Arabs, consequently, were proficient mathematicians—the word algebra, for instance, comes from them.[103]

---

[100] Findlay & O'Rourke, p. 17; Finer (1997b), p. 624; Gascoigne (2003), p. 112; Roberts, pp. 353-4.
[101] Roberts, p. 336.
[102] Roberts, p. 338.
[103] Roberts, p. 339.

In the preceding section I characterized the outcome of the wars between the Persians and the Greeks as one of world history's most consequential road choices—had the Persians won the extraordinary Athenian civilization would never have appeared and much would have been very different. Byzantium's successful defense of Constantinople against the Arabs' attacks may, in the same way, be considered a consequential road choice by world history. Had the Arabs succeeded in opening the northern route, and penetrated into Europe that way, much could have become very different. The courses of events which are to be described in the next section, and which have been of fundamental importance for forming the world we are living in today, might then have been replaced by completely different ones with other, unknown consequences. But this did not happen. Rather, the Caliphate itself soon perished. This happened when the Mongols (about whom I will write more in the section about China below), after a successful siege, conquered and destroyed Baghdad in 1258.[104]

Prior to its disappearance the Caliphate had, however, had other and less dangerous enemies than the Mongols, namely the European crusaders who ultimately aimed at re-conquering Palestine for Christianity. Within that enterprise the crusaders however also engaged in affairs affecting Byzantium. Inspired and supported by Venice—about which more follows in the next section—they succeeded, in 1204, in taking Constantinople by penetrating the city's weak, and since long neglected, defense against attacks from the sea.[105] They plundered the city and stayed there until 1261, when it was taken back by Byzantium. And this empire, once so great and splendid but now severely weakened, was to remain there for almost another two hundred years.

After the collapse of the Caliphate something which was destined to become the next big Muslim state—the Ottoman Empire—had begun to take form. The origin, again, was one of all those tribes, in this case the Turks. It was these Turks who finally, and definitely, succeeded in conquering Constantinople, which happened in 1453. To a large extent this depended on gunpowder.[106] A gradually more efficient gunpowder-artillery had been developed for some time, and the conquest of Constan-

---

[104] Finer (1997b), p. 670; Roberts, p. 379.
[105] Finer (1997b), p. 626; Hicks, p. 52; Roberts, p. 361.
[106] Derry & Williams, pp. 268-70.

tinople was this artillery's first big triumph. When the city, due to this, was transferred from Christianity to Islam, the Hagia Sophia church was equipped with the four big minarets it has today. The Ottoman Empire then grew and thrived for a long time until 1923, when Kemal Atatürk, following all sultans, became modern Turkey's first president.

The Byzantine culture was thus repudiated by the Muslims, but another people, those who were to become the Russians of the future, appreciated it all the more. The religion of Byzantium—the so called Eastern Orthodox variety of Christianity—thus gained adherents among them, and the Byzantine style of building, with big cupolas, became a characteristic feature of, for instance, Kiev as early as around the year 1000. When the Russian state gradually became more consolidated its rulers, who considered themselves successors to the Byzantine rulers, also adopted the title of the latter, namely tsar. The first one to be crowned as a Russian tsar was Ivan the Terrible (1530–84). Another, later tsar, whom we will meet in what follows, was Peter the Great (1672–1725).

So far I have not treated one of the most important neighbors of Byzantium, perhaps the most important, namely Venice. The story of that state will, however, be presented in the next section. Here, at last, I will just notice that when Constantinople fell in 1453, the very last part of the former Roman Empire also fell. And thereby, after about 2200 years, the sequence of events, which began at a little village at the mouth of the Tiber, came to an end.

WESTERN EUROPE AFTER THE FALL OF THE WESTERN ROMAN EMPIRE

After the fall of the Western Roman Empire the conditions in what is today Western Europe were chaotic. All organization and order which the Roman Empire, at its best, had delivered, was gone. People lived in statelessness and anarchy. The Roman road network had degenerated, and was to a large extent even destroyed. The economy had returned to self subsistence and the markets, and the well developed monetary system of the empire, were gone. At most a certain degree of barter economy existed. The collapse was almost total. There were no large, important monopolies of violence, but rather hundreds of small entities and beside them just anarchy.[107]

---

[107] Finer (1997a), p. 33; Finer (1997b), p. 855; Palmer, Colton & Kramer (2007a),

But still this western Europe would prove to be a fertile ground for interesting states of different kinds.[108] All the things that today are considered valuable characteristics of states, and that are now taken almost for granted, developed out of this chaos. It was here, and in no other place, that the modern, civilized state saw the light of day. All democracy that today exists around the world has social processes in western Europe, during the thousand year period after the fall of the Western Roman Empire, as its necessary precondition—and not only that period, but also the fall of the Empire as such. Had the Empire not fallen we would today, in all probability, live in a much worse world than the one we are, in fact, living in. To see this it may be enough to compare with China. China may be considered as the Roman Empire which did not fall— on the contrary the dictatorships were persistent and a space large enough for alternatives to grow never appeared.[109] In western Europe, however, different kinds of states materialized, and, among these, two in particular are interesting, each one in its own way, namely Venice and England. I will start with Venice in order to get to England later on.

After the collapse of the Western Roman Empire various Germanic tribes ravaged within its former area, and people living there were forced to flee in different directions. One such group of people—probably chased by the Lombards (the long-beards)—sought refuge in a difficult to reach, fragmented island world in a lagoon on the Italian coast in the northernmost part of the Adriatic Sea. It was this people which, at that place, founded Venice—probably at some time in the seventh century. The location by the sea, in combination with the difficulties of reaching the mainland, where anyway the hostile Germanics resided, forced them to become mariners. And the limited possibilities for subsistence in the small island world forced them into contacts with the surrounding world.

To some extent these contacts, in the same way as for most other states until about this time in history, consisted in conquering and plundering. But to some extent they also consisted in commerce, and even if states have traded with each other almost as long as there have been states, Venice became one of the first states in history whose riches mainly came from commerce. Perhaps the same may have been true for,

---

p. 23; Roberts, p. 290.
[108] Finer (1997a), p. 14.
[109] Finer (1997b), p. 738.

for instance, Phoenicia and Carthage[110], but the traditions from that time were anyway broken long since, and Venice, therefore, still became a pioneer of commerce.[111] True, the great incomes from commerce partly depended on Venice's capacity—a strong military naval power as it was—to create a commercial monopoly in the eastern Mediterranean. The monopoly started with the control of the river mouths in northern Italy, and was then enlarged successively. But even if the commerce thus, to a considerable extent, was monopoly commerce, it was, nevertheless, commerce.

Other states, about which I will soon write more, were to be inspired by this commerce, and these states all belonged to the western world which is the subject of this section.[112] In the beginning Venice's large incomes from commerce were however due to the contacts with Byzantium and the Caliphate in the east, and to some extent also with the Muslim part of Africa.[113] During Venice's early days Constantinople and Baghdad were, as we have seen, important centers of international commerce, while Venice's immediate neighborhood was undeveloped and chaotic. The two eastern empires were, therefore, of crucial importance for Venice's rapid and successful take off. The Venetians not only exported their own goods but also acted as intermediaries, and, with its successively larger and larger fleet, as freighters of others' cargoes. An early export product of their own was salt, which was of great importance for preserving meat and fish[114], and for the production of which the conditions within the lagoon were excellent. The water's salt content was excessive already from the beginning, and large evaporation basins could easily be built on the flat sand-banks constituting the islands. Large incomes were also generated by the export, to the Caliphate, of slaves and eunuchs—persons whom the Venetians sometimes bought from others, sometimes captured themselves in bellicose raids in their neighborhoods.[115] Many more kinds of goods, for instance wood and timber, could be mentioned, but that is hardly necessary. More important is to relate what I have said so far to the cultural movement which is called the

---

[110] Chrissanthos, p. 114.
[111] Lane, pp. 5-6; Findlay & O'Rourke, pp. 92-4.
[112] North & Thomas, p. 33.
[113] Lane, p. 26.
[114] Rosenberg & Birdzell, p. 75.
[115] Herrin, p. 204; Lane, p. 8.

Renaissance, and which had its beginning in Italy around 1400. Since Venice is considered one of the strongholds of the Renaissance it should be noted that this chapter came late in the history of the state. The exceptional, commercial expansion preceded the Renaissance.[116]

Venice was, however, not only a commercial state but also, as already mentioned, a military power, and, after some time, a very strong one. From its start as a small city-state in the lagoon it went on by conquering not only large areas to the north and east of the Adriatic Sea, but also considerable parts of the Aegean island world and Crete. A few steps in this expansion may therefore be noted.

I have already mentioned Venice's participation in the crusaders' plundering of Constantinople in 1204, but that story may be made more complete. By that time Venice, from having had friendly relations with Byzantium in the beginning, had become a militant enemy of the empire. In the beginning Venice was, in fact, a Byzantine satellite, since it lay just to the east of Byzantium's western border, and during that time the relations between Venice and the great empire were also cordial. The Venetians were, as we remember, completely dependent on Byzantium for their first commercial achievements. But it ended very differently, and an interesting testimony to that is the four bronze horses outside Saint Mark's Basilica in Venice. They and much else was taken in the plundering of Constantinople.[117] Another important part of Venice's foreign policy was the wars against Genoa from 1294 to 1381. They were about asserting supremacy over the eastern Mediterranean area, and Venice finally triumphed by winning the battle of Chioggia—one of the very first occasions when gunpowder canons were used on ships.[118] At about this time Venice's power was at its apogee, and the state had also fulfilled its important role in world history, to which I will return later on. Then and finally, after a long period of gradual decline, the state perished in the Napoleonic Wars.

At the same time as Venice was created there appeared, in quite another place in Europe, another state—and even here a Germanic tribe was involved. In this case the tribe did however not have the role of per-

---

[116] Hicks, p. 59.
[117] Lane, pp. 192, 206. The horses outside the church are in fact copies of the real horses, which however also are in Venice.
[118] Lane, pp. 189-96.

secutor as in the case of Venice, but rather created the state itself. The tribe, the so called Franks, had participated in the plundering of the Western Roman Empire, and the process thereafter followed a pattern, with which we now start to become familiar. First the state is created, then it grows by means of conquests to a great and glorious empire ruled by a dictator, and finally it collapses. The state this time was the so called Frankish Kingdom (481–843) or, during its climax, the Carolingian empire (772–814). At its largest it included almost all of today's continental Western Europe. Its capital was Aachen, situated close to the place where the borders of the Netherlands, Belgium and Germany meet today. This, thus, was—within the "main course" with which we are dealing here, and thus excluding for instance the Chinese states—the first great state which had its center outside, and without connections to, the so far dominating Mediterranean area. But the empire expired and thereafter—and excluding Venice—chaos returned to Western Europe.

This, however, was to change and slowly small states, or embryos for states, began to emerge. In some cases the process was about the same as it had always been—a ruler, or a series of rulers, occupies an area, and controls it, for a longer or shorter time. Processes like these will be analyzed in more detail in chapter 3, where I will introduce a mechanism called the "second invisible hand". This invisible hand can, in some simple cases, explain the appearance of national, stationary monopolies of violence.

In the Europe we are interested in here this mechanism was however complemented by another, new and interesting phenomenon, namely feudalism, which started emerging about the year 1000.[119] Even this phenomenon, with its preconditions and consequences, will be dealt with in more detail in later chapters. Here it is enough to say that the feudal society had several levels—in the simplest case two—between which a, at least temporary, power balance could prevail. At the higher level there usually was a king, and at the lower level a group of so called vassals or fiefs, who, with considerable freedom, ruled their own provinces, or fiefdoms, within the larger state of the king. The emergence of these levels was a result of the technical development of weapons, and of the difficulties involved in acquiring these weapons. The technical develop-

---

[119] Palmer, Colton & Kramer (2007a), pp. 29-31.

ment had resulted in a formidable weapon, namely the medieval knight, but at the same time the monetary economy had collapsed. The kings who needed the weapons therefore had to engage in bartering with those able to provide them, in particular great landowners. The landowners were allowed, on the whole, to govern their provinces as they liked—they became fiefs—in exchange for their commitment to deliver, when asked for, completely equipped, equestrian knights. These, thus, were feudalism's preconditions. If a society became feudal or not depended on the conditions of the individual case. And in a society which had once become feudal the balance of power could tilt, for instance giving the king all the power, or giving the lower level all the power.

Now, let us look at different parts of Europe and start at the Iberian Peninsula. There, at an early stage, appeared three states, which could be described as dictatorially governed kingdoms without any feudal structure at all, namely Portugal, Aragon and Castile.[120] Portugal had by the end of the fourteenth century become a very important, maritime power.[121] Even if this period of strength soon was to end, it was nevertheless long enough to be of utmost historical importance. Henry the Navigator (1394–1460) initiated early voyages of discovery and after him followed the great explorers Vasco da Gama (1460–1524) and Magellan (1480–1521). All three were Portuguese. During its period of power Lisbon also became an important center of international commerce. Going then to Aragon and Castile they became something very important when the king of the former state, Ferdinand, and the queen of the latter state, Isabella, married in 1469, and thereby founded what was to become the great power of Spain.[122] Even this state became an early and important maritime power. Christopher Columbus (1451–1506) came from Genoa, that is true, but it was Ferdinand and Isabella who financed and supported his voyages to America. And Hernán Cortés (1485–1547), who initiated the colonization of America, was a Spaniard.[123]

For the Portuguese and Spanish great powers feudalism was thus without significance, but in large other parts of Europe things were different. What was to become the great power of France thus began as

---

[120] Bloch, pp. 186-7.
[121] Roberts, pp. 508, 532-3.
[122] Palmer, Colton & Kramer (2007a), p. 74; Roberts, p. 508.
[123] Palmer, Colton & Kramer (2007a), pp. 74-5, 99-106; Roberts, pp. 532-4.

something rather fragmented. It consisted, in fact, of a number of small states ruled by their magnates. In 987 these magnates elected a common king[124], and in due time, at about the turn of the twelfth to the thirteenth century, the then king made himself the only ruler over the whole area. Thereby the French monarchy had been created, a state which at its climax was to be ruled by Louis XIV (1638–1715), the Sun King. It may be debated that he really asserted that "L'État, c'est moi" ("I am the State"), but it certainly could have been true. Anyway France went through the feudal stages upwards, from the partitioned state to the consolidated and centralized state.[125]

In Germany[126], and to some extent also in Italy, the process was the reverse one. There was, at an early stage, the so called Holy Roman Empire, about which the French philosopher Voltaire (1694–1778) at a later stage quipped that "this agglomeration which was called and which still calls itself the Holy Roman Empire was neither holy, nor Roman, nor an empire".[127] Germany went through the feudal stages downwards, and the country was not united, and did not get its modern form until the end of the nineteenth century. In Italy the process was similar and that country, too, was united late and just shortly before Germany.

Then we get to England, so important in this context and in the rest of this book. At first it was a consolidated kingdom, similar to the ones on the Iberian Peninsula, but then it got feudalism introduced from outside. The one who performed this was William the Conqueror from Normandy (circa 1027–87) who started by defeating the English at the battle of Hastings in 1066. After that he conquered all of England and introduced, there, the constitutional arrangement with which he was acquainted from his own country, the feudal one.[128] And this was destined to become of utmost importance, since the eventual council of vassals of the English feudalism was the embryo of the representative assemblies of representative democracy. All of this will be extensively dealt with in chapter 9.

Thus some larger areas were consolidated during the age we are talking about here, while other ones disintegrated, or were fragmented

[124] Palmer, Colton & Kramer (2007a), p. 30.
[125] Finer (1997b), pp. 919-35.
[126] Spruyt, p. 109.
[127] Palmer, Colton & Kramer (2007a), pp. 31, 190.
[128] Palmer, Colton & Kramer (2007a), p. 31.

from the start. But even these small entities harbored utterly critical possibilities for development. The pioneer, and source of inspiration, was
Venice. What happened was that a number of cities, extraneous to the
consolidated monarchies, and often situated at a coast or a river, were, or
made themselves, free. Among these cities were Genoa, Florence and Pisa
in Italy[129], Antwerp, Bruges and Ghent in today's Belgium, and a number
of cities such as Rostock, Lübeck and Stralsund along the coast of the
Baltic Sea[130]. Perhaps these cities succeeded in making themselves free
since feudalism's upper level already was weak, or perhaps it was the
other way round, that they, by making themselves free, contributed to
making that level weak. Anyway, a number of these cities applied for, and
was granted, status as free cities. Thereby they became, in effect, almost
free city-states. The mode of governing was in most cases oligarchic—the
cities were governed by means of a collegial cooperation between the
best-off citizens or families.[131]

　　All of these states were thus small, but in spite of this they not only
survived but were in fact quite wealthy. And the reason for this was that
they lived by commerce. It was their commercial activities which gave
them their great historical importance. A good example is the Venetians'
establishing in 1317 of the so called Flanders galleys which, regularly,
sailed between the Adriatic Sea and the North Sea.[132] The great economist
John Hicks (1904–89) has even argued that "[t]he fact that European
civilization has passed through a city-state phase is the principal key to
the divergence between the history of Europe and the history of Asia",
that is the key to why the West became rich.[133] Even if the constitutional
development, which started in England, also was a necessary condition
for the wealth of the West, Hicks's emphasis on the role of the small city-
states is nevertheless important. Within them commercial institutions,
which were to become of utmost importance, were developed, and a pre-

---

[129] Spruyt, pp. 130-50.
[130] Spruyt, pp. 109-29.
[131] Alesina & Spolaore, pp. 176-8; Finer (1997b), pp. 951-8; North & Thomas, pp.
33-5, 49-50; Palmer, Colton & Kramer (2007a), pp. 31-5; Roberts, p. 602;
Rosenberg & Birdzell, pp. 55-6, 77-8, 105.
[132] Palmer, Colton & Kramer (2007a), p. 100.
[133] Hicks, p. 38.

condition for this, as we will see in chapter 5, was, precisely, that the states were small.

But the limited size of the states also entailed problems, and in particular defense problems. At their Golden Age these cities could handle this problem by means of their fortified, defense walls—in some cases remaining from Roman times—and when they had to wage war outside their own borders they usually engaged mercenaries, which they could easily afford. But when gunpowder began to be used more extensively—from the end of the fifteenth century—the walls ceased to be a significant protection, and therefore the heyday of these city-states came to an end.[134] But by then their crucial historical mission had also been fulfilled.

The importance of this mission was however not so easy to re-cognize in its own time. I have already described how Plato criticized his own Athens, and similarly it is interesting, in this context, to focus on Niccolò Machiavelli (1469–1527), the author of the famous political-science book "The Prince". He dealt with the problem that the small states we are talking about here often were fighting each other—one example, but certainly not the only one, are the wars, mentioned above, between Venice and Genoa in the beginning of the fifteenth century. The problem, according to Machiavelli, was that the states were small, and his ideal, therefore, was the big, consolidated monarchies. His heroes were strong kings such as Ferdinand of Aragon, Louis XI of France and Henry VII of England. That England, at that time, harbored the embryo of a repre-sentative democracy could of course not be known by Machiavelli. It was not the feudal balance of the English state that he admired, but the, in spite of everything, considerable power of the Tudor king.[135]

So far I have concentrated on the monopolies of violence which appeared in Western Europe after the fall of the Western Roman Empire. But the processes were not always towards consolidation. Prevailing, or new, chaos was also important. About this I will write more in chapter 11 about statelessness. Here it may be enough to mention the Thirty Years' War from 1618 to 48 as an important example. This war, which took place roughly within the area which constitutes today's Germany, was, to a large extent, a war of everybody against everybody—troops from

[134] Alesina & Spolaore, pp. 179, 181.
[135] Palmer, Colton & Kramer (2007a), pp. 67-9.

several nations fought each other. Anarchy prevailed within the area and the devastation was horrific.[136]

What I have now said about Western Europe after the fall of the Western Roman Empire is, for the time being, enough. In the following chapters some related topics will however be taken up and elaborated in more detail. In particular the emergence of representative democracy will be described and analyzed in detail in chapter 9.

THE SIDE LINES

THE INDIAN STATES

The vast Indian subcontinent is effectively protected by the Himalayas to the north. From the outside there are only two narrow entries to the area—the one through the plains surrounding the Indus River in the west, and the other, correspondingly, along the Ganges in the east. Of these two entries the western one has, historically, been the most important. The existence of this entrance, it may be remarked, makes the charac- terization of the Indian states as a side line somewhat questionable, but it is not wrong either. The Indian states to a large extent developed in isolation, and their limited interaction with the outer world on the whole meant that they received impressions from outside—their own influence on the outer world was much more limited.

The first, important civilizations appeared in the western areas around the Indus. Here, from about −2600 until about −1700, big cities, among which Harappa and Mohenjo-Daro may be mentioned, were erected with a very advanced building technique. Each of them may have had around 30 000 inhabitants. They were protected by fortified towers and walls. The houses in the cities often had two storeys, they were partitioned into flats and rooms, and, in many cases, also included a bath room. There were also large drainage systems built by burned bricks. Taking all of this into account it thus seems as if these societies were consolidated enough to be considered states, or perhaps to belong to a single encompassing state, even if our knowledge about these matters is limited. The finds are mainly archeological, and there are hardly any written remnants.[137] It is however fascinating to realize how advanced

---

[136] Palmer, Colton & Kramer (2007a), pp. 135-41; Roberts, pp. 604-5.
[137] Burrow, pp. 182-4; Chrissanthos, p. 13; Cotterell (1980a), pp. 176-81; Roberts,

these societies were, in spite of their early place in history. Their age, as the dates above indicate, coincides roughly with last phase of the Egypt's Old Kingdom, or with the time when Sargon of Akkad ruled his empire.

The reasons for the fall of these societies are unknown, but it happened at a time, around −1700, when the Arians, a people coming from the west, invaded the area. About these Arians we know that they implanted their language in the area, but not much more. The descendants of this language in India would later prove to have important similarities with European languages. The discovery was made by the British lawyer William Jones (1746–94), employed by the British East Indian Company in Calcutta. He was the first to formulate the hypothesis about an Indo-European family of languages with a common origin.

After the Arian invasion there are four great Indian states which are particularly interesting, namely the Maurya Empire from −321 to −185, the Gupta Empire from about 320 to 647, the Delhi Sultanate from 1206 to 1334 and the Mughal Empire from 1526 to 1739. The accumulated life time for the first three of these states—with the years indicated—is 676 years. Compared to the total time of 3200 years from the Arian invasion to the creation of the Mughal Empire, this is a very short time. For long periods the Indian subcontinent was fragmented and a victim of almost perpetual war making.[138]

The states mentioned were also markedly different—there was nothing of the continuity over long periods as we have seen in Egypt, and will see in China. The first of the states, Maurya, was founded just after Alexander the Great had reached the Indus and turned back westwards— the creators of Maurya may have utilized the power vacuum that had appeared after Alexander's retreat.[139] The territory of Maurya included all of today's Pakistan and India except the southernmost part of the subcontinent. The state was interesting because, among other things, one of its rulers, Asoka (about whom more follows in chapter 6), after a personal crises, turned to Buddhism. Buddha lived in India from about −560 to about −480, and thus died about 150 years before the Maurya Empire appeared. But even if Asoka thus became a Buddhist, Hinduism as well had been present in India for a long time when Maurya arrived on

pp. 121-3.
[138] Finer (1997c), p. 1213.
[139] Thapar, pp. 62, 70.

the scene, and the same was true for India's unique and very special caste-system.[140]

The Gupta Empire was not as centralized as Maurya, it became more long-lived, and its territory was essentially smaller.[141] It did not reach as far westwards, and southwards, as Maurya's; it was limited to a belt across the northern part of the subcontinent including the Indus and Ganges areas.[142] The Gupta Empire is interesting, among other things, for the cultural achievements performed within it. It was here that the decimal numeral system, so important for mathematics, was created, and important mathematical results were also produced, as well as astronomical ones. The astronomer Aryabhata (476–550) calculated correctly the length of the year as well as π with several decimals.[143] Some of the major works of Indian literature also got their final form, in the Sanskrit language, in this empire.[144] The Gupta era is sometimes called India's classical age, a kind of correspondence to the first period of the Roman Empire.[145]

The Delhi Sultanate was neither large, nor long-lived, but still something completely new in India since it was Muslim. It was founded in 1206 by incoming Turks—a people related to those who, about 250 years later, were to conquer Constantinople. And even if the Sultanate expired, its appearance meant that Islam got foothold in India. It should also be said that the year for the passing of the Sultanate stated above—1334—is only partially true. Certainly a far-reaching, internal disintegration of the Empire started at that time, and in addition to that Delhi was plundered in 1398 by the conqueror Timur (1336–1405)—a warrior similar to Alexander the Great and Genghis Khan (1162–1227). But in spite of these strains the Sultanate continued to exist in a formal sense all the time until 1526. Then, however, it finally perished when, what was to become the Mughal Empire, was founded.[146]

The founder was the young prince Babur (1483–1530) originating from a place in contemporary Uzbekistan and descending from Timur

---

[140] Finer (1997c), pp. 1210-11.
[141] Thapar, pp. 136, 145.
[142] Finer (1997c), p. 1212.
[143] Thapar, p. 155.
[144] Roberts, p. 430.
[145] Roberts, pp. 429-30.
[146] Finer (1997c), p. 1213.

through his mother and from Genghis Khan through his father. He started by conquering Kabul in Afghanistan from where he went into northern India. In 1526 he captured Delhi and thereby the story of the Mughal Empire began. Mughal is the Persian word for Mongol, and the rulers were sometimes called Great Mughals.[147] They followed after each other in a long row, in which Akbar the Great (1552–1605) and Shah Jahan (1592–1666) are the most well-known. When they ruled the Empire expanded and came to include almost the whole subcontinent—it was larger than the Maurya Empire and the largest Indian state until then.

The only "soft" trait of this state was a long lasting religious tolerance. Even if this tolerance eventually ended, it was manifest in particular during reign of Akbar.[148] Although the state was Muslim other religions, and in particular Hinduism, were tolerated. There were high-ranking Hindu bureaucrats at the court, even a Hindu "minister of finance", and Hindu women in the harem.[149] But the "softness" stopped at that. The centralized administration was utterly harsh, and the tax-level high with continually recurring peasant revolts as a consequence.[150] And these were suppressed with despotic cruelty. Those revolting could be beheaded and, after that, as a deterrence for the future, the heads could be accumulated in large heaps and the bodies impaled along the road-sides.[151] But in spite of this the despotism was not complete. I have already mentioned the religious tolerance, and in addition to that there were no homogenizing mass-deportations of people.

The tax-incomes were, of course, used for military and police purposes—from the state Bukhara in Central Asia was imported, for instance, one hundred thousand (!) horses per year.[152] But after that the resources were almost completely devoted to a luxurious court life which in lavishness probably surpassed everything that had existed anywhere so far, and perhaps almost all that was to come. The opulence included, in particular, flourishing art and fantastic architecture. South of Delhi was created a new capital, Agra, where Shah Jahan built the extraordinarily

---

[147] Roberts, pp. 435-43.
[148] Gascoigne (1971), pp. 69-72; Roberts, p. 441.
[149] Roberts, p. 438.
[150] Eraly, p. 173; Gascoigne (1971), pp. 188-9; Roberts, pp. 440-1.
[151] Eraly, pp. 261, 305; Finer (1997c), p. 1253; Gascoigne (1971), pp. 62, 185-6.
[152] Anthony, p. 341; Eraly, p. 291.

beautiful mausoleum Taj Mahal for his deceased favorite wife. The equally well-known Peacock Throne, decorated with the world-renowned diamond Koh-i-Noor, was also created at this time for Shah Jahan. As an interesting detail it may further be mentioned that the personal body-guards of the Great Mughals were not, as in many other courts, eunuchs, but women—amazons—well versed in the use of bows and other weapons.[153]

But the Mughal Empire, as all empires, had its end, and, as usual, the reasons were a combination of inner disintegration and attacks from the outside. The disintegration started in 1712 when the first in a row of weak Great Mughals entered the throne, and the death-blow was then delivered when a Persian adventurer raided and looted the capitals and carried off the Peacock Throne.[154] By that time, however, the British had already started establishing themselves in India—the British East India Company had been founded in 1600—but this was not the cause of the fall of the remarkable empire. A new Indian state would, however, not arise until the break-down of the British Empire after the Second World War.

THE CHINESE STATES

The base for the Chinese states is the extremely fertile lands around the Yellow River and the Yangtze River. The areas around the Yellow River were exploited first and mainly for growing millet. In the southern later developed Yangtze area the main crop was rice.

At the outskirts of these fertile plains there were natural protections against invaders. To the east were the frontier waters of the Pacific, in the south the jungles towards the Indochinese peninsula, and in southwest and west the Himalayas. Only in the northwest and north, where the area meets the Central-Asian steppes, natural defense barriers were missing. At an early stage these natural barriers were however of limited relevance, simply because the area protected was so large. The states which were first created, and which could be created with the military technique then available, were much smaller than the protected area. The similarities with the early conditions in Mesopotamia were

---

[153] Eraly, p. 54; Finer (1997c), p. 1234; Gascoigne (1971), p. 73.
[154] Finer (1997c), p. 1260.

therefore considerable. When the states grew larger the barriers did however become more and more valuable, but at the same time the opening to the north and northwest became a problem. To this I will return, however.

Now and then, and in particular at an early stage, there could thus be several, or even many, states within the area. But still it is possible to concentrate on a sequence of states following each other. Among those Qin, which existed for a short period around the year −200, holds a key position. It not only gave China its name[155] but also, emphatically, imprinted its societal characteristics on the succeeding Chinese states. There is, considering the societal organization at large, and disregarding some intermediary periods, a very remarkable continuity from Qin to, at least, 1912 when the state of Qing ended, and possibly even longer. The arguments supporting a continuity into our own days are not absent. So even if the reasons are different, the Chinese states, nevertheless, are characterized by a continuity as outstanding and remarkable as that of the ancient Egyptian states.

Before Qin there were, however, two important predecessors, and I will start with them.[156] The first one, Shang, was founded by the leader of a tribe with the same name, and covered a rather small area in the Yellow River valley. It existed from circa −1600 until circa −1100, and thus, being approximately contemporaneous with Egypt's New Kingdom, lasted about 500 years. The other one, Zhou, the name of which also came from the founding tribe, existed from circa −1100 till circa −700, and hence was about contemporary with the Assyrian Empire.

In important respects these two states were similar to each other. That they could be created at all depended, to some extent, on the disposal, by the leaders to be, of advanced weapons. The technique for bronze casting was highly developed, and this did not only result in beautiful objects of art, but also in efficient weapons—above all heads for arrows and lances and fundamental parts of chariots (about which I will write more in chapter 4).

Furthermore the written language was of great importance in these first Chinese states, as well as in their successors, and this language was,

---

[155] This becomes more obvious if it is observed that Qin, in English, sometimes is written Ch'in. Finer (1997a), p. 444.
[156] Finer (1997a), pp. 442-69.

in the same way as those of hieroglyphs and cuneiform, difficult. The scribes, therefore, in the same way as in Egypt and Mesopotamia, constituted an important part of society's upper level. There was, however, one very important difference. The hieroglyphs and cuneiform have since long disappeared while the complicated Chinese writing has remained, and still remains today, and thereby, as well, much of the culture and social conditions associated with the writing.

Shang and Zhou were both characterized by a balance between the ruler and the great landowners, and the states were thus feudal (about which more follows in chapter 6). And below the ruler and the land-owners were the common people. These handled the agriculture but were also forced to carry out other kinds of work, above all building protective walls around the cities. But the common people, and slaves, were also used for other, more macabre, purposes—and in that case mainly in Shang. In graves large numbers of people, who were sacrificed at the funerals of the rulers, have been found.[157] Anyway Shang and Zhou were probably not particularly well consolidated—the power of the land-owners, and the building of walls around the cities, testify to that. The territory has vividly been described as an archipelago in which thousands of islands were surrounded by a wild and dangerous sea. The islands were strongholds such as walled towns, castles and military garrisons, while the sea was dominated by hostile villagers and alien tribesmen.

During a long time after Zhou—from about −700 to about −200—this fragmentation dominated.[158] The first part of this time is usually called the Spring and Autumn period, and the latter part the Warring States period. During this time the thinker and social philosopher Confucius (−551− −479), who was to become of considerable importance in the history of China, was active. It is interesting to compare Confucianism in China with Christianity in the Roman Empire. In both cases the adherents at first, during a long period, were persecuted, occasionally by very cruel means. But then, again in both cases, the philo-sophies were adopted as, almost, state ideologies, or, in the case of Christianity, as a state religion. The Confucianism, which in this way was promoted during the Han dynasty was however a somewhat diluted ver-

---

[157] Cotterell (1980b), p. 289; Morris, p. 212-3.
[158] Cotterell (1980c), p. 292.

sion which did not significantly impede the wielding of centralized, despotic power.[159] Preceding Han came however the formative period of Qin.

In spite of its fundamental importance this period was however extremely short. The state of the period, Qin, the name of which came from the founding chief, only existed during the few years from –221 to –207, that is for fourteen years in all. Before that the state in being had however been built up step by step—in the final phase during the years –230 to –221 by the then chief Shi Huangdi defeating competing minor kings in the area.[160] Shi Huangdi was a skilful and brutal warrior and he had weapons which had not existed in the times of Shang and Zhou. In the same way as in the western world the chariots had been substituted for by a combination of infantry and cavalry. Furthermore weapons made of iron, swords for instance, had been introduced, as well as the cross-bow, a Chinese invention which for its stretching mechanism was dependent on advanced metallurgy.[161]

The real reign of Shi Huangdi—starting when the state was created in –221—was to be short, but still he managed to accomplish a lot.[162] He enlarged the territory of the state—both westwards so that more of the Yellow River area was included, and southwards so that large parts of the Yangtze area were embraced as well. And within this total area a far-reaching centralization and homogenization was carried out. The feudal system, with its dependence on big landowners, was abolished and replaced by a harsh, centralized hierarchical administration. A large number of landowner families were deported to the new frontier areas. The Confucians were cruelly persecuted and their books burned. Shi Huangdi in fact created a despotic, top ruled state. The dictator in this survey to whom he, in these respects, is most similar, is probably Assyria's Ashurbanipal. It is hardly surprising that he much later, in the twentieth century, was celebrated as a hero in the communist China of Mao Zedong.[163]

---

[159] Morton & Lewis, p. 64.
[160] Finer (1997a), p. 472; Roberts, p. 445.
[161] Derry & Williams, p. 27.
[162] Cotterell (1980d), pp. 296-7; Fairbank & Goldman, pp. 54-7; Finer (1997a), pp. 469-75; Gascoigne (2003), pp. 48-53.
[163] Finer (1997a), pp. 473, 527.

Some of the undertakings of Shi Huangdi were however more constructive. The problem with the opening in the northwest— mentioned above—was now addressed more seriously. True, there were even earlier beginnings of what was to become the Great Wall of China, but it was only now that the first large scale activities were undertaken— activities to which some 300 000 humans are thought to have been assigned. Additional great building projects were carried through, or at least started. Among those was the Zhengguo Canal, which connected various watercourses of the Yellow River system with each other, large irrigation installations, and comprehensive road networks. Different kinds of measures, for instance for weight, were standardized.[164] And the remarkable army consisting of several thousand soldiers, a great number of horses, and so on, everything in life-size in terracotta, and discovered as late as 1974, was created during the reign of Shi Huangdi.[165]

After the death of Shi Huangdi in −210 the state disintegrated rapidly and in −206 it was gone. Then, with some intermediary periods in between, followed the well-known states with the names of their dominating dynasties, namely Early Han (−206–9), Late Han (25–220), Sui (589–618), Tang (618–907), Song (960–1126), the Mongol period or Yuan (1234–1368), Ming (1368–1644) and the Manchu period or Qing (1644–1912).[166] Here, it is hardly necessary to treat these periods separately. Since the main characteristics of Chinese society essentially remained the same since Qin at least until 1912, it is enough to describe in a summary form some of the most important episodes and changes.[167]

First it should then be said that the periods of consolidation, which the dates above indicate, were interspersed by periods characterized by various degrees of fragmentation and conflict. After Han, for instance, there followed what is called the period of the Three Kingdoms, during which three generals from the Han era governed one part each of the formerly unified state.[168] During other intermediary periods there was still more chaos. Of considerable interest are also the two periods during which successful invaders completely overtook the Chinese state and

---

[164] Finer (1997a), p. 472.
[165] Fairbank & Goldman, p. 56; Gascoigne (2003), p. 51; Morris, p. 282.
[166] Roberts, p. 453.
[167] Finer (1997c), p. 1303.
[168] Cotterell (1980e), p. 300.

ruled it. One of the emperors during the first of these periods, which we may call the Mongolian one, was Kublai Khan (circa 1215–94), grandson to Genghis Khan.[169] During the second of these periods it was the Manchu people, also coming from the northwest, who invaded and ruled China. But, remarkably enough, China preserved its main features even during these periods with foreign rulers. They ruled the state in about the same way as the emperors of the Chinese dynasties. The periods of foreign rule thus have some similarities with ancient Egypt's second intermediate period in which Hyksos ruled the state.

But then, what were those rather permanent features of the Chinese societies? First, China was during all the time a manifest two-level society. An upper level totally dominated the enormous lower level mainly consisting of peasants who were severely oppressed and taxed. Peasant revolts, and their brutal crushing, are almost permanently recurring phenomena in China's history[170]—even if the Ming period to some extent is an exception[171].

But even if the upper level constituted a very small share of the total population, its structure was quite complicated. In addition to the emperor, his family, court, harem, eunuchs and so forth, there were two other important groups. One was the great landowners. Certainly I wrote above that Shi Huangdi deprived this group of their power, and in that way brought the elements of feudalism, which had existed in Shang and Zhou, to an end. Occasionally this group managed, however, to regain some of its power.[172] The other group consisted of what may be called the professional bureaucrats. It is often contended that the Chinese society is very particular in the sense of being an extreme meritocracy. Ancestry and background are of no importance for an individual's career possibilities—what is important is rather the school-education received and the marks obtained. And by education is then meant education in the Chinese language, in Confucianism, etcetera—not matters of practical or scientific importance.[173] That school results were overwhelmingly important may perhaps be debated—ancestry has, for instance, not been with-

---

[169] Morton & Lewis, pp. 119-20.
[170] Finer (1997a), p. 523; Roberts, p. 452.
[171] Finer (1997b), p. 806.
[172] Finer (1997a), pp. 486-7.
[173] Finer (1997a), p. 443; Roberts, pp. 448-51.

out importance—but the general tendency indicated seems, nevertheless, correct. Anyway, in this milieu emerged and thrived the important group of people which sometimes, starting with Tang, are called the manda-rins.[174] Even this group has, in the same way as the emperors and the landowners, had its periods of weakness and of strength.[175] But these were just fluctuations. What is important, and provided the stability, is that there was, throughout, an upper level which, on the whole, had the same components and which brutally exploited the great mass of the population.

How, then, can this stability be explained? One of the reasons seem to be that China all the time was isolated, and even strived for isolation—at least it did not try to break the isolation. The non-martial contacts with the outer world were few and occasional. During Han, for instance, occasional discoveries finally resulted in the Silk Road—the caravan route which connected China with the Mediterranean area, and thanks to which Chinese Silk was sold at markets in Rome as early as before the year 0.[176] Silk was the great Chinese export commodity, but the Chinese were not interested in importing anything other than horses and the ornamental stone jade. Another non-martial contact with the outer world was made in the Ming-period when a eunuch made a few naval exploratory expeditions to the Persian Gulf and the coast of Africa.[177] But that was just about all.[178] It was—with some reservation for the earlier part of Tang—as if there was no interest in the world outside China.[179] Chinese behavior was completely different from that of the Europeans in similar conditions. And this, of course, leads to the next question, the one about the reasons for this lack of interest. Part of the answer is, perhaps, included in the often held contention that the upper level, because of its background and education, despised manual work and commerce. But this could hardly be the whole truth. The building of the Great Wall of China, which was done in stages during several dynasties, was, of course, a stunning physical, manual enterprise. Offensive military enterprises are, as well, obviously

---

[174] Finer (1997b), p. 764; Gascoigne (2003), p. 36.
[175] Finer (1997c), p. 1133.
[176] Gascoigne (2003), p. 77.
[177] Gascoigne (2003), pp. 153-4; Morton & Lewis, pp. 127-8.
[178] Fairbank & Goldman, pp. 137- 40.
[179] Morton & Lewis, pp. 84-5, 99.

physical, manual undertakings, and in the eras of Han, Tang and Qing there were a number of utterly belligerent emperors who made very considerable conquests.[180] In the Sui period a big canal, which connected the water systems of the Yellow River and Yangtze with each other, was built.[181] And, to continue, in Tang the then capital of China was transformed into a fantastically glorious city which the historian J. M. Roberts describes like this:[182]

> "The capital was then at Ch'ang-an, in Shensi, a western province. Its name means 'long-lasting peace' and to this city at the end of the Silk Road came Persians, Arabs and central Asians who made it one of the most cosmopolitan cities in the world. It contained Nestorian churches, Zoroastrian temples, Muslim mosques, and was probably the most splendid and luxurious capital of its day, as the objects which remain to us show."

Building a city like this was, again and of course, a first rate physical, manual achievement. The quotation also shows that a lot of people from the surrounding world made their way to China. Much later, during the Mongol era, the Venetian Marco Polo (1254–1324) visited China and even became a confident of Kublai Kahn.[183] But the Chinese themselves never explored the surrounding world in similar ways, and when they, later on, built more cities, they would be of a very different kind than the one at Ch'ang-an. During Ming the so called Forbidden City, the extensive imperial palace in Beijing, was built—a creation which possibly could be considered a symbol for isolation and seclusion.[184]

Anyway, and disregarding the reasons for the introversion, there remain some facts which, as far as I have been able to find out, are non-controversial. The Chinese state, and society, displays some features which are rather constant during all the time from Qin until at least 1912. To these belong, above all, the utterly harsh treatment of the large masses of people by the upper class, all the time structured in the same manner.

---

[180] Finer (1997a), pp. 510-11.
[181] Gascoigne (2003), pp. 90-1.
[182] Roberts, p. 455; See also Fairbank & Goldman, p. 78. A much earlier, similar city was Egypt's Naukratis, see Wilkinson, pp. 43-4.
[183] Roberts, p. 459.
[184] Finer (1997b), p. 822.

Certainly the Chinese states also lived in isolation and without being interested in the world around. The exceptions are conquests westwards during Han, Tang and Qing dynasties. But those were military enterprises—culturally China has all the time been isolated and, as it seems, wished to be so.

THE JAPANESE STATES

I wrote above that it was not without question to consider the sequence of Indian states as a side line, and the same holds true for the Japanese states. During certain periods the Chinese influences were considerable—concerning ideas and institutions, but primarily concerning the written language—but in spite of this the Japanese isolation has for long periods not only been considerable, but also self-chosen. So treating the Japanese states as a side-line seems, after all, quite reasonable.

Japan has some similarities with ancient Egypt as well as with ancient Greece. The similarity with Egypt consists in the geographical isolation from the world around. The sea between Japan and the continental mainland is wide and difficult to cross, and the military missions across this sea were therefore, until modern times, few. The Mongol emperors of China tried twice—1274 and 1281—to invade Japan, but were both times stopped by typhoons. In Japanese these were called *Kamikaze*, meaning Divine wind.[185] In 1592 the Japanese themselves tried to conquer Korea and thereby to start an expansion into the Asian continent, but failed. The similarity with Greece consists in the typography with small cultivable areas between mountains—it was difficult to unify the people and splintering tendencies were common. Cultivation of rice and fishing were the main means of subsistence.

The Japanese state building process is of a late date.[186] Around the year 700 the country—or rather the main island Honshu and the southern island Kyushu—were united in an Empire. The capital Nara, close to today's Kyoto, became a magnificent center where the emperors lived lavishly and thereby, as it seems, also became enervated. Anyway the military forces of the emperors were small, and various landowners and local magnates were strong, so the state fell apart and acquired, without

---

[185] Findlay & O'Rourke, p. 104.
[186] Finer (1997c), pp. 1077-85; Palmer, Colton & Kramer (2007b), pp. 552-9.

that being anyone's intention, a kind of feudal structure. Feudal anarchy it has even been called, and occasional violent conflicts also broke out now and then. All of this ended however in 1192 when one of the strongmen conquered the whole country and made himself dictator. And thereby was created a very particular, Japanese constitutional arrangement, which was to remain, with a few interruptions, for a long time.

What was so special was that the state got two dictators. One of them was the real, military dictator with the title shogun, and the capital of this dictator was Kamakura in the neighborhood of contemporary Tokyo—far away from Nara or Kyoto. The other dictator was the former emperor, who became a symbolic dictator. He lived isolated in his palace as a national symbol or as a cult object. This constitutional structure was then to prevail for a long time, even if a new feudal period followed between 1333 and 1600. That last year, however, the military comman-der Tokugawa created a new state which was to be called the Tokugawa-shogunate. The stability thereby created lasted all the time until 1868.[187]

The Tokugawa-shogunate was a despotic police-state, but it was nevertheless characterized by peace with the external world and, at least on the whole, internal order and stability.[188] And it seems as if the latter, paradoxically, became the cause of the fall of the regime.[189] In spite of its efforts the dictatorship did not succeed in penetrating the society all the way down. A certain amount of commerce developed and the economy grew.[190] People also started to long for an end to the long-term isolation imposed by the shogunate, and contacts with the surrounding world became more frequent. All of these tendencies led to a kind of inner dissolution and in 1868, finally, to a non-violent revolution, usually called the Meiji Restoration (The word "meiji" means "enlightened rule"). The shogunate ended and the emperor, who once again became the real dictator, moved his residence to Tokyo. Thereafter followed some moder-nizing, institutional reforms and also a certain amount of democrati-zation. That, however, brings us to Japan's modern history, which I will not take up here.

---

[187] Finer (1997a), p. 49.
[188] Finer (1997c), pp. 1123-8.
[189] Roberts, pp. 841-2.
[190] Hicks, p. 37; Rosenberg & Birdzell, p. 138.

THE AMERICAN STATES

Those humans who, long ago, crossed the Bering Strait, thereafter moved southwards across the North American continent and reached South America's Andes about 12 000 years ago. In some places, in particular in Middle America and in the western parts of South America, they created states. In the first area the state of the Aztecs appeared around the year 1400 and in the latter, what was to become the Inca Empire, in 1438. Both were however destined to be short-lived and they perished when conquered by the Spanish Conquistadors in 1521 and 1535 respectively.[191] But even if these states became short-lived their cultures and social patterns were, to a large extent, inherited from their predecessors.

As for the Aztecs, and starting with them, the well-known Mayas were among their predecessors and after them the Toltecs.[192] The Aztecs started by defeating the latter, and thereafter they expanded their state rapidly by conquering new areas. At its largest it covered a territory corresponding, roughly, to the southern parts of contemporary Mexico. The capital, Tenochtitlan, lay on an island in the middle of a lake with long bridges leading from the shores of the lake to the city itself. The city was also intersected by canals for transport purposes. The water was thus never far away and the similarities with Venice, in that respect, striking. The city was also most splendid—according to one of the Spaniards who first saw it, it surpassed even Rome and Constantinople, even if the most impressive buildings were pyramids rather than Roman large-spanned vault buildings.[193] That the Aztecs were skilful sculptures and artists must also have been obvious. But the capital, with an estimated hundred thousand inhabitants, was not the only city. There were, within the state, several big cities.

The state was ruled by a dictator—a king from a royal family—with, according to the available literature, a combination of relative liberalism and brutality. Starting with the first, there were, in the cities, markets with an extensive, relatively free commercial activity. Among the products exchanged were the mineral obsidian and food products of various kinds, above all maize but also different kinds of meat. The state

---

[191] Palmer, Colton & Kramer (2007a), p. 103.
[192] Bernal, pp. 318-25; Diehl, pp. 332-6; Santley, pp. 325-32; Willey, pp. 336-42.
[193] Roberts, p. 486.

also was fairly liberal in the sense of being decentralized. It contained, within itself, a number of smaller kingdoms—sorts of vassal states— which to a considerable extent seemed to be allowed to do what they wished as long as they paid the required taxes to the central state.[194]

Then we get to what is less liberal. A considerable part of the taxation consisted of forced labor. Since the state was belligerent and expansive, military activities were important. Already at the early age of ten most boys were taken from their families to be trained as soldiers[195]— a system of the same kind as Sparta's, which will be described in more detail in chapter 8. And then we come to what is really appalling. Ritual sacrifices of humans were part of the activities of the Aztec state, and even if the information is varying and uncertain, thousands of individuals were affected.[196] Those who were to be sacri- ficed were taken from slaves and prisoners of war, and those sacrificing could also, after the killing of the sacrificed, eat parts of their bodies.[197]

When the Aztec state was conquered by the Spaniards in 1521 it was only somewhat more than a hundred years old, and it was also, as it seems, stable and consolidating after earlier conquests. There was no internal disintegration—at least, and so far, no visible one. The fall of the state was entirely due to the Spanish conquest.

The Inca Empire was—apart of the obvious similarity that both were dictatorships—in many ways another kind of state than the Aztecs'.[198] The societies, or small states, which had preceded the Inca Empire, were much more primitive than the Aztecs' predecessors. The degree of civilization, or even high culture, which, at least to some extent, had characterized the Aztecs, was therefore missing.

The state was created in 1438 when one king among several— Pachakuti—succeeded in conquering the territories of his neighbors. When his enterprise was fulfilled by his son, and the son's son, the empire covered all the land from contemporary Ecuador in the north, southwards along the coast all the way to about the middle of today's Chile, and eastwards a long way up into the Andes. It was thus a very large state, and

[194] Roberts, p. 485.
[195] Nicholson, p. 345.
[196] Morris, p. 213; Roberts, p. 486.
[197] Nicholson, p. 347.
[198] The whole text here is based on Conrad, pp. 348-55.

the military successes were probably a consequence of the rulers' administrative skill. Their weapons were primitive and no better than their
enemies'. But internal struggles for power were to become fateful. When
the son's son mentioned above died a war of succession broke out, and
when the Spaniards arrived a few years later, in 1532, the former empire
was already headed for its fall.

How, then, was this large but short-lived state constituted? First
and foremost it had a strictly hierarchical system of command. At the top
was the king, or the emperor, with a group of chiefs below him. Each of
these chiefs, in their turn, commanded chiefs below them, and so forth, all
the way down to individuals who were the chiefs for a small number—
often ten—of families. The rules determining people's possibilities to
move, or to choose with whom to marry, were utterly restrictive.
Deportations of people for the sake of homogenization were carried out.
Education was uniform and controlled. The economy was a clear-cut
storage-redistribution economy—there were no markets and no money.
Everything was owned by the state. "The Incas began," writes an
authority, "but never completed, the task of moulding their extremely
heterogeneous subjects into one nation with one language, one religion,
and one culture."[199] The Inca state was a predecessor to the modern
totalitarian dictatorships, about which I will write more in chapter 6.

---

[199] Conrad, p. 348.

3

BASIC THEORY

INTRODUCTION

In the previous chapter I presented a survey of some of the most important states in the history of mankind. The presentation was to a large extent chronological and in that respect in accordance with what is customary in history books. When working with this book I have also to a large extent relied on presentations of this kind—it would, in fact, have been just impossible to write it without sources like that. But here, in this book, there will hardly be any more history like this, history which I call sequential history. After the preceding chapter the chronological presentation is, with one important exception, finished. The exception is the description of the emergence of representative democracy in chapter 9. This type of democracy appeared, as I wrote in chapter 1, in one single sequence of improbable events, just once in the whole history of mankind. It might quite easily never have happened. In order to understand the appearance of representative democracy it is therefore necessary to examine, step by step, this crucial sequence of events. This is, in fact, a case of what is often called *path dependence*—the path is essential and it is impossible to explain the final result without referring to that particular path. But apart from this exception—this coming back to sequential history—the approach in this book is a different one.

A basic idea in this approach is that different states—in particular within each of the categories dictatorships, direct democracies, oligarchies and representative democracies—have so much in common that they, more or less, can be considered as entities in statistical populations. From this basic idea follows that it should, to a considerable extent, be possible to generalize about states. Take, for instance, dictatorships. Even if they may seem different on the face of it, for instance because the ruler happens to be called king, pharaoh, caliph, sultan, tsar, shah, emperor or shogun, they also have—according to the approach adopted here—considerable similarities with regard to important matters such as how they come into existence, how they develop and use their power, the nature of their vulnerability, the mechanisms leading to their fall, and so forth. In his great, classical work "Decline and Fall of the Roman Empire" Edward Gibbon (1737–94) analyzed the breakdown mechanisms of one particular—but very interesting—state. That the same problem can be formulated and discussed also with respect to other states goes without saying, but—and that is the basic approach and hypothesis adopted in this book—one will also in many cases get very similar results.

It is similarities like that, but also differences between matters basically similar, which we are interested in here. I will thus feel free to compare states from different geographical areas, and from different epochs, irrespective of the particular, and unique, historical backgrounds which also characterize them. What we are striving for is, ultimately, generalizations. How were the various states created, what properties did they have, and how did they fall? Which were, in these circumstances, the fundamental mechanisms? Questions like these are the central ones. Or, to put it somewhat differently, this is a book of social science, not of history. And if social science is to be of any value it should of course—in relevant parts—be valid for all human societies at all times.

I wrote in the introductory chapter that a purpose of this book is to present an outline for a comprehensive theory about states, and here I will make my motives for this ambition more clear. There is a saying attributed to the English physicist Arthur Stanley Eddington (1882–1944), namely that "one should never believe any experiment until it has been confirmed by theory."[200] At first this may perhaps seem somewhat mysterious—the common idea seems, rather, to be the opposite one, that empirical results support theory—but, when thinking further about it, the saying is not only interesting, but also at least as relevant for social science as for natural science.

Both are *empirical* but natural science is also, to a very large extent, *experimental*, while social science hardly is that at all, and could not be. The empirical results of social science are therefore always more disputable than those of natural science. It is not possible, as in the natural science experiment, to isolate the interesting variables and eliminate all others. In social science the uncertainty always remains. Will I get the same result when determining the correlation coefficients next

---

[200] Weinberg (1993), p. 101.

time on new empirical material? How do I know that irrelevant factors, or factors I have not thought about, have not intervened in some treacherous way? In order to eliminate—at least to some extent—uncertainties like that, a good theory is a necessity. Theory and data must always support each other. All social science worthy of the name has to include a well developed, separate and easily identifiable theoretical part. There is no such thing as a purely empirical social science.

Having said that I will now continue with theory.

THE SECOND INVISIBLE HAND

THE BASIC MODEL

In spite of the fact that there have been innumerable state monopolies of violence during the course of world history, and that the world today is full of them, the mechanisms behind their appearances are, by no means, obvious. On the contrary, it is quite problematic to explain these phenomena, and in particular that is the case, as I have already said several times, with the appearance of the representative democracy. This latter problem will however not be dealt with until chapter 9. Here I will start with much simpler monopolies of violence, and, in that context, introduce the mechanism called "the second invisible hand". In order to put this mechanism into perspective it may however be appropriate to start with the first invisible hand, the one which was discovered by the Scottish philosopher and economist Adam Smith (1723–90).

In one of the most quoted passages in the whole of social science literature Smith wrote, in his book "The Wealth of Nations", that "[i]t is not from the benevolence of the butcher, the brewer, or the baker that we expect our dinner, but from their regard to their own interest."[201] For the mechanism involved Smith uses the expression "invisible hand". When the actors in a market follow their own interests they are led, as by an invisible hand, towards results which are favorable even for others.

But this invisible hand described by Adam Smith is not the only one. When monopolies of violence are created another invisible hand may be at work, and the one who discovered this hand was Mancur Olson. This happened when Olson studied monopolies of violence which did not have the size, and relative permanence, of states, and which, therefore, perhaps

---

[201] Smith, p. 119.

also were easier to analyze. What he was interested in was the chaotic conditions in China during the 1920s. At that time the empire, as we saw in chapter 2, had already fallen (that had happened in 1912). Furthermore Japan, after the fall of the Shogunate in 1868, had embarked on an aggressive and expansive foreign policy, and tried, although with limited success, to conquer parts of China. And after that came the First World War. There was therefore a power vacuum and stability did not return until 1928 when the movement Kuomintang, perhaps best known because of its somewhat later leader Chiang Kai-shek (1887–1975), took over. The situation in China, in which Mancur Olson was interested, thus had considerable similarities with the chaotic, primordial state of affairs in Hobbes' Leviathan. The most detailed version of Olson's theory is presented on a few pages in his posthumous book "Power and Prosperity".[202]

At the period we are considering large parts of the Chinese territory were in the hands of war lords with their own armies. Some of those war lords, usually the ones with the best or largest armies, conquered demarcated areas, established themselves as rulers within these areas, and taxed the people living there continuously and heavily. Other war lords, whose troops had less capacity, rather ravaged around and plundered whatever victims they happened to find, sometimes here, sometimes there. In Mancur Olsons terminology the first kind of war lords are *stationary bandits*, and the second kind *roving bandits*, and the interesting point, now, is that the ordinary people preferred the stationary bandits to the roving ones. This was Olson's point of departure. How come, he asked himself, that the common people preferred the war lords who stole from them continuously to those who did so only now and then?

Let us start the discussion about this problem by comparing the incentives of the two kinds of bandits. When a roving bandit meets an ordinary human being, or perhaps a group of them, he knows that he probably will not meet these same people again, at least not in the same condition. Therefore he takes everything they have, the looting is total. The roving bandit can be likened to a roaming beast of prey, or a human hunter lacking control over the game he is hunting. When he sees the game he shoots, since, in all likelihood, he will never see it again.

---

[202] Olson (2000), pp. 6-14.

The incentives of the stationary bandit are very different. He controls his area and the people living within it, and he disposes of weapons for keeping roving bandits outside. He, therefore, sets for himself long-term goals—he wants the people he is taxing, or stealing from, not only to survive but also to remain productive. The result is that he taxes them hard, but not too hard. For if he did so, he would not only reduce their willingness, but also their capacity, to work, and thereby also diminish his own rents from their activities. There thus seems to be a certain optimal tax rate that the stationary bandit, in his own interest, should reach, but not surpass.

But the stationary bandit favors his ordinary people also in other ways than his limited taxing. As I have already mentioned he is, of course, interested in keeping roving bandits away from his area, since they otherwise would steal his resources. But that kind of defensive effort is obviously beneficial for common people as well. Furthermore the stationary bandit may very well find it profitable, for himself, to invest in roads, irrigation, etcetera, within his land. This is good for the productivity and therefore also for the stationary bandit's economic benefit, but at the same time it is also good for the people within the area. In the same way as the settled farmer cares about his cattle, the stationary bandit cares about the people, whose work is his tax base.

After this account of the incentives of bandits, the roving and the stationary ones, it is not difficult to understand why the common people preferred the latter. Within their areas they could, in spite of everything, live in peace in a society characterized by order and security, and even have a margin for a certain, although limited, consumption. In the areas outside those of the stationary bandits, where the totally plundering roving bandits were permanent threats, everything was different. For ordinary people it was therefore much better to live within the area of a stationary bandit than not to do so. Furthermore, if they initially lived outside such an area, they had strong incentives to try to move into one.

Now, to complete the picture a further look at the incentives of the bandits is needed. How did they look upon the roving and the stationary predicament respectively? About this Mancur Olson says that the bandit who disposes of sufficient resources of violence, and thus is able to become stationary, also will opt for that. Perhaps he even puts on a crown and calls himself king. From what I have said hitherto this should be quite clear. Compared to the roving bandit the stationary one is obviously in a position to create and accumulate resources of various kinds of a totally different magnitude—he may become rich. The incentives are the same as those of the nomad hunter who settles in order to become a cattle breeder with real estate and land of his own. The latter situation usually entails much greater possibilities for wealth and long-term development.

A stationary bandit thus enjoys a monopoly of violence within his area, and this monopoly is favorable not only for the monopolist or the bandit, but also for the ordinary people within the area, which means that it is *mutually* beneficial. There are thus—that is the conclusion—two mechanisms which are linked to each other, and which lead to a spontaneous establishment of monopolies of this kind. These mechanisms are:

- Bandits, who are strong enough to establish a demarcated area and thereby become stationary, will do so.

- Ordinary people prefer living within the area of a stationary bandit to living outside such areas.

It is the interaction of these two mechanisms which Mancur Olson calls "the second invisible hand", and he writes:[203]

> "This second invisible hand is as unfamiliar and perhaps counter-intuitive as the first hidden hand was in Adam Smith's time, but that does not mean it is less important. There can be no satisfactory theory of power, of government and politics, or the good and the harm done by governments to economies, that leaves out the second invisible hand."

With this there is every reason to agree and it is also easy to find other examples of the workings of this hidden hand than those from China in the nineteen twenties. When discussing big land-owning families in Chinese Han and Tang, and comparing them with similar families in the late Roman Empire, Samuel Finer, writes, for instance, as follows:[204]

> "These great families were as rich as they were noble. As occurred in late Rome, many of the smallholders fled to them for protecttion—against the taxman as much as against bandits—and they

---

[203] Olson (2000), p. 13.
[204] Finer (1997b), p. 741.

turned their vast estates into fortified, self-sufficient haciendas, filled with dependants and retainers of every variety."

Even if this is about establishments of secondary monopolies of violence within a larger, and possibly disintegrating, entity, it is, nevertheless interesting, and obvious, that the mechanism described by Finer is basically the same as the one analyzed by Mancur Olson.

MODIFICATIONS OF THE BASIC MODEL

But even if it is easy to agree with Mancur Olson about the importance of the second invisible hand the reasoning about it may be modified in various ways. So far I have only presented the reasoning as, on the whole, it is put forward by Olson himself. It is simple and clarifying, but thereby also to a considerable extent, schematic. It has, unmistakably, the character of a *model*. And this, as so often, is an advantage rather than the opposite. It is proper and straightforward to start with a simple model and thereafter, when needs arise, bit by bit, introduce modifications and thereby develop the model. In this section I will do so.[205]

The first modification deals with the possibilities of creating stationary monopolies of violence at all. Hitherto we have, without any reasoning, just taken for granted that some war lords have resources for creating such monopolies, while other ones, lacking such resources, have had to remain roving. But this is not necessarily the case. It seems perfectly possible that no war lord is able to create a stationary monopoly of violence, and if so, the question arises why is that? One possibility is that the resources of violence, in an assumed initial situation, are so evenly distributed that no war lord is able to defeat any other one. Another possibility is related to the conditions for attack and defense respectively. If attack is easy and defense difficult, it may perhaps be impossible to create monopolies of violence. Anyway, and irrespective of the reasons, there have, during the portion of world history we are interested in, and in particular during the early phases, been large geographical areas that,

---

[205] Francis Fukuyama's criticism of Olson's model may be mentioned here. After some positive, but also slightly ironic comments, he writes that "The only problem with Olson's theory is that it isn't correct". Fukuyama, p. 304. This is however much too simple. Fukuyama basically gives only one counterexample and disregards all corroborating examples. He thereby also disregards the possibilities for modifying or developing the theory.

during long periods, have not harbored any monopolies of violence at all. A possible reason is that it has been impossible to create such monopolies.

The next modification is about the incentives and options of the stationary war lord. So far I have only assumed that such a war lord wants to become rich and therefore prefers to be stationary rather than roving. And I have also assumed that he, in order to become rich, taxed his people until a certain limit, but no more. This may however be modified by assuming that the war lord not only wants to become rich, but *as rich as possible*. And from that follows the question about what he can do in order to achieve that goal. In the basic model no other activity than taxing the people was mentioned, but he can do more than this. His possibilities for getting rich are, obviously, to a large extent determined by the number of people he can tax, and that number, in turn, is determined by the size of his territory. The larger that area is, the more resources of production, for instance land to cultivate, and the more inhabitants, it probably contains. The war lord will therefore, to the extent possible, and by military means, expand his territory and make it larger and larger. Here it is appropriate to distinguish between two kinds of areas which may be taken on in this way.

- The first type is areas which are uninhabited or characterized by anarchy, and which therefore are not controlled by any monopolist of violence. In this case we talk about *claims*.

- The second type is areas which are already controlled by another monopolist of violence. In this case the defense is obviously much stronger than in the preceding case, but if the war lord is strong enough, he will succeed anyway. In this case we talk about *conquests*.

Perhaps it may be commented that in today's totally nationalized world no possibilities for claims remain. One of the last great claims was the European colonialists' movement westwards on the North American continent in the eighteenth and nineteenth centuries, and not even this was a case of pure claim. The areas taken certainly belonged to the Indians, but their resistance was weak, and their tribal societies were not states.

The conclusion following from the modification introduced here is that monopolies of violence, which are governed by dictators, tend to expand since the rulers thereby may become richer. The ruler who is able to expand his territory by claims and/or by conquests will do so.

A further modification is related to the distinction between stationary and roving war lords. In some cases this distinction may be less sharp than at first it seems. A war lord may, for instance, control a core area effectively while, simultaneously, having some, although not complete, control over adjacent areas. But such a war lord may still undertake raids and plundering expeditions into these bordering areas. And, if so, he is a stationary and a roving war lord at the same time. He is stationary within his own core area, and roving in surrounding areas. The Assyrian kings[206] and the Roman emperors acted, for instance, periodically in this way. Another example is provided by the Portuguese in their early Indian colonies—from these well established monopolies of violence they undertook extensive plundering expeditions into the subcontinent.[207]

The next modification is related to the particular conditions prevailing at the time of creation of the monopoly of violence. Reasonably the personal relationships between the eventual ruler and the rest of the people are of great importance. About this Olson does however not say anything—the relation between the war lord and his future people is completely depersonalized. But, obviously, there is always some kind of relationship, and this relationship will in all likelihood contribute to determining the properties of the monopoly and its development. Do, for instance, the ruler and the ordinary people know each other or not? And if they know each other, are they in conflict or not?

Of particular interest here—again—are our tribes. In many cases in history, as we have seen, monopolies of violence, which have become very great, have originated from minor tribes. Such a tribe may originally have been a small group of closely related people in the same family living as nomads by hunting, fishing and gathering. Then, as the tribe grows, various kinds of options as well as problems may easily arise. Possibilities for ending the nomadic life and settle may for example appear, or other,

---

[206] Roux, p. 285.
[207] Findlay & O'Rourke, p. 155.

competing tribes may become increasingly threatening. Changed conditions like that may require a more firm, and more coordinated, rule, and
this requirement may be dealt with in various ways. One possibility is
that someone—by being pushy himself, or by consent from the others, or
by some combination of these mechanisms—becomes chief of the tribe.
And such a person may very well turn into a dictator later on. But it is also
possible that the common members of the society, perhaps together with
some elected chief, continue to take part in the decision-making in some
kind of direct democracy. Still another possibility is that the decisions will
be taken by a selected group of some kind—for instance elderly members
of the tribe, or particularly rich ones, or as especially prudent-considered
ones—in association, perhaps, with a chief.

When talking about particularly rich tribal members it may be
appropriate to mention the roles played by great land owners in many
circumstances in world history. Here, obviously, I am not talking about
ownership in a strict legal sense, but it may still be the case that some
tribal members, when a tribe has begun settling, have succeeded in
getting control over large parts of the common area. Such persons, or land
owners, may then, as a consequence, also get a lot of influence over the
common decisions. Perhaps the causal order could also be reversed, so
that individuals with a lot of decision-making power thereby also succeed
in acquiring large chunks of land. Anyway, processes that give great land
owners important roles are extremely frequent. Again and again great
land owners have been quite influential. Examples will appear in the
following chapters.

A primitive tribal society may thus, depending, among other things,
on the initial relations between the humans involved, develop in different
directions, and thereby be transformed into other kinds of societies.
These matters will be dealt with in later chapters. Transformation from
tribal society to dictatorship will be exemplified in chapter 6, to direct
democracy in chapter 7, and to oligarchy in chapter 8. Already here it may
however be said that a transformation from a tribal society to our fourth
type of state—representative democracy—has never occurred. Representative democracy is, as we will see later on in this chapter, the only kind of
state which cannot evolve directly out of a tribal society.

At last I will add something which hardly is a modification, but
rather a deviation, and *an important deviation*, from the basic model. The
deviation concerns the relationship between the ruler and the ordinary

people, and the incentives of the ordinary people. In the basic model it was assumed, we remember, that the ordinary people were better off within the area of the ruler than outside it, and therefore did not want to leave it. And for the same reason people who lived outside such an area, would like to move into one. But it need not be so. If the stationary bandit at some time, shorter or longer after the creation of the monopoly, is able to close the outer border, so that people cannot move away from the area, he will also be able to tax them still harder than before. Still, of course, he has to take into account the impact of his taxes on people's willingness and capacity for work, but he needs no longer care about the risk that people, if they find the conditions too oppressive, will flee from his land.

This deviation, as we will see in chapter 6 about dictatorships, is of utmost importance. Some of the dictatorships in world history have been open and people have remained in them since they found that best. Other dictatorships on the contrary, as for instance the Soviet Union, enclosed its people behind its borders. But there are also, in particular in earlier historical eras, interesting cases in between the open and the enclosed ones. The states then could be so large, and the means of transport so inefficient, that a dictator, even without closing his borders, could exploit people utterly. They could not leave the territory anyway. Their option rather was to revolt, and revolts of that kind were common. Several examples will be given in chapter 6.

After these modifications of the basic model I will now continue by making the assumptions behind it explicit and precise.

Basic Social Science Principles

In the reasoning about the second invisible hand two kinds of individuals are acting—ordinary people and war lords. But in spite of being two kinds of actors they have one property in common, namely that they, in their acting, try to weigh the alternatives available against each other, and choose the best one. If a war lord is able to choose between being stationary and roving, he chooses to become stationary. And if an ordinary human being is able to choose between living inside the area of a stationary war lord and outside such an area, she or he chooses the former alternative.

The behavior of individuals is thus assumed to be the result of decisions, and the reasoning is in that sense decision-oriented. Each individual considers the alternatives available for him or her, tries to infer the consequences of the alternatives in various respects, and chooses the alternative which, for her- or himself, appears as the best one. We may also say that the individuals are steered by their incentives, or that the reasoning about their behavior is based on an assumption of rationality. And the same holds true for Adam Smith's butcher, brewer and baker— they as well as their customers, the dinner eaters, were steered by their incentives. This rationality assumption is methodologically fundamental and characterizes large parts of today's social sciences. It will also be of fundamental importance throughout this book.

While writing this I remember with pleasure what Mancur Olson once said, in a telephone conversation, when, in one sentence he encapsulated the most important lesson of social science, namely that "people react to incentives". So it certainly is, but here in this book which is about states, we may add that incentives are not created haphazardly. Modern institutional theory—pioneered by, among others, the British social scientist Ronald Coase (1910–2013) and his American colleague Douglass North (born 1920)—tells us that incentives to a large extent are formed by the institutional milieu in which people live. Various institutions result in various kinds of incentives—and if there are no institutions at all as, for instance, in Hobbes' primordial state, that will bring about incentives characteristic for that very special state of affairs. This institutional aspect is obviously of great significance in this book, since the state is the most important of all human institutions. In what follows there will be many examples of how incentives are formed by institutions.

But the reasoning about the second invisible hand is not only characterized by incentives and rationality. It is also important that only single, individual human beings are taken into account. This assumption, or approach, is often labeled "methodological individualism". The expression was originally coined by the Austrian social scientist Joseph Schumpeter (1883–1950).[208] The basic idea is that all human behavior, ultimately, has to be explained by starting from acts of single individuals. Only individuals are able to ponder alternatives, and only individuals are in possession of a will. The common idea about a "will of the People" is thus clearly in conflict with methodological individualism. There is no

---

[208] Mitchell, p. 74.

"will of the People" any more than there is a "heart of the People" or any "kidneys of the People". All of these things—wills, hearts and kidneys—can only be attributes of individuals. The Marxist idea about classes as basic actors is thus clearly in conflict with methodological individualism. Classes can never act in the same sense as individuals since they cannot think, compare and evaluate in the way that individuals do. It is, by the way, interesting to note that the tendency to individualize the People was particularly endorsed by the totalitarian, Nazi dictatorship of Hitler. The expressions then used were "Volksgeist" (spirit of the People) and "Volks-seele" (soul of the People).[209] In order to make things perfectly clear it should perhaps be added that methodological individualism is a me-thodological principle, and nothing but that. It does not have any ideo-logical implications whatsoever—a methodological individualist may, for instance, without any problems, be a socialist and an advocate for collec-tivistic solutions of various social problems.

Thus far I have only said that the individuals are steered by their incentives, but I have not said anything about the nature of those incen-tives. What is most common—and that tradition is a long one with Machiavelli as one of the pioneers—is the assumption that the individuals follow narrow, egoistic interests. It need, however, not be that way. It is, from a theoretical point of view, perfectly possible to combine the rationality assumption with for instance an assumption about altruistic incentives, and this has also been done even if it is not all that common. An example is the American social scientist Anthony Downs (born 1930), about whom I will write more in chapter 10, who, in his book "Inside Bureaucracy", makes assumptions about incentives with altruistic com-ponents.[210] In this book I will, myself, however stick to, or at least start from, the narrow self-interest tradition. But I will also try to be open-minded and aware of the possibility of other kinds of incentives, and thus also introduce them into my reasoning when that is appropriate. That, at least, is my ambition.

But then, what constitutes self-interest? How may it be described and made more precise? Here, I will again start from Mancur Olson. It may be said that his whole scientific achievement is founded on one basic

---

[209] Friedrich & Brzezinski, pp. 121, 164.
[210] Downs (1967), pp. 79-91.

assumption about the nature of incentives—an assumption which he exploited to the uttermost. But even if Olson, in all of his works, starts from this assumption, he has, as far as I know, never formulated it explicitly. Rather, it is there implicitly, just below the surface and constantly recurring. My attempt to make the assumption explicit goes as follows.

The assumption concerns individual actors and in particular Olson is interested in actions which have consequences not only for the actor itself but also for others and thus have so called external effects. The assumption then says that the actor normally considers only the consequences for itself and thus ignores effects on others. This basic assumption may then, depending on the impact of the incentives, result in *passivity*, or in *activity*. We thus get the following two versions of the basic assumption.

- An individual usually does not carry out an action which is negative for the individual him- or herself (the disadvantages outweigh the advantages), even if the totality of advantages, for all those affected, outweigh the totality of disadvantages.

- An individual usually carries out an action which is positive for the individual him- or herself (the advantages outweigh the disadvantages), even if the totality of disadvantages, for all those affected, outweigh the totality of advantages.[211]

This assumption is, as we see, very similar to the basic assumption in economic theory about the behavior of the so called *economic man*. In both cases the reasoning starts by considering individuals evaluating available alternatives, and in both cases these individuals maximize their

---

[211] The compatibility of the phrases "the totality of advantages, for all those concerned" and "the totality of disadvantages, for all those concerned" in this and the former assumption with methodological individualism may perhaps be questioned. The phrases may however be interpreted by means of the so called Pareto-criteria (further explained in the section "Incentive oriented theories" in chapter 10) or, perhaps better, by means of the modified, less rigorous version of the Pareto-criteria usually called the Kaldor Hicks-criteria. The passivity assumption, interpreted in that way, may then be as follows: "An individual usually does not carry out an action which is negative for the individual him- or herself, even if it is Kaldor Hicks-effective." And correspondingly for the activity assumption.

self interests in a narrow sense. But in spite of these similarities there are also important differences. First, in economic theory there are, in the normal, or basic, case, no external effects. These are introduced only later on when the theory is developed in various ways, for instance in so called welfare economics. Second, in traditional economic theory all decisions are assumed, at least implicitly, to take place within a consolidated legal structure, within a system with well developed market institutions. And, third, the actions dealt with in economic theory usually include several parties—the concluding of a mutually beneficial agreement is, for instance, a basic act, which, necessarily, includes more than one party.

But on these very points Mancur Olson differs. He considers already from the beginning external effects—perhaps because he thinks that in reality such effects are always present. Furthermore, his basic assumption does not presuppose any already existing legal structure. Or, to put it somewhat differently, his assumption is not limited to applications within an institutionalized market economy, it is equally valid for criminals acting in societies ruled by law and for anarchists or robbers acting in environments without any laws whatsoever. It is these properties of the assumption that makes it so useful in the contexts discussed in this book, contexts in which institutions cannot be taken for granted. Rather, the institutions may not only be of very different kinds, they may also be totally absent, and for all of these situations we are interested in forming ideas about people's behavior.

Now, it may of course be argued that the basic assumption presented seems too simple, and that, therefore, it does not realistically portray people's often far more complicated incentives or motivations. Sometimes people's motivations are perhaps not only more complicated than in the basic assumption, but also very different from that assumption, and perhaps even incompatible with it. So it is in all likelihood. I have, for instance, mentioned the possibility of altruistic incentives, and it seems obvious that at least some people, sometimes, are guided by these and similar incentives.

This, however, does not negate the expediency, from a theoretical point of view, of starting with the simple, in order to introduce complications later on, if and when the need arises, but only then. There is a well-known intellectual principle of parsimony which, honoring its originator the Englishman William Occam (circa 1285–1349), is called Occam's razor, and which says that an explanation should not include more elements than needed for explaining that which should be explained. Or, in other words, an explanation should be as uncomplicated or simple as possible. In this context, and in this book, this principle means that we will try, as far as possible, to explain various phenomena related to monopolies of violence by using the basic assumption as presented above in its versions of activity and passivity respectively.

If it proves necessary, however—but only then—the basic assumption may be modified or perhaps even replaced. The explanations we are striving for should be as simple as possible, but not *too* simple. Starting with the simple in order to, thereafter, and if and when it becomes necessary, make the reasoning more complicated, has great advantages. The Englishman Francis Bacon (1561–1626) described these advantages elegantly by contending that "truth emerges more readily from error than from confusion".[212] If the simple, with which one starts, proves wrong, it may be relatively easy to discover this and to make the corrections necessary. If, however, one has started with an unnecessarily complicated theory or model, it may, when faults are discovered, be much more difficult to find out exactly wherein these consist. The situation may easily get messy, and the proper corrections towards a successively more well-founded theory difficult to find.

Following Occam and Bacon we will thus strive for simplicity. The use of Mancur Olson's basic assumption entails however more than pursuit of simplicity in this sense. The simplicity we are striving for is always the *same* simplicity, since it is the same basic assumption that is used all the time. Or, in other words, we are striving for generalizations. We want—to the extent possible—to put as many phenomena or processes as possible under the same theoretical hat. Or, to express it in still another way: we want, as far as possible, to avoid explanations which are made for the special case and which are thus, according to common terminology, *ad hoc*.

This pursuit of generalizations is nothing particular to this book but rather fundamental in many scientific endeavors. The idea is to explain as much as possible from a certain set of premises, or to reduce as much as possible the number of premises needed for explaining a certain set of phenomena. Well-known is the anecdote about how Isaac Newton (1643–

---

[212] Weinberg (2001), p. 202.

1727), sitting under an apple tree, discovered the law of gravitation. When an apple fell on his head he realized that it was pulled by the same force as the moon in its orbit around the earth. The only difference was that the moon also moved perpendicularly to the direction of the fall with such a speed that the result was an almost circular orbit around the earth. The apple and the moon, and all other smaller or bigger bodies in the universe, were thereby incorporated in a common theory.

Pursuit of simplicity and generality will thus be fundamental in what follows. Expressed in a somewhat different way this means that we are more interested in similarities—to the extent that they exist—than in differences. It seems for instance obvious—and returning to an example already mentioned—that there are great differences between different dictators with various fine titles, but probably there are also very important similarities, and it is those that we are interested in here. What Newton saw, and what gave rise to a generalization, was an until then neglected similarity between the moon and the apple—only the very striking differences had been observed. Simplicity and generality are thus important goals in the following. This intellectual attitude is sometime labeled "reductionism".

It is fascinating to realize how well these principles are followed by Mancur Olson for one. In the trilogy containing the lion's share of his work—namely "The Logic of Collective Action"[213], "The Rise and Decline of Nations"[214] and "Power and Prosperity"[215]—he deduces consequences from his basic assumption in wider and wider circles. This very fact that one and the same idea is used all the time has made some commentators talk about him as "a one-idea thinker", and in this there is a lot of truth. Those who have said so have however also, as it seems, considered this way of thinking as limited, and thus as something negative. Against this I will, on the contrary, insist that it is quite an achievement to recognize the fertility of a simple, single idea and, by means of ever new deductions demonstrate this fertility. The reasoning about the second invisible hand, already presented, could be considered an example of this, and more examples will be given below.

---

[213] Olson (1965).
[214] Olson (1982).
[215] Olson (2000).

Social science is thus, as we have seen, empirical in the same way as natural science, but, contrary to large parts of natural science, it cannot, on the whole, be experimental. An important consequence of this is that social science hardly admits specialization in the same way as natural science. If the factors or variables one is interested in cannot be isolated in an experiment, they cannot, in all likelihood, be isolated in a particular discipline either. The fact that most social scientists of importance—or perhaps almost all of them—have been generalists is therefore hardly surprising. The great social scientists have, practically always, been familiar with several disciplines—or were active before the division into separate disciplines started to gain momentum—and have therefore also had a good intuitive feeling for a large range of relevant mechanisms, irrespective of their disciplinary home. About this the social scientist Friedrich A. von Hayek (1899–1992) has written as follows:[216]

> "The physicist who is only a physicist can still be a first-class physicist and a most valuable member of society. But nobody can be a great economist who is only an economist—and I am even tempted to add that the economist who is only an economist is likely to become a nuisance if not a positive danger."

Hayek is here talking about economists but the same thing could, I contend, be said about other specialized social scientists as well.

After this general account of the basic theoretical points of departure I will now turn to two particular somewhat more matter-of-fact applications which are—now and then—of interest in what follows. The one comes, again, from Mancur Olson and the other one from the German-American social scientist Albert O. Hirschman (1915–2012).

THE LOGIC OF COLLECTIVE ACTION

In the political science of the nineteen-fifties there was a movement that gave interest organizations an indispensable role in modern democracies. The organizations were, together with the parties, considered as necessary actors, and the government's constant interactions with them were thought to be almost as important as elections. According to this view all interests became, to the extent possible and reasonable, satisfied, and the

---

[216] Hayek (1967), p. 123.

result therefore optimal. The most elaborated version of this view was presented in the book "The Governmental Process" (1951) by the American political scientist David Truman (1913–2003).[217] The death-blow against the theory was delivered fourteen years later, in 1965, by the then young Mancur Olson. In "The Logic of Collective Action"[218] he showed that a necessary condition for the theory was not fulfilled.

The condition was that all interests get organized. The political scientists had, without further arguments, taken that for granted—if there was an interest, then there was also an organization. Olson showed however that this occurred only sometimes, and under special conditions. Important interests could very well remain unorganized for a very long time, or even forever.

For an organization to be created it was not, according to Olson, enough that it was beneficial, that is that it yielded benefits greater than the costs it incurred for the total collective of potential members. It was also necessary that the incentives for those individuals, who might take the initiative in creating the organization, were favorable, which could not be taken for granted. The potential initiators might, for instance, have to pay a disproportional amount of the costs of creating the organization without getting more advantages from it than all other members and, if so, they would not take the initiative. This is a straight-forward consequence of the earlier mentioned basic assumption in its passivity version. The organization of large, heterogeneous collectives such as, for instance, consumers or taxpayers, faces, according to this reasoning, the greatest difficulties, while it will be easier with small, well-defined professional collectives.

Mancur Olson's reasoning had its point of departure in a basic distinction introduced by the American economist Paul Samuelson (1915–2009) in a couple of papers in the middle of the nineteen-fifties, namely between individual and collective goods or utilities.[219] What characterizes an individual good is that its consumption by one person excludes its consumption by anyone else. If, for instance, A has eaten an orange—an individual good—then it is impossible for B also to eat it. A collective good, however—and organizations are typical such goods—can

[217] Truman
[218] Olson (1965).
[219] Samuelson (1954) and (1955).

be useful for several or even many people. The "consumption" of the utility by one person does not exclude its "consumption" of others.

Organizations provide however but one example of collective goods. There are many others, and they also can be of different kinds. They may, for instance, be either concrete or abstract. Roads and communication networks of different kinds, and irrigation systems, are examples of the former. Among the latter may be mentioned legal systems in civilized societies. Such a system is beneficial for all those affected by it, or at least almost all—the one's benefit does not exclude that of anyone else. The organizations which Mancur Olson analyzed may, I think, be placed somewhere in between the abstract and the concrete. In what follows we will, now and then, meet with various kinds of collective goods, and especially abstract ones. Common to them all is—in the same way as for organizations—that their "production" is not straight-forward. It is not enough that they, when once existing, entail advantages surpassing the costs of their creation. There also has to be some kind of creational mechanism which is compatible with methodological individualism, and which, thus, directly or indirectly, relates their creation to the incentives of specific, single individuals.

I have already said several times that it is difficult to explain the emergence of representative democracy and the reason for this difficulty, we can now state, is that this kind of democracy is a collective good. For getting some perspective on this problem it may be interesting to consider earlier phases in the history of political philosophy. It has thus been argued that states with ruling systems beneficial for the citizens have been created by means of agreements between the citizens to be— they have, by means of social contracts, created their states. And if that has been the case in history, it should be so in the future. The most well-known, and most articulated, proponent of this view is the French-Swiss philosopher Jean-Jacques Rousseau (1712–78), who, in his book "On the Social Contract" ("Du contrat social"), developed the theme.

But Rousseau was hardly right. Complicated social systems cannot be created in the way he described and recommended. It conflicts with the logic of collective action. About this Mancur Olson writes that "[t]here is no case in the historical record that I can find where any substantial population has, through voluntary collective action of any kind, established a peaceful order."[220] Returning to representative democracy it thus cannot, and not any more than other complicated social orders, have been created by means of a social contract—the process of its emergence must have been of some other kind. What actually happened will be told in chapter 9. What is important here is the formulation of the problem involved. The representative democracy is a collective good and the important problem about its appearance therefore has no simple, obvious solution.

With oligarchies, and possibly also with small direct democracies, it is different. For them social contracts should not be totally excluded, even if the creational mechanisms in many cases also may have been of other kinds. The possibility of social contracts here is however, again, a consequence of the logic of collective action. Obviously the potential contracting group is much smaller than in the case with a large population, and therefore the costs for those taking the initiative will be much lower while, at the same time, their gains may be considerably greater—in particular this may be the case with oligarchies.

Mancur Olson was, at least in "The Logic of Collective Action", quite pessimistic about the conditions for creating collective goods, and now I am again talking about collective goods in general. He thought that the creation of such goods, practically always, required the cooperation of several, or many, individuals, and that this kind of cooperation, for the reasons I have given, usually did not come about. But in addition there is one more difficulty. Since we are talking about a collective good it can, almost by definition and after having been created, be freely used by anybody. It is, as it is usually stated, easy to *free-ride*. And the more those are who, before the creation of the good, intend to do that, and thus not to take part in the creation of the good, the more difficult it becomes to create the good.

This pessimism was however hardly completely justified. At about the same time as Olson published "The Logic of Collective Action" the American social scientist James Buchanan (1919–2013) issued the paper "An Economic Theory of Clubs" in which Samuelson's ideas also were developed, but in another direction than Olson's.[221] Buchanan's main argument was that goods or utilities did not need to be clearly individual

---

[220] Olson (2000), p. 90.
[221] Buchanan (1965).

or clearly collective—there were also goods in between, and this led to challenging problems. Buchanan's handling of these problems may, however, be left aside here. What is interesting for us, rather, is Buchanan's comment, almost in passing, that a collective good, at least in principle, may be created by a single individual acting according to his narrow self-interest. What is required is some means for keeping free-riders away from the good. If such a barrier can be established the entrepreneur, who has created the collective good, can charge those wanting to use it and thereby make the undertaking profitable for himself. Buchanan gives the example of an entrepreneur who builds and encloses a swimming-pool—the collective, or at least partly collective, good in the example—and thereafter charges those who want to pass the entrance in order to bathe in the pool.

But the examples need not be so peaceful, or enjoyable, as in this case. Let us have a look at our war lords in China with Buchanan's spectacles. The peace and order created by such a war lord may be considered as a collective good which is beneficial for all the people within the area. But still, as we remember, the war lord—or, using Buchanan's language, the profit maximizing entrepreneur—created this good entirely for his own purposes. Individual action led to the creation of a collective good.

Monopolies of violence may thus, in some cases, be created by profit maximizing entrepreneurs, and most probably there are more cases than those of the Chinese war lords. In fact, and as we will see in chapter 6, a considerable number of the dictatorships in world history falls into this pattern. Also interesting is, however, the question whether other kinds of states than dictatorships, and more civilized ones, may be created in the same way. In a later section in this chapter—"Entrepreneurs and democracy"—I will discuss this problem.

TRANSACTION COSTS

Collective goods, as we have seen, do not materialize as a matter of course. The main reason is that the necessary initiators work, or costs, consisting in matters such as contact-making, discussions, negotiations, persuasion, and so forth, may be very high and higher than their potential benefits from the resulting good. And, if so, the initiative will never be taken. The collective good will never materialize however beneficial and cost-effective it would have been if it became real.

These mechanisms may also be described in terms of transaction costs, a concept introduced by Ronald H. Coase in the two essays "The Nature of the Firm" and "The Problem of Social Cost".[222] Here we may forget about the particular problems which led Coase to the discovery and introduction of the concept, and which are presented in the two essays. The concept is clarifying even in other contexts and I will therefore return to it at various places in what follows. Here and now we can begin with the production of collective goods. I have just talked about "contact-making, discussions, negotiations, persuasion, and so forth", and all of this, taken together, constitutes transaction costs.

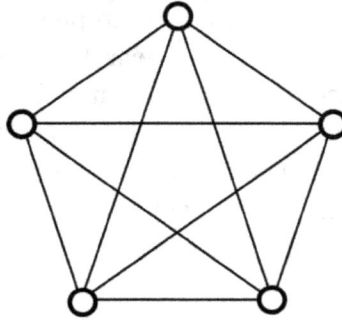

Figure 2: Transaction cost example

For understanding how these costs depend on group size we may think of a situation such as the one in figure 2. Let us assume that there is some collective good which would be valuable for the illustrated group consisting of five individuals, and that they start a discussion with each other about creating the good. In the very simple case illustrated in the figure, with very few group members, they will in all likelihood succeed. They may perhaps get together and, after a common discussion, take a decision about the good, but even if they cannot meet each other in that way the number of contacts which need to be taken is still quite limited. Between the five members of the group there are, altogether, only ten "dialogue possibilities" (the lines in the figure).

---

[222] Coase (1937) and (1960).

But let us then assume that the group, or the society, gets bigger. If so, the number of dialogue possibilities will obviously also grow rapidly. For those interested in formulas this assertion may be given a more precise form. If the number of individuals is n, then the number of dialogue possibilities becomes

$n(n-1)/2,$

which means that the number of dialogue possibilities increases, roughly, with the square of the number of individuals. If, for instance, we consider a population of 1000 individuals, the number of dialogue possibilities will be 499 500. But even a society with 1000 individuals is a very small society. Societies, and states, usually are much bigger, and therefore the number of dialogue possibilities much, much bigger.

It is exactly because of this that large groups cannot reach the point of decision-making, for the creation of collective goods, by means of general talk and discussion. The initiative has to come from some individual or some small group of individuals. There must be some minor constellation promoting the issue. And for this constellation the costs for the initiative may be prohibitively high.

The size of the transaction costs do however not only depend on the number of individuals, but on other factors as well. One such factor, which is important in this book in particular, and which also may be mentioned in order to underline Mancur Olson's argument, is related to the properties of the collective good at issue. Thus, and generally speaking, the more abstract, and the more complex, the good is, the higher the costs will be as well. The abstractness and complexity certainly will make the necessary communication, discussions and negotiations still more difficult, which entails further difficulties for the creation of the good. And representative democracy—returning once again to that phenomenon—is not only a collective good, it is furthermore an abstract and very complex such good. Which makes its appearance still more remarkable.

EXIT AND VOICE

THE GENERAL PROBLEM

Albert Hirschman, in his book "Exit, Voice, and Loyalty—Responses to Decline in Firms, Organizations, and States", formulated and analyzed the problem arising when people get dissatisfied with a collective, or an institution, to which they belong. How do they react?[223] The analysis, as the subtitle of the book makes clear, does not only concern dissatisfaction with states but also with, for instance, clubs, religious communions, one's own family, corporations, enterprises, and so forth. In this book, which is about states, I will however limit myself to the subjects', or the citizens', dissatisfaction with their own state. And by *subjects* I then mean, here and in what follows, the common inhabitants in dictatorships, whereas *citizens* will stand for the inhabitants in oligarchies and in direct and representative democracies.

Hirschman discusses two kinds of dissatisfaction reactions, namely "exit" and "voice". *Exit* means that the dissatisfied individual leaves the state he or she is dissatisfied with. *Voice*, rather, means that the dissatisfied individual makes the reasons for the dissatisfaction public, for instance by talking or writing, hoping that that may lead to changes.

Using this terminology we may now say that the exit reaction is typical, primarily, for dissatisfied subjects in dictatorships. For them the voice option is severely circumscribed since mass media in which critical opinions may be published hardly exist. Furthermore the critique, even if published, is most probably meaningless since those in power certainly will ignore it. And not only that, the critique may even entail reprisals and thus be dangerous for the originator. The most available option therefore might be exit. But not even that can be taken for granted. It not only presupposes that the dissatisfied subject is able to leave his or her own state which—as I made clear in the section "modifications of the basic model" above—is far from certain. It also presupposes that there is something more attractive, for instance a state which is considered better, which in fact may be entered. And this, again, is far from sure—the borders may be closed. Obvious examples in the present world are the obstacles around the whole of the EU-area and along the southern border of the US towards Mexico. Finally it may be added that the exit-reaction also has been described as "voting with the feet". This expression is due to the American social scientist Charles Tiebout (1924–68), whom we will meet later on in this chapter.

But even if the exit-reaction thus is typical for dictatorships, it should be underlined that this is the case only when dissatisfaction in fact

---

[223] Hirschman (1970).

is present. And this need not be so. In the world of the Chinese war lords, we remember, the ordinary people, with good reason, thought that they were better off within the lords' protected areas than outside them. The same has certainly been the case with many other dictatorially ruled states in world history.

So far I have taken for granted that if a dictatorship's subjects prefer to remain within it, then it is also tempting or attractive for individuals outside to move into it. And if so, such a dictatorship may be called attractive. But matters are seldom as simple as that. It could for instance be the case—and probably often is—that even if the subjects of a dictatorship, or at least most of them, prefer to remain in it, there are still very few outsiders who would like to move into it. So even if the dictatorship's own subjects are satisfied with their state, it need not be attractive for outsiders. It is for situations like these that Hirschman uses the concept of *loyalty*. The reason for the relative satisfaction of the subjects may be their loyalty. But those living outside, or at least most of them, obviously have no reason to feel any loyalty like that. Therefore I will not, in the following, talk about attractive dictatorships. I will rather make a distinction between *repressive* dictatorships—that is dictatorships which the subjects want to leave—and *non-repressive* dictatorships—that is dictatorships with which the subjects are satisfied.

If exit thus is the typical dissatisfaction reaction in dictatorships, voice, rather is the typical dissatisfaction reaction in democracies. In democracies there even exist a number of institutions designed and established just for the purpose of facilitating the exercise of the voice-option. There are mass media, political parties, interest organizations, and so forth, which all, among other things, are forums for debate and for criticism of the ruling and the rulers. And ultimately, of course, the election procedure is an institutionalized method for taking the citizens', and in that case all citizens', opinions—critical as well as supportive—about the rulers into account. But in spite of all of this some citizens may nevertheless find the exit-option attractive.[224]

---

[224] An interesting case of combined exit and voice is the emigration to Belgium, and the acquiring of Russian citizenship and passport, by the French actor Gérard Depardieu around the New Year 2012/13. The reason was the tax increases initiated by the new French president François Hollande. See the article "Adieu Obélix" in The Economist, December 22nd, 2012.

Before continuing it may be interesting to relate the theories of Mancur Olson and Albert Hirschman to each other. Olson's concepts may be directly applied to Hirschman's strategies. It is thus easy to see that the result of exit is an individual good, whereas the result of voice is a collective good. When the exit strategy is at all available it is immediately effective for, and only for, the one who is dissatisfied. The one choosing the exit-strategy thus chooses to produce an individual good. The one choosing the voice strategy, on the contrary, chooses to produce, or at least to take part in, or perhaps to initiate the production of, a collective good. The result of the critique expressed will, if and when it is successful, be beneficial, not only for the criticizing individual her- or himself, but also for many other citizens, or perhaps even for all. But still the individual, or the small group, which formulates and delivers the critique usually also will have to pay the costs—which may be quite demanding. A lot of criticism which, from the point of view of the many, would have been valuable, may therefore never be expressed. It may even be the case that some critical ideas, however potentially beneficial they may be, never suggest themselves to anyone. And the reason, if so, is that it not only requires efforts, but also may seem quite meaningless, to study and investigate issues and topics which, however important they may be from a general point of view, are to be dealt with in collective, democratic processes. It may often be better—using a common expression for this and similar phenomena—to remain *rationally ignorant*. Here, as well as in other cases, people do not, without further incentives, take part in the production of collective goods.[225]

Olson's and Hirschman's ideas may thus be linked to each other in the way just described, but still, as far as I have been able to find out, this is hardly noticed in the relevant literature. In fact, I only know of two remarks about the matter, both from Hirschman himself. The first one, no more than a suggestion, appears in "Exit, Voice and Loyalty" in a context where much smaller collectives than states, namely groups of buyers in markets, are dealt with. There Hirschman writes, explicitly referring to

---

[225] An illustrative example is given by Joseph Schumpeter when describing the dilemma of a citizen in a democratic country. The citizen, he writes (Schumpeter (1942), p. 261) "is a member of an unworkable committee, the committee of the whole nation, and this is why he expends less disciplined effort on mastering a political problem than he expends on a game of bridge."

Mancur Olson, that the voice reaction is likely to be effective in particular if the group is small.[226] The other, more explicit, appears in Hirschman's autobiography "A Propensity to Self-Subversion" and goes like this: "Moreover, to be effective, voice often requires group action and is thus subject to all the well-known difficulties of organization, representation and free riding."[227]

DISCONTENT, REBELLIOUSNESS AND TERRORISM

Voice-reactions in Hirschman's sense can be very different—anything from general, diffuse and unarticulated discontent to well articulated and argued written articles, or even books. Hirschman also writes himself that "[voice] is a far more 'messy' concept [than exit] because it can be graduated, all the way from faint grumbling to violent protest."[228] Critique thus can be of many different forms and this is of great importance for the probability that the critique will become manifest. Much potential articulated criticism never materializes however beneficial it would have been. The costs for the few, necessary initiators easily surpass their "incomes" or advantages.

General discontent, on the contrary, appears most easily and also spreads equally easily among the masses of a population, and the same, for that matter, is true about general enthusiasm. Just assume that there is some reason, or event, which gives rise to discontent. It may be some measure from above, such as more taxes, or perhaps something which cannot be directly connected with the rulers, as for instance a bad harvest. In such situations some people, or even many, will probably think and react in similar ways, and individuals will also talk to each other. More than that is not needed for a general mood to appear, a mood which easily may spread in wider and wider circles and perhaps also grow in intensity. General discontent thus can grow into something which, for the ruler, may become serious, threatening and difficult to handle. None of this is incompatible with the logic of collective action.

Criticism, which for the ruler is difficult to handle, may however be of another character than general discontent. Terrorism can thus be

---

[226] Hirschman (1970), p. 41.
[227] Hirschman (1995), p. 12.
[228] Hirschman (1970), p. 16.

described as a voice-reaction in Hirschman's sense—acts of terrorism are executed because of dissatisfaction with something, and in order to get the ruler to change this. What is special about the terrorist action, in comparison with many other critical reactions, is that it need not cost the performer very much. To explode a bomb in crowd does not, for instance, require any tremendous effort. If, however, we make a distinction between efforts and costs, the terror action may in a certain sense be costly. It might, for instance, cost a suicide bomber his or her life. But if the bomber believes that she or he, in some heaven, will be rewarded for the achievement, this cost turns into a benefit. Anyway, in our discussion about states and their stability, we have to include terrorist acts as a very important, even if also very particular, kind of voice-reaction.

A FUNDAMENTAL MECHANISM OF CHANGE

In the last three sections of this chapter I will take up a few applications of the preceding reasoning which are of particular interest in this book about states. The first one concerns the mechanisms operating when new institutions are introduced, or already existing institutions are modified. I have already argued that such changes cannot be brought about by concerted action by all those affected except in small and uncomplicated societies. And even in such cases, when changes have occurred, it need not have happened in that way. But then, in all those cases in which institutional changes in fact have occurred, how did they come about. How were all those complicated institutions which have existed, and which exist, created, and how did they, in the many cases that that has happened, develop after that? Which mechanisms were operating? In more general terms the problem may be phrased as follows:

- What may come from below?

- What has, because of the logic of collective action, to come from above?

- How can the two levels interact with each other?

Figure 3 which—schematically—depicts a state or a society with a ruler at the top, and a large mass of subjects below him, may serve as a point of departure for a discussion about these questions. Let us assume that the subjects are dissatisfied with something, and perhaps also have some idea about changes they want. This may then give rise to more widespread discontent and rebelliousness of the kinds I mentioned in the preceding section. It may perhaps also—and perhaps in particular when the discontent is concentrated in small groups—lead to terrorist actions of some kind.

○

[   ]

Figure 3: A fundamental mechanism of change

What, then, will the ruler do in such a situation? What kind of action suits, according to his own judgment, his own interest best? The answer is that rulers, in situations like the one assumed, almost always have used brutal violence for punishing the dissatisfied, for crushing revolts or threatening revolts. World history is full of reactions like that. But it has not always, in all situations, been so. There are also situations in which the ruler has considered it to be in his own interest to concede in some way, to undertake measures which at least to some extent favor the dissatisfied, or which he, at any rate, believes do so. In the relatively few cases when that has happened the states affected have probably also become more productive, economically and culturally. An outstanding example is the birth of the Athenian direct democracy, about which I will write more in chapter 7, but more examples than that will be presented in subsequent chapters.

The important, theoretical conclusion is the following. The combination of unarticulated, widespread discontent, and adaptations to this by the ruler, in his own interest according to his own judgment, is a very important, fundamental mechanism of change, and often also of improvement, in the institutional history of states. And it is also not only a main mechanism but perhaps even almost the only mechanism of improvement for the subjects. The mechanism, obviously, is fully compatible with the logic of collective action.

ENTREPRENEURS AND DEMOCRACY

Earlier in this chapter I raised the question whether other kinds of states than dictatorships could be created by profit-maximizing entrepreneurs, and then I thought primarily about democratic states. Now, when we are familiar with the concepts of exit and voice, this question may be addressed anew.

In democracies, as we know, the voice-strategy is not only an important corrective, but also to a considerable extent institutionalized. It is however possible to imagine a completely different kind of state, in which the influence of the citizens is exercised by means of exit rather than voice. States like this may, at least in principle, be created by profit-maximizing entrepreneurs—the procedure would be about the same as when baths were created by entrepreneurs in Buchanan's club theory. In a world consisting of states like that common, ordinary people move to the state they consider best. Using a metaphor it may be said the people in this case moves into the *hotel* they find best, and, continuing with the same kind of metaphor, our common, voice-dependent democracies could be called *homes*. The state-creating entrepreneurs thus compete with each other for recruiting guests, and one may thus talk about "competing monopolies of violence" or "competition in government".

In the real world mechanisms like this are however scarce. They are only to be found, sometimes, as means of competition between local communities in ordinary states, and between provinces or states in federations—and when they appear they are hardly ever fully developed. The reason for this scarcity seems to be that a fully developed, institutionalized exit-mechanism requires some kind of overarching legal system upholding the competition. Local communities and provinces both are parts of greater, overarching states providing such systems. Ordinary states, however, do not enjoy any asset like that. For such a purpose the international legal structure is much too weak. Saying this it is also interesting to note that the only existing, elaborated, theoretical model of competition of the kind we are talking about—at least as far as I know—deals with competing local communities, not states. The model is presented in a well-known essay entitled "A Pure Theory of Local Expenditures", authored by the above mentioned Charles Tiebout.[229]

For making the point about the need for an overarching legal order more obvious it may be interesting to make a comparison with cooperative enterprises, that is enterprises which are governed by their owners,

---

[229] Tiebout (1956).

whether consumers or producers, rather than by market mechanisms. Even if there are enterprises of this kind also in rich countries they are by far most common in developing countries, that is countries which are lacking exactly that kind of overarching legal structure which reliance on the market requires. Better then to take everything in one's own hands, to found an association and to do everything within that structure. In the same way ordinary democratic states could be considered as coopera- tives—it is only that they are cooperative states rather than cooperative enterprises. But the fundamental, explaining precondition is the same, namely the lack of a reliable, overarching legal order.

HIERARCHIES

All states, of all kinds, have to be administered in some way. Most important, of course, is that the monopoly of violence must be handled adequately. Violence should be used when, and only when, the rulers judge it appropriate. But many other decisions also have to be based on some kind of information, and to be executed by somebody, and this requires some kind of organization. Obviously these organizations may be very different in different kinds of states, and also, to some extent, have very different purposes. But in spite of all differences there are also con- siderable similarities. In all likelihood there is always something which may be called administrative or bureaucratic hierarchies.

Such a hierarchy is, in principle, structured as shown in figure 4. The figure is, however, only an exemplification—the number of levels may for instance vary, as well as the number of actors on the different levels. At the top there is a chief giving orders, indicated by arrows, to the functionaries on the level immediately below his own. These functio- naries, in their turn, then give orders to those at the lowest level. An organization of this kind makes it possible to execute a very large, admini- strative task, since it is distributed among a great number of individuals, and at the same time keep the enterprise controlled and coordinated in a way that would not have been possible if the individuals involved had acted independently of each other. But for this to work it is not enough to have centralized orders—the functionaries at the different levels, and in particular the chief at the top, must also, in one way or another and in relevant respects, be kept informed in order to be able to perform their tasks. One possibility is that the organization in the figure is used for that purpose as well—for example by functionaries at lower levels informing those higher up. If so we get flows of information going upwards in the organization, rather than downwards as shown by the arrows indicating orders.

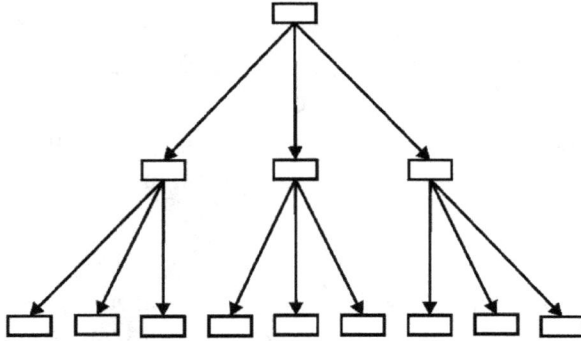

Figure 4: An administrative hierarchy

The orders sent down in the hierarchy may be about individual actions, but it need not be so. In many cases it may be preferable to formulate goals and send them downwards, thereby giving the functionaries below a certain freedom of action. Such a functionary may for instance be in possession of temporary but relevant information which, even according to the chief, ought to affect the actions taken. If so it may be better to send precise goals downwards rather than orders about specified acts. But still we are dealing with a hierarchy. It is still the top that rules—it just rules by goals rather than by ordering actions.

When going downwards in a hierarchy the number of acting units thus increases. The principles behind the division into units may however be of different kinds. One possibility is that it is subject matter oriented. Within a military hierarchy there may, for instance, be units for armies, for naval forces and for air forces. But the division may also be region-oriented. If so the top level is responsible for the whole area or region administered, while the levels below, in due order, handle successively smaller regions within the main region.

Hierarchies of the kind described have been objects of theorizing, and among those having contributed to that are the already mentioned Anthony Downs and the American social scientist Gordon Tullock (1922–2014).[230] An inspiration for this theorizing has been the realization that hierarchies usually do not work as smoothly and effectively as my simple presentation so far may have suggested. A fundamental problem is that orders on their way down, irrespective of their being about acts or goals, may be misunderstood or tinkered with, and the same, of course, may happen with information on its way upwards. The reasons for this, in turn, may be of different kinds. First, there are always difficulties of communication, and if so it is a matter of transaction costs of the kind we have already made acquaintance with. But in addition to this the problems may be due to conscious manipulation by functionaries at different levels. At an early stage in this chapter I introduced an assumption about self-interest, and this, of course, also applies to those operating in a hierarchy. If an actor's self-interest differs from the over-all goal of the hierarchy, and if the actor is able to satisfy his own interest at the expense of the hierarchy's goal, he will do so.

In his book about hierarchies—"The Politics of Bureaucracy"— Gordon Tullock has analyzed the consequences of the assumed selfish behavior of the functionaries. One hypothesis is that the functionaries, possibly correctly, believe that the passing upwards of information, which from the point of view of the superiors is annoying, may be unfavorable, or even dangerous, for the informers themselves. And if so, they choose to cleanse the information and send only positive messages upwards. Another hypothesis is that every person in a hierarchy, as far as possible, acts in ways which are appreciated above all by his or her closest superior. If so, the reason should be that the closest superior, more than anybody else, holds the keys for the functionary's future career.

These two hypotheses lead, in turn, to further hypothetical consequences. One such hypothesis is that the top level of a hierarchy will consist of conformists—this is so since the persons in the top level have made successful careers, and such careers are facilitated by acquiescence. Another hypothesis, which rather is about the lower levels of hierarchies, is that large hierarchies easily become uncontrollable. Those at the lower levels may become almost independent of, or disconnected from, the goals and orders from the top. Such a situation, it is not difficult to understand, will easily materialize if the hierarchy is large enough and the communication problems in combination with the self-interested beha-

---

[230] Downs (1967) and Tullock.

vior of the various functionaries therefore distorting enough. And if so the hierarchy will not succeed in fulfilling its purpose. Or, in other words: there is a limit to the size of hierarchies—sooner or later they become unmanageable. In this book this phenomenon is interesting in particular in connection with expanding dictatorships.

Hierarchies of the kind described are thus always, in one way or another, used for the administration of states. Apart from the more general properties presented here their specific features may however vary considerably. And hierarchical structures may also be combined in various ways with each other. In what follows—in particular in chapter 6 about dictatorships—I will write more about this.

Summary

The theory presented in this chapter aims at arriving at generalizations rather than ad hoc explanations. For making that possible two basic principles, which are to be adhered to, are introduced. The one is methodological individualism—there is no such thing as the will of the people, all explanations, basically, must start with individuals. The other one is rational choice—the individuals are steered by their incentives. A theory which does not treat politics as a result of human ambition can hardly be successful.

To be more specific the theoretical approach developed is to a large extent inspired by Mancur Olson. According to his logic of collective action a large collective cannot undertake complicated actions, and this result can be applied in more specific situations. Thus his explanation of the emergence of small monopolies of violence—or pseudo-states—by means of a "second invisible hand" starts from this result. And the same is true for my "fundamental mechanism of change", which is presented in a separate section of the chapter. This mechanism can explain constitutional changes favoring larger parts of populations, and it has, in fact, as will be seen in the following chapters, been working again and again in the history of states.

Apart from Mancur Olson Albert Hirschman and Ronald Coase are also of great importance for the ideas developed in the chapter. In fact, as demonstrated, the results of these three scholars may be integrated far more than is usually realized. The reason why a large collective cannot undertake complicated actions can thus be formulated in terms of

Coasean transaction costs. Furthermore, someone choosing Hirschman's exit option produces a so-called individual good, whereas the one choosing the voice option rather produces, or takes part in producing, a collective good.

4

DEVELOPMENT AND SIGNIFICANCE OF THE TECHNIQUE OF VIOLENCE

INTRODUCTION

Since a state is characterized by its monopoly of violence it goes almost without saying that at least parts of the development of the technique of violence must be dealt with in a science of states, that is in political science. In this chapter I will therefore present a few steps in this development. The presentation will be far from complete or totally encompassing—I will confine myself to aspects relevant for the problems dealt with in this book. And there are three main kinds of ramifications of the technique of violence for government and society which are of interest here.

The first one regards the possibility of creating monopolies of violence at all, the second one regards the possibilities of keeping such monopolies once established intact, and the third regards the influence of the technique of violence on the inner structures and constitutional patterns of states. Ramifications of all these kinds are discussed in different parts of the book. In chapter 2 I mentioned, for instance, the relevance of military technique for the constitutions of Athens and the Roman Republic, and more of that kind will follow in succeeding chapters. In order to connect these parts of the various chapters with each other, and in order to give them a common foundation, it is however expedient to discuss the technique of violence as such coherently, and in some detail, in one place. Doing so is the purpose of this chapter. I will start by saying a few words about the three types of ramification.

First there is the problem of creating monopolies of violence at all. In the section "Modifications of the basic model" in chapter 3 I wrote that it could not be taken for granted that such monopolies, always, could be created. Anarchy over a large geographic area could very well prevail for long periods. What determines the outcome is however not easy to say—a lot of very different conditions seem to be relevant. The natural, topographic conditions are obviously important as we saw when comparing Egypt and Mesopotamia in chapter 2. In the section "Modifications of the basic model" in chapter 3 I also mentioned factors such as size differences between troops and other resources of different war lords or military commanders, and moreover the relationship between the conditions for attack and defense. If the technique of violence make defense relatively easy, it ought to be fairly easy to create monopolies of violence, but if the weapons of attack are the most effective, it ought to be the other way round.

This whole complex is however more difficult to analyze than at first it may appear, one reason being that what is an attack in a smaller context may be a defense in a larger context. Assume for instance that an attacking force is entering a foreign area and approaching a city or some other strategic target, and that the defenders, from an ambush, attack the intruders in the flank. This operation is then, from a tactical point of view, an attack, but from a strategic point of view, a defensive measure. Another complication is related to the purpose of the attack—is the purpose to establish a new monopoly of violence or to destroy one already existing? An interesting example is the establishing of the Japanese Tokugawa-shogunate, and thereby, the unification of Japan after a long period of anarchy. It has been argued that the availability of firearms—muskets—facilitated this unification. Due to these weapons, which reasonably are attack weapons as much as defense weapons, the unification came about much earlier than otherwise it would have done. The weapons made it possible for one of the war lords to eliminate his main rivals.[231]

The whole issue about the relations between weapons of attack and of defense is thus complicated, and, in addition to that, our basic question about the conditions for attack and defense may concern other matters than the characteristics of weapons. Decisive may rather be matters such as the skill of commanders, the length of lines of supply, and so forth. But in spite of these problems there are still undertakings which may be characterized as pure defense. What I am thinking about are those walls of defense which were in use from the very first beginning of the history of states and at least until 1500.

---

[231] Findlay & O'Rourke, p. 171.

About the second type of ramification of the technique of violence, the one about the possibilities to keep monopolies of violence intact once established, I need not say anything at all here. These matters will be addressed when they become pertinent—for instance in the section "Threats against the dictatorship and countermeasures" in chapter 6. About the third type of ramifications, those related to the inner structure and constitutional patterns of monopolies of violence, there is, however, considerable reason to say something.

These ramifications are not only critically important but also, on the whole, quite unobserved and unanalyzed. For a start it may however be said that for a very long time the relationship between infantry and cavalry was of prime importance. Very roughly it may be said that the impulses favoring democracy have been particularly strong when infantry has dominated. Correspondingly, the impulses leading to various forms of oligarchic rule have been strong when cavalry has been most important. And this seems quite natural since infantry soldiers are many and recruited from large parts of the population, whereas the equestrian warriors with their horses and supplementary expensive equipment are much more of an elite. During the cavalry's periods of strength great landowners therefore often became quite influential, whereas power was spread in much wider circles when infantry was most important. But this is just a rough generalization and there is one exception of utmost importance. Cavalry, not infantry, was a necessary condition for the representative democracy—without the horse no representative democracy. The reason—and here I will just indicate it—is that the assemblies of the medieval knights, or fiefs, constituted the embryo of representative democracies' representative assemblies. This, however, does not exclude that infantry also was important for the development of the representative democracy—that was the case later on when the medieval assemblies, the embryos, began developing towards real democracy. In chapter 9 I will deal with these matters in much more detail. Anyway, and quoting Samuel Finer: "The way in which military power is distributed among the various sections or strata of society is decisive for the form that regime takes."[232] The importance of this can hardly be underlined enough.

---

[232] Finer (1997a), p. 15.

These are then the three kinds of ramifications of the technique of violence that I am interested in, and I will only deal with matters which are of direct relevance to them. This entails the following limitations. First, I will follow the development of the technique of violence only until, about, the year 1500. The main reason for this is that, at about that time, the basic conditions for representative democracy were established, and that therefore, the historical period in which the techniques of violence were of importance for the constitutional development also, in all essentials, had come to an end. Another reason is that the nationalization of the world—in the sense I have used that concept—although not completely finished, had proceeded a long way at that time. On the whole—and in spite of exceptions such as the American and African continents—considerable parts of what could be claimed had also become claimed. Another limitation is that I will, in the following, only deal with land warfare and its techniques. Certainly there was naval warfare even early in history— we have already, for instance, made acquaintance with the battles of Salamis and Mycale—but this, as it seems, has not been of great importance for the problems at issue here. The limitations indicated furthermore mean that matters as important as the internal combustion engine, and the still later atomic bomb, are left without any comments in this chapter, and the same is the case with the modern techniques of surveillance which have been used, and are used, in, above all, totalitarian and other dictatorial states. But even if these well-known techniques are left aside in this chapter I will, of course, when appropriate, mention them in later chapters.

Having said that I now turn to the technique of violence proper. First comes a section about defense walls, and thereafter one about the varying relationship between cavalry and infantry.

DEFENSE WALLS

In the Bible we are told about how trumpet blowing destroyed the wall of Jericho, and in the Iliad about the penetration of the wall of Troy by means of the ingenious Trojan horse. These are myths and tales, but they have a background as real as anything. Already the Sumerian city states— the very earliest states in Mesopotamia—were surrounded by high walls of clay bricks.[233] Real threats, most certainly, lay behind the erection of these big and resource requiring constructions. And for a very long time humans were to continue building walls of this and similar kinds. For clarification I think it is appropriate to make a distinction between city walls and border walls. City walls are used for the defense of individual cities or settlements. A border wall, on the contrary, is part of the defense of a territorial state. It is built along a part of the outer border, which is considered particularly threatened.

The city walls did not enclose the whole state but only one, or perhaps a few, densely populated towns or villages, and then, in particular, the capital. The Sumerian states for instance, in spite of being called city-states, also disposed of considerable areas of cultivated land outside the city itself—the main mean of subsistence was, after all, agriculture—but only the city was enclosed by the wall. If we stay in Mesopotamia, but move forwards in time, we will find more exact descriptions of these matters. It has, for instance, been estimated that the Babylon of Nebuchadnezzar had about 100 000 permanent inhabitants, but that the city, when need arose, could harbor about 250 000.[234] In time of war those living outside the city could thus flee into the security behind the wall.

Walls of this kind have been erected practically everywhere where there have been states—from the very first states until at least a long way into the fifteenth century when, because of the more frequent use of gunpowder, they lost their value. Here are some examples from the almost infinite set. In addition to the walls in Mesopotamia there were also walls around the cities in the Indian Harappa civilization[235] and in the Chinese state of Shang[236]. Antique Athens had a wall as well as Constantinople. Even the city of Rome was, in a late phase of the Empire, equipped with a wall.[237] Still later, after the fall of the Western Roman Empire, walls were built around practically all greater cities in medieval Europe.[238] Defense walls were thus very common, and so common, indeed, that they have left noticeable imprints on languages. The German word "Bürger", for instance, originally meant those citizens living inside

---

[233] Bertman, pp. 262-3; Roux, p. 126.
[234] Roux, pp. 390-1.
[235] Cotterell (1980a), p. 176.
[236] Cotterell (1980b), p. 288.
[237] Browning, p. 261; Roberts, p. 279.
[238] Finer (2007b), p. 952; North & Thomas, p. 11.

the "Burg", that is inside the defense wall[239], and the Chinese word "ch'eng" means city as well as city-wall[240].

The city-walls were, during the long period when they were built, very effective means of defense. Usually they had the form of a complete ring surrounding entirely the object—the city or the city-center—to be protected. And they could be quite impressive. The already mentioned defense which Nebuchadnezzar II built consisted, in fact, of two walls— the one outside the other one—with a moat in between. The outer wall was about 8 kilometers long, which implies a diameter of quite 2.5 kilometers, and had on its top a road broad enough for four horses, or two chariots (see nest section), abreast. When needed the wall could therefore, also, be utilized for transport purposes.[241] Another much later wall was built at the end of the fourteenth century by the early Ming emperors around their capital Nanjing. This wall, which was about 20 meters high and about 30 kilometers long, was probably the biggest city wall in the history of the world, and one of the last as well.[242] But city walls did not have to be formed as closed rings. Athens's wall, for instance, protected the central, densely populated area and the road to the harbor Piraeus, but it was not closed since the sea was relied upon for the remaining defense.[243] The defense of Constantinople, which lay on a tongue of land, was similarly arranged. The wall, even if it had the form of a closed ring, was nevertheless much higher and stronger towards the land side, then along the sea shores.[244]

These city walls were thus very effective and breaching them required considerable effort.[245] Ladders were used, of course, and sometimes the attacker also tried to dig tunnels under the wall. High, wheeled towers, which could be rolled up to the wall, and which had soldiers at their tops, were used. Battering-rams and varying types of catapults were developed. And the ammunition used for bombing the target included not only heavy stones and incendiary torches but also dead, contiguous hu-

---

[239] Finer (1997b), p. 952.
[240] Cotterell (1980b), p. 288.
[241] Roux, p. 391.
[242] Morton & Lewis, p. 123.
[243] Roberts, p. 189; Willetts, p. 275.
[244] Lane, pp. 39-40.
[245] Lane Fox, pp. 265, 270.

man and animal bodies.[246] The breaching of defense walls was, in fact, considered so important that some states—for instance Assyria during the imperial time and Philip's and Alexander's Macedonia—developed, for the purpose, what must be considered full-fledged corps of engineers.[247]

In addition to these direct methods for attacking walls sieges, often lasting for many months, were also used to force the starving population inside to surrender. Some attackers—for instance Assyria—could furthermore, after a successful siege, turn on the inhabitants. They were killed atrociously and some of them were also hanged on poles so that they could be seen from far and wide. The purpose was to induce other cities, not yet besieged, to open their gates straight away. It seems to have worked.[248] Sometimes the attacker could also successfully cooperate with some conspiring traitor inside the wall as was probably the case when the Persians finally conquered Babylon[249], or make use of some kind of acquired expert knowledge about weaknesses in the wall as when the crusaders crossed, from the sea, the threshold to Constantinople in 1204[250].

These methods of attack—the direct assault and the siege—were sometimes successful, sometimes not. Numerous examples of both can be given. But in spite of the very high costs city-walls were built all around the world for more than 4000 years. The development of successively more and more effective methods of attack testifies to the very considerable value of that which was protected. Taken together, the very frequent use of city-walls in many states for a very long time, and the tremendous efforts undertaken for breaching them, including appalling cruelties of various kinds, is a testimony as good as any regarding the importance of violence, theft and conquests in the history of man.

Then we get to the border walls, about which I can be briefer. They are much fewer and their effectiveness also less obvious. The biggest endeavor of this kind, of course, is the Great Wall of China, with its length of 3000 kilometers, or, if secondary fortifications are included, 6000 kilometers. On top of the wall there is also a broad road facilitating the

[246] Lane, p. 19.
[247] Bertman, p. 267; Roberts, p. 213; Roux, p. 349.
[248] Grayson (1980b), p. 106.
[249] Roux, p. 391.
[250] Herrin, pp. 263-4; Horodowich, pp. 40-1; Lane, pp. 40-1.

defender's troop movements. The first big parts of the wall were built during Qin and Han, but since the material used at that time was clay, the results have by now, to a large extent, withered away.[251] For defense they were not either, as it seems, all that effective. As we saw in chapter 2 the Mongols, in spite of the wall, succeeded in invading the country and even ruled it during the so called Mongolian period (1234–1368). But after that, when the Chinese had taken their country back and the Ming era had started, the Mongols still constituted a threat. The wall, as we know it today, was to a large extent built during Ming, and it also seems to have been effective.[252] When the eventual new rulers, the ones from the Manchu people, succeeded in penetrating the wall, they were assisted by a Chinese general who, treasonously, opened the wall.[253]

But even if the Great Wall of China is by far the most well-known of all border walls, there have also been others. Thus, and as mentioned in chapter 2, during Third Dynasty Ur walls were built along the empire's northeastern border, and, much later, the Roman emperor Hadrian had a wall built across England.

THE RELATIONSHIP BETWEEN CAVALRY AND INFANTRY

INTRODUCTION

The horse was fundamentally important in fighting and warfare long before the appearance of the first states about five thousand years ago and kept its crucial role long into the twentieth century. This—a stupendously long period of effective use—attests to the enormous importance of the horse. Roughly the horse has had two main roles in warfare. In the one role the horse itself is active on the battlefield, in the other the horse, rather, has been used for pulling in heavy transports. It could have been transport of troops to the battlefield, for instance Roman legionaries on the Roman road network, or, in later times, transport of heavy artillery cannons or loads of ammunition.

About this second role I will only say that an important technical innovation, namely that of an efficient horse-collar, was a necessary prerequisite. Before that the harness was laid around the throat of the horse

---

[251] Gascoigne (2003), pp. ix-x; Roberts, p. 448.
[252] Fairbank & Goldman, pp. 57, 139; Morton & Lewis, p. 46.
[253] Roberts, p. 461.

and was therefore, in fact, almost an apparatus for strangulation. With the new, developed collar the horse was not intimidated in that way but could rather pull with its breast and shoulders and thus mobilize its entire weight and power. This development started in China at some time before the year −200.[254] In Europe, and in that case in the Roman Empire, the technique appeared much later, around 200 as it seems.[255]

After this comment I will confine myself to the horse on the battle-field, and in particular to those cases in which the warring soldier fights riding on the horse's back. In this way horses have been used during the whole of that very long period we are interested in, but even so the ca-valry has often, more or less, been complemented with other kinds of forces, as for instance infantry. There are also periods in which other means of violence have been efficient enough for reducing the role of the cavalry most considerably. During one of those periods the so called chariots—light-weight wagons drawn by horses—were dominating and almost eliminated the cavalry. At other periods the infantry, rather, and due to technical development, became the most important weapon. About these competitors I will write more in what follows, but before that I will say more about the cavalry itself, its problems and the solutions for these problems which have gradually emerged. This is important since it was these problems which, among other matters, opened the field for the chariots and the infantry. For understanding the roles of these latter weapons it is therefore necessary to know a little about the cavalry and its problems as well.

THE CAVALRY

The horse was first domesticated by those nomadic peoples to the north of the Black Sea and the Caspian Sea which I wrote about in chapter 2. They started by hunting wild horses as game for eating; they then learned that it was possible to keep the horses behind fences in the same way as cattle is kept today; and still later they learned that it was possible to communicate with the horses, that they could be domesticated. The time for this domestication has been determined quite precisely. In graves re-

---

[254] Morris, p. 395; Morton & Lewis, p. 27.
[255] Fairbank & Goldman, p. 77; Lane Fox, p. 270; Palmer, Colton & Kramer, (2007a), p. 28-9; Roberts, p. 516.

mains of horses have been found and after a certain time the teeth of the horses are weared in way which has been interpreted as coming from a rein of some kind. The conclusion is that human beings started riding horses at about the year −4000, that is some thousand years before the appearance of the first states.[256]

But the first riders faced several problems. First, the horses were smaller and more feeble than today, and could therefore not be ridden long distances or carry much more load then the rider himself. By means of a more or less conscious breeding[257] the horses did however, gradually but slowly, become bigger and stronger. Still it is difficult to specify any particular steps in this development, and I therefore just state the fact. Breeding has resulted in horses successively bigger and bigger, and stronger and stronger.

Other problems were related to the very riding on the horseback. In the beginning there were no saddles so the riding was bare-back or perhaps the rider was sitting on some simple piece of cloth. Furthermore, there were no stirrups. And all of this meant that fighting from the horseback was difficult. The cavalry soldier could not stand up working with his whole body, not mobilize his whole weight for throwing a javelin or for handling a lance or a sword. The greatest danger facing the fighter may, indeed, have been falling off the horse rather than the actions of the enemy. These problems were however to be solved successively. The saddle was developed bit by bit and did not only become more stable and solid but was also fastened around the horse by means of saddle-girth. The developed iron stirrup came to Europe from the east at some time during the eighth century or perhaps somewhat later.[258] The exact origin is unknown as well as the exact time. Clear is however that the stirrup, when it came to Europe, had been used in its place of origin—possibly China—during several hundred years.[259]

In this way, and during a long time, the horses as well as the equipment for the riding were developed. In the thirteenth century—that is more than 5000 years after the age of the first riders—a culmination was reached with the medieval knight. Since the horses had become

---

[256] Anthony, p. 460.
[257] Oppenheimer, p. 34.
[258] Finer (1997a), p. 22; Finer (1997b), pp. 876-7; Roberts, pp. 90, 324.
[259] Fairbank & Goldman, p. 77.

bigger and stronger the knight could carry a metal helmet and protect his body with armor or chain-mail and even the horse could be protected by plate armor of its own. Due to the saddle and the stirrups, the knight also sat or stood steadily and could therefore handle his weapon with great efficiency. The lance was a main weapon and the knights usually attacked in a group. The shock cavalry charge, in which a large group of knights rode towards the enemy with their lances heading forwards, was a formidable method of attack.[260]

During cavalry's early phases—before the era of effective saddles and stirrups—the handling of several weapons such as javelins, lances and swords from the horse-back was thus difficult or impossible. One weapon, the bow, was however available, at least in principle, since it did not require that the rider worked with his whole body and body-weight. Even here there was however a difficulty, namely that the first bows were too long and therefore difficult to maneuver from the horse-back. It was difficult to freely change the shooting direction in the way necessary. And if the bows were made shorter they lost shooting power. This problem did however get a solution quite early—about the year −1700 as it seems—with the so called composite bow.[261]

For understanding this important innovation it helps to know a little bit about the physics of bow shooting. One important quantity is the power needed for drawing the bow. That this power should be as great as possible with respect to the arm strength of the archer is obvious. Another important quantity is the length of the drawing. The further the archer can draw the string—from the undrawn to the fully drawn state—the better it is. The reason is that the energy of motion, accumulated in the arrow leaving the bow, increases not only with the drawing power but also with the drawing length—the longer that length is the longer is also the time during which the string accelerates the arrow. And it is exactly these relationships which are problems with respect to short bows. The shorter the bow is, the shorter is also the drawing length—at least as long as the basic construction of the bow remains the same.

In the composite bow the very basic construction was however changed. Lengthwise the bow was built up by different materials—for

---

[260] Finer (1997b), pp. 876-7, 1028.
[261] Derry & Williams, pp. 245-6.

instance sinews, wood and horn—which were glued together. In that way the bow's bowing properties could be made very good—the different materials could be placed in a way maximizing the arrow's energy of motion. But the use of several materials also made it possible to change the bow's curvature to some extent. The thickness of the bow along its length could be varied more freely than earlier, and the same was true for the exact form of its curvature. And this was utterly important since it meant that the drawing length could be quite extended in spite of the bow being short. In addition to this the arrows were also made better and also given about the same shape and size so that the soldier could carry them in a quiver on his back.[262]

During all the time we are interested in there has thus been a cavalry weapon, and it has also developed most considerably in various ways. What in the beginning were bare-back riders on small horses became, step by step, ultimately the medieval grandiose, armored knight. But this development has not been without problems and during some periods, as I have already mentioned, other kinds of weapons have been the most important. The following sections are about these alternatives.

THE CHARIOTS, FROM −1700 TO −600

Small and rather weak animals, and lack of saddles and stirrups, were thus major problems when horses began to be used for belligerent purposes. At first these problems were however not directly addressed, they were rather "solved" by the introduction of a very different kind of weapon, the chariot. And this is hardly surprising. The possibility of getting bigger and stronger horses by breeding was perhaps vaguely recognized, but it required anyway a lot of time, and better saddles and stirrups became really interesting only when the horses had improved. The small horses had to be used in other ways and hence the chariot. In a common design it was a very light-weighted, two-wheeled wagon pulled by two horses and serving as a platform for two soldiers, one driver and one archer. The latter often used the composite bow, since even here mobility was of crucial importance.

Since the wagon was light the lack of good harnessing was no problem, and neither the horses' limited power since more than one horse

---

[262] Bertman, p. 264; Chrissanthos, p. 2.

could be used for the pulling. The lightness of the wagon also made the equipage very fast, and speed contributed significantly to the strength of the chariot weapon. But a prerequisite for all of this was an innovation of utmost importance—even this one emanating from the peoples to the north of the Black Sea and the Caspian Sea—namely the spoked wheel.[263]

Since the wheels had to be light they could not consist of solid wood, they had to be built up by a hub, spoks and a wheel rim. That the making of wheels like that, in the age at issue, met with challenging problems goes without saying. We are, in fact, dealing with an, for its time, utterly advanced carpentry. The wheel rim must, for instance, have consisted of a number of separate parts so that the wood's grains everywhere roughly followed the rim. In addition to that essential components of iron or bronze were used in the wheels and the wheel-suspension.[264]

A considerable limitation of the weapon was, of course, its dependence on a reasonably flat ground. But in spite of this it was, during its age, widely spread. The estimations of the exact occurrence of this age varies somewhat—one reason being that the wagons were gradually developed from, in the beginning, use for peaceful purposes to, after that, the much more requiring belligerent use. Here I have however settled for the period –1700 to –600.[265] The weapon was thus used by the Hyksos tribe when it attacked Egypt around –1700, and then successfully by the New Kingdom in its expansion to the north-east. In the greatest chariot battle ever—the battle of Kadesh in Syria about –1275—Egyptian and Hittite forces stood against each other. According to some estimates no less than 5000 chariots were taking part—who won is unclear.[266] Chariots were also used extensively by the Assyrians and the Babylonians. The chariot period indicated above coincides in fact quite well with the period from the appearance of Assyria and Babylonia until their disappearance about 1300 years later. Above all chariots were used intensively and successfully when Assyria entered its expansive, imperial period.[267]

---

[263] Anthony, p. 462; Derry & Williams, pp. 190-4; Finer (1997a), pp. 102-3.
[264] Grayson (1980b), p. 103; Roberts, p. 90.
[265] Anthony, p. 18; Finer (1997a), p. 234.
[266] Anthony, p. 44-5; Leick, p. 207; Mieroop, pp. 220-1; Morris, p. 199; Roux, p. 261; Wilkinson, pp. 304, 324-30.
[267] Bertman, pp. 265-6.

But chariots were also used in totally different places. Thus chariots were of great importance when the Chinese state Shang was consolidated, and so even in Zhou. At the time of Qin the period of the chariots was however over. But anyway, during its period of strength the chariot weapon was thus widely spread, which is interesting since it indicates contacts over very long distances. This opinion has been expressed by for instance Samuel Finer, arguing that such an advanced innovation as the chariot hardly is done in several places without contact with each other.[268]

The chariot period had thus, on the whole, come to an end about –600, but the reason was not that the cavalry had improved enough to substitute for chariots. Certainly the cavalry had become more efficient during the chariot period, and the Assyrians, just to take one example, used, beside their chariots, also an advanced cavalry mounted with composite bows. But the decisive factor, nevertheless, was the very considerable development of the infantry. And therefore it is also interesting to note that the time when the chariots disappeared roughly coincides with the entering on the scene of the Persian Empire, the Greek city-states and the Roman Republic.

INFANTRY'S FIRST PERIOD OF STRENGTH, FROM –600 TO 400

The development of the infantry was started by the Assyrians even if it was to gain its greatest importance in other states.[269] In Athens and in Sparta the new type of effective infantry soldiers were called hoplites, in the Roman Republic they were called legionaries and in the Persian Empire there was an elite force called "the ten thousand immortals".[270] This much improved infantry was, of course, to develop further and gradually, but in the beginning it basically looked like this:

The soldiers were well equipped, with armor as well as with weapons. They wore helmets, their breasts and legs were protected, and they also carried a shield with their left arm. The weapons, often swords or lances, were maneuvered with the right arm. All of this equipment was a result of technological development, particularly metallurgical, and required a good supply of metals, above all iron. Metal was not only used for

---

[268] Finer (1997a), pp. 446, 448; Morris, p. 220.
[269] Kriwaczek, p. 236.
[270] Finer (1997a), p. 311; Hansen, pp. 116-7.

the soldiers' armor but also in the weapons. It should be noted that the initial phase of infantry's first period of strength coincides roughly with the time for the passage from the bronze- to the iron-age.[271]

Not only the individual soldier and his equipment were important however, but also the formation of the larger fighting group. In this the soldiers walked side by side in long rows, the one row behind the other. In every row every soldier protected, with his shield, his closest neighbor to the left. This mutual dependence made it imperative that the formations were kept together on the battlefield—discipline was of utmost importance, the formations must not split.

This indicates still an important condition for the emergence of the infantry, namely that a well organized society of some kind, a state, already existed. Lacking that it should hardly have been possible to mobilize the large, cohesive and disciplined entities we are considering. And this was something new—the early cavalry did not face any requirements like that. A small group of riding soldiers, or of chariots, could certainly, without much organization, terrify its opponents effectively. But for a small group of infantry soldiers that was hardly possible. For them the large number, the organization and the discipline were of crucial importance in a totally different way. And the first entities of this kind, in contrast to the first cavalry, also appeared in states already established—which indicates an interesting, causal chain. In chapter 2 I wrote that some of the Greek city-states and the Roman Republic were the first known states in history to adopt a precise, generally known and respected system for political decision-making. The pattern may now be enlarged as follows: first a state, then infantry, and then a detailed and precise system for decision-making, that is a constitution.

The infantry I am talking about here had its period of strength from about −600 to 400, that is for about a thousand years. And during this time it was also developed and improved in various ways. Thus Philip of Macedonia and Alexander the Great not only developed the infantry technique as such but also complemented the infantry with cavalry in new, efficient ways. The cavalry was thus used for protecting its own infantry's vulnerable flanks, for splitting the enemies infantry formations, and, perhaps most important, for chasing and massacring the enemy infantry

---

[271] Derry & Williams, p. 126; Morris, p. 233.

after its formation was split.[272] But the infantry technique as such was also developed—in particular by the Romans who longest of all, far into the Empire period, stuck to infantry warfare. As early as in the Republic they introduced, for instance, formations which were smaller and more mobile, and therefore also more efficient in many situations, than the original, sometimes too rigid, row constellation. The weaponry of the soldiers was also somewhat changed—javelins to be thrown, or bows, could for instance be included.[273]

But in spite of all these improvements infantry's first period of strength was destined to end. Cavalry gradually became more and more important and would, in due time, dominate completely. And the climax reached was not only characterized by the heavily armored medieval knight, but also by the so different light and indefatigable cavalry of the steppes under Genghis Khan (circa 1162–1227).

INFANTRY'S SECOND PERIOD OF STRENGTH, FROM 1300 TO 1500

But even for this very effective cavalry, and especially for the knights, there were limits. During the fourteenth and fifteenth centuries infantry entered into a new period of strength and the background, again, was new and more efficient weapons, but possibly also a successively more and more widespread monetary economy.[274] To this latter aspect I will return towards the end of this section.

Among the new weapons was a new bow, the so called long bow, which had been developed in England. Since it was an infantry weapon it could be admitted to be long, and so it was—about as long, or high, as the archer using it. And therefore it was possible to achieve simultaneously, without any changes of the curvature or measures like that, great drawing power and long drawing length. There was no need for man-made layers of various materials as in the composite bow. The bow was made of one single piece of material—yew wood—but in such a way that both the softer sapwood and the harder heartwood were included. Thereby an interaction between the materials, similar to that in the composite bow, was obtained. The result was an infantry weapon with long reach, great

---

[272] Chrissanthos, pp. 73-5; Derry & Williams, p. 17; Roberts, p. 213.
[273] Lane Fox, pp. 474-5.
[274] Palmer, Colton & Kramer (2007a), p. 73; Rosenberg & Birdzell, pp. 63-7.

precision and, in many cases, power enough to penetrate a knight's armor. Among the new shooting weapons was also the cross-bow, originating in China.

Other weapons, developed in particular in Switzerland, were better lances and so called halberds. The former, which were used especially for defense against knights, were now made of metal altogether rather than, as earlier, having a metal head and a wood shaft. Thereby it became impossible for the knight to crush the lance. The halberd, which was used in closed combat after the splitting of a knight formation, was a kind of very long axe by which the knight could be deadly injured. And the halberd also had, on its head, a hook by which the knight could be grappled and pulled off the horse.[275] At the end of the period we are talking about the infantry weaponry also began to include firearms, so called muskets. These, however, had their teething problems, and did therefore not dominate from the beginning but were rather used as a complement. The appearance of the muskets does therefore not change or diminish the importance of the long bows, the lances and halberds for the infantry's renaissance.[276]

Parallel with this development in weaponry the formations of the soldiers, so important in infantry warfare, were also remodeled. One example is the so called Swiss Square which consisted of about ten rows behind each other with about ten soldiers in every row. This constellation was quite flexible. The lances—the weapon usually used—could quickly be mobilized in whichever direction of attack was wanted, and in defensive situations the lances could, from the four sides of the square, aim in all directions.

Infantry's new strength was not only demonstrated in a long row of important battles, but it was also further developed in the process. For the English the so called Hundred Years' War (1337–1453), in which the English kings tried to conquer France, was especially important. The English first won important victories in the battles of Crécy 1346, Poitiers 1356 and Agincourt 1415. The efficiency of the new weapons, and especially the longbows, was demonstrated and the knights on the French side could not resist in spite of support from cross-bow soldiers. When

---

[275] Finer (1997c), pp. 1267-8; Steinberg, pp. 21-2.
[276] Derry & Williams, p. 39.

most successful the English had conquered about half of France. But finally they were nevertheless driven back from all of it but Calais. Led by Joan of Arc the French triumphed. Contributing to this was that the French began using firearms earlier than the English.[277] 1453 was the year of gunpowder. That year the French won the Hundred Years' War by means of muskets, and that same year the Turks, using gunpowder artillery, penetrated the until then impenetrable land-wall of Constantinople.

The Swiss development of new weapons is directly related to the creation of the Swiss state, to which I will return in chapter 7. Here it suffices to say that a number of forest cantons united at the end of the thirteenth century, that these cantons were direct democracies and that they had a common problem of defense. The solution was infantry—and a very advanced infantry. The Swiss could register a number of great successes. In the battles of Morgarten 1315 and Sempach 1387 Swiss infantry defeated foreign, hostile forces of knights.[278] And a Swedish example, by the way, is the battle of Brunkeberg 1471. There the Swedish infantry, consisting of otherwise farming people, defeated the attacking Danish cavalry of knights.

And so, finally, to the question about the infantry and the monetary economy. In chapter 2 I wrote that the conditions leading to the European feudalism were the development of the knight weapon in combination with a moneyless economy. But these two conditions disappeared just about simultaneously, although gradually. That the knight weapon was substituted for by a successively more efficient infantry we already know, but at the same time the use of money spread more and more widely. And that meant that the kings who needed soldiers could buy them on markets rather than being bound by the restrictive barter deals with feudal fiefs. Infantry's second period of strength is therefore also the great age of mercenaries. Infantry soldiers, operating on markets, offered their services to the one paying most—questions about the purposes of fighting, or about loyalty, were at most of secondary importance. One example of mercenaries of this kind is the so called Swiss Guards, originating from Switzerland. A prominent critic of this entire system was Machiavelli, contending that the mercenaries were cowards, dishonest and unreliable.

---

[277] North & Thomas, pp. 81, 94-7, 121.
[278] Finer (1997b), p. 957.

The Prince who aimed at being strong and free should not use them.[279] To this it may be added that the mercenaries, when not engaged by anybody, ravaged and plundered widely on their own behalf.

SUMMARY

In the first chapter I introduced the monopoly of violence as the most important defining characteristic of a state, and in the third chapter I then described a mechanism, the second invisible hand, by which monopolies of violence may be created. A precondition was that the impending creator disposed of sufficient and appropriate means of violence. But the technique of violence is not only relevant for the possibilities to create, and to defend, states, but has also, during a long part of world history, been of great importance for the inner structures, or for the constitutional properties, of states. This being so the technique of violence must obviously be dealt with in some detail in a theory of states, and that is the main purpose of this chapter. Here are some main results.

During considerable periods of time, and over large areas, there have not been any states at all. Statelessness and anarchy have dominated. A common reason for this, in all likelihood, is that the properties, and the distribution, of the means of violence did not allow for the creation of any states.

But when and where it has been possible to create states they have been attacked since they represented richness, and thus they had to be defended. Nothing makes these basic conditions more clear than the defense walls which were built in states of all kinds and everywhere for 4 500 years—from the very first states until about the year 1500 when they lost their value because of the arrival of gun powder. During that time, because of the great values protected by the walls, very considerable, and sometimes successful, efforts for penetrating them were also made.

As for the relevance of the technique of violence for the constitutional patterns of states the relationship between infantry and cavalry has been of great importance. Basically infantry gives impulses towards democracy since the infantry soldiers, requiring influence in the decision making, constitute a large part of the population in their state, whereas

---

[279] Machiavelli, p. 43.

cavalry, typically recruited from the much fewer great landowners, gives impulses towards oligarchy. Even if horses always have been used in warfare it is therefore important that infantry has dominated during two periods.

The first of these period of strength, from about −600 to 400, is particularly important. It started when the iron age had followed the bronze age and weapons and armor of iron thus began to be used. In ancient Greece the infantry soldiers were called hoplites, in the Roman state legionaries, and in the Persian Empire there were "the ten thousand immortals". The hoplites and the legionaries, in particular, required influence, and the fundamental mechanism of change, described in chapter 3, worked. The result, as will be described in more detail in what follows, was ancient Athens's direct democracy and the Roman Republic. Even if the latter state was not a democracy its arrival, after a prior dictatorship, was a development in the direction towards democracy.

5

POLITICS AND ECONOMY

INTRODUCTION

So far I have only talked about political matters in a wide sense, hardly at all about economic ones. The economic conditions of a society are however of greatest importance—not only by themselves, but also because of their interaction with politics. And this interaction is complex. In the same way as for political phenomena it is expedient to make a distinction between matters which may grow from below as a result of individuals acting at the grass root level, and matters which, because of the logic of collective action, must be decided about and implemented from above. What I particularly have in mind are all those economic institutions of various kinds which today we take for granted. When did they appear, and due to what mechanisms?

To bring some clarity into this subject area I have divided the time we are dealing with into three periods. The first one, which I call the period of emerging markets, is long, about 4000 years, and stretches from the time of the very first states all the way to the appearance of the Italian city-states, and among them Venice in particular, somewhat before the year 1000. In these city-states the economic entities we call "firms" or "companies" in a modern sense began appearing for the first time in history, and hence a new period. By "modern" I mean not only that the firms were private, and that they were run by full-time officers for the sake of profit, but also that they became more and more institutionally sophisticated. Italian double entry book-keeping was, for instance, introduced at this time, but not only that—the whole institutional milieu in which the firms acted gradually developed. And this is the reason for which I call this second period the period of institutionalization. In spite of this development the firms were however still, and on the whole, engaged in commerce rather than in manufacturing. But this changed with the industrial revolution in England about 1700 which launched the third period, the period of industrialization in which we still are living.

This division is interesting partly because the methods available for those wanting to become rich, whether state leaders or single individuals, have been very different in the three periods. But this is not the only reason for the division. In the three periods state leaders may also have viewed differently the methods used by individuals, or perhaps enterprises, for becoming rich—they may have suppressed some such methods, and they may have tolerated, or perhaps even encouraged, other methods. About this I will try to say something in what follows and thereby give a picture of the relations between politics and the economy over the course of history. When have, one may ask, the political and the economic developments within states worked together and supported each other, and when have they, on the contrary, rather worked against each other, or even been in direct conflict? These are the main questions in this chapter, the outline of which follows the three periods just mentioned.

THE PERIOD OF EMERGING MARKETS—FROM −3000 TO 1000

THE EARLY MARKETS

My calling this period, about four thousand years long, the period of emerging markets should not be misunderstood. Especially during the early phases of the period markets were small and uncommon and, in many states, did not exist at all. If we start by looking at the individual state with its own resources—and thus disregard conquests and similar matters—the rulers were of course always interested in increasing the production, and in distributing it according to their preferences. But the instruments for this were not markets but directives from above. The rulers gave orders about what was to be produced, for instance grains of specified kinds, and about the distribution of the resulting crops. The economies were, on the whole, so called storage-redistribution economies.[280] But in spite of this small markets may very well have appeared, and they could perhaps even grow and gradually become larger and more important.[281] And this is the reason why I include the early storage-redistribution economies in the period of emerging markets.

How then did the first markets come about, or how could it have happened? Human beings are social and cooperate with each other, and

---

[280] Finer (1997a), p. 20.
[281] Mieroop, p. 238.

an important element in this cooperation is exchange. Someone has more of something, or is perhaps particularly skillful in producing it, and someone else is, rather, good at something else. Situations like that, which have always been present, frequently lead to exchanges. If I get this from you, you get that from me. The basic element of commerce is the mutually beneficial exchange. Both parties consider themselves better off after the exchange than before. The goods and the activities become better distributed. For making these matters still clearer it is however important—in particular for early states—to make a distinction between domestic trade and foreign trade. In this section I continue with domestic trade in order to deal with foreign trade in a later section.

Even in very primitive societies without generally accepted rules, and without a monetary system, some exchanges will certainly take place, at least between people close to and trusting each other. Under primitive conditions like that it is also possible, or even likely, that some kind of means of exchange—primitive money one may say—emerges and becomes used more and more. In a pure system of barter, that is a system in which goods and services are exchanged directly with each other, it is not enough for a person wanting to sell something, say a stone axe, to find someone wanting the axe—this other person must also be in possession of something wanted by the first person, say a pot of clay of some specified kind.

Restrictions like these are obviously very limiting, but may to a considerable extent be eliminated by means of exchange of various kinds. Assume for instance that the prospective buyer of the stone axe does not have the clay pot required, but has some other object which is durable and considered beautiful, rare or valuable—for instance a piece of metal of some kind, a rare stone or a beautiful shell. If so, it is perfectly possible that the "seller" of the axe accepts this object as a "payment". And it is furthermore equally possible that the seller, rather than keeping the object, bears in mind the possibility of using it for buying something from some third person, for instance the wished for clay pot. Already very simple means of exchange of this kind enlarges the area of possible transactions most considerably and thereby contribute to the welfare of human beings. It is also well known that means of exchange like these have been in frequent use. In Mesopotamia measured quantities of grains or silver were used as "money" as early as about −2000.[282] In the first Chinese states bolts of silk and cowry shells were used in the same way.[283] And the Aztecs used cacao beans and cotton mantles of standardized size.[284] More examples could easily be given.

Primitive markets like these, with their means of exchange, can be created by individuals within, initially, very small groups. All of it is easy to explain by assuming rational human beings, there is no need for a superimposed state level. There is therefore every reason to believe that there have been markets of some kinds in all states, even the earliest ones. Thus there seems to have been markets in the capital of Egypt's Old Kingdom Memphis and in Thebes, the capital of the Middle Kingdom, in Assyria's Nineveh and in Babylonia's Babylon.[285] Going a long way forwards in time, there were also significant markets in Chinese Song.[286] And still later the Aztecs did also have large markets, not only in the capital Tenochtitlan but in several other cities as well. So even if the dictators' activities have dominated in all these early states—in Egypt, in Mesopotamia, in China and in the Aztecs' state—spontaneous markets have nevertheless existed and also been permitted.

As long as there have been states there have thus also been markets, more or less extended, like the ones described, but their importance was nevertheless, and for two reasons, probably quite limited. First, in order for all potential, mutually beneficial exchanges to materialize, institutions much more sophisticated and reliable were required and institutions like that did not appear until the period of institutionalization. Second, the possibilities for creating saleable added values by development and innovation were quite limited. For sure there was a significant, gradual development concerning for instance handling of animals, growing of vegetables and the use of metals, but this development was nevertheless slow and erratic. The great change in this respect did not come until the beginning of industrialization, that is in our third period.

---

[282] Roberts, pp. 92-3.
[283] Finer (1997a), p. 82; Morton & Lewis, pp. 27-8.
[284] Nicholson, p. 344.
[285] Hicks, p. 32.
[286] Morton & Lewis, p. 103.

CLAIMS, PLUNDERING AND CONQUESTS

Even if there thus were markets at a very early stage in the history of the states, it was not by them that wealth was created—and the wealth that is important in this era is that of the rulers. Their wealth was achieved by other means. In the theory chapter I described how the ruler who wished to become rich quickly could utilize the work and resources of other people. First there was the possibility of taxing the subjects within the ruler's own state severely, for instance by taking away from them parts of the results of their productive work, or by forcing them to perform specified labor of various kinds. But in addition to this the ruler could also, if he was strong enough, claim new areas outside his own state, undertake plundering raids outside his own borders, or conquer areas from other states. These methods for creating wealth—claims, plundering and conquests—were not only extremely frequent during the four thousand year period we are here considering, they were also, by far, the most profitable methods. When wealth appeared the reason was practically always transfers of these kinds. And this was true not only for the valuables of dictatorships and their leaders. States of other kinds, although few, behaved similarly. The Roman Republic lived to a very large extent by conquests—grains from conquered Egypt for instance—and Athens, the direct democracy that I described in chapter 2, benefitted from the large taxes taken from the other members of the Delian League. If there was a difference between these states and the dictatorships it consisted at most in the use of the resources taken. Perhaps they were somewhat more evenly distributed in the non-dictatorships.

Wealth was thus, during the era considered, to a large extent created in so called zero sum games—the gains of the plunderers and conquerors were the losses of the victims. But there was one more method by which the state leaderships could enrich themselves—and which was not a zero sum method—namely the already mentioned foreign trade. And this takes us back to the mutually beneficial exchanges.

FOREIGN TRADE

The local markets were thus, in spite of their possible value for ordinary people, of minor importance in the great, stately contexts. In these foreign trade was however of major importance from the very beginning. Foreign trade, in fact, seems to have developed long before domestic trade, at least if reasonably large volumes are considered.

Thus the very first states in Mesopotamia were traders. Their own valuable commodity, which could be exported, was above all bitumen. It could be used as a building material, for mosaics, for packing, as fuel and even as a drug. But even if there was bitumen in Mesopotamia other commodities were missing—for instance stone, metals and high quality wood. These products could however be imported from Lebanon, Egypt, Persia and India.[287] Some trade routes passed over land and in the beginning donkeys were used as beasts of burden. Around the year –1500 they were however gradually replaced by camels, the domestication of which then began to succeed.[288] But sea routes were also used, especially for the Indian trade.

These are thus some examples of very early international trading, and the activities grow steadily during the first long period we are considering. Further details are however not necessary. More generally it should only be added that the trading routes between Central Asia and the Mediterranean area became of great importance after the time of Alexander the Great—a period usually called the Hellenistic one. Among the commodities transported along these routes were gold, ivory, spices, incense, precious stones, dates, wool and grains.[289] Especially important among the routes was the Silk Road between Chinese Han and the Roman Empire, which opened just before the year 0. On this road were transported, mainly, silk in the one direction and wools, gold and silver in the other.[290]

Thus, and from the time of the very first states, there was a considerable foreign trade. But why, one may ask, did the states trade at all? Why did they not just steal the goods they wanted, as they did in so many other cases? Why did the states sometimes steal, and sometimes trade? About this it is obviously difficult to say anything for sure, in particular concerning individual cases. But it easy to imagine that pure opportunism was decisive. If the goods wanted were present in areas close to one's own country one probably tried to conquer those areas—in many cases such a

---

[287] Cotterell (1980a), p. 180; Roux, pp. 12-3.
[288] Leick, p. 269; Roberts, p. 91; Roux, p. 13.
[289] Roux, p. 415.
[290] Encyclopædia Britannica Online, title word "Silk Road".

military enterprise probably looked quite possible. But if, on the contrary, the goods existed only far away, a military conquest could have been difficult, or even impossible. And if, additionally, a continuous supply of the goods was wanted, the problem could not be solved by a one time plundering raid. It was rather necessary to establish good and stable relations with those in possession of the desired goods. One had to be able to return again and again. And this may explain how foreign trade, which really to a very large extent was long distance, appeared.

An interesting case is Egypt's Old Kingdom. Commodities of interest for this state were present both in nearby Nubia to the south and in the more distant Lebanon in the north-east. Nubia had above all gold, but also other luxury goods such as ebony and ostrich eggs and feathers.[291] The Egyptian method for gaining access to these goods was, at least mostly, theft. What was interesting in the more distant Lebanon was the cedar timber which was used for building the ships operating on the Nile. And this timber was, as should be expected, and at least for long periods[292], acquired by trading, even if the means of exchange may have varied.[293] Sometimes goods produced in Egypt may have been used, and sometimes, perhaps, some of the goods stolen from Nubia.

From the beginning foreign trade was thus important, and those trading with each other were states.[294] Using a modern term the early states were state-trading countries. And it was not just trade in general. I have already mentioned a number of goods traded and, apart from some important raw materials, the goods involved were almost exclusively various kinds of luxuries. This clearly indicates that those trading with each other were the states' leaderships, striving for wealth and luxury. The commodities traded were not affordable by any one else. In the beginning, therefore, the traders were the state leaderships. Later on merchants, acting on orders from the state leaderships, may however have become involved, and still later merchants who, trying to become rich themselves, acted more independently.[295]

---

[291] Brewer & Teeter, p. 40.
[292] Although not always—Wilkinson, pp. 172-3.
[293] Walters (1980a), p. 27.
[294] Finer (1997a), p. 186.
[295] Leick, p. 201; Morton & Lewis, pp. 27-8.

MONEY PROMULGATED BY THE STATE

The means of exchange mentioned in the section "The early markets" were created by the common people themselves, and they were thus introduced "from beneath". In the same way it could have continued and, to some extent, it probably also did. At least some of the actors in the markets could, for instance, have manufactured pieces of some valuable metal and stamped on them figures indicating their weight. In principle there is no difference between such an activity and the production of the earlier mentioned bolts of silk or cotton mantles, and the stamped metal pieces would thus constitute perfect money. Perhaps that is also what happened, at least for a start. Thus real coins, according to some information, may have been used in Assyria as early as, or even before, –700.[296] More often it is however argued that the first documented coins appeared around –600 in Lydia at the eastern coast of Aegean Sea—an area favored by suitable mineral resources.[297] These coins may very well have been introduced from beneath. But if so, this was soon to be changed. About –560 the Lydian dictator Croesus started promulgating coins himself— coins thus introduced from "above"—and he was soon followed by dictators in other states.[298] And these dictators not only stamped the values on the coins but also pictures of themselves.[299]

But why did the dictators do this? Which were their interests? Sometimes it is argued that state book-keeping was facilitated by the introduction of money, and that is possibly part of the truth. But more important was probably that money made possible a harder and more extended taxation. For seeing this it is enough to consider a society with a pure storage-redistribution economy, for example Egypt's Old Kingdom. Taxing there, as we saw in chapter 2, consisted in taking from the subjects what they produced—essentially grains—and in forcing them to do work, to build pyramids for instance. But with such a system it became most probably, and gradually, more and more difficult to reach all actors or activities. Even if most people were cultivators they could, now and then, buy or sell things on markets, and some people may also have tried to

---

[296] Roberts, p. 92.
[297] Finer (1997a), pp. 281, 289, 323.
[298] For instance in Egypt—Mieroop, p. 337.
[299] Hicks, pp. 66-8.

make a better living by adopting some craftsman occupation. At the time of Croesus market tendencies like these had of course become much more widespread than in the Old Kingdom. And therefore the problem of taxation had also changed and become more difficult. The challenge was to find a method by which these various market activities also could be taxed. Here the introduction of money opened a possibility. With money the tax system could be given a wider coverage, and a better penetration, and thus make possible a greater total amount of taxes.[300]

But was this possibility also, in fact, the reason for which money was introduced by the state? Actually it seems as though it was. A few decades after Croesus's monetary reform Lydia was occupied and incorporated into the new and rapidly expanding Persian Empire. Taxes in this empire consisted to some extent in labor, to some extent in goods of various kinds, and to some extent in money. That last form of tax-paying was common especially in the western parts of the empire where the monetary system was most established. And this was exactly the area of the former Lydia. A reasonable interpretation is that the Persians took over Croesus's tax system.[301]

But the monetary systems had more advantages for Croesus and other dictators. If a dictator had money he could also himself lead a richer and more diversified life. Commanding forced labor or craftsmen to produce luxurious commodities was probably often more complicated and less rewarding than letting markets develop and thereafter utilizing them—either by buying the desired goods directly, or by buying the labor of those able to produce those goods. So even in that way the flexibility resulting from money was probably beneficial for the dictators.

Stimulating the development of markets by promulgating money thus favored the interests of a dictator. The dictator could for instance force some people to do the works necessary for producing the coins, and thereafter, himself, use the money for buying at the markets, or for paying his employees. In that way the coins could be spread wider and wider, and thereby also become more and more used in exchanges between common people. Possibly those common people also thought that coins with the picture of the dictator stamped on them were more safe than

---

[300] Finer (1997a), p. 81.
[301] Finer (1997a), p. 302.

coins promulgated by, say, some merchant—perhaps the dictator's autho-
rization conveyed a feeling of security.

If so this feeling of security could however be exploited treache-
rously by a dictator wanting to do so. If he successively decreased the
coins' metal value by reducing their content of precious metals, he,
himself, could gradually buy more and more for less and less—or, in other
words, the taxing became harsher. Such a policy could however be implemented in various ways. One possibility was to give the new coins such
an appearance that their reduced metal value could not be recognized.
This happened in, for instance, the Indian Maurya Empire.[302] Another
example are those faked silver-coins—in reality copper-coins covered by
silver—by which roman soldiers in the early Empire were paid.[303] Rather
than disguising the reduced metal value it was however also possible to
stipulate that the new, inferior coins had to be accepted as means of exchange. An example is the so called "Notgeld" (emergency money)
promulgated in Sweden during the last years of the Swedish Empire in
the beginning of the eighteenth century—the former "coins" made of big
copper plates were replaced by small coins with a radically reduced metal
value. True, this happened after the end of my period of emerging markets, but it is nevertheless illuminating, and furthermore Sweden, being
late in its development, had hardly entered the period of institutionalization at the time concerned. We do however not need to go into these
matters, or similar problems of monetary economics, any further. The important upshot is that money deterioration is a frequently used method of
taxation, and not only in dictatorships.

So far I have only talked about coins used in domestic trade, and for
the reasons given it is also that use which, from the point of view of the
dictator, should have been most important. This does however not
preclude the use of coins even in foreign trade, and perhaps the use of
coins actually started that way. But since the foreign trade to such a large
extent, at least in the beginning, was trade between state leaderships, it
could probably, without much difficulty, be conducted by means of bartering. However this may be it is well known that the use of coins in domestic trade increased rapidly—archeological finds demonstrate that the

---

[302] Thapar, p. 89.
[303] Liebeschuetz, p. 258.

values of the coins became successively lower and lower.[304] This gives additional support to the contention that the dictator's taxation interest was the force driving the coining of money.

THE INTERACTION OF POLITICS AND ECONOMY

The question about the interaction between politics and economy during the period of emerging markets seems easy to answer. There were no major conflicts. The markets which existed, and which gradually grew, did not, as it seems, bother the rulers, usually dictators, even if they to a large extent were initiated from below. Often, and most likely, the rulers on the contrary appreciated the markets. The political measures undertaken from above were in accordance with this. For sure the measures, and in particular the promulgation of coins, aimed at making the rulers richer by means of a more efficient taxation, but even so the common actors on the markets were also aided in a way they certainly found beneficial. And so there were no important conflicts between politics and economy during the long emerging market period—at least no severe conflicts related to the basic properties of the political and economic systems. But neither were the conflicts totally absent. Politically planned and implemented devaluation of money in particular is likely to have caused conflicts. It is also interesting to note that established monetary systems now and then collapsed. Chinese Han's monetary economy disappeared for example to a large extent during the following period of Tang.[305] I do however not know of any conflicts related to this.

Here a distinction between system-conflicts and distribution-conflicts may perhaps be clarifying. What I am interested in is above all system-conflicts, that is conflicts between the functioning of the political system and of the economic one, and I thus contend that conflicts like that have been few or perhaps even nonexistent. That does however not exclude common distribution-conflicts. An interesting case in-between the two kinds of conflicts is the competition between the Chinese state, during Tang for example, and great land-owners about the taxed common cultivators.[306] The land-owners' taxing was less harsh, and the cultivators

---

[304] Hicks, p. 67.
[305] Finer (1997b), pp. 768, 785.
[306] Morton & Lewis, p. 95. See also the comment about Han and Tang, and the late Rome, at the end of the section "The basic model" in chapter 3.

therefore migrated into their lands, whereby the taxes delivered to the state decreased.

THE PERIOD OF INSTITUTIONALIZATION—FROM 1000 TO 1700

INTRODUCTION

This period, lasting from about 1000 to about 1700, is much shorter than the previous one. Its main characteristic is the emergence of a number of crucial market institutions. Before turning to them it should however be recognized that transitions between periods of the kind I am using never are clear-cut. Much of what was new took a long time to acquire importance, and simultaneously much of what was old remained in place. Here it is thus important to note that claims and conquests, with state leaderships as main actors, continued to be of great importance during the institutionalizing period. The great geographical discoveries were, we remember, made during this period, as well as the colonizing that followed. Here we are however interested in the new institutions. Some of them were good, others bad.

THE GOOD INSTITUTIONS

The basic element of commerce, as already noted, is mutually beneficial exchange. But exchanges could be more or less complex, and the exchanges taking place in the markets described in the preceding section were quite simple. Usually it was about some kind of chattel and if so the whole transaction could be carried out without any precautions or other impediment. The parties just exchanged the good and the payment and thereafter left each other without any problems then or afterwards. An economy working like that is sometimes called a bazaar economy.

For more complicated affairs the simple bazaar economy is however not sufficient. More developed institutions of various kinds are required. Above all precise and reliable rules about *property-rights* and about *contracts* are necessary. The buyer needs to know that the seller really owns what he or she wants to sell, and the seller needs to know that the buyer really owns the money, or other means of exchange, with which he or she intends to pay. If someone wants to buy a piece of land, or some real estate, the seller's assurance is hardly enough for making his or her ownership perfectly trustworthy—something more is needed. Gradually the need for even more complicated property rights—above all for

immaterial objects—also became pertinent. Most important here is perhaps the patent which gives the innovator of a new apparatus or technique—for a limited period of time—monopoly on the commercialization
of the innovation.

But even rules about contracts are important. When property rights
are exchanged it is important for both parties to know that the contract
stipulating the conditions is valid and safe. One reason for this, but not the
only one, is that the payment for the property bought, according to the
contract, may come long after the transfer of the ownership—that, as we
know, is what characterizes a credit deal. Exchanges over long geographic
distances in which seller and buyer do not know each other, and therefore have no mutual confidence to start from, are also problematic. How,
in such cases, do the parties know that the contracts concluded will, in
fact, be honored? Part of solution, in all these cases, is more precise rules
about property and contract, but that is not enough. What is also required
is some kind of power competent and able to enforce the contract if that
should be needed. In cases like these one usually talks about contracts
requiring *third party enforcement.*

Having its monopoly of violence the state is a possible such third
party and gradually more and more states also undertook that role.[307] In
the beginning it was however not so. Rather the merchants themselves
developed their own judicial system. This system, called *Lex Mercatoria*,
developed bit by bit out of the gradually larger pool of judgments already
taken, the precedents, and in this sense it was similar to the British so
called Common Law. Judges were persons familiar with the conditions of
commerce and enjoying a reputation for impartiality. The merchant who
did not bow to sentences arrived at in this way was excluded from the
community of merchants—their implicit association one may say—and
thereby his commercial options were severely reduced. Such was the
threat by which enforcement was achieved.[308]

Lex Mercatoria was thus a complicated, institutional system created
by the merchants themselves—that is by activities from below—and one
may therefore wonder about the compatibility of this development with
the logic of collective action. Since the system could be built step by step

---

[307] North & Thomas, pp. 6-7; Rosenberg & Birdzell, pp. 115-7.
[308] Benson, pp. 30-6; North & Thomas, pp. 56-7.

this need however not be a serious problem. It could all start by a few merchants, familiar with each other, agreeing about a few relatively simple rules. After that more and more merchants could join the group at the same time as the rules were made more specific and more applicable to complicated affairs.

During the period of institutionalization the rules about property and contract were thus developed, but that was not all. Much more happened.[309] Another important development was that firms started acquiring a separate identity of their own. Earlier—and concerning for instance firms built by and around a family—the allocation of responsibilities over the firm and the family, and over the individual members of the family, was basically unclear. The borderlines were messy which made affairs unnecessarily diffuse or complicated. Someone who bought something from an enterprise, or sold something to it, did not exactly know with which party he or she was dealing—nor about that party's capacity, for instance economically, for arriving at agreement. This was however to be changed. An important step was the introduction of Italian double entry book-keeping.[310] Another step was the introduction of the concept of *legal personality*. Further steps in the same direction included institutionally more complicated enterprises, such as joint stock companies (or limited liability companies), which greatly increased the supply of capital for the enterprises.[311]

With new more sophisticated types of enterprises it also became possible to start commercial activities in other areas than the traditional ones. Commercial banks engaged in depositing as well as lending money began to appear, which facilitated new investments—with the banks as intermediaries the capital found its way to the places where it was most productive. But that was not all. The development of banking also led to new financial instruments such as, above all, the *bill of exchange*.[312] This was very important, in particular for long distance trade, since payments were made simpler and safer. After having sold something far away the merchant did not have to return with a large amount of bulky, metallic

---

[309] Roberts, pp. 556-7.
[310] Rosenberg & Birdzell, pp. 114, 126-7.
[311] Hicks, p. 80.
[312] Findlay & O'Rourke, pp. 97, 109; North & Thomas, p. 141; Rosenberg & Birdzell, p. 117.

money easily detected by robbers or pirates. Instead of that he just had a single, easily hidden piece of paper, which he could exchange for pure money when he got home. And, when the instrument was further developed, the bill could be used directly as a means of payment. Beside the banks even commercial insurance companies began to appear at this time, which hardly was a coincidence.[313] First insurance companies are in important ways similar to banks—in both institutions money that is not to be used immediately, and which therefore could be lent out, is accumulated—and, second, there was a strong demand for insurance services. Again the riskiness of long distance transportation was a big problem and the availability of insurance therefore appreciated.

All the institutions mentioned greatly facilitated various kinds of commercial activities and in the beginning especially trade. Taken together these institutions constituted a market system fundamentally different from that of a bazaar economy, which allowed for much more complicated and welfare enhancing business deals of various kinds. The full potential of mutually beneficial exchange was exploited.

This institutional development occurred in different places, and there were also early historical predecessors. Thus there seems to have been some kind of banking system in Babylonia, and in the ninth century tea merchants in China developed an instrument similar to the bill of exchange called *flying money*.[314] But even if there were predecessors like these they did not lead to a continued, unbroken development. The great development, the one which has persevered uninterrupted until our own time, was started by the small west European city-states mentioned in chapter 2. Among these the Italian ones were the earliest, and most important was the pioneer Venice. Venice inspired the other city states to commercial activities similar to its own. Thereby these other states also became contributors to institutional development.

THE BAD INSTITUTIONS

Later in the period of institutionalization—from about the beginning of the sixteenth century—other less beneficial institutions and ideas did however also appear, namely guilds[315] and mercantilism[316].

---

[313] Rosenberg & Birdzell, pp. 118-9.
[314] Kriwaczek, pp. 181-2; Morton and Lewis, p. 96.

A guild is an association of craftsmen enjoying, within a specified region, a monopoly of the exercise of their particular profession. The education of those wanting to join the profession also took place within the guilds, and the career included the three steps *apprentice, journeyman* and *master craftsman*. The basis of the guild system was a mutual interest between the ruler-king on the one side and the different groups of crafts-men on the other. In his role as leader of the state the king could get sorely needed incomes by selling monopoly rights to groups of craftsmen, who thereby got protection from competition.[317] In the long run this was obviously not good for the economic development, but possibly that was not recognized. Anyway the short-term special interests, those of the king as well as those of the craftsmen, determined the outcome. An example, thus, of the working of Mancur Olson's basic assumption in its activity version as described in the section "Basic social science principles" in chapter 3.

The emergence of the guild system is thus easy to explain, but mercantilism, which became important especially in the big kingdoms, offers more challenging problems. Mercantilism did not only consist of a certain kind of policy but also included a quite elaborated supporting theory.[318] Books in which the theory was described and explained were written and this was, perhaps, the first more-or-less coherent economic theory. Adam Smith's later great work "Wealth of Nations" includes a harsh criticism of the mercantilist ideas, and even if Smith was critical this indicates that the mercantilist works were part of the theory deve-lopment within the science of economics.[319] There may, of course, be a problem about what came first, the mercantilist practice or the mercanti-list ideas. But, irrespective of this, what did mercantilism actually mean, in practice as well as in theory?

Basic was the contention that a state should export much and im-port little—the trade balance should have a great surplus. Already this

[315] Palmer, Colton & Kramer (2007a), pp. 34-5.
[316] Rosenberg & Birdzell, pp. 134-6.
[317] North & Thomas, pp. 57, 100.
[318] Schumpeter (1954), pp. 335-92.
[319] It may however be noted that even if there was a mercantilist practice, and ideas supporting that practice, long before Adam Smith, it was in fact he who coined the very term "mercantilism". Coward, p. 93.

may seem strange. For a modern mind the export's *raison d'être* is that it generates incomes which can be used for import—thus, and again, the mutually beneficial exchange. But if one continually exports without importing correspondingly the scarcity of goods in the country will increase and the conditions for subsistence get worse. The state will become empty of goods and filled with uneatable money. Only the one part of the mutually beneficial exchange is carried out.

But obviously the mercantilists did not look upon matters like this. The drawbacks mentioned above were not, for some reason, considered serious, and possibly there were also advantages to be counted with. For understanding these matters it is, I think, first important to recognize that foreign trade was not a great part of the total economy of the countries considered, and never could become. In addition to this the export incomes that were valuated above all were those consisting of precious metals. And for these incomes a monetary theory which was not unreasonable was developed. It was argued that the availability, within the state, of precious metal money not only stimulated economic activity and thereby economic development, but also erased internal barriers to trade and thus turned the whole state into one single, large market. More specifically it was also argued—correctly and in accordance with the quantity theory of money of later times—that when the circulating quantity of money increased prices would also rise. And these higher prices, in their turn, would stimulate economic activity. This last point may perhaps be understandable, but it is hardly correct. Enterprises do not only sell their final products, for which high prices perhaps may be welcome, they also buy producer goods and labor, for which low prices rather should be favorable. Furthermore high prices impede the export trade.

To all of this we may now add a final comment, perhaps the most important one. The rulers or kings in the countries we are talking about were dictators representing special interests of their own. From their point of view it may have been favorable—in the same way as for Croesus—that taxing became more efficient when the amount of circulating money of precious metals grew bigger. And in contrast to Croesus these rulers had, at most, very limited mineral resources of their own, and therefore had to use the export generated incomes. Mercantilism may therefore, together with the guild system, be considered as the ruler's means for increasing his tax incomes and thereby also his own fortune. Certainly it is true that the guilds fragmentized the domestic market while the mercantilist practice worked in the opposite direction, but that need not have been important. This conflict was only about the general functioning of the economy and the markets, not about the ruler's interests. If one only takes the latter into account, and only shortsightedly, it seems quite possible that the guild system and mercantilism worked in the same direction.

THE INTERACTION OF POLITICS AND ECONOMY

In the same way as for the period of emerging markets I will now, for the period of institutionalization, try to draw some general conclusions about the interaction of politics and economy. At first it may be stated that there were no really sharp conflicts between politics and economy in this period either. If we start with the guilds and mercantilism these phenomena hardly stimulated the economy, on the contrary they rather intimidated its development. But even so this did not lead to any conflicts between the political actors and the commercial ones. The reason, in all likelihood, was that the destructive special interests of the two parties to a large extent overlapped. The rulers got their incomes and the craftsmen got their markets protected.

The really interesting question concerning the relations between politics and economy during this period is rather about the mechanisms behind the emergence of the good institutions—that is the more detailed and exact rules about property and contract, sophisticated new forms of enterprises, etcetera. Institutions like these could hardly have emerged in dictatorships; for this they were too exclusively favorable for private interests. And that did not happen either. Rather the institutions emerged in the small Italian city-states, particularly in Venice, and in those states the rulers also were merchants. These oligarchic states, about which more follows in chapter 9, were run by influential merchant families. So in these states there was obviously no conflict between politics and economy. But another conclusion is still more important, namely that if only dictatorships had existed and no merchant oligarchies, then the beneficial welfare-creating market institutions had probably never appeared.[320]

---

[320] In the section "Western Europe after the fall of the Western Roman Empire" in chapter 2, I mentioned John Hicks' contention about the crucial importance of the European small city-states for the richness of the West, and here I do the same again. Hicks, p. 38. And still, it may be added, Fukuyama is very brief and vague

But even if these new institutions thus had the merchant oligarchies as a precondition, they were hardly, when once existing, restrained in the dictatorial monarchies. Even there enterprises, which at least to some extent used, or were dependent on, the new institutions, were created. And everywhere, as it seems, this occurred without any noticeable friction between the dictatorial states and the private merchants. Rather, the merchants were probably considered an asset in the dictatorships.[321] The upshot thus is that, on the whole, there were no conflicts between politics and economy in the institutionalization period either.

THE PERIOD OF INDUSTRIALIZATION—FROM 1700 AND FORWARDS

What we call the industrial revolution began in England during the eighteenth century. The core of this revolution was innovation and development of goods, and mass production of the goods developed. But even if the passage from the former period into this one really was revolutionary it was nevertheless, in same way as the passage from the emerging markets period to the period of institutionalization, gradual. Even before the industrial revolution technical development had taken place in some areas, and production centers, which must be called factories, had also existed. The technique of plowing had been repeatedly improved which, in combination with a shift from two to three field crop rotation, had led to substantially increased yields.[322] Wind and water had begun to be used for power, weaving-mills were built in several places with those in Flanders as pioneers, and in Venice there had since long been impressive shipyards.

But however important all of these were, they were nevertheless occasional phenomena. Beginning with the industrial revolution the development of existing products, and the inventing of new ones, became systematic in a totally new manner, and the discoveries of the natural sciences were increasingly used for the purposes. The improvement of the steam engine with the Scottish mechanical engineer James Watt (1736–1819) as the great practical pioneer and the French military engineer Sadi

about this important point. See for instance Fukuyama, p. 271.
[321] Palmer, Colton & Kramer, (2007a), pp. 207-9.
[322] Findlay & O'Rourke, p. 82; Palmer, Colton & Kramer (2007a), p. 29.

Carnot (1796–1832) as the theoretical giant may serve as an example of development of existing technique. The invention of electric apparatus of different kinds, with the American Thomas A. Edison (1847–1931) as a front-rank figure, may serve as examples of totally new innovations. Furthermore an increasingly large amount of fixed capital for production was created. The systematic mass production by means of machines began. As a symbol for this part of the revolution no one could be more fitting than the American Henry Ford (1863–1947). For the production of the Model T car he introduced, as one of the pioneers, the assembly line process.

The industrial revolution thus followed after the institutional development which hardly is remarkable. All of those ideas about improvements and innovations, that the individuals in all kinds of positions in a society have, will not materialize into new products without appropriate incentives. And those incentives were provided by the new institutions. When it became easy to found profit making enterprises it also became possible to transform ideas into money. Furthermore there appeared, without that ever being the intention, a sophisticated signaling system that steered the entrepreneurs in proper directions. The prices of the free markets informed them about interesting possibilities for trade, for product improvements and for innovation. The knowledge and the ideas spread all around society were thereby coordinated without any central planning organization or institution being active—apart from the legal system with its supporting monopoly of violence. And not only that. The means of coordination also produced efficiency. The resources were made to move to those places where they were most useful. The invisible hand, which Adam Smith was soon to discover, was already fully active.

Here it may be appropriate to take up, parenthetically, an often discussed problem, namely why there never was an industrial revolution in China in spite of the many innovations made there at a very early stage.[323] Among these innovations were for a beginning the cross bow. In chapter 2 I mentioned that the Chinese, as early as Shang and Zhou, were very skilful bronze casters and that this skill was used for producing the bow's crucial levering mechanism. And even iron casting was pioneered by the Chinese. After having cast iron for several centuries they succeeded,

---

[323] Fairbank & Goldman, pp. 93-4; Gascoigne (2003), pp. 127, 172; Morris, pp. 395-6; Morton & Lewis, p. 87; Roberts, pp. 446, 457, 464.

around the year 0, in achieving still higher temperatures in their ovens by means of piston-bellows driven by water wheels. This iron technology, by the way, is probably what explains why the iron stirrup came to the West from the East as described in chapter 4. The ability to produce high temperatures was also of fundamental importance for the outstanding, later Chinese porcelain art. And the Chinese also pioneered ship parts—at an early stage, and long before any others, Chinese vessels thus had stern-rudders. Still further Chinese innovations include paper and book prin-ting—China hade movable types long before Gutenberg. The Chinese also were first with the compass, and with gunpowder, which they disposed of as early as around the year 1000. And the Chinese also—thanks to a cru-cial innovation—had well functioning mechanical clocks long before the rest of the world. But in spite of all these early, pioneering and important innovations the Chinese never had an industrial revolution. Why?

A possible answer, following the reasoning above, is that the insti-tutions necessary for the exploitation of the inventions never were allow-ed to emerge in China. The regime, including the mandarins, was always too repressive, even if the degree of repressiveness varied. During Song—about the year 1000 and between Tang and Ming—repression was for instance comparatively mild and markets and the economy were stimula-ted.[324] But this relative freedom, probably due to the rulers' laxity at the end of Tang and lasting during Song, was not tolerated by the following Ming dictators who restored order.[325] In Europe, we remember, the insti-tutions necessary for economic development had been created by the ruling merchants in the small city-states, not by the kings in the big king-doms. But there were no city-states like that within the Chinese area and the Ming dictators were as little interested in economic institutions as the European kings. And so things turned out as they did—China's enormous potential possibilities never materialized.

But back to the main track. In the beginning of this chapter I wrote that at the time of the first states there was no other way to become rich than by stealing from others. Then, as markets and commerce emerged, additional options gradually became more important. Occasional techni-cal development also gave similar results. The really big change did how-

---

[324] Findlay & O'Rourke, pp. 61-6; Finer (1997b), p. 776.
[325] Gascoigne (2003), p. 155.

ever not come until the industrial revolution. At that point the possibilities to become rich by other means than theft had expanded enormously. And this was so not only for single, individual, successful entrepreneurs or builders of corporations—such as Bill Gates or Ingvar Kamprad (IKEA) in our own days—but also, increasingly, for ordinary people. After the industrial revolution—in those parts of the world affected by it—wages have grown practically incessantly, and faster than ever before in mankind's history. The former zero-sum game has turned into a game in which—as a matter of principle—everyone can get it better without anyone losing out.

This is of utmost importance. Prior to the industrial revolution there were, as we have seen, no serious conflicts between politics and economy. For sure the Ming dictators, as I have said, erased the liberties which had prevailed during Song, and more examples like that could certainly be found. But these conflicts, in spite of everything, were nevertheless small or almost latent. With the industrial revolution all of this changed dramatically. The conflict between politics and economy became sharp and severe. The related issues became urgent and explosive as never before. Part of the background was the approximate simultaneity of the industrial revolution and the beginning of the development of representative democracy—a combination of economy and politics which were to prove unprecedentedly and extraordinarily successful. It is therefore paradoxical that this lead to severe conflicts, but so, in fact, it did. But recognizing this is one thing, explaining it is something else and much more difficult. One reason may have been the social misery which sometimes accompanied early industrialization, another may have been that freedom of debate and the possibilities of making one's voice heard were considerably greater than before, still another one that large groups of citizens still lacked the right to vote, and, finally, perhaps, the emergence of new social theories. Prominent in this development of theories and ideas were Karl Marx (1818–83) and Friedrich Engels (1820–95).

The details of this early debate will however be left aside here. I will rather, unbounded by these early circumstances, try to discuss the relation between politics and economy in the period of industrialization in more general terms. A main question in such a discussion concerns the compatibility of different political and economic systems. Could, for instance, democracy be combined with a planned economy? Or could dictatorship be combined with a free market economy? A first comment on these questions is that they are surprisingly little discussed in the scholarly literature. There has been some discussion, it is true, by for instance the social scientists Joseph Schumpeter and Friedrich Hayek and by the economist Oskar Lange (1904–65). But these are exceptions, and somewhat dated exceptions as well. In today's social science widespread lack of interest in the questions is what is most striking. Perhaps the reason is that political science and economics are separate disciplines at the universities with different, and even incompatible, "cultures", and that interdisciplinarity is held back rather than encouraged.[326] For certainly the questions posed are interdisciplinary. But they are also complicated and I will therefore proceed stepwise. The two next sections may be considered as preliminaries. Not until after those passages, in the section "Politics and economy in the age of industrialism", will I take up the main discussion.

THE SECTOR, AND THE DOMAIN, OF THE STATE

Hitherto I have used the expressions *state* and *society* without much discrimination, sometimes perhaps even almost as synonyms, and in the so far very general and broad discussion this has hardly been unreasonable. The state, as we have seen, provides, by means of its monopoly of violence, the protection within which societal life goes on. If we look at matters from within, from the point of view of the subjects, or the citizens, things do however become different. It becomes necessary to make a distinction between state and society.

For making these matters precise the concepts of public sector and private sector are often used. These concepts are economic and the measure usually used is per cent. A common measure of the size of the public sector, even if not the only possible one, is the public expenditures'

---

[326] The tendency described here certainly prevails on the whole, but even so a few important exceptions have appeared recently. One is Acemoglu & Robinson and another North, Wallis & Weingast. In both of these works the interaction of political and economic phenomena is treated extensively and in a very interesting manner. On the whole the conclusions are also the same as the ones arrived at here in what follows. Perhaps also Fukuyama could be mentioned but this book is, in spite of the author's declared intention, much more of a history book than a work of social science. And, indeed, it is only a book of partial history. Thus, and for instance, ancient Greece, the Roman Republic, the Roman Empire and Venice are hardly dealt with at all.

share of the gross national product. For modern market economies it is relatively easy to determine this quantity, but for dictatorships it could be much more difficult—market prices in a real sense may not exist and national accounts may be unreliable or misleading. And it is still more difficult to work this out for states far in the historical past.

But the "public sector" concept also suffers from other problems. First the very expression itself is debatable. In a book such as this one it might be better to talk about the "state sector" rather than the "public sector" and in what follows I will, at least on the whole, do so. The reason for the common use of the expression "public sector" is that local communities usually are included, but about local communities I will hardly say anything so there should be no risk of misunderstanding.

Another problem is that the concept is economic and therefore sometimes may be misleading. For a state may intervene in the lives of the subjects or citizens in many other ways than by taxing them and thereby make public expenditures possible. Thus laws and rules of various kinds may affect the lives of the common people most considerably without involving any money transactions whatsoever. So if one wants to talk about the influence of the state generally, and the resulting, remaining free space for ordinary people, which often is of interest, the "state sector" is hardly a suitable concept. A better concept is the "domain of the state". That concept has the advantage of adequately giving the associations intended, but the drawback that it is not obvious how it should be quantified empirically. Various solutions of this problem may therefore give somewhat different results.

Obvious however is that the domain, in principle, may vary from being very small to being very big. A pure so called night watchman state[327]— that is a state which does nothing but upholding inner and outer security—exemplifies the former. And totalitarian dictatorships exemplify the latter. Even if these dictatorships will not be dealt with until the next chapter the very word "totalitarian" conveys an idea about what is meant. The state does not only try to steer all possible aspects of the subjects lives, but also aims at redoing them, to form their characters and personalities according to a blueprint considered ideal. An example—

---

[327] The phrase was originally coined by the German socialist Ferdinand Lassalle in a speech in 1862.

although a literary one—is the state portrayed in George Orwell's book "1984".

THE IDEA OF A DEMAND STEERED UNMIXED STATE ECONOMY

I mentioned earlier the discussion between Lange, Schumpeter and Hayek. In that discussion Lange and Schumpeter stood on the one side and Hayek on the other.[328] One point of departure for Lange and Schumpeter was their contention that a pure market economy could result in unreasonably large inequalities of income and of fortune. Another their contention that the pure market economy, even if it ultimately led to optimal results, did so much too slowly. Would it not be possible, they asked, to cure these evils with some kind of planning, and, at the same time, keep the advantages of the free market. And they not only asked the question, they also answered it in the affirmative.

What they had in mind was a system which, to begin with, did not include, and was not allowed to include, any private enterprises. All production was done by the state, and the complete production apparatus was run by a great state bureaucracy. The running should however be such that the prices became the same as on a free market. The marginal costs of the production could be calculated by the bureaucrats them-selves, and the demand should result from the activities of all those human beings living freely in the society. If equilibrium was not imme-diately achieved the bureaucrats could put that right by adjusting the quantity produced and thereby the marginal cost. In that way supply and demand of all imaginable goods could be made to balance each other making the final result optimal in the same way as on a free market. But all inequalities would disappear and the steering bureaucrats would also reach the optimal equilibrium state much quicker than the blindly fumb-ling market mechanisms.

So this was a kind of planned economy, albeit a very special one. But could an economy like the one described really work? Lange and Schumpeter naturally answered in the affirmative, but Hayek, the foremost critic, emphatically rejected the whole idea and considered it to

---

[328] Hayek (1944); Lange & Taylor; Schumpeter (1942), pp. 165-302. Even the economists Ota Sik and János Kornai have put forward opinions similar to those of Lange and Schumpeter—see for instance Judt pp. 428, 437.

be based on much too simple ideas about market mechanisms. Among others he contended that the role of prices in connection with the introduction of new products, and the development of already existing products, was much more subtle and intricate, and much more important, than understood by Schumpeter and Lange. If the steering bureaucracy were to be able to act in the way suggested it was obviously required that all properties of all products were well known from the beginning, but that is never the case, and never could be. In a real market economy existing products are developed all the time and new products are also continuously introduced, and for this there is no place in Schumpeter's and Lange's system. So certainly Hayek's criticism was correct. To this it may be added that some products necessarily change all the time. This, for instance, is the case with modern daily newspapers with their continuously and rapidly changing content. How could matters like that be produced by a steering state bureaucracy?

POLITICS AND ECONOMY IN THE AGE OF INDUSTRIALISM

INTRODUCTION

After these preliminaries I will now start the discussion about the relation between politics and economy in the age of industrialism, and I depart from a very simple schematization. As for the political systems I make a distinction between democracy, which here means representative democracy, and dictatorship, and for the economic systems I distinguish between market economy and planned economy. This gives us the four combinations shown in figure 5 and the main question is about their possibility. Which combinations are possible, which ones are not?

	Dictator-ship	Demo-cracy
Market economy	1	4
Planned economy	3	2

Figure 5: Combinations of political and economic systems

The classification into four types of states is obviously utterly schematic since a representative democracy, a dictatorship, a market economy and a planned economy all may come in multiple varieties. And of course the compatibility, or incompatibility, of a political and an economic system may depend on variations like that. Nuances must therefore be introduced into the discussion and I hope to be able to do so within the framework of the four main cases.

DICTATORSHIP AND MARKET ECONOMY

Let us begin with the combination dictatorship and market economy (cell 1). A first comment is that the modern dictatorships—and I am then primarily thinking about the great dictatorships of the twentieth century—hardly would have been possible without the industrial revolution preceding their establishment. Without the products of industrialism they hardly would have been able to supervise their subjects, and to control their societies, in the ways they actually did. But in spite of their dependence on the industrial revolution their economies were hardly market economies. That a dictatorship is incompatible with a fully developed market economy seems clear, but what, exactly, are the reasons for that? The main problem is that a dictatorship is unable to tolerate, or to get along with, all those liberties which not only characterize the market economy, but also are its prerequisites. The political system is threatened by the economic one.

In a market economy, as we know, people are allowed—within very wide limits—to produce commodities and services freely and to sell these products to those wanting to buy them. In the fully developed market economy enterprises may be freely established, and there is furthermore a legal system guaranteeing equality before the law. The former, the free establishment of economic enterprises, increases drastically the probability that innovations likely to add to human welfare will, in fact, materialize in new marketed products. And equality before the law is also of paramount importance for the good functioning of markets. It is, for instance, a prerequisite for free competition on equal terms.

But these freedoms of the fully developed market economy do, of course, constitute problems from the point of view of the dictator or the dictatorship, and most important is probably the freedom to establish enterprises. Some kinds of private enterprises may be quite innocuous, but there are also those which are obviously problematical.

Take for instance newspapers and other mass media enterprises. Can such enterprises be allowed to establish freely? Hardly. Such enterprises may obviously, and naturally, be used for information about politics and for political debate and opinion formation. But clearly a free political opinion formation process can never be tolerated within a dictatorship. A dictatorship cannot accept a free press or other free mass media enterprises, which thus severely restricts the free establishment of enterprises. Enterprises of this kind have to belong to the domain of the state.

Are there other kinds of enterprises which cannot be tolerated? Yes, certainly. Take for instance all kinds of enterprises dealing with techniques which are used for, or could be used for, the propagation of opinions of various kinds. Here there are not only enterprises manufacturing paper for printing on, printing presses, printer's ink, and so forth. There are also, in particular in the modern society, enterprises dealing with electronics such as computers and computer communication. Enterprises like these obviously constitute threats for the regime and therefore cannot be allowed to act freely. If they are allowed at all their freedom must be circumscribed considerably—for instance by forbidding them to sell their products to private clients, that is to all possible clients but the dictatorship itself.

Another important issue is about wealth and the creation of fortunes. In a fully developed market economy people are allowed to become rich, and even very rich, and this very possibility is an important incentive for many important activities such as the founding of enterprises. But clearly a dictatorship cannot accept unlimited possibilities for fortune creation. Large private fortunes, it is easy to imagine, may be used for undermining the regime—at the extremity for financing coups. Important, furthermore, is the issue about private actors' international activities. Even minor things such as travels abroad, or establishing of contacts abroad, may be threatening for the regime. Placing of financial capital in foreign banks is another threat. Therefore the dictatorship cannot accept these market activities either, at least not fully. They must to a large extent be brought into the state domain.

These restrictions for fortune creation and contacting imply, in turn, one further most important restriction. It is hard to imagine a dictatorship giving full freedom to that very important, or even basic, part of the fully developed market economy which is constituted by the innovation activity. Innovation presupposes free thinking, and far-reaching possibilities for exploiting commercially the results of this thinking. That a dictatorship cannot accept innovation activities like these, including all their consequences, seems again obvious. And to this it may be added—returning to the mass media—that enterprises have to be able to market their products. In particular this is so for newly founded innovation-based enterprises. For this marketing the availability of free mass media, which are natural vehicles for advertisements and marketing, as well as for more impartial consumer information, is of crucial importance.

It thus seems clear that a dictatorship cannot live with, or tolerate, a fully developed market economy in the long run. An interesting case with respect to this hypothesis is today's China. That the country is a dictatorship is obvious, but equally clear is that the development towards a fully developed market economy has gone far. If the arguments above are correct this combination is not stable. In my opinion we will soon—probably within ten years—see a transformation in China. Either the market-driven actors will enforce considerable political changes towards democracy, or else the dictatorship will strangle the markets.[329]

Here it is interesting to compare India's and China's economies since they both, as a consequence of liberalizing reforms, have grown spectacularly in the recent past. But the differences are also great. The Chinese manufacturing industry is to a considerable extent based on foreign innovations—so called contract manufacturing—and in many cases foreign enterprises have also invested directly in China. The share of new foundations based on Chinese innovations is comparatively small. In India the situation is very different. There the domestic innovation activity is burgeoning and masses of small enterprises, based on innovations, are founded.[330] So, one may ask, what will happen in China when an innovation activity like the one in India begins emerging there?

---

[329] Here it may be noted that Fukuyama puts and discusses the question about China's stability but without giving a definite answer. Fukuyama, pp. 481-3. On this very point I am thus, in contrast to Fukuyama, putting my foot down.
[330] See for instance "India's surprising economic miracle—The country's state may be weak, but its private companies are strong", The Economist, October 2nd,

A dictatorship—going back to the main topic—can thus not tolerate a fully developed market economy. Some very important restrictions must be implemented. But a certain amount of market economy may still be accepted. Possibly, as we will see in the section "Dictatorship and planned economy" the dictatorship may even have interest in such an arrangement. But before getting to that we shall discuss the combination democracy and planned economy.

DEMOCRACY AND PLANNED ECONOMY

Dictatorship and market economy are thus incompatible and the combination democracy and planned economy (cell 2) has similar problems. The strict schemata of the planned economy are incompatible with the liberties necessary for the workings of democracy. While the free formation of opinions, and all entrepreneurial and commercial activities depending on this freedom, threatened the dictatorship, all of these things are rather necessary conditions for democracy. However the democracy, in its details, is constituted—and there are as we will see in chapter 10 several basic models—it requires, unconditionally, open, free and public discussion, debate and opinion formation, and commercial freedom for entrepreneurs and enterprises. Democracy is a continually proceeding, dynamic process. There must be no obstacles to a free and open discussion. And this, of course, makes a completely planned economy incompatible with democracy. It must be possible to found freely not only enterprises but also organizations which in one way or another deal with formation and propagation of opinions. Enterprises and organizations like these must be allowed full freedom outside the domain of the state.

But granting this, would not a partially planned economy, one not affecting the opinion formation processes, be feasible? This possibility is interesting since steps in that direction have been taken. One example is the British Labour government immediately after the Second World War.[331] Even Sweden at about the same time is interesting. The real measures undertaken did not go as far as in Britain but an important political debate, the so called "Planned economy debate", did nevertheless take place. Concerning both these cases it is however important to make clear

2010, p. 11.
[331] Palmer, Colton & Kramer (2007b), p. 887.

that all that was at issue was making some enterprises in base industries state owned. Planning in the real sense of the word—that is production according to adopted plans, for instance Five-Year Plans—was never an alternative. So the activities mentioned never really threatened democracy.

More interesting from that point of view is the India of Jawaharlal Nehru (1889–1964). When Nehru, in 1947, became free India's first prime minister he introduced Five-Year Plans.[332] They were inspired by the Soviet ones, but were not equally far-reaching. There were still a considerable amount of free economic activity, and opinion formation was not restricted in any way. Now this planning is since long obsolete and freedom has taken over in most areas. Irrespective of the exact causal mechanisms here we may anyway state that the empirical facts available so far, and I am then talking not only about India but also about Britain and Sweden, do not contradict the main contention advanced here. Namely that democracy and a reasonably complete planned economy are incompatible.

DICTATORSHIP AND PLANNED ECONOMY

The next question is about the compatibility of dictatorship and planned economy (cell 3). At first the answer may seem self-evident, namely that the two fit each other perfectly well. But even if it is like that in the main, there are important nuances to be added.

In the section about a demand steered unmixed state economy I described a system which possibly could be characterized as planned. But this kind of system, even if it certainly does not reach the efficiency of a market economy, is much too complicated to be handled by a dictator's bureaucracy. And a fully developed system like that has, consequently, never existed. When we talk about planned economy it therefore has to be something much simpler and much less subtle. Subtleties such as marginal costs and consumers' demand must be kept away. Basically the ancient storage-distribution economies and the economies of our own time's dictatorships—for instance the Soviet one—therefore were quite similar. The state just determined what was to be produced. A basic problem with such an approach is however that it is much easier to plan

---

[332] Palmer, Colton & Kramer (2007b), p. 918; Watson, pp. 164-70.

the production than the consumption. Even in the harshest of dictator-ships humans themselves—at least to some extent—decide what to consume, and what not to. There is thus a problem in making ends meet. Some goods produced will not be consumed.

Possibly this problem could be solved by distributing the goods directly to the intended consumers or, perhaps easier, by sending coupons for which the consumers could acquire the goods. But even so some goods would remain unconsumed. The only way to solve that problem, or at least for making it less pertinent, thus seems to be to allow the consumers to exchange goods with each other. And exchanges like that would certainly be facilitated by the introduction, by the state, of a monetary system. But this is tantamount to a certain, even if small, departure from the fully planned economy, and an equally small step towards market economy.

It thus seems as if even harsh dictatorships—for instance ones with almost completely implemented Five-Year Plans—have, in spite of everything, a need for some form of minimal, circumscribed markets. There is a need for shops and for money. The kind of economy which I above called bazaar economy is perhaps perfect for dictatorships. And if so there is a limit for the compatibility between dictatorship and planned economy—the planned economy must not be too complete. There is, as it seems, an area between the fully developed planned economy and the fully developed market economy which suits dictatorships.

DEMOCRACY AND MARKET ECONOMY

The next and last combination is the one between democracy and market economy (cell 4). That these two are compatible may seem self-evident, and on the whole this also is so. The very simple fact that so many countries, for such a long time, have lived so prosperously with the combination of market economy and democracy, testifies, of course, emphatically to this compatibility. But this does not exclude problems.

A first one is that the liberties present—and then above all the political liberties—may be used for crushing all liberties. This possibility was demonstrated when Germany, in a free election, assisted Hitler on his way to dictatorial power. Clear-cut examples of a corresponding utiliza-tion of the economic liberties for undermining the political liberties are more difficult to find, but Italy during Silvio Berlusconi's period of power, may be thought-provoking.[333]

But these risks for quick erasements of existing liberties are perhaps, after all, not all that menacing. Some long-term, slow processes seem more important and interesting, and I am then thinking about the threats involved in the continuously ongoing, democratic decision-making. The resulting decisions are to a large extent intended to change the results of the markets—for instance by redistribution of wealth, by regulating prices, and so forth. These market interventions do, almost necessarily as it seems, result in growing public sectors and domains. If this, in the long run, entails problems, that is hardly strange. I will address this topic anew in the last section of chapter 10.

The combination of democracy, and now I am always talking about representative democracy, and market economy is thus fully possible, but the reasoning may be advanced further than that. The discussion in this section and the former ones has made clear that the only economic system which can prevail in a democracy is market economy, and that the only political system which can prevail in a market economy is democracy. Representative democracy thus implies market economy, and market economy implies representative democracy. Or, in other words, the two systems are but different aspects of the same thing, of a more fundamental legal and liberal system. The one aspect cannot be taken away without the other one also disappearing.

SUMMARY

The main idea underlying the discussion in this chapter is that politics and economy cannot be treated separately. The two areas overlap to a large extent, and affect each other considerably, and must therefore be dealt with simultaneously. From that main idea follows directly the basic problem addressed in this chapter, namely that of the compatibility of economic and political systems in different kinds of states.

For the discussion of this problem I have divided the time we are interested in into three main periods. The first one—by far the longest—I have called the period of emerging markets. It endured from about –3000

---

[333] See for instance "The man who screwed an entire country"—a 14-page special report on Silvio Berlusconi's Italy, The Economist, June 11th–17th, 2011.

to about 1000. To the extent that markets evolved during this period they were institutionally unsophisticated. One may talk about bazaar economies. The second period—from about 1000 to 1700—is the period of institutionalization. It is, among others, characterized by the development of a number of important economic institutions and techniques, for instance more rigorous concepts of property and contract, third party enforcement of contracts, developed banking and insurance activities, bills of exchange, double entry book keeping, and so forth. The third and final period, in which we are still living, is the period of industrialization, starting at about 1700 with the industrial revolution. Its main characteristics are the systematic innovation and development of products of various kinds, to a large extent by the use of scientific advances, and the mass-production of these products.

Now, and going to the conclusions, there were no important conflicts between politics and economy during the two first periods. In all states the two areas existed together quite peacefully. Certainly the new institutions which characterized the second period were developed in small city-states—and hardly could have appeared elsewhere—but once developed they were also accepted in other kinds of states. During the period of industrialization everything became however different. Conflicts between politics and economy arose and became severe. "The Communist Manifesto" by Karl Marx and Friedrich Engels may be seen as a symbol of these conflicts.

After this historical account the chapter ends with a more analytical discussion about the relation between economy and politics in the industrial period. The main conclusions are that market economy and dictatorship are incompatible, and that the same is true for democracy and planned economy, whereas planned economy and dictatorship go well together as well as market economy and democracy. For the last two combinations some further comments are however also added for making things more precise. Thus even planned economies in dictatorships will benefit from prices, and therefore from some kind of primitive markets, for instance such as those of a bazaar economy. And market economy and democracy not only go well together. They also require each other. They may even be considered as just two aspects of a more fundamental legal and liberal system.

6

DICTATORSHIPS

DICTATORSHIPS IN THE HISTORY OF THE WORLD

A dictatorship is a state which—in principle—is run by one single individual, the dictator. In practice it is however seldom, perhaps never, like this. Around the dictator there is a group of persons who give him advice in different matters and who may have a considerable influence even in other ways. The size of this group could vary and it could also be structured in different ways. Differences like these may give rise to different types of dictatorships. A dictatorship is however not only characterized by the ruling group but also by the absence of precise and respected rules for governing. Since the dictator himself, together with his group, governs, no such rules are needed. And if any rules like that should happen to be present, there should be no need to respect them anyway. Since the dictator is dictator he is not responsible to anyone, he decides himself.

The dictatorship is by far the most common type of state in the history of the world. During long periods there have not been any other kinds of states at all. The representative democracy appeared, as I have already said several times, very late in the history of states; the direct democracies that there have been have since long disappeared; and the oligarchies have never been many. For the rest, and all through history, we are dealing with dictatorships.

If we look at the sequences of states described in chapter 2 the pattern becomes still clearer. Practically all states in the sequences there called side-lines are dictatorships. The Chinese states have all the time been dictatorships and in India and Japan the dictatorial continuity was not broken until the twentieth century. The states in the American side-line—the Inca Empire and the Aztecs' state—were dictatorships as well. Early, significant exceptions from the dictatorship rule therefore occurred only in the sequence which I called the main course—for instance the Athenian direct democracy and the Roman Republic. But these early exceptions did not break the general tendency. After them followed, in the main course, still another long row of dictatorships. First came the Roman Empire, then the Byzantine Empire, and then a number of European states run by dictators entitled King.

Then, taking a long jump forwards, there appeared in the twentieth century after a long period of more general democratization, the modern dictatorships among which Nazi Germany, the Soviet Union and communist China were among the most horrible dictatorships ever. And even if Nazi Germany and the Soviet Union are gone, all have not disappeared. In spite of the very considerable liberalization China must still be considered a dictatorship, and in Russia the dictatorial features have never totally disappeared and even seem, at present (2014), to be growing. But apart from these states there are quite a number of dictatorships in the present world. More about them follows in the Appendix.

Of particular interest are the modern Latin American dictatorships since they, in important respects, differ from most other dictatorships. This whole topic is in fact so atypical—and so closely related to a certain kind of democracy—that it could not be treated until after, or perhaps within, chapter 10 about democratic politics. I have chosen the latter and the Latin American dictatorships will then be dealt with as democratic failures—as democracies run off the rails.

But this chapter is about the great main bundle of dictatorships. Since they have been so many, and present in all times, they must of course, in some respects, differ from each other. But, since they have all been just dictatorships, there must also be important similarities. A systematic disclosure of these differences and similarities therefore should be an important and interesting task, but it has hardly been a priority in political science even if the interest has started growing.

An example of this new interest, perhaps the most important one, is Ronald Wintrobe's volume "The Political Economy of Dictatorship", 350 pages thick. Even if Wintrobe is an economist, not a political scientist, the subject matter nevertheless belongs to political science. I sympathize with Wintrobe's methodological points of departure but still his book, as I see it, is of limited value. The expression "much cry, but little wool" is uncommonly fitting. The "cry" consists in masses of mathematical formulas—differential- and integral-calculus—spread all over the pages (a misbehavior which has become more common in parts of the social sciences in recent years). And the lack of "wool" becomes evident in the really meager final, concluding chapter. In spite of Wintrobe's frequent references to historical facts one gets the impression that his understanding of them is superficial. The fundamental difference between dictatorships before and after the industrial revolution (which will be dealt with later on in this chapter) is, for instance, not mentioned and not recognized. Rather, pure formalism takes over and steers. There are also clear oddities. Thus, as an example, Wintrobe writes that he has been unable to find any female dictators in the historical past, except possibly Indira Gandhi for a short period.[334] And yet on fact there have been lots of female dictators as will become evident below. My devoting here a whole paragraph to Wintrobe's book does not only depend on its representing a growing interest. It has also been extravagantly praised by individuals as well-known in parts of social science as Barry Weingast and Dennis Mueller.

The discussion about dictatorships and their properties which I will undertake in this chapter is thus another one than Wintrobe's. As the chapter proceeds I will point out distinctions which I find interesting from a theoretical point of view. In the final section I will then present a classification of dictatorships departing from these distinctions.

THE DICTATOR'S INCENTIVES

Since the dictator is the absolute governor of the dictatorship it seems reasonable to start the discussion about the properties of dictatorships by examining the incentives of the dictator. What does he want, what characterizes his decisions? In the section "Modifications of the basic model" in the theory chapter I suggested an incentive, namely that a dictator—or in that case a war lord—wishes to become as rich as possible, and therefore tries to acquire many subjects who could be heavily taxed. But this incentive is not only simple, it is obviously *too* simple. It is easy to agree with Carl J. Friedrich and Zbigniew K. Brezezinski when they, in their book "Totalitarian Dictatorship & Autocracy", write:[335]

> "For whereas tyranny was conducted for the benefit of the tyrant, as Aristotle pointed out, it is not very realistic to make that kind of egoism the basis of an interpretation of totalitarian dictatorship. Whatever Lenin's new type of state was, it was not conducted in the personal interest of Lenin."

---

[334] Wintrobe, p. 12.
[335] Friedrich & Brezezinsky, p. 4.

But then, how complicated are the incentives of dictators? How far, and in which directions, do we have to distance ourselves from the simple idea in the theory chapter? Is it really possible to generalize about dictators' incentives? At first this may undeniably seem difficult, but I believe that it could be easier than it seems. Even if the outwardly perceptible manifestations of dictators' ambitions vary enormously there are, I contend, traits beneath that are more uniform. But let me start with the easily discernible, outer characteristics.

Some dictators such as the pharaohs of Egypt have considered themselves to be gods, or at least as intermediaries to gods, and in this respect they are not the only ones.[336] A number of dictators in Mesopotamia behaved in the same way.[337] The dictators of the Aztecs considered themselves gods.[338] And similar patterns have characterized many other dictatorships as well. In the Roman Empire a number of emperors were declared gods—albeit, in this case, after having died.[339] The Chinese emperors were, during long periods, regarded as "Sons of Heaven" which again entails a godly, or at least un-earthly, origin.[340] The Arab word "caliph", which means "successor" or "substitute", originally stood for "the successor of God's representative" but later on, more pretentiously, for "God's substitute". The sun-god religion of the Incas was, in reality, a deification of the ruling dynasty's first ancestor.[341] Kings claiming divine right to rule are almost countless. There are however also dictators having aspired for completely other things than godliness, and thereby we get to the differences in the outer appearances. Sargon II in Assyria, Nebuchadnezzar II in Babylonia, Xerxes in the Persian Empire, the emperors of the Byzantine Empire, Charlemagne, the Great Mughals of the Mughal Empire, Peter the Great and Louis XIV all wished to create luxuriously decorated great palaces, or even entire cities. Dûr-Sharrukin, Babylon, Persepolis, Constantinople, Aachen, Agra, Sankt Petersburg and Versailles testify eminently to this. Colossal, lavish opulence of various kinds, as well as big harems for the more intimate pleasures of the dictator, could also

---

[336] Finer (1997a), p. 39; Mieroop, pp. 194, 217.
[337] Roux, pp. 156-7.
[338] Finer (1997a), p. 39; Roberts, p. 486.
[339] Stockton, pp. 161-3.
[340] Fairbank & Goldman, p. 69; Roberts, p. 139.
[341] Conrad. p. 354.

be included in the requisites. But still other dictators, for instance Charles XII of Sweden and Napoleon Bonaparte, seem to have been more ascetically inclined and mainly devoted themselves to war-waging. Then there are dictators, such as for instance Ramses II (governing 1279–13) of Egypt's New Kingdom[342] and, much later, Hitler, who have been absorbed by an enormous ambition or hubris and thus have strived to be remembered as the Greatest in the history of the world. And the dictators Lenin and Mao Zedong seem to have been driven by the ambition to spread certain social philosophies or social systems.

So these are some of the most common, easily identifiable incentives, and then there are of course also combinations of them. The pharaohs of Egypt's New Kingdom did not only consider themselves gods—they eagerly fought wars as well. Peter the Great did not only build his capital but also was a first rate warrior. But irrespective of these combinations, and of the exactitude of the short characterizations given above, the great variation is the essential point here. At first sight the incentives of the dictators in world history really seem very different. And so it may be, but it may also be, at least to some extent, a delusion. It is thus most likely that at least some of the dictators who, in one way or another, have laid claim to divinity, have done so in order to enhance their own power—and that consequently the claims, in fact, have been intended pretences. A grandson to the Mesopotamian king Sargon of Akkad found it for instance necessary, in order to solve a political crisis, to present himself as a god.[343] And with Egyptian pharaohs it may, according to some information, have been similarly.[344] But still there remains a most considerable variation. In spite of this variation, and behind it, there is however, I contend, an important common factor. All of the incentives are such that they, for their fulfillment, require far-going exploitation of a lot of people, the subjects of the dictatorships.

The pharaohs were not just any religious or pious individuals, they wished to have pyramids, temples, palaces and statues. Lenin and Mao Zedong were no common social philosophers, they also wished to implement their ideas by means of resource-requiring violence. The hubris or ambitiousness of dictators have not been of the same kind as the

---

[342] Wilkinson, pp. 330-4. Se also pp. 10, 16.
[343] Leick, p. 100; Wilkinson, pp. 477-8.
[344] Finer (1997a), p. 140; Wilkinson, p. 455.

ambitions of for instance artists or scientists—they have always been of a kind requiring great material resources and violence for their fulfillment. So, irrespective of all easily discernible variations, and irrespective of the intensity or seriousness of these variations, dictators' incentives have always been such that they, for their fulfillment, require exploitation of subjects. The dictator needs his subjects. The subjects are necessary since it is only by means of them that the dictator can realize his ambitions.

The Egyptologist Toby Wilkinson, when describing the attitudes of some of the pharaohs of the Middle Kingdom, writes that "... resources— human as well as material, native as well as foreign—were to be exploited for the benefit of the crown. People were merely another commodity ...".[345] And Friedrich and Brzezinski, in a similar vein, write that "Hitler was not primarily interested in the German people and was basically motivated by his totalitarian mission, as he conceived it; for this the German people was merely the tool."[346] This seems correct, and even if Hitler was an unusually atrocious dictator, the same holds, according to the reasoning conducted here, for many other dictators as well, such as for instance the Egyptian pharaohs. Maybe it even holds for most of dictators. Their peoples were their tools.

The reasoning thus leads to the following main hypothesis. Dictators' incentives have always, in all dictatorships and in all times, been such that extensive exploitation of many subjects has been necessary for their fulfillment. The dictators have therefore tried to exploit their subjects as much as possible, and also to increase the number of subjects. This hypothesis is obviously closely related to the one advanced in the theory chapter, which also emphasized the utilization of the subjects. The difference just is that the pursuit of wealth was the only aim of the utilization mentioned there, whereas, as we have now seen, it may be used for other purposes as well. Furthermore, for the utilization of the subjects the dictators may have used different methods. The conditions may have varied with the geographical location and the period of time. And the dictators themselves have of course differed most considerably with respect to intelligence, temperament, and so forth, and therefore acted differently. For these reasons, and in spite of the main hypothesis'

---

[345] Wilkinson, p. 173.
[346] Friedrich & Brezezinski, p. 141.

emphasizing of dictators' similarities, different dictatorships have had different properties.

The main hypothesis is thus fundamental, but still there may be dictators who are not captured by it. It is even easy to point at mechanisms giving rise to such dictators. Thus it is quite common that the dictatorship is inherited within the family of the founder (see the section "Transfers of power" below). And under conditions like that dictators with really strange incentives, or even perhaps almost lacking incentives, may obviously appear. There is no scarcity of dictators with limited intelligence, or else badly or bizarrely equipped.

The most interesting deviations from the pattern described are however not the handicapped dictators, but those, if such ones have existed, who have had all forces and capabilities and who used these resources wholeheartedly for something totally different than the hitherto mentioned purposes, for instance for the betterment of their subjects. What in particular deserves attention—for the sake of contrast—are dictators with an altruistic inclination. Have there been any such ones? Have there existed any dictators who have not considered their subjects essentially as means for their own ends, but who have really cared for them for other reasons? Logically this is of course not excluded and trying to find such dictators is of great interest. First this is of course interesting for the very simple reason that it is always nice to be able to register the presence of decent people. But it is also interesting from a theoretical point of view. Precisely since we have used an assumption about self-interest as our starting point it is important keep our eyes open for possible, existing counter-examples. The theory must not be *too* simple. After having discussed various aspects of dictatorships I will therefore, in the final section of this chapter, raise the issue about dictators' incentives anew. Above all I will then focus on altruistic dictators, if there are any.

THE EMERGENCE OF DICTATORSHIPS

Specifying a creational mechanism for dictatorships is not difficult. The second invisible hand described in the theory chapter may bring at least small, dictatorial, stationary monopolies of violence into being. In the theory chapter I also explained how a tribal leader could make himself an absolute leader. Furthermore I pointed to the incentives of the monopolist to enlarge his territory by conquests. The basic model thus indicates a possible mechanism for the emergence of dictatorships. But is the model also correct? Have the processes actually been like that when dictatorships of the real world have emerged?

A first comment is that the basic model is relevant only for the transition from a stateless or anarchistic situation to dictatorship, or the transition from a simple tribal society, possibly with some kind of simple, direct democracy, to dictatorship. But obviously dictatorships have been created in other ways as well, for instance by the transformation of other kinds of fully developed states. Processes like that must of course be dealt with in the discussion here, but let us start with the simple transition from anarchy or primitive tribal society to dictatorship.

It seems likely that all, or practically all, of those early dictatorships mentioned earlier in this chapter and in chapter 2, emerged, or at least could have emerged, in the way described. And the reason for the reservation "could have emerged" is not the presence of any obvious, manifest counter-evidence but rather that the details sometimes are unknown. The origin of the two states Upper and Lower Egypt, which together were to constitute the Old Kingdom, is for instance unclear[347], and the same is true for the background of several other early states, as for instance the Sumerian city-states. We do however also know about cases where the traces are clearer and where the mechanism described seems likely. This is so, for instance, for the first Chinese states Shang, Zhou and Qin, for the Persian Empire originating from the Medes tribe, and for Rome which was created by a tribe at the Tiber, and which, at its very earliest, was a dictatorship. A much later example is the kingdom of Charlemagne, the origin of which was a German tribe, the Franks. Going forwards in time it then seems likely that the early European, dictatorial kingdoms mentioned in chapter 2, that is Portugal, and Aragon and Castile which were to unite into Spain, and early England, had similar backgrounds. For none of these dictatorships is the mechanism by which they emerged at all mysterious. The same is the case with the French kingdom which was created by the uniting of a number of very small states, with a stage of feudalism in between. Also Russia was created by the unification of smaller areas run by their chiefs even if there was no feudalism included here. It would be easy to give more examples than the ones already mentioned.

---

[347] Wilkinson, pp. 23-7.

But dictatorships do not only emerge out of primitive societies of various kinds. Also highly developed societies may be turned into dictatorships. An early, outstanding example of passage from oligarchy to dictatorship is, of course, the transition of the Roman state from the Republic to the Empire—this occurred, as was described in chapter 2, after the long republican period which, in its turn, had followed the very short, initial, dictatorial, period already mentioned. A much later example is the transition from one type of dictatorship—Russia of the tsars—to another type of dictatorship—the Soviet Union. This transition was a long, drawn-out process including hunger revolts, the degeneration of the tsarist regime and even the beginning of a process towards European style democratization and liberalization. And then, in connection with the set-backs during World War One, Vladimir Lenin succeeded in getting the upper hand by means of the so called October Revolution in 1917. After a civil war lasting until 1920 the new dictatorship was then established. In Italy Benito Mussolini, aided by his fascists, made himself dictator in 1926. Still later, as another example, the German representative democracy of the interwar period, the Weimar Republic, was transformed into the dictatorship of the Hitler period. In this case the general elections of 1931, which made the Nazi party the largest in the parliament, were of crucial importance. But since the party did not achieve a majority of its own this was however not enough. Using violence and threats of various kinds Hitler could however supplement the electoral success and in 1934 the process was brought to an end—thus a transition from democracy to dictatorship by means of, at least to some extent, democratic means. And some years later the Spanish representative democracy was turned into a dictatorship as a consequence of the civil war 1936–9. Here it was a professional soldier, the general Franco, who, using violence, made himself dictator.

The last four examples—Russia, Italy, Germany and Spain—are interesting since they belong to the modern age, the age after the industrial revolution. The transitions occurred in societies which were much more developed than those less modern societies we have previously considered. And that means that the conditions for establishing a dictatorship were different. What should be changed was more consolidated and therefore the organization for achieving the change also had to be more elaborate. It was not, as it could be in older times, enough for the aspiring dictator just to murder the incumbent one. The organization required could however be of different kinds.

In Russia, Italy and Germany grass root level parties were created.[348] These parties then recruited more and more members, made themselves known by aggressive behavior and then, finally, took over the running of the state. Certainly the processes were somewhat different in the three cases but even so a main characteristic is that they all started from below. And this is perfectly compatible with the logic of collective action. At least from that point of view nothing is difficult to explain. At first a small group of similarly minded individuals may have formed the embryo for a party, and within that group someone may have been a natural leader already from the beginning, or made himself leader later on. Similar processes, leading to what may be called party dictatorships, have also taken place later on in other places, for instance in North Korea at the end of the 1940s, in China in 1949, at Cuba in 1959 and in Iraq, with its Baath party and Saddam Hussein, in 1979. The parties operating in these sorts of processes are however not necessarily created for the purpose of founding a dictatorship. A variation is that of liberation movements in colonies during the colonial era continuing as dominating parties in their respective countries after the achievement of independence. Such a party could maintain its position by founding a dictatorship. That happened in for instance Algeria, Tunisia and Zimbabwe.

In Spain the organization was however of another kind. In a developed country there is usually, beside all public administrations and authorities, all companies, and so forth, also a military apparatus with all its equipment, all its employees, and among the latter in particular the career officers. And such a situation is always potentially dangerous since the military disposes of the most important means of violence. If some high officer, or group of officers, wants to take hold of the ruling power, and if the rest of the soldiers are loyal to them, their prospects are good. In Spain there was a situation almost like this. The future dictator, Francisco Franco, was a professional solder, and together with parts of the army he tried to overthrow the republic and its democratically elected government. He did however not succeed immediately, partly because he did not have the full support of the armed forces. Rather a long, horrible

---

[348] Friedrich & Brzezinski, pp. 21-2, 25.

civil war came to pass (1936–9), a war in which foreign forces intervened on both sides. At last Franco however succeeded. The result was what may be called a military dictatorship, and of such there have been many. To them belong, among others, the Latin American dictatorships, but about them I will, as I have already mentioned, write more in chapter 10. There are however many more, and often the coups have been successful without any long civil wars. Modern examples are Egypt which was turned into a military dictatorship by the professional soldier Gamal Abdel Nasser in 1956, Burma which was similarly transformed by the country's Chief of Army in 1962, and Libya where the colonel Muammar Gadaffi seized power in a military coup in 1969. And in these cases there is also nothing that is difficult to explain—everything is compatible with the logic of collective action. The necessary organization—the military apparatus—had been in place from the beginning, built up by former governments. But if a party dictatorship grows from below a military dictatorship is, on the contrary, imposed from above.

So these are two main processes by which modern dictatorships may be created even if other ways should not be excluded. What is important is that there hardly is anything mysterious involved. Explanations compatible with the logic of collective action are never difficult to find. Transitions from oligarchy or representative democracy certainly require, for making the explanation complete, that the emergence of the oligarchy or the democracy also is explained, but those explanations will not be presented until chapters 8 and 9 respectively. Here, in this chapter, I only cover the ground needed to explain transitions to dictatorship.

Before continuing I shall however make a further comment on the distinction between party and military dictatorships. The distinction, as explained above, is related to the way in which the dictatorship is created. After being created the two types of dictatorships may however become more and more similar. That a dictatorship which is created by a party will very soon also have to acquire a military apparatus of its own is obvious—without that the new dictatorship would in all likelihood not survive for long. An example of a quick militarization is the Russian revolutionaries' creation of the Red Army as early as in January 1918. That a party dictatorship, beside its party, very soon will dispose of a significant military apparatus should therefore not be surprising. Less expected is however, perhaps, the appearances of parties in military dictatorships.

An interesting example is Egypt. After the establishment of the dictatorship a later dictator, Anwar Sadat, in 1978 founded the National Democratic Party. This party has, as it seems, two main functions. One is that it is included in, and amplifies, the dictatorship's aspiration for a democratic façade. The other is that it provides a demarcated and controllable institution for the careers of the functionaries of the dictatorship. Even in military dictatorships parties may thus be valuable.

The essential conclusion of this section is that dictatorships easily emerge from anarchistic conditions or from direct democracies, and that all kinds of societies, as it seems, sometimes and quite easily may be turned into dictatorships. Dictatorships have also, totally independent of each other, appeared in many parts of the world in all times. There has not been any early prototype dictatorship serving as inspiration for followers, and neither has there been any need for such a prototype. The dictatorship is therefore, and in this sense, the most "natural" kind of state.

TRANSFERS OF POWER

THE PROBLEM

The problem of succession is, in a dictatorship as in every stately monopoly of violence, of greatest importance, but also complicated and peculiar. Characteristic for dictatorships is that the succession is much less regulated by rules, and in particular by formal rules, than in other kinds of states. But some rules, even if implicit, and often also ignored, have nevertheless almost always existed. This section is about the more regular types of succession in dictatorships. But certainly power has often also been transferred in other ways, for instance by murdering the incumbent dictator. Shifts like that will however be dealt with later on, in the section "Threats against the dictator".

Let us, following our earlier way of reasoning, start by looking at the succession problem from the point of view of the incumbent dictator. Let us furthermore assume that this dictator is extremely egoistic—he thinks about nothing but himself and his own interests. Even such a dictator, interestingly enough, has every reason to consider the succession problem seriously, and to handle it in a credible way. If the subjects—when the dictator approaches the end of his life or becomes regarded as threatened in some other way—suspect that the succession is not properly arranged, this may be enough to trigger disturbances and disorder in the state. Facing the coming uncertainty a growing number of people may then conclude that it is better to forestall than to be forestalled and thus start breaking formerly respected norms and rules, whatever they may be. And this may happen irrespective of whether the subjects have supported the dictator or not. Therefore, in order to avoid unrest and perhaps chaos, it is in the interest of even the most egoistic and self centered dictator to address the succession problem convincingly. To the extent that he succeeds with this he has also contributed to stability and to his own personal security in the final days of his regime.[349]

An interesting example of these mechanisms is provided by the events that followed the murder of Philip of Macedonia by one of his body guards in the year −336. Since no one expected that Philip's son Alexander, then only twenty years old, would take over, uprisings started everywhere in the realm created by Philip.[350] Alexander, however, proved himself master of the situation and did not only pacify his father's territory but also continued in order to become known as "the Great". But had Alexander not been who he was, he obviously could have failed. And therefore the disorder erupting after the murder of Philip clearly demonstrates the importance of orderly succession.

In reality there has almost always also been some kind of rule or principle for the succession and part of the reason may be an understanding of the mechanisms just described, even if other explanations are imaginable as well. The dictator may, for instance, have been equipped with somewhat more empathy than hitherto assumed and in fact cared about his family and offspring. However that may be, more or less clear rules of succession have been quite common and in the subsequent sections I will consider two basic models. In the first one, the family model, the successor comes from the dictator's own family, and in the other one, the party model, from the dictator's party. Beside these two main models there have also been some other courses of action.

THE FAMILY MODEL

The family model is by far the most common in the history of the world. In its most widespread variety it means that one of the dictator's child-

---

[349] Olson (2000), pp. 25-8.
[350] Chrissanthos, pp. 77-8.

ren—for instance the eldest son, or the eldest child, or the child considered most suitable by the dictator—takes over. The dictatorship is thus inherited and thereby so called dynasties are brought into being. World history is full of well-known dynasties. In Egypt's Kingdoms a long row of dynasties ruled—somewhere around 30 depending on how one counts. In early Assyria members of the same family ruled for more than two hundred years.[351] The names of the Chinese states are those of their main dynasties. The English and Scottish dynasties Tudor and Stuart are well-known. On the European main land the House of Habsburg is one important dynasty. And many, many more examples could be given. The ones mentioned should however suffice for conveying an impression about the spread of the family model.

But then, what is the reason for this extensive spread of the model? For a start it is quite simple, and, as I have already noted, some dictators may also have wished to favor their own family for pure sentimental reasons. But more important is probably that the family model is the model giving least influence to persons outside the dictator's own circle. If, for instance, the dictator himself should select his successor from a group of confidents—a model which has been used—this immediately opens the door for various kinds of influences from outside. The dictator is no longer as much of a dictator. So perhaps it is its combination of simplicity and closeness which explains the spread of the family model.

But irrespective of the reasons for the spread of the model the political consequences have been enormous—and this, of course, depends on the links between higher politics and family life, and sometimes even amorous affairs, established by the model. About –1350 the rulers of Egypt and Babylonia improved the relations between their countries using the diplomatic means of their time—the Egyptians gave gold to the Babylonians who countered by sending princesses to pharaoh's harem.[352] In the year –1261 history's first known peace treaty—between Egypt's New Kingdom and its enemy the Hittites—was agreed upon, after which Egypt's pharaoh confirmed the treaty by marrying a Hittite princess in –1246, and then still another one in –1235.[353] About –600 Babylonia and

---

[351] Roux, p. 282.
[352] Grayson (1980a), p. 92.
[353] Chrissanthos, pp. 9-10; Wilkinson, p. 304. For still more examples see Wilkinson pp. 260, 269-70.

Media enforced their at that time existing alliance by means of a marriage between the Babylonian king's son Nebuchadnezzar—the future great king—and the daughter Amytis of the king of Media; and after that the two states together crushed the Assyrian Empire.[354] But marriages, or invitations to marriages, were not only used for enforcing the links with allies, but also for appeasing enemies. Thus an emperor in Chinese Han, trying to make the hostile neighbors in north-west stop their aggressions, bestowed them with a princess—in that case without success however.[355] New and bigger states could also be created by marriages as when Ferdinand of Aragon and Isabella of Castile married in 1469. Thereby the Spanish kingdom—which was to become a veritable super power in its own time—came into existence. And—with the risk of being repetitive—almost countless examples like these could be given.

But the mixture of great politics and family life does not stop with matters as simple as marriages. In a world in which the dictators own their countries, and fight each other to increase or protect their scope, there are greater games than that. The Spanish super power which was created by means of a marriage would later on dwindle because of a family conflict about a will, a conflict which led to the war of the Spanish succession (1701–14).[356] This was not, as its name perhaps may lead one to guess, a Spanish civil war, but a major European war, or even, according to some historians, the first world war of the modern age.[357] The French king Louis XIV was married to one daughter to the Spanish king who died in 1700 and the Habsburg emperor of the Holy Roman Empire to another one. Both therefore hoped to be able to place some younger member of their own family on the Spanish throne. But the Spanish king, in his will, had given the whole of Spain, including all its non-European territories, to the grandson of Louis XIV, thereby leaving the Habsburgs without anything. And thereby the field was open for that great war which led, among much else, to the splintering of Spanish territorial holdings.

Before leaving the family model it may be interesting to mention some variations on the theme. Families take different forms and dictators

---

[354] Roux, p. 376.
[355] Gascoigne (2003), p. 74; Morton & Lewis, p. 52.
[356] Palmer, Colton & Kramer (2007a), pp. 183-4.
[357] Roberts, p. 661.

with many wives are, for instance, quite common. And that, as well as other family constellations, may, of course, entail problems. Which child should inherit the throne? In the Egyptian Kingdoms problems like these seem to have been frequent and it occurred that pharaohs married their sisters in order to strengthen the position of their own family.[358] In the Persian Empire the ruling dictator chose—when the rules were followed—his own favorite.[359] Chinese Han adopted the rule that, if an emperor died before his wife, the widow should choose the successor from the family of the deceased.[360] But several widows, in Han as well as later on, circumvented this rule by appointing a weak successor from the family of the former emperor permitting a strong man from her own family in reality, even if not formally, to take over. In the Inca Empire the rules were utterly strange. The emperor or dictator could have many wives, but he had to have one of his full sisters as his principal wife. The one of the sons with this wife who the emperor considered most fitting was appointed successor. These rules were based on the idea that the emperor was a god, and that the divinity was upheld by the bloodline. Even the rules of inheritance were interesting. Nothing of a dead emperor's very large possessions could be inherited. They were rather assembled at a cult place where his mummy was placed as well. Every new emperor therefore had to accumulate anew the very large and expensive belongings necessary for his dignity. It has in fact been argued that these inheritance rules were the main reason for the ever new conquests by the Inca state.[361] Perhaps it was so. Anyway the result was a very harsh exploitation of the subjects and in that sense in accordance with our main hypothesis about the dictator's incentives. The Inca rules were thus fairly strict even if bizarre. In the Mughal Empire they were on the contrary almost nonexistent even if the family model, on the whole, was implicitly adopted. If an emperor unexpectedly died a fight between the pretenders to the throne inevitably ensued. When for instance a dictator had died in 1627 both Shah Jahan—he who built Taj Mahal—and his brother claimed the throne. Shah Jahan triumphed and thereafter executed all his male relatives. The next transfer of power even if of a quite different kind, was

---

[358] Mieroop, pp. 67, 170; Wilkinson, p. 222.
[359] Wiesehöfer, p. 85.
[360] Fairbank & Goldman, p. 59.
[361] Conrad, p. 353.

also, in its own way, interesting. Shah Jahan's son captured his father, put him into prison, and made himself dictator.[362]

Above I wrote about the political influence of the Chinese emperor widows, and in relation to that it may be appropriate to say something about female dictators. Of such there have been many, in particular within the family model. In Egypt's New Kingdom Hatshepsut, daughter to the former pharaoh, was queen from –1490 to –1468.[363] The last ruler of Egypt was also a woman, namely Cleopatra (–69– –12). When she, together with her lover Mark Antony, had committed suicide Egypt was made part of the Roman state. Zenobia who ruled the country Palmyra—about the same as today's Syria—from 240 to 274 was a remarkable, dynamic dictator. When her husband, the former dictator, had died, she seized power and started a revolt against the Roman Empire. In the beginning she was successful and conquered Egypt, where she made herself dictator. Finally, however, she was defeated by the Romans.[364] In Chinese Tang a woman, the formidable Wu, took the throne from her sickly husband.[365] She ruled iron-fistedly from 690 to 705—for instance by continuously exchanging ministers, or even by executing them—but in the end she was forced to abdicate. A later vigorous and charismatic Chinese dictator was the empress dowager Cixi, who ruled China until her death in 1908.[366] Other well-known female dictators are Catherine II, "the Great", of Russia (1729–96), the Tudor queens Mary I, "Bloody Mary", (1516–58) and Elizabeth I (1533–1603), and the Stuart queen Mary II (1662–94). The list could easily be made longer.

Another example of the family model—or rather a failed family model—is the Caliphate. Muhammad's death in 632 came as a surprise and the appointment of his successor, the first caliph, therefore became tumultuous. After some more caliphs Muhammad's cousin and son in law, Ali, became the fourth one. After that, when Ali had been murdered in 661 and been followed by another caliph, a conflict broke out in the Muslim world. Ali's supporters held that caliphs should be recruited from Muhammad's family, and thereby they disqualified not only Ali's successor

---

[362] Eraly, p. xx; Finer (1997c), p. 1233; Gascoigne (1971), p. 217.
[363] Roberts, p. 83; Wilkinson, pp. 228-36.
[364] Morris, p. 311; Walters (1980b), p. 55.
[365] Finer (1997b), pp. 752-6; Morris, p. 340; Morton & Lewis, p. 88.
[366] Morton & Lewis, p. 167.

but also the three first caliphs as well as all the following ones.[367] These adherents to the family model were to be called Shiites. The others, those not sympathizing with the Shiites, were the Sunnis. In this way, what was to become a main conflict in the Muslim world, started. The conflict has more elements than the succession issue, but it was with that issue that it began.

The family model has thus been most important in world history, but lost, essentially, its significance in the societal transformations following the industrial revolution. It is however not completely gone. There are remains in some Arab countries which still have their dynasties. Possibly the explanation is that the dictators of these countries, with their great oil resources, are able to live well without suppressing their subjects all that much. But these are reminiscences, even if some efforts to enliven the model also have been undertaken. North Korea, in which shifts from father to son have occurred twice, the first time in 1994 and the second time 2011, is one example.[368] In Burma[369] there have been similar tendencies, at least before the present, potential democratization, and the same was true for Libya[370] before the death of Gadaffi in 2012. But in spite of this the family model has in all likelihood ended its sway. As main model it has been replaced by the party model.

THE PARTY MODEL

Let us start with Benito Mussolini's Italy and Adolf Hitler's Germany. In these states the dictator was also the leader of the only political party permitted—the National Fascist Party and the National Socialist German Workers' Party respectively. There were however no shifts of power. The Italian and German dictatorships were short-lived and expired together with their leaders in the Second World War. In the communist dictatorships—and then in particular in the Soviet Union and China—which also use the party model, a considerable number of power transfers have

---

[367] Finer (1997b), pp. 685-6; Roberts, p. 333.
[368] Briefing Succession in North Korea: Grief and fear. The Economist, December 31st, 2011, pp. 15-17; Obituary: Kim Jong Il. The Economist, December 31st, 2011, p. 70.
[369] This relates to the former general and dictator Than Shwe, who clearly had ambitions of creating a ruling dynasty of his own.
[370] Libya: A civil war beckons. The Economist, March 5th, 2011, p. 42.

however taken place. Common to all of these transfers is that the new dictator, or in some cases a small interim group, always has come from the top level of the only permitted party. Formal rules have hardly been followed and brutal violence has been common.

In the Soviet Union, after the death of Vladimir Lenin in 1924, Joseph Stalin finally triumphed in a brutal fight against Leon Trotsky.[371] Then, after Stalin's death in March 1953, a new, intense fight for power followed. An early ingredient in this fight was a trial against one of the main candidates, the former chief of the secret police (more about this secret police follows in the section "Communication routes, intelligence systems and police" below) Lavrentiy Beria. Those remaining after that were Georgy Malenkov, Nikolai Bulganin and, at first waiting in the coulisses, Nikita Khrushchev. The last one finally won and immediately engaged in efforts to consolidate his own position—primarily by criticizing his predecessor Stalin intensively at the twentieth party congress in 1956. In particular he condemned the so called cult of personality during Stalin's reign.[372] After that he ruled absolutely until 1964 when he, himself, was outmaneuvered, but not executed—he lived in the Soviet Union, arrested in his own home, until he died in 1971. The ones who expelled him, once again a small group, were Leonid Brezhnev, Alexei Kosygin, Nikolai Podgorny and the, in the very top level of Soviet politics long-established, perpetual survivor Anastas Mikoyan. But this group, in the same way as earlier groups of a similar kind, only became an interim solution. Brezhnev forced the other ones out and thereafter ruled as dictator until his death in 1982. After him followed in order, and until the breakdown of the Soviet Union, Yuri Andropov, Konstantin Tjernenko and Mikhail Gorbachev.[373] These later power transfers were more peaceful than the earlier ones, and perhaps even rules were followed to some extent. Possibly the institution which announced the leaders appointed—the executive committee of the communist party, the Politburo—also had a certain amount of real influence.

Characteristic of the party model thus is that the new leader always comes from the only party permitted, and that there is no previously obvious, generally agreed upon, successor. Rather a fight for power en-

---

[371] Friedrich & Brzezinski, pp. 72-81.
[372] Friedrich & Brzezinski, p. 33.
[373] Judt, p. 594.

sues, a fight between some main aspirants which is often settled quite brutally. In these respects the Chinese patterns are similar to the Soviet ones. During Mao Zedong's last years a rival power group—the Gang of Four—appeared. The members of the group were however imprisoned and sentenced to death by the dictator who took over after Mao's death in 1976, Hua Guofeng. Later on the death sentences were changed to life time imprisonment. And Hua Guofeng, after only two years, was forced out by Deng Xiaoping in 1978. Before that Deng Xiaoping had long since been the central man in the party and, after having taken over, he acted as dictator until his death in 1997. It was Deng Xiaoping who introduced the market liberalizing reforms and he also restructured the state's ruling institutions in some respects.[374] But even so it is still a party dictatorship. The dictators having followed Deng Xiaoping are Jiang Zemin (1989–2002), Hu Jintao (2002–12) and, from 2012, Xi Jinping.[375]

Before leaving the party model I shall take up an important similarity between this model and the family model. The families were always limited—only very few individuals in the states concerned could belong to them—and furthermore those in power often tried to control in-marrying so that no ill-suited individuals were included. The parties at issue here were, and are, similarly controlled. They were, as we have seen—or at least became in due time—the only party permitted in their respective state. And in addition to that the membership was restricted. There was always some kind of adoption procedure in which the wheat was sifted from the chaff. It was a privilege to belong to the party. Correspondingly a member, as a punishment for some real or alleged impropriety, could be expelled. The party constituted an elite and was used for strengthening, in this elite, attitudes and behavior regarded as desirable. At most the members of the party could amount to about 10 percent of the population, but often the figures were essentially lower.[376] For the Soviet Union, at about the middle of the twentieth century, the figure 2–3 percent of the adult population has been mentioned.[377]

---

[374] Morton & Lewis, pp. 222-4.
[375] The Economist, November 17th, 2012, the articles "China's leaders: Changing guard" and "China's economic performance: The paramountest leader".
[376] Friedrich & Brzezinski, pp. 22, 56-7.
[377] Palmer, Colton & Kramer (2007b), p. 744.

OTHER COURSES OF ACTION

What I call other courses of action can, to a large extent, be described as
mixtures. In ancient Egypt, for instance, deviations from the principle of
inheritance sometimes took place. Dictators could, if they thought it fitting, go outside the own family in order to find a suitable successor, and
sometimes did so.[378] In the Roman Empire adoptions were not unusual—
Marcus Aurelius was for instance adopted by the emperor he succeeded.
There were also, in the Empire, occasional shifts between, or mixtures of,
different methods. During some periods the Senate, still formally existing
as a holdover from the Republic, had some influence, at least in legitima-
ting transfers of power; during other periods the army was quite influential and effectively appointed the dictator from among its own officers;
and during still other periods the family model prevailed.[379] Turning then
to European kingdoms there have been some instances of election, or at
least some kind of legitimation afterwards from some smaller group or
assembly, when new kings have taken power. In Sweden, for instance,
such a principle was introduced as early as about 1350, in a law promulgated by the king Magnus IV.[380] After that the principle has been inter-
mittently adhered to. During long periods it has not been followed at all,
during other periods the transfer of power has only been legitimated following the introduction of new dynasties. The House of Vasa was for instance established when Gustav Eriksson was elected king, Gustav I of
Sweden, by an assembly of leading men in 1523.[381] In a similar way the
first Russian tsar of the House of Romanov was elected in 1613—a house
or dynasty to which the later dictator Peter the Great belonged. Peter,
being dissatisfied with his own son, did however abolish the inheritance
principle and declared that every tsar was free to appoint his own successor.[382] For safety he thereafter also killed the son.[383]

What is important, in point of principle, among these other courses
of action are the elements of election. Here groups or assemblies of one

---

[378] Finer (1997a), p. 134; Wilkinson, pp. 222-3.
[379] Chrissanthos, p. 174; Finer (1997a), p. 544; Herrin, p. 186; Roberts, pp. 277, 282.
[380] Herlitz, p. 21; Kent, pp. 27-8.
[381] Kent, p. 51.
[382] Palmer, Colton & Kramer (2007a), p. 220.
[383] Palmer, Colton & Kramer (2007a), p. 223; Roberts, p. 623.

kind or another have acted, for instance the Roman senate or the Swedish assembly of leading men. The emergence of these groups must be explained, and the explanations must be compatible with the logic of collective action. I will return to these issues in chapters 8 and 9.

Finally the modern military dictatorships discussed in the earlier section "The emergence of dictatorships" have to be commented on in this context as well. Their only principle of succession seems to be that the new dictator should be a professional soldier. The Spanish example is hardly interesting since there never was a succession—after Franco's death in 1975 the transformation into a modern democracy was, on the whole, quiet and peaceful. In Burma several power shifts have taken place and, even if they have been rowdy, the new dictator has all the times been a military officer. In Egypt the dictators have also, continuously, been military officers. After Nasser came Anwar Sadat, and after him Hosni Mubarak. The transitions also seem to have been quite orderly. Sadat, for sure, was murdered, but he was not replaced by the murderers. They were on the contrary punished by the surviving and continuing military regime. In the spring of 2011, the Arab spring, this succession pattern was however broken. Mubarak was forced out and a transitional development started. The results of this transition, which is still going on when this is written (late 2014), are uncertain (see the section "Flight, inner exile and rebellion" below).

THE ECONOMY OF DICTATORSHIPS

INTRODUCTION

Let us start from the previously assumed main hypothesis that the dictator runs the dictatorship completely in his own interest. If so he should reasonably strive to acquire as many and as valuable resources of various kinds as possible. The more he has, or can lay his hands on by taxing, conquests, and the like, the further he can advance his own ambitions whether they consist in building pyramids, waging wars, or whatever. As we saw in the preceding chapter three main methods have, during the course of history, been available for increasing wealth, namely first claims, plundering and conquests, second foreign trade, and third development of the own economy. All of these methods have also been extensively used even if their relative importance has changed over time. If one should draw a dividing line somewhere it is natural to do that at the time of the industrial revolution. This revolution not only led to enormous technological changes, its capitalistic production methods also were poorly suited to dictatorships, and, finally the possibilities to become rich by means of claims or conquests were, at about this time, drastically reduced. So even if the dividing line obviously not is sharp, I will nevertheless distinguish between the conditions before and after the industrial revolution.

BEFORE THE INDUSTRIAL REVOLUTION

The first method at a dictator's disposal for increasing his resources, that is claims, plundering and conquest was, as has been made obvious in several places above, utterly commonplace, or even the main method, during a long period in the beginning of the history of states. Since I have already described this method in some detail I may however leave it aside here. And the same holds for foreign trade which I dealt with in the preceding chapter. I will rather turn directly to those efforts which dictators undertook, before the industrial revolution, for improving their own economies. These efforts were in many cases considerable.

I mentioned in chapter 2 that the Assyrian dictators, in spite of their brutality and intensive war-waging, also ordered the building of extensive irrigation systems to benefit agriculture. More generally it may be stated that the Mesopotamian dictators persevered at building and extending canals, dams and dykes and also continuously tried to keep them functioning.[384] The same applies to a great extent to the Egyptian and Chinese dictators.[385] Many more examples could be mentioned. In the Indian Maurya Empire great investments in different kinds of infrastructure were made.[386] And, taking a long jump forwards, Russia's Peter the Great undertook far-reaching, and to a large extent successful, efforts for developing, as far as possible at that time, the Russian economy. He travelled himself, for purposes of study, to England and Holland, and also employed a large number of experts from these countries who, in Russia, helped modernizing the country.[387] Mining and metallurgy were developed, as

---

[384] Roux, pp. 323, 409.
[385] Finer (1997a), p. 86.
[386] Thapar, p. 83.
[387] Rosenberg & Birdzell, p. 71.

well as the textile industry and in particular the armaments industry, commercial companies were founded, and so forth.[388]

Many dictators thus tried intensively, with the resources available, to develop their own economies, and possibly Peter the Great went furthest of all of them—certainly he went to extremes. But there were also dictators who behaved quite differently, who relied totally on plundering, conquests and foreign trade, and who did not care at all about their own economies. The Indian Great Mughals are strong candidates for an extremist position in that respect—investments in productive infrastructure seem to have been virtually non-existent, all building activities were focused on the fantastic monumental buildings and on control systems to be mentioned in the section "Communications routes, intelligence systems and police" below.[389]

AFTER THE INDUSTRIAL REVOLUTION

With the industrial revolution these patterns began to change. Let us start by looking at the method "claims, conquest and plundering". Certainly it was tried in some cases even in the twentieth century, and then by dictatorships. A first interesting example is the Japanese aggression in Manchuria in the 1930s. At first the Japanese army operated on its own without its government's sanction. Then Japan—through a military coup, including the murdering of the prime minister—was transformed from a kind of "half democracy", a budding representative democracy, to a military dictatorship, and the expansionist policy continued. Other examples are Mussolini's occupation of Ethiopia in 1936[390], and Hitler's large-scale attack eastwards—operation Barbarossa[391]—in 1941. All of these conquering efforts were at least partially economically motivated, but all also failed. Japan, Italy and Germany were the great losers of the Second World War. So even if great conquests have been tried far into modern times, and perhaps should not be excluded in the future, a long time has anyway passed since such operations were successful. Going then to the time after the Second World War, when one of the victorious powers, the Soviet Union, occupied the whole of Eastern Europe, the motives were

---

[388] Palmer, Colton & Kramer (2007a), pp. 219-22.
[389] Eraly, pp. 15, 267-8; Finer (1997c), p. 1257.
[390] Palmer, Colton & Kramer (2007b), p. 831.
[391] Lee, pp. 241-5

hardly economical. The ambitions to create a military buffer zone towards West, and to spread communism, were probably more important.[392]
Anyway Eastern Europe gradually turned into an economic burden for
the Soviet Union.[393] China's occupation of Tibet in 1950 was also not, in
all likelihood, undertaken for economic reasons. The time for making
oneself rich by conquests seems, on the whole, gone.

The two other methods for creating wealth, that is by foreign trade
and, above all, by developing one's own economy are, however, more interesting. As I wrote in the preceding chapter there was, until the industrial revolution, hardly anything in the economic institutions developed
which was unacceptable from the point of view of a dictator. But then
things changed. Dictators could not accept the free market institutions
such as they were after that revolution, but at the same time they wished,
of course, to enjoy the fruits of industrialization. So they had to go their
own ways. Here I will say something about how this was done in the Soviet Union, in Nazi Germany and in communist China.

From an economic point of view these countries were very different
at the time of the establishment of the dictatorship. The Soviet Union was,
even if basically an agricultural economy, still industrialized to some
minor extent. In Germany the situation was very different. The country
was, when the Nazis took over, not only industrialized but a leading industrial country, or perhaps even the leading industrial country in the
world. Enterprises such as Krupp, Mercedes, IG Farben, Siemens, Porsche,
and so forth, are well-known. China finally, was practically nothing but an
agricultural country. It is interesting to compare with the Soviet Union. In
1950 China's population was four times larger than that of the Soviet
Union in 1920, but its national product per capita only half as big.[394] The
conditions of departure were thus very different in the three countries. In
the Soviet Union there was a certain, even if minor, industry to start from
when the large industrialization was launched; in Germany an already
existing and very advanced industry could be utilized from the very beginning; and in China, finally, a completely new industry had to be created
from scratch. Because of these differences I will start with the Soviet
Union and China, and then take Germany after that.

---

[392] Judt, pp. 118, 130, 166-7.
[393] Judt, pp. 576-84.
[394] Fairbank & Goldman, pp. 359, 369.

In both the Soviet Union and China targets for the production of various goods were specified in Five-Year Plans. The first Soviet plan was issued in 1928 and the main purpose was to industrialize the country. The first Chinese plan appeared in 1953 and the objective was not only industrialization but also a far-reaching restructuring of agriculture.[395] In both countries private enterprises were, for all practical purposes, forbidden and in both countries agriculture was almost entirely nationalized.[396] From this also followed, with respect to foreign trade, that both countries continued the old tradition of state-trading. The states, the dictatorships, traded themselves since no private actors were allowed. But the really interesting thing, of course, is the development of the national economy.

An important question is about the use of prices and money in these economies. With the possible exception of China soon after the establishment of the communist dictatorship—a China which at that time was quite similar to the storage redistribution economies of older times[397]—prices and money were extensively used.[398] Superficially things thus looked much the same as in contemporary democratic countries—but why were there prices and money at all, what were their functions?

Obviously the prices did not have the same function as in free market economies, they were not the result of supply and demand, and they did not steer production and consumption. Had something like that been the case it would immediately have collided with the plans. And clearly nor was it a sophisticated system à la Lange—that is a system like the one described in the section "The idea about a demand steered unmixed state economy" in the preceding chapter.[399] Lange's ideas never became anything more than an intellectual exercise, even if they left some impressions in Tito's Yugoslavia (more about that in chapter 11) and in Hungary[400]. But, in that case, what were the prices and the money for?

Part of the answer is that prices and money facilitated the distribution of the production as described in the section "Dictatorship and planned economy" in the preceding chapter. Furthermore the prices were used

---

[395] Friedrich & Brzezinski, p. 219.
[396] Nove, p. 29.
[397] Fairbank & Goldman, p. 348.
[398] Fairbank & Goldman, p. 354.
[399] Nove, pp. 288-303.
[400] Judt, p. 428.

to make the fulfillment of the plans easier. In the Soviet Union there were for instance separate price systems for exchanges between manufacturing enterprises, for common consumption goods, and for agriculture. Within these areas the prices were determined independently of costs, or of supply and demand, in such a way as to facilitate goal realization. And whatever may be said about this, it was probably better than if no prices at all had been used. An interesting example of the use of prices and money for steering—namely the Soviet taxing system—will be described in the next section.

Prices were thus important for steering in certain contexts, but they could never become more than that. Since we are dealing with planned economies the goals for the production to a large extent had to be specified in physical terms, and so it was. This was however not without problems. If, using an often quoted example, a nail producing industry had a goal given in tons, it was much easier to meet this by producing a small number of very big nails than a large number of small nails.[401]

But possibly this example may seem to crude—does the dictatorship really have to behave that casually when determining its production goals? Would it not be possible to specify the size of the nails as well? Well, yes, but the problem is still there. One problem is that, for every added specification, the number of goods increases as well as their number of properties, and therefore the planning bureaucracy also becomes more unwieldy. Another problem is that the specifications must be very precise and go very far if all possibilities for unwanted manufacturing evasions are to be eliminated. Basically, therefore, there are no other reliable incentives than those of a market economy—the ones consisting in entrepreneurs wanting to make profits by satisfying the customers. But this is exactly what cannot be fully accepted by a dictatorship.

But even if the planning systems in the Soviet Union and in China thus were similar, they also had some interesting, special traits. One such is the deviation from total state planning in the Soviet Union which consisted in the small, private plots at the large state kolkhozes for collective farming. The owners were allowed to handle these plots as they wished, and the productivity was drastically higher than in the rest of the agriculture.[402] Another peculiarity is the use in China of large, country-wide

[401] Nove, pp. 94-5.

campaigns for inciting the masses to something, for instance to harder working. The most outstanding example is "The Great Leap Forward" 1950–60. This campaign included, as typical for China at that time, small-scale production entities—for instance small back-yard iron smelters. The result was however no success, but rather a most horrible catastrophe. Not only were the farmers forced to use inefficient production methods, in at least one of the years the agriculture also suffered from unsuitable weather. When the tax functionaries had taken their part of the production there remained, for the farmers and their families, often much less than needed for survival. It has been estimated that something between 20 and 30 million people died from starvation.[403] This may be compared to the more than 6 million people who lost their lives in "The Holocaust", about which more follows later on.

The economies of the two countries were thus noticeably inefficient. The breakdown of the Soviet Union was to a large extent the result of its badly functioning economy. The failure of the Chinese economic methods was indicated by the "Great Leap Forward" example above. More emphatically, and more generally, the failure has been demonstrated by the market economy reforms of later years, reforms initiated by Deng Xiaoping. The result, as we know, is a virtual economic explosion.

And so the economy of Nazi Germany remains. Here there are both similarities and differences in relation to the Soviet Union and China. A similarity is that the German dictatorship, in the same way as the Soviet and Chinese ones, introduced planning. Thus a German Four Year Plan, with the motto "guns rather than butter", was promulgated in 1936. The intention was to eradicate unemployment and to prepare for war. But the plan differed from the communist ones in one important respect, and at least superficially, since private enterprises were allowed to continue their activities. But even if the companies with their names, and their earlier officers, remained, party functionaries with considerable authority were nevertheless installed in strategically important company leaderships. Under the surface the German system therefore, in spite of everything, was more similar to the communist systems than one at first, per-

---

[402] Friedrich & Brzezinski, p. 267; Judt, p. 423.
[403] Fairbank & Goldman, pp. 368-82; Morton & Lewis, pp. 212-3. In a later source the estimation of the number of people starved to death has increased to 36 million. Book review in The Economist, October 27th, 2012, p. 71.

haps, would have guessed.[404] To this it should be added that the German industry already from the start had a composition making it suitable for the intended production and thus easily adapted to the new requirements.[405] Leading German industries competed, for instance, for the orders for the gas chambers of the concentration camps.[406] About the effectiveness it is difficult to have an opinion. The dictatorial economy was in function for a very short time and to a large extent engaged in production of weapons and other war materials. Perhaps it was, during its short time, effective in doing just this. But if so that is a very particular measure of efficiency.

TAXATION

In the preceding section I discussed the total economy of the dictatorships, the total result of their productive efforts. But since the dictator, according to our main hypothesis, wants, for his own disposal, as much as possible of this result or at least a very large part of it, there have to be instruments for that. And this leads to taxation. In most dictatorships it has been harsh even though the forms have varied.

Starting with the early, moneyless storage-redistribution economies—among those are for instance all the first river states—the taxes, obviously, were in kind, for instance goods of various sorts. The methods for paying these taxes may however have varied, and perhaps they were not paid at all. Many of the subjects could have been slaves, or at least have been forced to perform specified productive tasks occasionally, and if so it was the dictator, or his underlings, who gave the orders and therefore also, primarily, got hold of the results of the work. Thereafter these functionaries could supply the subjects with what was necessary for their subsistence. Systems of this general character were common for a long time.[407] Even slavery was common, and not only in dictatorships, but also in those few states of other kinds that existed. The first more complicated societies, which were not based on slavery, were in fact those of Medieval Europe.[408] But even if the importance of forced labor gradually, and

---

[404] Friedrich & Brzezinski, pp. 21-2, 240-4, 272.
[405] Lee, p. 217.
[406] Lee, p. 232.
[407] For a detailed description of the conditions in Egypt's New Kingdom see Wilkinson, pp. 364-8.

generally speaking, has diminished, dictatorships have continued utilizing it. The labor camps in Nazi Germany and in the Soviet Union are clear-cut examples, and the method is also in use in the present dictatorship of North Korea.[409]

In the beginning there were thus only taxes in kind, forced labor and slavery, but later on important innovations were introduced. In chapter 5 I described how the dictator Croesus introduced money thereby hoping, in all likelihood, to be able to simplify and increase the taxing at the same time. Another example of the same thing, that is of the value of money for the one taxing, is given by the development in Europe following the decline of feudalism. An important prerequisite for feudalism was, as we saw in the section "Western Europe after the fall of the Western Roman Empire" in chapter 2, the lack of money. But when money gradually came back not only did feudalism disappear, the rulers also discovered that the taxing could be made harsher and more spread out and penetrating. And the result of the taxation, the taxes collected, could also be used more flexibly. Instead of being dependent on a number of knights, contracted by means of barter deals, the rulers could freely buy mercenaries on the market. If there is a difference between the antique rulers and their medieval counterparts it is that the former, themselves, initiated the introduction of money while the latter, rather, got it as a gift. Anyway money, even in dictatorships, for long times has been a good servant for extensive and efficient taxation. Samuel Finer writes that "Wherever and whenever possible, governments have preferred to take the taxes in cash."[410] This, on the whole, seems correct, but as we soon will see, Stalin's Soviet Union was an exception.

Before that however, and since I have just taken up medieval Europe, it should also be mentioned that dictators could acquire monetary incomes by other means than taxation. The selling of various kinds of privileges, for instance charters to cities making them independent in important respects, monopoly rights to guilds, and so forth, thus gave rise to substantial incomes for dictators at this time. Not exactly taxing, but important incomes for the dictator nevertheless. And the technique with

---

[408] Palmer, Colton & Kramer (2007a), p. 29.
[409] Friedrich & Brzezinski, pp. 197-201; North Korea's gulag—Never again?, The Economist, April 21st, 2012.
[410] Finer (1997a), p. 81.

state monopolies has also been used in totally other places, and at other times, than in medieval Europe. The Chinese states claimed, for instance, monopoly rights for the production of iron and salt. And these monopolies were enforced by prohibiting ordinary people from producing the goods mentioned. Producing salt by evaporating water in one's own pan was thus, for instance, criminal in Han.[411]

And so we may turn to the Soviet Union, and thereby also advance far forwards in time. By means of an interesting innovation the dictator, Stalin, succeeded in obtaining a, perhaps, unprecedented level of taxation. For understanding how ingenious this system was it may be fitting, just for comparison, to start with an ordinary progressive taxation system of the kind existing, or having existed, in a number of modern, western democracies. In such a system people, as we know, have to use proportionally more of their incomes for taxes the higher the incomes are, and therefore the income differences after the taxing become smaller than those before. Irrespective of all possible advantages of such a system it results easily in reduced incentives for work. If someone, after having worked a full day, wants to earn a bit more, and therefore thinks about carrying out some available extra work, that is perhaps not all that tempting if that extra work is taxed more than the ordinary work.

But Stalin had a solution to this problem which roughly looked like this. By means of competitions and the like—among others the system with so called working heroes or "Stakhanovites"—the state could form an idea about the maximum amount of work obtainable from every individual.[412] Then the individual worker did not receive any payment at all until having—almost—reached the limit of his or her capacity. After that, however, the worker got everything paid in money. In that way an equality after taxing, similar to the one in a progressive system, was achieved, but with amplified incentives for work rather than diminished incentives. And neither was the tax basis reduced as in a progressive system. So the resulting tax level became extraordinarily high.[413]

---

[411] Finer (1997a), p. 514.
[412] Friedrich & Brzezinski, p. 251; Lee, p. 81; Palmer, Colton & Kramer (2007b), pp. 755-6.
[413] The main source for the description of Stalin's taxation system is Olson (2000), pp. 115-29.

Taxing in dictatorships has thus always, or at least almost always, been harsh, even if the degree of harshness as well as the methods of taxation have varied. And this is important for the classification of dictatorships. In the theory chapter I introduced, it will be recalled, a distinction between repressive and non-repressive dictatorships, and the nature of the taxation is, of course, of great importance for the labeling in this respect. An example of a non-repressive dictatorship is the early Roman Empire in which the taxation was moderate or even mild. But this was so only during a short time. In due time taxation was to increase, and finally even to become unsupportable.[414] The Empire thereby turned from having been non-repressive to repressive. Most dictatorships have however, as it seems, been repressive from the very beginning. An extreme example is the Mughal Empire. There the taxation level was not only extraordinarily high—the punishments for tax evasion were also utterly brutal. Enforced selling of wives, children and cattle, as well as torture and other corporal punishments were included in the arsenal.[415] Perhaps it is fitting to conclude this section by quoting Jean-Baptiste Colbert (1619–83), the minister of finance of Louis XIV, one of the dictators of world history most devoted to luxury, lavishness and grandeur. The art of taxation, argued Colbert, consisted in "so plucking the goose as to obtain the largest amount of feathers with the least possible amount of hissing."

THE ADMINISTRATION OF DICTATORSHIPS

INTRODUCTION

A dictatorship is a large and complicated apparatus. The territory is often large. In older times when claims and conquests were important sources of income it was furthermore often expanding. And within the territory taxes should be collected, order should be upheld, and so on. Obviously the dictator himself could not carry out all of these tasks. He had to dispose of an administration of some kind, and such there have always been. There must be functionaries able to implement the wishes and orders of the dictator, not only in the capital but also in other places of the dictatorship. The creation of an administration for these purposes is however not easy—the problems involved are substantial. The administration, from

---

[414] Finer (1997a), p. 594.
[415] Eraly, pp. 263, 277; Finer (1997c), p. 1259.

the point of view of the dictator, is there to solve his problems but it consists, necessarily, of human beings with their own goals and ambitions. In a dictatorship those ambitions may become not only strong but also dangerous for the dictator. The functionaries in the administration may use their positions to challenge or threaten the dictator. So even if the administration is the dictator's instrument it is nevertheless also a potential threat and we must deal with both these aspects here. And thereby we also begin approaching a theme which will be further developed in later sections, namely the threats, coming from within the dictatorship, directed against the dictator himself. Here in this section, I will however concentrate on the first aspect, the one about the administration's main function. And for that purpose it is expedient to make a distinction between top-down administrations and feudal ones.

TOP-DOWN ADMINISTRATIONS

Top-down administrations are of the same kind as the hierarchies described in the theory chapter. The dictator steers from the top and under him there are functionaries in successively smaller and smaller regions. A division into regions like this is probably always present, but in addition to that there may also be divisions into subject areas. But irrespective of this the steering, as noted in the theory chapter, is never without problems.

A first problem is that orders going downwards and information going upwards may be, not only misunderstood, but also consciously distorted by functionaries with their own interests. It seems, in fact, most likely that the functionaries in a dictatorship may have interests of their own which are not only stronger, but also more in conflict with those of the top, than the functionaries in, for instance, an ordinary administration in a representative democracy. An extreme example of information adjustment comes from China during "the Great Leap Forward". At the time of the already mentioned crop-failure harvests more than double the size of the real ones were reported upwards.[416] Independently of the motives in this particular case dictators, in many times and in many places, have searched for ways of avoiding problems like these. One problem is that functionaries have been able to build power positions of their own and to

---

[416] Fairbank & Goldman, p. 372.

hinder this some dictators have used rotation systems—the functionaries were moved around at fairly frequent intervals. This method was used by, for instance, Rome's first Emperor Augustus, in Chinese Tang and in the Mughal Empire.[417] As an interesting contrast it may be mentioned that the top positions in the extensive administrations of the Egyptian Kingdoms were inherited, and the same was true for the Aztecs' state and for the Inca Empire.[418] I have however not succeeded in finding any information about the consequences of these arrangements.

Another problem which I also described in the theory chapter, and which in fact is a consequence of the first one, is that top-down administrations work worse the larger they are so that, finally, they do not work at all. This problem is particularly pertinent for dictatorships. During the long period when claims and conquests were important sources of income the territories of the dictatorships, as we have seen, often expanded. And that expansion necessarily led to larger and larger administrations more and more difficult to control. In the end such an administration, as was explained in the theory chapter, could become totally uncontrollable.

The magnitude of these problems does however not only depend on strength of the functionaries' own ambitions and the size of the dictatorship. Of great importance, as well, are the ambitions of the dictator himself. How much does he want to control? How much does he want to interfere with the lives of his subjects? How harshly will he tax? The further he wants to go in these respects, the more difficult the administrative problems are likely to become. To discuss these problems it may therefore be in order to make a distinction between *hard* and *soft* top-steering.

The dictator aiming for hard top-down direction may try to handle his administrative problems by making the administration "denser", that is by making the regions, if we are talking about a regional administration, smaller and more numerous, by engaging more bureaucrats, and by giving them more extensive, and more precisely formulated tasks. But even if such measures could facilitate the carrying out of a repressive po-

---

[417] Chrissanthos, p. 169; Eraly, pp. 82, 245; Finer (1997b), p. 766, Finer (1997c), p. 1258; Gascoigne (1971), p. 96.
[418] Conrad, p. 353; Mieroop, pp. 107, 177; Nicholson, p. 345; Wilkinson, p. 372. Still it has been argued that a rotation system also was used in the Egyptian Kingdoms—see Finer (1997a), p. 161.

licy, the drawbacks are also obvious. Thus the communication problems I have talked about—and which originated from misunderstandings and conscious distortions—easily become greater when the number of functionaries increases. Still there are indications that the method described has been used. Thus repressive China[419], during long periods, had a very large bureaucracy while that of the initially mild Roman Empire was much smaller. In relation to the population Chinese Han had four times as many administrative functionaries as the Roman Empire at the same time.[420] The Kingdom of Charlemagne, in which the top-down control certainly not was hard, had almost no administration at all.[421]

But even if there thus are examples of soft top-down control they nevertheless seem to be exceptions. Most dictatorships have been top-down controlled in the hard way and have also aimed at that. I have already mentioned the obvious example of China during long periods, and there are many more. The Akkadian and Assyrian Empires were of that kind from the very beginning, and continued like that as long as they existed.[422] The Inca Empire and the Mughal Empire also belong to this category. The two later states are also interesting with respect to another important, administrative similarity. In the Inca state the down-going chains of command ended with commanders over small groups of individual families, and in the Mughal state with commanders over the individual villages.[423] All the states mentioned were thus top-steered in the hard way, and many more, all the way to modern times, could be mentioned. The big dictatorships of the twentieth century—Germany, the Soviet Union and China—were, of course, extreme in this respect.

In these later states the top-down steering was furthermore elaborated in an interesting way. They were, as we know, one-party-states and the party, the only one permitted, was of utmost importance in various contexts. Of particular interest here is the relation between this party and

---

[419] Finer (1997b), pp. 756-7.
[420] Finer (1997a), p. 65.
[421] Finer (1997a), p. 13; Finer (1997b), p. 856.
[422] Jacobsen (1980b), p. 88; Roux, pp. 305-6. It has however also been argued that the top steering of the Assyrian Empire did not reach the state's peripheral areas—see Mieroop, p. 293.
[423] Conrad, p. 352-3; Eraly, pp. 231-2, 273; Finer (1997c), pp. 1242, 1245-6.

the common administration, and in connection with that also the organization of the party in relevant aspects.

Starting with party organization the parties were hierarchically organized just like top-down administrations in general. Hitherto, when describing such hierarchies, as in the theory chapter, I have only talked about vertical communication, whether orders downwards or information upwards. But obviously the functionaries in such an organization also can communicate with each other horizontally—for instance within the same section, or between different sections at the same level—and certainly such communication often also takes place. In a hierarchical party organization horizontal communication like that may however be purposely impeded, or perhaps even forbidden. If so an important reason could be the leadership's wish to strengthen its control of the organization, but the aim to make the organization secret by concealing it from the surrounding environment may also be crucial. For both of these reasons it may in fact be imperative to hinder horizontal communication, in particular at the organization's lower levels. At the communist parties' lowest level there were thus cells with just a few members who knew each other well, but who's contacts with members of other cells were limited or non-existent.[424] The success was however not always complete. In Nazi Germany Gestapo (see below) did for instance manage to identify and eradicate a great number of the cells of the forbidden and hostile communist party. [425] When talking about cells it is, by the way, also interesting to notice similarities with the previously mentioned families and villages at the lowest levels of the Inca and Mughal Empires respectively.

Going then to the relation between the common administration and the party hierarchy it should be noted that these, often, were very close to each other or even grown together. In the Soviet Union all high functionaries were also party members and this group, or class, of persons, often called the "Nomenklatura", enjoyed special, far-reaching favors.[426] Their residences and country houses—so called "Dachas"—were often grandiose and luxuriously arranged and furnished. At the higher levels of

---

[424] Bealey, title-words "Cell" and "Democratic centralism"; Friedrich & Brzezinski, p. 349; Palmer, Colton & Kramer (2007b), p. 744.
[425] Lee, p. 221.
[426] Bealey, title-word "nomenklatura"; Bogdanor, title-word "nomenklatura"; Friedrich & Brzezinski, pp. 51-2, 207-8; Nove, p. 22.

the hierarchy it was however also more difficult than at lower levels to restrict horizontal communication. The members of the nomenklatura could easily come to know each other in a way which was dangerous for the dictator—or which, at least, he easily could consider as dangerous. As we will see later on in this chapter that, in turn, could entail extensive purges. Finally it should be mentioned that even in the modern military dictatorships different hierarchies could interpenetrate each other, so that, in particular, the military hierarchies merge into the civilian ones.

FEUDAL ADMINISTRATIONS

A top-down administration is thus afflicted with considerable, difficult problems. The other main type of administration, the feudal, lacks some of the problems of the top-steered type but has, on the other side, some weaknesses of its own. Basic in this model, which may be described schematically as in figure 6, is the separation of central and regional power. In the regions of the dictatorship there are local chiefs enjoying considerable freedom. A common arrangement is that they are allowed to do whatever they want with their regions and subjects as long as they pay the taxes agreed upon to the dictator at the top. It is because of this that the lines between the dictator and the regional chiefs in the figure are broken rather than continuous—they do not represent orders as in the top-down model. This does not preclude, however, that the regional chiefs may top-steer their own regions, which, in that case, is represented by the continuous lines in the figure.

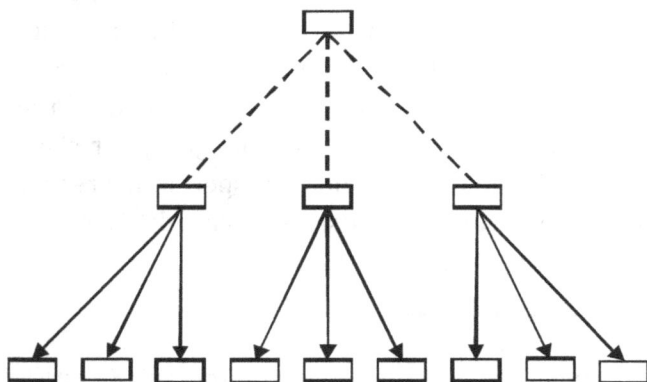

Figure 6: A feudal administration

It is easy to imagine the advantages and disadvantages with the feudal model. If the central dictator essentially is interested in the tax incomes, and believes that he will receive them, and for the rest is able to tolerate differences of various kinds, such as cultural ones, it may work well. Yet, to my knowledge, there are not many dictatorships in history which, from the beginning and consciously have considered this model the best one and therefore settled for it. Much more common is that they have been forced into it. But the Persian Empire[427] was an early dictatorship which adopted the feudal model from the beginning, and the Caliphate[428] a later one. So let us have a look at the Persians.

The first dictator there, Cyrus, purposely behaved as a liberator in the conquered new areas (see chapter 2). He tried to gain the loyalty of the new subjects by encouraging their own local traditions, cultures and religious beliefs rather than frightening them into obedience.[429] And this tactic also included his substituting his own regional chiefs for the former despised dictators. But the tasks given the new chiefs by Cyrus were limited. Basically they consisted in paying the taxes agreed upon.[430] This system was then continued by Cambyses and Darius, the third dictator, institutionalized the system formally by dividing the empire into a good twenty so called satrapies, that is a kind of regional states. And thereby the Empire got its feudal structure. The next dictator, Xerxes, differed however from his predecessors' policy in this respect—and not just in that one actually—and initiated a transformation towards top-down steering.[431]

The feudalism of the Persian Empire was thus voluntary, but what were the conditions in all the other more common cases when a dictator was forced into the feudal model? Which forces were then active? To understand this I think it helps to consider feudalism as a result of mutual agreements, as something which, at least implicitly, has the character of a contract. From the dictator in the top the regional chief gets more or less far-reaching rights to govern his region as he likes, and in exchange for that the dictator gets guaranteed tax incomes from the region.

---

[427] Finer (1997a), pp. 297-8.
[428] Findlay & O'Rourke, p. 17; Roberts, pp. 334-5.
[429] Roux, p. 386.
[430] Roberts, p. 162.
[431] Young, p. 151.

But what makes the two parties interested in a mutual agreement like this? Why does not the dictator himself take all the power in the regions rather than sharing it with the local chiefs? And why do not these latter break away completely to found their own states, rather than staying within the larger entity? As for the dictator the reason may be that he lacks the military resources, or the power, necessary for conquering the regions completely, but he may also have problems with top-down steering of the kinds I have already described. And the regional chief may consider it better, for defense purposes, to be a member of a larger state than to found a small one of his own—the whole group of regions within the dictatorship may in fact be functioning as a defense alliance. But at the same time as this reasoning shows wherein the mutual interests may consist it also indicates an instability inherent in the system, a delicate balance mechanism. If the conditions change it may tip in the one direction or the other—either by the dictator taking over some or all regions, or by some or all local chiefs breaking away completely. Both processes are common in the history of the world.

Perhaps I shall also, for the sake of clarity and before continuing, say that the European, medieval feudalism, which plays such an important role in this book, in particular in explaining the birth of representative democracy in chapter 9, is a special case of the feudalism I have just described. What is special is the nature of the obligation of the regional chief towards the dictator. In the European case this obligation consisted in supplying the dictator, when asked to do so, with a fully equipped knight and horse, and nothing but that. This particular kind of feudalism, which was widely spread in Europe during the Middle Age, has hardly existed in other places, possibly with the exception of the Japanese samurais who were a kind of counterpart to the European knights.[432]

The more general kind of feudalism has however existed in many places at different times in world history and for different reasons. A first reason is that it was a necessary step towards fully established top-down control. Egypt's Old Kingdom thus had clear feudal traits, and so even, to some extent, the Middle Kingdom.[433] In the New Kingdom the administration was however centralized—the development was in the direction of

---

[432] Finer (1997c), pp. 1086-93; Rosenberg & Birdzell, p. 138.
[433] Finer (1997a), p. 74; Wilkinson, pp. 61, 100, 112, 175.

top-down control.[434] In China the conditions were similar. The two first states, Shang and Zhou, were clearly feudal, while a hard top-down control was introduced in Qin.

It may however also be the case that the top in a top-down dictatorship shows signs of weakness and that, therefore, a process towards feudalism is forced through—the power balance tips in favor of the regions. Even here China provides examples. Periods of weakness within the dynasties or states—from Han to Qing—and even the more complete break-downs between the dynasties, thus had, in several cases, causes like these. Great land owners have always been important in imperial China and when they have succeeded in advancing their interests a certain amount of feudalism, more or less, has resulted.[435]

The Chinese conditions are however more interesting and more complicated than that. The landowners did not always succeed in upholding their interests even if they were relatively strong. A weak dictator sometimes could be aided by his administration. The Chinese class of bureaucrats or administrators was not only very large and well educated, but also very uniformly educated. This class, the so called mandarins, was therefore politically important. Sometimes when the dictator was weak these mandarins could—being loyal to the dictator or at least to the dictatorship—take over. If so, the state was still steered from the top, but by the mandarins rather than by the dictator.[436] A similar pattern sometimes prevailed also in ancient Egypt,[437] and in the Roman Empire. The Romans thus to a large extent used the army rather than civilian bureaucrats for their administration, and during periods with weak emperors the army could take over the role of the emperor, or even appoint a new emperor from among their own. The Roman army thus could play a role similar to the role played by the Chinese mandarins.

---

[434] Finer (1997a), pp. 188-9. The centralization was however not complete—see Mieroop, pp. 189-91.
[435] Finer (1997a), p. 453-4.
[436] Finer (1997a), pp. 526-7.
[437] Wilkinson, p. 185.

THREATS AGAINST THE DICTATORSHIP AND COUNTERMEASURES

FLIGHT, INNER EXILE AND REBELLION

So far I have concentrated on the normal, routine aspects of dictatorships. I started with the incentives of the dictator, continued with the taxation and after that came to the necessary administration. But this is not the whole picture. Dictatorships and dictators are usually threatened in various ways. Some threats are directed against the territory of the dictatorship and those threats may come from within or from the outside. They may come from hostile neighboring states wishing to attack or conquer the dictatorship, or from rebellious subjects within the dictatorship. Threats like these, and countermeasures for dealing with them, are treated in this section. Threats directed at the dictator himself will be dealt with in the next section.

The exploitation of the subjects by taxation is a basic problem. The taxation is, as we have seen, extensive in most dictatorships even if the degree of extensiveness may vary and thereby also the consequences. There are, as I have written several times, cases where the subjects, in spite of high taxes, consider themselves favored by the policies of the dictator and therefore prefer remaining within his territory to leaving it. Dictatorships like that have existed and there have even been those with low taxes. An example is the early Roman Empire with its *Pax Romana*, which was appreciated by many subjects.[438] Rebellions were rare and it was even, in the Empire, a severe punishment to be expelled from it. But this is an exception. As a rule taxation in dictatorships has, rather, been harsh or even very harsh.

But even if the exploitation of the subjects is a basic problem, there are other problems as well. During the long period we are here considering dictatorships have often, as we have seen, been expansive with the purpose of increasing their material resources by means of conquests. But irrespective of the purpose of the expansion it has often entailed problems. If it has been vast enough the state has almost necessarily become multi-cultural and multi-lingual and thus heterogeneous, and this heterogeneity has often formed a fertile ground for separatist tendencies or insurrections threatening unity. Even if there are dictatorships which have

---

[438] Finer (1997a), p. 564.

not had any severe problems like this—examples are the early Persian Empire, the early Roman Empire and the Caliphate—they are exceptions. For most dictators the heterogeneity has on the contrary, and in particular in combination with the harsh taxation, contributed to instability, especially in the peripheral parts of the dictatorships' territories.

The subjects' possibilities for fleeing out of the dictatorship—to leave it—have however always been severely restricted. In older times this was difficult for pure, technical reasons. Since the territories of the dictatorships often were large the escape routes, with some exceptions for the subjects in peripheral regions, were impassibly long. And in later times with better communication techniques the dictators have kept the subjects locked in by means of fences or other obstacles at the borders. The Soviet Empire with the Berlin Wall (1961–89) as the most known and visible part of such a fence is one example, and North Korea of our own days another one. In a similar way the Chinese communist regime, after having taken power in 1949, closed the border to Hong Kong, at that time British.[439] In spite of this the dictatorship did however allow some emigration. Visas were given to individuals who, due to age or weakness, only constituted a burden for the regime anyway.[440]

Flight has thus often been difficult or impossible and the alternatives remaining therefore were inner exile and rebellion. The former means that people, often agricultural workers, leave their common, ordered labor and take to the roads, possibly as brigands. Behavior like that occurred, for instance, in Egypt's New Kingdom.[441] And the behavior was replicated in the otherwise, and mainly, so stable early Roman Empire. When the farmers in Egypt—by then the granary of the Empire—about the year 170 were forced to produce more grains than they were able to they departed, in this way, from their habitual occupations.[442] More examples, from the western part of the later Empire as well as from Byzantium, could be mentioned.[443] Even in other dictatorships, and at other times, in-

[439] Friedrich & Brzezinski, p. 168.
[440] *Hong Kong: Refugee Dilemma*. Time Magazine, April 27th, 1962 (the article is available on the Internet).
[441] Wilkinson, pp. 365, 480-5.
[442] Walters (1980b), pp. 52-4.
[443] Finer (1997a), pp. 597-8; Finer (1997b), p. 659.

ner exile was used as a protest strategy. A very large inner exile movement did, for instance, contribute to the fall of Chinese Tang.[444]

Rebellion is a more severe and sharper, and perhaps also more des-
perate, reaction than inner exile, and the history of the repressive
dictatorships is full of rebellions. Sometimes, but far from always, they
have resulted in greater or smaller concessions by the dictator—and if so,
the fundamental mechanism of change described in chapter 3 was working. A rebellion in the Assyrian Empire made, for instance, and quite unusually, the dictator Sargon II take away some of the subjects' burdens.[445]
In the Chinese states large-scale peasant rebellions, usually resulting in
no concessions but rather in brutal suppression, have been almost perpe-
tually recurring.[446] In France of 1789 the storming of the Bastille on the
14 July was a typical rebellion. The background was, among others, high
taxes in combination with crop failure resulting in increased prices for
bread.[447] This rebellion however, in contrast to most other ones, was not
suppressed, but rather led to concessions—at least occasional ones (more
about this in chapter 9). Advancing further in time—to the Soviet Empire—there were several rebellions, above all the Hungarian Revolution
of 1956[448], the so called Prague Spring in Czechoslovakia in 1968[449] and
the strikes at the Polish ship yards in 1970[450].[451] All of them were suppressed even if there were, in the last case, at least some verbal concessions. In all cases part of the background was economic oppression, but
national separation efforts of the kind mentioned above were also important. Both Hungary and Czechoslovakia lay at the border of the dictatorship and therefore, possibly, hoped for help from the West, but if so in
vain. The threat of nuclear war definitely excluded any such support.[452]

But the time for rebellions has not come to an end. Since the end of
2010 a revolutionary wave of protests has gone through North Africa and
the Middle East. It all started in Tunisia in December 2010 when the

---

[444] Finer (1997b), p. 798.
[445] Roux, p. 311.
[446] Finer (1997a), pp. 14, 598.
[447] Palmer, Colton & Kramer (2007a), pp. 359-60.
[448] Judt, pp. 313-23.
[449] Judt, pp. 436-47.
[450] Judt, 585-90.
[451] Friedrich & Brzezinski, pp. 279-89.
[452] Judt, pp. 497, 501.

street vendor Mohamed Bouazizi, protesting against the harassments and humiliations he had suffered at the hands of the authorities, set himself on fire. This became the igniting spark. Large scale, intensive protests followed first in Tunisia, the so called Jasmine Revolution, and after that in, among other countries, Egypt, Bahrain Libya, Morocco, Yemen and Syria. The protesters were to a large extent recruited from the youth, a youth which, in the countries concerned, constitutes large shares of the total populations. Of crucial importance for the spreading of the protests were the new, electronic, social media. Facebook and Twitter made their high political debut. The protests were not only about—perhaps even not essentially about—material conditions. Requests for liberalization in a more general sense were also of great importance.

When writing this (late 2014) the revolutionary processes are still ongoing, and nowhere is a stable and peaceful order yet restored. Tunisia, the country where it all started, has however come a long way towards this goal. Not only is the former dictator overthrown, but a new constitution has also been adopted and two parliamentary elections have been held as well as a president election. Furthermore, the secular political actors have, peacefully, got the upper hand. In Egypt the former dictator was also overthrown and a political process similar to the one in Tunisia started but evolved in a different way. A new constitution and popular elections led to victories for the Muslims. And after that the Muslim president Muhammad Morsi has been ousted and even jailed by the military. At least for the moment Egypt thus seems to have returned to a military dictatorship. In Bahrain the rebellion was crushed by military means. Libya got rid of its dictator but also disintegrated after that. In Morocco the king has promised a constitution. In Morocco some constitutional changes in democratic direction have been implemented, but without going the whole way. Yemen, unstable from the beginning, has fallen apart. And in Syria, finally, the regime engaged in violent and atrocious suppressions which still are going on.[453]

Inner exile and rebellion thus have been constant problems for the dictators of the world, but in addition to this there are also threats from the outside. Always—or at least almost always—there have been such

---

[453] An extensive and detailed description of the of the events up to the summer of 2013 is given in the 16-page special report "The Arab Spring—A climate of change" in The Economist, July 13th 2013.

threats. A possible exception is Egypt's Old Kingdom, and possibly also the Middle Kingdom, at least during its first phase. Since these states were protected by vast deserts they had no significant enemies. But for the rest—as illustrated in chapter 2—it has been different. External enemies have just about always been present.

But even if there have been enemies like that the dividing line between them and inner rebels has, nevertheless, in many cases been fuzzy. The sharp borderline between West and East which, together with the presence of nuclear weapons, made interventions in Hungary and Czechoslovakia impossible is a late phenomenon. Earlier in history when matters were more unclear it was quite common that outside enemies and inner rebels cooperated. Rebellious minorities, in particular in the peripheral parts of a dictatorship, could be stimulated by outside enemies who considered themselves too weak to attack without help. The Assyrian Empire, for instance, during its great power phase, suffered from indirect attacks of this kind.[454] In other cases it even happened that outside enemies, after having changed sides, made remarkable careers in the state they had formerly attacked. Thus a number of individuals from German tribes were promoted to very high positions in the late Roman Empire.[455] In China (as we saw in chapter 2) it even happened that earlier enemies, during two long periods, took over the ruling of the whole empire, namely first the Mongols and then the Manchu people. To succeed in this they had however to adopt the Chinese way of ruling.[456] The basic features of the Chinese dictatorship were not changed by these visiting rulers.

Thus, the distinction between inner and outer threats has not always been all that clear. The one may imperceptibly transform into the other, in particular in the dictatorship's peripheral parts. But whatever it is, the consequence for the dictator is that he must protect the territory he considers his. The following sections deal with this subject. The first one is about the physical means for controlling the territory.

---

[454] Roux, p. 311.
[455] Liebeschuetz. p. 257.
[456] Finer (1997a), p. 9.

COMMUNICATION ROUTES, INTELLIGENCE SYSTEMS AND POLICE

I have already mentioned that the Nile was an important communication route which the Egyptian pharaohs could use for quickly moving police or military units to rebel areas. And this capacity was further improved by a system of signal fires, beacons, which could be used for summoning troops when needed.[457] In the late Assyrian Empire not only a widespread road network was built—an extensive, internal communication system including, in addition to beacons, written messages carried by human couriers was also developed.[458] In the Persian Empire this system was further elaborated. Among others metal mirrors were used for signaling.[459] Going then to the early Roman Empire the Mediterranean, constituting at that time a Roman inland sea, made sea transport to many parts of the dictatorship's vast territory possible. In addition there was built, in the European parts of the territory, a dense, extended road network of a quality easily surpassing anything having previously existed. Defense and control were the main reasons for creating this network.[460] Legions, that is entities consisting essentially of infantry soldiers, were placed not only along the borders but also in the interior of the territory, and could easily be moved to places where they were needed. The great canals in China described in chapter 2 obviously had several purposes, but one of them was facilitating transports of the troupes necessary for the control of the country.[461] And the Inca Empire also had an impressive road network. Along the length of the country there were two main roads, the one close to the coast and the other one higher up in the Andes, and these two roads were connected by a number of transversal roads. Only military troops and the very important human couriers were allowed to use the roads—there were no horses. The messages of the couriers were not written—there was no written language—but rather formulated by means of an ingenious system with knots on colored cords. On a main cord a number of side cords were attached, and on these side cords knots were knitted according to specified rules.[462] And, for taking a final ex-

[457] Wilkinson, p. 177.
[458] Roux, pp. 306, 348.
[459] Wiesehöfer, pp. 76-7.
[460] Lane Fox, p. 524.
[461] Morris, p. 337.
[462] Conrad, pp. 353-4.

ample, the Mughal Empire had, in spite of the generally underdeveloped infrastructure mentioned above, an utterly well developed intelligence system, including among others homing pigeons.[463]

Particularly interesting from the point of view of control are the defense walls built around cities for long periods. Even if these walls were built to meet urgent needs, they could also turn into being problems of themselves. An example is the Akkadian Empire in Mesopotamia. According to some interesting information the first dictator there, Sargon, had the walls encircling the cities within his rapidly expanding state destroyed.[464] When these cities had been independent city-states they had needed the walls for their protection but in Sargon's larger empire they could serve separatism and were therefore not wanted. In the same way, and for the same reason, the creator of China and its first dictator, Shi Huangdi, destroyed some of the walls at that time protecting many Chinese cities.[465]

But even for dictators ruling over vast territories the walls could, now and then, be an asset, and China, again, provides examples. Within the walls the cities were planned in a way facilitating the control of the subjects. The streets or roads were straight, and perpendicular to each other, so that all buildings became rectangular. The guards patrolling the streets thus got a perfect view through the area. Furthermore curfew was upheld during the nights, between exactly specified hours, and all doors were locked and opened from the outside, by the guards having the keys. This, as it seems, was an effective system of control at the dictator's disposal.[466] And similar systems were used in other cities in other dictatorships, for instance in ancient Harappa and Mohenjo-Daro in the Indus valley[467] (mentioned in chapter 2), in Egypt's Middle Kingdom[468], in the Mughal Empire[469] and in the Japanese Tokugawa Shogunate[470].

But even if the control systems were well developed in many early dictatorships they were, nevertheless, more extensive, more penetrating

---

[463] Eraly, pp. 229-30; Finer (1997c), pp. 1242-3, 1252; Gascoigne (1971), p. 94.
[464] Jacobsen (1980b), pp. 85, 88; Leick, p. 120.
[465] Fairbank & Goldman, p. 56.
[466] Gascoigne (2003), p. 79.
[467] Cotterell (1980a), p. 178; Roberts, p. 121-2.
[468] Mieroop, p. 105.
[469] Eraly, p. 234; Finer (1997c), pp. 1224, 1244-5.
[470] Finer (1997c), pp. 1107-9, 1244-5.

and more brutal, in later dictatorships, and then in particular in the big dictatorships of the twentieth century. In Germany the paramilitary organization SA (Sturmabteilung), or the "brown-shirts", were important in particular during the Nazis' rise to power. They acted, at least formally, as a kind of order keeping police at the Nazis' propaganda meetings, but also, in reality, worked up the agitation by provoking quarrels with adversaries, especially social democrats and communists. But SA could also be used for directly upsetting the prevailing order. The organization was thus fully active at Hitler's failed *coup d'état* in Munich in 1923, the so called "beer hall putsch." When Hitler had reached power in 1934 the organization, having essentially finished its role, was substituted for by the SS (Schutzstaffel). In the beginning this was a body guard for Hitler, but soon, led by Heinrich Himmler, it grew into a large police organization with obvious military characteristics. Thus the SS came, in due time, to administer the very extensive concentration camp activities. But the organization was not only engaged in what might be called the inner order, it also actively took part in fighting at war fronts—then in the form of the special entity Waffen-SS. The activities of the SS, and of the SA before that, were outwardly manifest and easily recognized—their personnel wore easily identified uniforms. Beside the SS, and in due time merged into the SS, there was however also a secret police, namely the Gestapo (Geheime Staats-polizei), led by Reinhard Heydrich. This police was eventually to acquire very substantial entitlements. It could thus, without being observed from the outside, and without being scrutinized by any higher authority, on its own investigate, and sentence, in cases of treason, espionage and sabotage directed against Germany or the Nazi party. In particular the organization could completely on its own, and without any further investigation, arrest anyone, whosoever, placing him or her in so called protective custody (Schutzhaft). In this way thousands of people disappeared to the concentration camps.

In the Soviet Union there was created at a very early stage an organization which could be called a political police—a police which above all should suppress threatening ideas and opinions, more or less deviating from those of the leaders, that is, especially, Lenin's. This police, created as early as in 1917, was in fact the first of all institutions which were to be established by the regime—the Red Army was not founded until 1918.[471]

Under various labels this police was then to remain in continuous existence until the fall of the Soviet Union. At first, using the pronunciation of its abbreviation, it was called "Cheka". In a later period it was called KGB (an abbreviation for Committee for State Security in Russian). During the reign of Joseph Stalin this police executed hugely extensive purges and, powerful as it was, was also purged itself. More about this follows in the section "Threats against the dictator" below.

LEGAL SYSTEMS

Even if dictatorships usually lack rules for the ruler himself there may be other kinds of rules. I have for instance already dealt with rules for transfers of power. In many dictatorships there have also been various kinds of ceremonials and rituals, for instance related to the dictator's public appearances, which have been strictly adhered to. This section is however not about these mattes, but about the legal systems of various kinds directly affecting the subjects. The reason for my talking about *legal systems* rather than about *judicial systems* is that the distinction is important, especially when dealing with dictatorships. The term judicial system easily leads to thoughts about justice in a modern, civilized sense, and the occurrence of that kind of justice in dictatorships is rare. Their laws are often of a very different kind, or perhaps even non-existent.

From the point of view of the dictator it is easy to understand the existence of laws as well as their absence. That some dictators considered it in perfect order to punish behavior they did not approve of, without the support of any rules at all, is hardly strange—perhaps it was also quite a natural step of development since the creation of laws reasonably could take some time. But neither are the efforts of the Babylonian dictator Hammurabi difficult to understand. He was, as mentioned in chapter 2, a pioneering law-maker, and it seems quite clear that laws can contribute to order. It may, from the dictator's point of view, be much better if the subjects are well aware of what is, and what is not, permitted, than if they, in these respects, are badly informed. That many dictators after Hammurabi have introduced legal systems specifying punishments for unwanted acts is, therefore, not surprising.[472]

---

[471] Palmer, Colton & Kramer (2007b), p. 738.
[472] An early example is the Egyptian pharaoh Horemheb in the New Kingdom.

To get some perspective on the legal systems of dictatorships it may be suitable to start with an extreme case, namely the system in the Chinese states. This system is, at first, old—the essential parts were in place already during Qin and Han, and even if some important revisions were made later on, especially during Tang, the basic principles nevertheless remained the same at least until the fall of the Empire in the beginning of the twentieth century. The crimes punished most severely were activities directed against the state such as treason and rebellion. Other crimes were related to family life. Failing to observe the required period of mourning after the death of a family member was for instance criminal. The punishments for different crimes included branding of the forehead, cutting off of the nose, cutting off of the feet, castration and death. The last of those, the execution, could be effectuated by throwing the victim into boiling water.[473]

Important in this system was also the principle of collective responsibility. All members of smaller groups—especially families—were considered responsible for all actions of all other members.[474] And not only that. Informing was required, and the one failing to inform was severely punished. Furthermore there was no equality before the law. Society's upper levels, for instance great land owners, were more or less unaffected by the system described. Still another ingredient was related to the principle of proven guilt. This principle was upheld in the sense that proof was considered necessary for condemnation, but it was also the case that confession was considered proof, and that confession could be obtained by means of torture. Trials often, in fact, seem to have started by brutally assaulting the one suspected.

If anything positive should be said about this whole system it is that the rules were very exact, and also rigorously followed. It is, as we know, often emphasized that a good legal system should make anticipation possible, which means that those affected should be able, in advance, to foresee the legal effects of their actions, if any. The Chinese legal system has been credited with this kind of predictability. And another possibly positive aspect, the right to appeal a conviction, was institutionalized.

Wilkinson, pp. 313-4.
[473] Finer (1997a), pp. 516-8; Finer (1997b), pp. 776-81; Finer (1997c), pp. 1154-5; Gascoigne (2003), pp. 52-3, 66-7.
[474] Finer (1997a), p. 480.

Furthermore death sentences could not be pronounced in lower instances—at least not from Tang and afterwards—and also needed to be re-
affirmed several times. But in the end, and bearing in mind that confessions always could be achieved through cruel torture, one must still wonder about the value of these positive aspects.

The Chinese legal system has thus for a very long period been utterly repressive. Taking into account that we are here dealing with an
extreme dictatorship this should not be surprising. But even other dictatorships have had similar systems. In the Persian Empire—which was, as
we have seen, less centralized and repressive in other respects—the punishments for actions not allowed could be utterly cruel. The arsenal included measures such as impalement, crucifying and the cutting off of
nose, ears and tongue.[475] And the principle of collective responsibility was
upheld in for instance Egypt's New Kingdom, the Japanese Tokugawa Shogunate and the Mughal Empire.[476] Even in Soviet law a stipulation about
collective responsibility for some crimes was introduced in 1934.[477]

A very special kind of law, present only in dictatorships, is the Muslim so called Sharia law. The origin is the maxims in the Quran and other
early sources about a good and righteous life. This origin thus is a kind of
correspondence to Christianity's Ten Commandments. And in the same
way as in the Christian case the area of application is quite limited, essentially it is about family life. In the Muslim case the religious maxims have
however also become law. What is sinful is also criminal. But within this
general framework there are variations. There are various interpreta-
tions of the grounds for conviction, and there are also different ideas
about what to do in all of those areas where the grounds are not applicable. That this later problem has become increasingly difficult as time
has passed and social life has become more complex is hardly surprising.[478]

That dictatorships have had legal systems of the kinds so far described is not strange—after all they are dictatorships. But there have
also been dictatorships with quite different legal systems. One such system, the so called Roman law, was developed in the Roman Empire, and
another one in the France of Napoleon Bonaparte. These legal systems

---

[475] Kriwaczek, p. 111; Lane Fox, p. 101.
[476] Finer (1997c), pp. 1117, 1253; Wilkinson, p. 366.
[477] Friedrich & Brzezinski, p. 180.
[478] Savory

were not only developed in dictatorships, they were also, each of them in relation to the general ideas in their own times, to a large extent civilized and predecessors to the modern state of justice. The systems did not only include—using common juridical terminology—criminal law but also a considerable and important civil law, in France called Code Civil. And this is interesting. In which way could this be valuable for the dictator?

If we start by looking at the Roman system it is at first important to recognize that it had—beside the "civilized" parts—also "Chinese" parts. There was thus no equality before the law—the higher social strata were clearly privileged. Ordinary subjects, on the contrary, and after summary trials including torture for achieving the confessions needed, could be sentenced to being burned alive, to crucifying or to be given as prey to wild animals, often exposed to large masses of spectators. But within a legal system with parts like these there was thus also developed a civil law which was not only advanced, but which also was destined to serve as an ideal for much of the civil law development in large parts of the world later on—above all in the democracies which were to emerge more than a thousand years later. And this is not easy to explain. How could the dictators—and this question applies not only to the Romans but also to Napoleon—be interested in a civil law like this?

I can imagine two hypothetical answers to this question, answers which do not necessarily exclude each other. The one is that it may be an irritating problem—even for a dictator—if there are unsolved conflicts between subjects out there in society. This may lead to quarrels, and if there are many conflicts, or if the parties are strong, for instance great landowners, this may become threatening. And therefore the dictator could have an interest in participating in the solving of the conflicts, which could be done by means of civil law. The other answer is already hinted at in this first answer. It could also have been the case that the criminal law, essentially, was intended for the large masses, the real subjects—in the Roman Empire called *humiliores*—whereas the civil law was intended for the upper class, for instance big landowners—*honestiores*. In this way the two answers may complement each other. The conditions in the Roman Empire seem quite compatible with this idea. [479]

---

[479] Finer (1997a), pp. 79-80; Liebeschuetz, p. 257; Matthews, pp. 404-5. A late ancient Egyptian state also had a double system of this kind—see Wilkinson, pp. 476-7.

The legal systems in the modern dictatorships are, at least at a first glance, somewhat different. Germany, as we know, was in contrast to Russia and China a modern, developed country when converted to dictatorship. At this time Germany therefore had an extensive, Western legal system, and important parts of this system was preserved during the Nazi time, and thereafter.[480] But even if this is true in a formal sense the reality was different, at least for activities which had, or could be claimed to have, some kind of political significance.[481] Hitler made this perfectly clear in 1938 when, after an acquitting verdict, he declared that "this is the last time a German court is going to declare someone innocent whom I have declared guilty."[482] Rule of law was thus overthrown in the modern dictatorships, but in spite of this the values of the modern state of justice were used for camouflaging purges. They were presented as results of justice done.[483] As we will see in a later section—"Threats against the dictator"—show trials were common in both the Soviet Union and communist China.

CONTROL AND DIRECTION OF PUBLIC OPINION

It is, of course, of greatest interest for a dictator to keep himself informed about, and if possible also to steer, the subjects' opinions about his rule. Since he, according to our main hypothesis, uses the subjects for his own purposes, and in some cases may go very far in that respect, dissatisfaction may obviously arise easily. If this gets strong, and spreads in wide circles, the problems for the dictator may be considerable. The countermeasures at his disposal are of three kinds. First, he can try to keep informed about the actual state of opinions, and its changes; secondly he can try to suppress or counter opinions unfavorable for him; and thirdly, he can actively try to foster new ideas and opinions he considers beneficial. The two last kinds of countermeasures may of course overlap, and in modern times in particular it has often been so. The fostering of a new opinion may go hand in hand with the erasing of an old one, and by use of the same means. But it needs not be so. In what follows I will try to keep the two things apart when appropriate.

---

[480] Friedrich & Brzezinski, pp. 119-20.
[481] Lee, p. 205.
[482] Friedrich & Brzezinski, p. 55.
[483] Friedrich & Brzezinski, pp. 183-202.

But even if dictators at all times have had reasons for dealing with public opinions the technical conditions for the relevant activities have changed radically in well known ways. The invention and spread of the printing press—in China about the year 1000 and in Europe some 400 years later—and thereafter the modern, printed newspaper, made it possible for the subjects to form and spread ideas harmful for the dictator. This development reached a kind of culmination in 1848 when the new telegraph, railways and daily newspapers multiplied the impact of the uprisings across Europe (about which more in the section "The spread and diversification" in chapter 9). After that further steps followed with the development of radio and television, and, still more with the appearance of modern electronic devices such as mobile phones and the Internet. An interesting, current example of the importance of the new media is the suppression in China of Internet information—about the Arab revolts and about other topics considered threatening by the rulers.[484] Generally speaking the new media have affected the dictators in different directions. They have made it easier for the subjects to communicate with each other, and thereby to promote their ideas. They have however also made it easier for the dictators, and the functionaries of the dictatorship, to trace communication between the subjects, and they may also have made indoctrination of the subjects easier.

Dictators' interest in opinions is thus an old phenomenon. I start with the efforts to register what was going on in the depths of the masses. Naturally dictators have always tried to use the functionaries in their administrations for this purpose, but, as I have already mentioned, this source of information may in many cases have been quite unreliable. Other institutions may therefore have been important complements. The assemblies in medieval, feudal Europe which I have also mentioned, and which consisted at first of vassals or knights and later on perhaps of estates, may, apart from the other functions, also have served as sources of information for the dictator.[485] He met them often, they knew what was happening in the regions, and since these dictatorships probably were relatively mild the disinformation need not either have been all that seri-

---

[484] China has in fact gone very far in this direction. In a 14-page special report The Economist describes these activities in considerable detail. "China and the Internet—A giant cage", The Economist, April 6th, 2013.
[485] Roberts, p. 512.

ous. On the whole the vassals may have been cooperative. And, as we will see in the Appendix, almost all dictatorships in our present world also have quasi representative assemblies of various kinds, and one of their functions may be to provide information.

In addition to these comparatively open and regular methods for collecting information there are also other ones. In Egypt's New Kingdom there operated, at least during some periods, a well developed spy- and security organization and the same was true for Assyria.[486] The Indian Maurya Empire had a far-reaching secret police and a well developed intelligence organization. In the state's "government manual"—the Arthashastra—spies disguised as recluses, householders, merchants, ascetics, students, mendicant women and prostitutes were advocated.[487] The later Gupta Empire had a well developed internal intelligence system as well.[488] And the Byzantine dictator had at his disposal a numerous, omni-present secret police labeled—most fittingly—the *curiosi*.[489] At last it may be mentioned that a Caliph in Baghdad, Harun al-Rashid, disguised, strolled around on the streets in the evenings so as to listen and find out for himself what was going on.[490]

Then we get to the suppression of unwelcome opinions. Again the Assyrian dictators are early pioneers. Their empire was, we remember, large and therefore also heterogeneous. Groups of subjects with a common background, in point of culture or language, could revolt or even try to break away from the Empire, and to hinder this the dictator, around –750, undertook great reallocations of people. In some cases those affected could amount to some tens of thousands of individuals, but it also occurred that more than a hundred thousand were involved in a single operation.[491] In the Inca Empire large groups of subjects were also, as mentioned in chapter 2, replaced for the same reason.

Mass-deportations in dictatorships are thus not anything new, and the same holds for the destruction of displeasing literature. Long before Pol Pot's book burnings during the nineteen seventies and those in Nazi

---

[486] Roux, p. 348; Wilkinson, pp. 252-3.
[487] Roberts, p. 425; Thapar, p. 84.
[488] Basham, p. 186.
[489] Roberts, p. 346.
[490] Friedrich & Brzezinski, p. 135.
[491] Roux, p. 307; Grayson (1980b), p. 105; Wilkinson, p. 431.

Germany in 1933, the Egyptian pharaoh Akhenaten established himself in the trade by elevating the god Aten and at the same time systematically destroying all references to other gods in tombs, in temples, on obelisks, and so forth.[492] Later on the creator of the Chinese state, Shi Huangdi, behaved in a similar way. He considered the philosopher and religion founder Confucius dangerous and therefore, in –213, that is about 250 years after the philosopher's death, ordered that all of his writings should be burned. And that was not enough for the dictator—all writings all through, except those dealing with medicine, agriculture and soothsaying, which were considered matters of practical importance, should be burned. Furthermore, in the process, 460 Confucians were put to death— according to some information, though contested, by being buried alive.[493] The Confucians were thus persecuted in early China and so were the Christians in the early Roman Empire. This Roman persecution reached its climax in 303 when the dictator Diocletian ordered that all Christian writings should be burned, all churches erased, and all Christian principals arrested and killed.[494] Ironically, however, not only Christianity in Rome, but also Confucianism in China, were to be restored to places of honor and even almost to become state ideologies.

A later example of opinion suppression is the so called St. Bartholomew's Day massacre in France in 1572.[495] The French protestants, the Huguenots, were in conflict with the Catholics, supported by the dictator Catherine de' Medici. The massacre started at her instigation and when it was over many thousand (estimations vary from 5000 to 30 000) Huguenots, all over France, had been killed. Going forward in time we find many more examples. During the collectivization of Soviet agriculture in the years around 1930 Stalin removed those relatively affluent farmers, the Kulaks, who were opposed to the transformation. Estimates of the number removed, either by being killed or by deportation to labor camps, are uncertain and differing, but it might very well have been several millions. A still later example of crushing of unwelcome ideas is the massacre at the Tiananmen Square in China in 1989. Students fighting for a democratization of Chinese society had assembled on the square and the

---

[492] Wilkinson, p. 292.
[493] Finer (1997a), pp. 465, 475; Gascoigne (2003), 48-9.
[494] Roberts, p. 285.
[495] Palmer, Colton & Kramer (2007a), p. 132.

dictatorship, led by Deng Xiaoping, attacked the demonstrators with tanks. The assessments of the number killed vary between 500 and 2500.[496]

The repression of unwanted opinions has thus in many cases been most brutal. But not always, and paradoxically modern dictatorships have sometimes been quite mild. An interesting, but not unique, case is the folk music singer Wolf Biermann.[497] He was born in Hamburg in 1936 but, having become a convinced communist, emigrated to East Germany in 1953. Disappointed by the conditions there he however began to write and perform songs directed against the regime. The latter finally solved its problem by giving Biermann, in 1976, permission to leave the country for various engagements in the West and, after that, refusing to let him in again.[498] This was thus a very mild form of expulsion. The reason for this mildness probably was that Biermann was a well-known artist, and that modern dictators sometimes care more about comparisons with the world around and about international opinions than earlier dictators did. Perhaps the Soviet regime had wished to treat the nuclear physicist and political opponent Andrei Sakharov (1921–89) similarly, had it not been for the fact that Sakharov was in possession of so much strategically important information. So, instead of that, he was deported in 1979 to the closed city Gorky from which he was released, by Gorbachev, as late as 1986.[499]

And so, at last, we get to the active indoctrination of the subjects and I start with the milder methods. Dictatorships trying to gain the support of the masses by popular undertakings—bread and circuses—are not uncommon. In the Roman Empire bread, oil and bacon were, periodically, freely distributed to parts of the population and gladiator games were important.[500] Later examples of "circuses" are Hitler's Olympic Games in Berlin in 1936 and the Olympic Games in Beijing in 2008. If we then turn to real campaigns, more or less intensively conducted, the already mentioned elevations of Christianity and Confucianism to, almost state ideologies, in Rome and China respectively, are interesting examples.

---

[496] Judt, pp. 628-9; Morton & Lewis, pp. 238-41.
[497] Judt, p. 612.
[498] Judt, pp. 573-4.
[499] Judt, p. 575.
[500] Finer (1997a), p. 546.

Large scale, aggressive indoctrination is however a different kind of matter, essentially belonging to later times. One reason is that the technical means for the indoctrination have improved[501], another that modern dictatorships have been founded by parties rather than by families. From their very beginnings these parties were vehicles for, and were kept together by, ideologies such as nazism, communism and fascism. But even so aggressive indoctrination was accomplished in various ways. In the Soviet Union the show trials already mentioned were for instance important.[502] The late dictatorships also tried to mold their subjects from their very youths, not only through the schools but also with specialized youth organizations.[503] Examples are Hitler-Youth (Hitler-Jugend) in Germany and Komsomol (the Communist Union of Youth) in the Soviet Union. And even science was affected. In the Soviet Union the plant physiologist Trofim Lysenko, who held that acquired traits could be inherited, was supported by the regime for a long time.[504] His ideas were considered to provide strong, scientific support for the Soviet ideology. In Nazi Germany "Jewish physics", as represented by for instance Albert Einstein, was abolished.[505]

At last the most remarkable "Hundred Flowers Campaign" in communist China 1956–7 should be mentioned. Mao Zedong, believing that no more than 3 per cent of Chinese intellectuals—that is persons educated above a certain level—were against Marxism, started the campaign convinced that it would support the dictatorship. But when the results began to show up in the spring of 1957 the campaign was instantly interrupted and replaced by the so called "Anti-Rightist Campaign" 1957–8. Some 500 000 educated individuals were removed from their jobs, labeled "enemies of the people" and substituted for by functionaries less suited for the tasks.[506]

---

[501] Friedrich & Brzezinski, pp. 4, 17.
[502] Judt, p. 187-9.
[503] Friedrich & Brzezinski, p. 62.
[504] Judt, p. 174; Nove, p. 128.
[505] Lee, p. 210.
[506] Fairbank & Goldman, pp. 364-7.

ETHNIC CLEANSING

We have already seen that mass-deportations of people within large dictatorships, aiming at reducing the risks of uprisings, have occurred at many times in world history. There are however also cases in which substantial population groups have been ousted or even annihilated. In such cases one talks about "ethnic cleansing" and somewhere I have to write about that. A dictatorship chapter not dealing with this subject is just unreasonable. But where should it be dealt with? Here, or somewhere else? The problem is the nature of the incentives for such cleansing. Does the dictator consider the unwanted population group as a threat against the dictatorship? Or does the cleansing rather constitute a part of his own, personal incentives? Or does the dictator perhaps believe that the cleansing will add to his popularity? Or are incentives like these perhaps combined in some way? I do not know, and so I address the subject here.

The most important example, of course, is the annihilation of Jews and Romani in Nazi Germany. Germany is, as far as I have been able to find out, the only country in world history which has, for reasons of so called "scientific racism", undertaken the extermination of parts of its own population. The "Holocaust", the large scale persecution of Jews, was initiated by the so called "night of broken glass" (Kristallnacht) between November 9 and 10 in 1938.[507] Some hundreds of human beings were murdered, tens of thousands arrested and sent to concentration camps, and a large number of synagogues and shops vandalized. When these activeties were brought to an end by Germany's defeat in the Second World War about 6 million Jews had been killed and, according to some estimates, almost a million Romani.[508] It may be added that before the Holocaust, an expulsion of all Jews—to, among other places, Madagascar—was considered, but this "solution" was soon seen as impracticable. And so the "final solution" was embarked upon.[509]

But even if this is the great example, there are other ones as well—smaller, that is true, but with important similarities as well. To take one more example most of Poland's Jews, in humiliating forms and at great personal expenses, were driven out of the country after the six-day war

---

[507] Lee, p. 232; Palmer, Colton & Kramer (2007b), p. 817.
[508] Judt, p. 804; Lee, pp. 259-71; Roberts, p. 964.
[509] Lee, p. 232.

between Israel and Egypt in 1967—the war provided a plausible alleged reason.[510]

THREATS AGAINST THE DICTATOR

The preceding section dealt with threats such as uprisings, separatism and the like against the dictatorship itself, threats being caused by repression of the subjects. The threats which will be discussed in this section are rather directed against the very person of the dictator, and usually have completely different grounds. Since the dictator, according to our main hypothesis, manages the dictatorship for his own sake and in order to obtain things he considers valuable, for instance riches, it is hardly surprising that others may wish to take his place. A rather common way of trying to realize this is to murder the incumbent dictator, even if there are also examples of other, less bloody, kinds of coups. Probably dictators have been murdered more frequently than "members" of any other "professional group". Certainly governmental leaders of other kinds of states have also been murdered as for instance Abraham Lincoln, John F. Kennedy and Olof Palme, but such murders are much less common, and the motives are also very different—the murderers' motives, whatever they have been, have never been the ambition to replace the one murdered. When a dictator is murdered that ambition is however often the important one—the murderer wants to become dictator himself.

Threats like these may have different origins, they may come from persons in the immediate neighborhood of the dictator—for instance from his family, from his closest advisors and confidents, or from functionaries and other power holders throughout the country.[511] Keeping himself informed about all possible threats like these, and countering them when discovered, are perpetual problems for the dictator. But complete success in these efforts is hardly possible, so other strategies have been used as well. One possibility is hiding. Shi Huangdi, the hard-fisted dictator of Qin around −220, used a vast complex of different palaces, between which he moved on covered roads, so that no outsider should know where he was.[512] The dictator Chandragupta in the Maurya Empire

---

[510] Judt, pp. 434-5.
[511] For interesting examples from ancient Egypt see Wilkinson pp. 107, 296, 361-3.
[512] Gascoigne (2003), p. 51.

changed his bedroom every night for fear of assassination.[513] Another possibility, common in particular in China, was the use of eunuchs as the emperor's confidents.[514] Since these could not form families of their own they were considered relatively safe, but it may also be noted that the Chinese eunuchs, at least during long periods, were allowed to adopt children.[515] So in the end it is difficult to form an opinion about how it all worked. It seems, however, that the murder of dictators were comparatively few in China—at least within the long dynasties, those which have given the states their names.[516]

Furthermore, and to protect himself, a dictator can form a personal guard. That was for instance done by the first Roman Emperor Augustus and those after him continued the tradition. This force, the so called Praetorian Guard, consisted of 9000 men stationed around the central parts of today's Italy. The guard's soldiers had higher wages, and shorter terms of service, than ordinary legionaries. It was thus a kind of elite force and it was not only used for protecting the emperor but also for suppressing rebellions in the ordinary units.[517]

But the precautionary measures of dictators may also be more active than the ones hitherto mentioned. Dictators have now and then actively taken custody of persons they have had suspicions against, and suspicions like that have certainly been frequent. A dictator is, it is easy to imagine, and from the beginning, almost necessarily quite a lonely person, and therefore also likely to become suspicious. But when the suspicions grow, so does, most probably, the loneliness, and therefore the suspicions are aggravated. The suspiciousness may therefore, quiet independently of whether it was justified from the beginning or not, escalate rapidly in a self-enforcing process. And that has happened many times with extensive purges as results. Thus the Roman emperors Tiberius, Caligula, Claudius and Nero, on very weak grounds, executed not only persons suspected of planning murders, but also their whole families.[518] Another interesting example comes, in spite of what I just wrote about China above, from Chi-

---

[513] Basham, p. 186.
[514] Gascoigne (2003), p. 64; Roberts, p. 451.
[515] Morton & Lewis, p. 62.
[516] Finer (1997a), p. 15.
[517] Chrissanthos, pp.171-2.
[518] Finer (1997a), p. 545.

nese Ming. The dynasty's first dictator decapitated his prime minister in 1380, suspecting him of conspiracy. But that was not enough. He went on by killing another 40 000 persons.[519] These examples, by the way, point to still another motive for murdering a dictator, another motive than the ones already mentioned. The examples clearly show that individuals around a dictator are living risky lives, and therefore it may be prudent to pre-empt. Better murder the dictator than to become murdered oneself.

Even in the recent, large party-dictatorships extensive purges took place, and even if there were several motives for them a main motive was the elimination of competitors dangerous to the dictator. I have already mentioned the military police SA of the German Nazis and this organization, led by Ernst Röhm, rapidly grew into a very significant power. In 1934, the year in which Hitler definitely had established himself as dictator, it had become an army of 600 000 men and Hitler considered Röhm a threatening rival. So, in the operation called the "night of the long knives", Röhm and a number of other leaders in the organization were captured, and after that all of them were killed. After this, as mentioned above, the SA was replaced by the SS.

In the Soviet Union, at the end of the 1930s, extensive purges within the party's own ranks were also carried out, even if more brutal, and in a sense also more refined, than those in Germany. It all started in 1934 with the murder of a friend of Stalin, and one of the first revolutionaries, Sergey Kirov. Who was behind the murder is unclear, but for Stalin it anyway served as a pretext for a number of trials against high level party functionaries, the so called Moscow trials. And these differed in one important respect from the more openly brutal purges in Germany. On the surface the trials had the character of perfect justice done. The charges were about anti-state and anti-party activities, and all those prosecuted, seemingly in full possession of their senses and without any signs of having been tortured or otherwise mal-treated, confessed unconditionally and were put to death. Out of the total 139 members of the Central Committee—the second highest organ of the party—at least 98 were killed. Similarly large parts of the corps of officers were sentenced and killed—the most well known among them the marshal Tukhachevsky. By these means Stalin got rid of all apparent, potential rivals. But not only

---

[519] Fairbank & Goldman, pp. 129-30, 403.

high ranking individuals were affected by this terror. All together some 300 000 persons were killed and about seven millions were deported to labor camps.[520]

Even in communist China there were purges similar to those in Germany and the Soviet Union. The so called Cultural Revolution, initiated in 1966, was a remarkable, multi-facetted phenomenon, which, among other things, and in particular in the beginning, aimed at eradicating "revisionist" thinking. And had this been the only aim the portrayal of the revolution would have belonged in the earlier section "Control and steering of public opinion". Gradually, however, the revolution became more and more directed against party functionaries, and high ones, and thus took on the character of a real purge. The revolution started by the ordering of some 15 million students from non-scholarly families—the so called Red Guards—to attack, at first, "intellectuals" in general, and then, increasingly, party functionaries. The result was a chaos so extensive—almost civil war—that Mao Zedong finally considered it necessary to engage the regular military forces—the People's Liberation Army—to restore order. By then about 60 per cent of party functionaries had been ousted and the result became clearly visible at the meetings of the party's Congress and Central Committee in 1969. The delegates in military uniform were then many more than earlier—in the Party Congress they constituted two thirds.[521]

DECLINE AND FALL OF DICTATORSHIPS

A dictatorship can come to an end in various ways. It may be crushed by external enemies in its heyday as for instance the Aztecs' state, Mussolini's Italy or Hitler's Germany. Or the fall may be the result of internal power struggles, or of the ascendance to the throne, by inheritance, of some incompetent or degenerated individual. Processes like these are hardly surprising. More interesting are those cases in which the dictatorship, in spite of a fully competent dictator, suffers from a gradually proceeding, internal disintegration. And this, in turn, may take different forms. A late example is the fall of the Soviet Empire, which was caused by a badly working, stagnating economy in combination with enormous ex-

[520] Friedrich & Brzezinski, pp. 187-95; Lee, p. 68.
[521] Fairbank & Goldman, 383-405; Morton & Lewis, pp. 215-9.

penses for three main purposes. The first one was the upholding of a military apparatus roughly corresponding to that of the other superpower, the United States, the second one the support of the equally badly working economies of the East European satellite countries, and the third one the maintenance of an acceptable standard of living for its own population.[522] These three, simultaneous tasks finally became overwhelming and the empire collapsed. Economic difficulties have also contributed to the Arab Spring and to the fall of dictators in at least Tunisia and Egypt, even if other factors as well have been important. Thus the demand for freedom, a freedom of the same kind as in democratic countries, has been important. So far, however, only a few dictators have fallen, and the future of these dictatorships still remains uncertain. But some of them may disappear, as well as others for similar reasons. Possibly Cuba and North Korea might be next.

In the historical past there is however another, completely different, mechanism of decline and fall which has worked again and again. It is in fact so common so that there seems to be something almost fated in the process, something that almost necessarily must occur. A dictator who wishes to increase his resources as much as possible often tries, as we have seen, to expand his territory, and thereby his tax base, by means of claims and conquests. But when the territory becomes larger it also becomes increasingly more difficult to control. The distance from the central part of territory to the outer border becomes greater and greater, which entails longer lines of supply and more severe communication problems. It becomes increasingly more difficult to detect and suppress revolts within the area, partly because the administrative systems necessarily have to expand and therefore also work less and less well for the reasons mentioned earlier in this chapter and in the section "Hierarchies" in chapter 3. The quest for greater resources therefore makes the defense of the outer borders, and the maintenance of order within the territory, increasingly difficult. And there are no simple solutions. Further expansion in order to increase the resources only make matters worse. Consequently the dictatorship falls.

---

[522] These economic problems are described by for exemple Judt, in particular at the pages 166-7, 248 and 632.

Mechanisms of this and similar kinds are thus common. They were operating in the Roman Empire about which Edward Gibbon wrote the great work "Decline and Fall of the Roman Empire". In this case however, and interestingly enough, the problems were recognized at an early stage. The emperor Hadrian (76–138) considered the empire too large and even abandoned some eastern provinces conquered by his predecessor Trajan.[523] The emperors following Hadrian basically accepted his idea, but then it was too late. The Western Roman Empire collapsed as a result of a combination of inner disintegration and attacks from the outside.[524] And the same was the case with a number of earlier as well as later dictatorships. Sargon's Akkadian Empire finally fell because of attacks from the outside, but prior to that it was seriously weakened by power struggles and an ill-functioning internal administration. When Third Dynasty Ur collapsed attacks from the outside were certainly important, but the inner disintegration was also important—whole regions seceded.[525] The rapid founding of Hammurabi's Babylonia entailed severe hardships for those conquered and thereby also threatening discontent. Certainly there were outer enemies—Hittites, Hurrians and Kassites—but they were not the real cause of Babylonia's fall. When the empire, after the death of Hammurabi, crumbled the reasons were rather internal disintegration and weakness.[526] The Assyrian empire exploited it subjects with utter harshness and in the peripheral provinces the revolts were almost perpetual. So the empire nurtured, within itself, the seed for its own departure.[527] And, to take just a few more examples, Chinese Han[528], and the much larger Tang[529], fell because, among other things, military commanders in the provinces, whom the central government could not control, took over. The states therefore disintegrated and were dissolved. And the weakening of the Inca Empire, as a last example, did probably not depend on superior strength, if any, of external enemies, but rather on too long internal supply lines.[530]

---

[523] Chrissanthos, p. 173.
[524] Roberts, pp. 290-3.
[525] Roux, p. 179.
[526] Roux, pp. 241-2.
[527] Finer (1997a), p. 229; Roux, p. 288.
[528] Roberts, p. 447.
[529] Finer (1997b), pp. 783-4, 802.
[530] Conrad, p. 352.

All of these examples show that the inner consolidation, even if ultimately perhaps unachievable, nevertheless is of utmost importance. Some impending dictators, such as Alexander the Great or Genghis Khan[531], neglected it almost completely. Other, on the contrary, understanding its importance, made considerable consolidation efforts from the very beginning. Among these are the first pharaohs of the eighteenth dynasty in the beginning of Egypt's New Kingdom, who strived to establish themselves firmly within their own state before starting conquests in the outer world.[532] Other members of this group of dictators are Hammurabi—in spite of what was just said above he in fact waited and consolidated before making the first expansionary moves[533]—the founder of the Assyrian Empire Tiglathpileser III[534], the Persian king Darius[535] and the Roman emperors Hadrian and Diocletian.

The perspective adopted here perhaps also throws a new, interesting light on the remarkable stability of Egypt's Old Kingdom. So far I have only said the state was easy to control and impossible to attack from the outside because of the surrounding vast deserts. One may, however, also turn the reasoning upside down and say that the Egyptian dictators themselves, and again because of the vast deserts, could not engage in any outward expansions. And this could have been favorable. Had expansionism been possible the dictators might have been hit by the problems of the expanding state much earlier.

A CLASSIFICATION OF DICTATORSHIPS

INTRODUCTION

In the reasoning in the preceding sections of this chapter I have, now and then, indicated differences between dictatorships which could be used for a more systematic classification. There are, in particular, three differences which I have in mind. The first difference is the one between early and late dictatorships, and then I put the borderline, which in reality obviously not is sharp, around the time for the industrial revolution. The

---

[531] Findlay & O'Rourke, pp. 101-8; Finer (1997a), pp. 296, 314; Morton & Lewis, pp. 115-9.
[532] Roux, p. 254.
[533] Roux, p. 197.
[534] Roux, pp. 305-6.
[535] Roux, p. 408.

second difference is the one between repressive and non-repressive dictatorships. This difference is related to the conditions under which the subjects are living, not to the situation of the more or less extensive upper strata, but still, of course, it is not sharp. There may, at the same time, be groups of subjects satisfied with the regime and groups dissatisfied, for instance with being persecuted or discriminated against. But this does not mean that the distinction is meaningless as a starting point for a discussion. Finally we have differences which are related to mechanisms of power shifts and founding. Here I differentiate between dynastic dictatorships, party dictatorships and military dictatorships.

By putting these differences together we get the classification shown in figure 7. For a start the whole figure is of interest. The coloring of some cells in grey is related to the conclusions of the impending discussion. The explanations will follow in due order, especially in the final paragraph of this section.

	Early		Late	
	Repressive	non-Repressive	Repressive	non-Repressive
Dynastic dictatorships				
Party dictatorships				
Military dictatorships				

Figure 7: A classification of dictatorships

EARLY AND LATE DICTATORSHIPS

Let us at first have a look at the difference between early and late dictatorships. This distinction is important for several reasons. First the late dictatorships are unable to use fully the kind of liberal, market economy which has proved so successful in the surrounding democratic countries, but for the early dictatorships there was no economic system conflict of this kind. Second, and that is perhaps almost the same, the world around the late dictatorships is very different from that of the early ones. For the late dictatorships this world contains industrialized, democratic countries with a widely spread high standard of living, with which the dictatorships' subjects can compare their own situation. Certainly the surrounding world could sometimes look tempting even for the subjects of earlier dictatorships, but if so probably only for occasional reasons rather than because of systematically working factors as for the late dictatorships. And in addition to this the technical development, epitomized by the emergence of the Internet, has made comparisons much easier. But countering all of this, and thirdly, the technical possibilities for supervising and controlling the subjects are also much greater in the late dictatorships than in the early ones. And the same holds true for the facilities available for keeping the subjects hemmed in.

After this we can look a bit more closely at the early dictatorships. Of what kinds have they been? Obviously there have been lots of dynastic dictatorships. But have there also been any party dictatorships, or military dictatorships? As I wrote above the mandarins in China, or the army in the Roman Empire, occasionally could take over the dictator's role if, for instance, he was weak. These two powerful strata thus seem to have similarities with later days' parties. So the question is if we are dealing with party dictatorships when these groups took over. And, considering particularly the Roman Empire but also some other early dictatorships, are we dealing with military dictatorships when high militaries made themselves dictators?

My answers to these questions are however in the negative. Even if there are some similarities with the modern dictatorships there are also considerable differences. If we first look at the question about parties it is a fact that those parties which gave rise to the modern dictatorships always were founded prior to the dictatorship at issue, and usually also with the purpose of creating that dictatorship. With the Chinese mandarins and the Roman army that was not so. The mandarin class emerged and grew in a dictatorship already established. And the Roman army, even if it existed before the dictatorship, was not created for the purpose of creating the dictatorship. So we are hardly dealing with party dictatorships. And the answer to the second question, the one about military dictatorship, is also in the negative. The Roman Empire and other early dictatorships[536] run by military dictators were not military dictatorships in a

---

[536] For instance the military dictator Horemheb in ancient Egypt. Wilkinson, pp.

modern sense. The modern military dictatorships differ from early dictatorships governed by military officers in at least three ways. First, the modern military dictatorships are founded in societies where the military
profession is just one among many specialized professions—but with the
early dictatorships run by militaries it was not so, they were rather societies militarized all through. Second, the militaries who founded early dictatorships almost always had a dynastic purpose—with the modern ones
it is hardly ever so. And thirdly, when modern military dictatorships are
founded, they often take the place of a democratic regime—with the early
ones it was never so.

Among the early dictatorships there were thus very few military
and party dictatorships—perhaps these were even almost non-existent.
But there is at least one exception, and an interesting one. The reasons for
considering the Caliphate a party dictatorship are thus, I contend, strong.
In the same way as modern party dictatorships the Caliphate was, to a
large extent, created from below. It was supported by a large mass of
loyal believers and the leaders, first Muhammad and after him the following caliphs, were a kind of party leaders. The movement also had, in the
same way as modern political parties, an ideology, in this case the Islamic
religion. Furthermore it was obviously not a dynastic dictatorship—the
caliphs were not recruited from the same family, even if the Shiites
wished to have it so. And neither was it a military dictatorship. It had not
been imposed from above in the way characteristic for a military dictatorship. So for these reasons I classify the Caliphate as an early party dictatorship. Possibly the same could be said about the likewise Muslim
Ottoman empire.

The upshot thus is that almost all early dictatorships were dynastic
but that there is at least one exception, namely the Caliphate which was a
party dictatorship.

Turning then to the late dictatorships there are obviously many
party as well as military ones. Several examples are already mentioned.
But there are also dynastic dictatorships. The Arab kingdoms, Saudi
Arabia for instance, are of this kind. That these dictatorships are at all
possible depends reasonably, at least to some extent, on their vast oil resources. Thanks to them they are not subject to normal economic condi-

305, 311.

tions. The whole issue about the superiority of free market economy to the planned economy lacks relevance for them. In spite of the existence of several dictatorships of this kind they therefore, nevertheless, have to be considered exceptions or anomalies.

The main conclusion thus is that almost all dictatorships before the industrial revolution were dynastic, while after that revolution, the main types rather were military and party dictatorships.

REPRESSIVE AND NON-REPRESSIVE DICTATORSHIPS

After this we turn to the question about repressiveness and non-repressiveness. I start again with the early dictatorships. That, among them, there have been innumerable repressive ones should by now be obvious. The interesting question therefore is about the existence of non-repressive ones. Have there been any such? A way of bringing that question to a head is to ask about the existence of altruistic dictators. Since it is in the nature of a dictatorship to be shaped by its dictator, dictatorships with altruistic dictators are probably also non-repressive.

An early candidate is the ruler Urukagina in the Sumerian city-state Lagash around −2350, but about him not much is known.[537] More is known about Asoka who ruled the Indian Maurya Empire from about −270 until −232. This Asoka, sometimes called the Great, started off as a successful warrior, but later on, after having been confronted with the human suffering caused by the fighting, went through a personal crisis. That made him a Buddhist and he started advocating, and even writing about, tolerance and non-violence. For all of this he has become well-known, but still it is not evident that he should be described as an altruistic dictator. Certainly he travelled widely in his empire and kept himself informed about the subjects' conditions, but nevertheless he was rather a philosopher and teacher of wisdom. He was clearly paternalistic and practical, material undertakings in an altruistic spirit are difficult to find.[538] Another much later dictator of the same kind was Marcus Aurelius. During most of his rule he was occupied by military defense operations at the north-eastern border of the empire, but still he managed to become himself, by his writing, an important stoical philosopher.

---

[537] Kriwaczek, pp. 101-4.
[538] Basham, pp. 186-7; Roberts, pp. 425-6; Thapar, pp. 70-91.

To the extent that Asoka and Marcus Aurelius did anything for their subjects, it was thus as philosophers, not by undertaking practical measures. And even if this perhaps was not all that bad, it was not very significant either. But there are more interesting dictators. During the fourteenth century, as we saw in chapter 2, Portugal emerged as an important Great Power. A remarkable ruler in the beginning of this period was Dinis of Portugal (1261–1325), who had inherited the throne after his father. Dinis tried to avoid wars, solved conflicts with the church, and considered it his main task to organize the state. He developed the Portuguese criminal law and civil law. He travelled around the countryside in order to detect and cure injustices, redistributed land, improved the infra structure and initiated the creation of farmer communities. He founded what was to become the great Portuguese fleet, as well as several shipyards. He developed mining and foreign trade. He founded the University of Lisbon. He also had intellectual and literary interests of his own and was an active and competent poet and troubadour. Of all dictators I have read about while writing this book this Dinis, sometimes called the "righteous" and sometimes the "farmer king", is, I think, the one who most of all, most unequivocally, stands out as an altruistic dictator.[539] But there may have been more of the same kind. A clear candidate is Henry IV of France and Navarre (1553–1610). He succeeded in bringing to an end the earlier mentioned conflicts between Huguenots and Catholics, and he undertook important measures for the development of agriculture, commerce and communications. He wanted, as he put it himself, "there to be no peasant in my realm so poor that he will not have a chicken in his pot every Sunday."[540]

The hitherto discussed dictators have in one way or another—practically or philosophically—directly and explicitly cared about their subjects. But beside them there remains an important group, perhaps the most important. These are the dictators who, even if they have had substantial interests of their own, nevertheless have done much good for their subjects as well. I have already mentioned the three first dictators of the Persian Empire who undoubtedly seem to have been of this kind. A later dictator in this category—perhaps the greatest of them all—was Au-

---

[539] Disney, pp. 70-142; Saraiva, pp. 13-44; Encyclopædia Britannica Online, title word "Dinis".
[540] Palmer, Colton & Kramer (2007a), pp. 133-5.

gustus (–63–14), the first emperor of the Roman Empire. He did not expand the territory any further, and he laid the ground for what was to become *Pax Romana*.

And of dictators like these there have been several. During Qing China was ruled, as we have seen, by emperors from the Manchu people in the north-west. A number of these were not only very capable in general, during their period China also benefitted from an inner stability, and development, which surpassed almost everything experienced before or after. The most remarkable of all of these emperors was Kangxi, the fourth in his dynasty, with the extremely long governing period 1661–1722.[541] Since he entered the throne at the early age of eight he had for sure regents, especially his grand-mother, during his early years, but still he ruled for a long time. Even if he waged wars to expand the territory he also improved domestic conditions significantly. The top-steered administration was made more efficient. Differing from most other Chinese emperors, who usually stuck to their palaces, he travelled much and often in the empire to learn about the conditions of the ordinary people. His own way of living was also, at least when compared with other Chinese emperors', unpretentious. In his harem he had for instance only 300 women, which may be compared with 3000, or at another occasion even 6000, during Han.[542] The subjects' tax burden was, for the Chinese, moderate. Intellectual pluralism was encouraged. Canals, irrigation systems, schools and hospitals were developed. Samuel Finer concludes his presentation of Qing and Kangxi as follows: " ... China was much happier under the [Qing] than under the Han or under any previous dynasty, and as happy, if not happier, than any other state in the whole world."[543]

Above I have mentioned Peter the Great several times, and then mainly positively. The reader may therefore well wonder if Peter belongs to the same category as Augustus and Kangxi. But so it is not. For certain he was eminently skilful but his efforts essentially aimed at winning wars, and it was also in those pursuits that he was most successful. After having lost against Charles XII of Sweden at Narva in 1700 he modernized the army and was soon rewarded. He got his revenge at Poltava in 1709

---

[541] Fairbank & Goldman, pp. 143-61; Gascoigne (2003), pp. 179-82; Roberts, pp. 461-2.
[542] Finer (1997a), p. 488.
[543] Finer (1997c), p. 1160.

whereby Russia became a Great Power. But the large masses in this empire, the peasants in villeinage, were throughout this time exploited extremely by the society's upper strata.[544] Peter the Great had many capabilities, but he was not his subjects' benefactor.

The dictators of the early dynastic dictatorships were thus, for summing up, quite different, and therefore also their states. There have been states in which the subjects have lived quite well, as measured by the standards of their own time, states in which the conditions have been atrocious, and states in between these extremes. But not all early dictatorships were dynastic—at least the Caliphate was a party dictatorship. And I think it was a non-repressive one.

Then we turn to the late dictatorships. Among these the party and military dictatorships have almost always been repressive, possibly with the exception for a euphoric first stage. During a considerable part of Nazi Germany's short life span—at least until about 1940—the enthusiasm for Hitler was thus firm and spread.[545] In the long run such an enthusiasm can however hardly remain intact, among other things depending on dictatorships' necessarily badly functioning economies. Normally these dictatorships are therefore repressive. The Soviet Union and Communist China up to Deng Xiaoping are clear examples. Today's China, as I have already written, and according to my contention, is in an unstable transitional phase. The question about the repressiveness is therefore not only difficult to answer, perhaps it is also irrelevant. The question, clearly, is mainly intended for relatively stable dictatorships.

When discussing late dictatorships the concept of totalitarian dictatorship should also be addressed. In their book "Totalitarian Dictatorship & Autocracy" Friedrich and Brzezinski write that the totalitarian dictatorship captures, and intends to shape, the subject, the complete individual, in all respects, into the innermost soul, according to one single mould. Furthermore they argue that this is an historical innovation, something which has never existed prior to the big dictatorships of the twentieth century.[546] This seems reasonable, but if so the reason is that the necessary technical facilities have not been there before. If one rather looks at the ambitions, they have been present several times previously, for

[544] Roberts, pp. 620-3.
[545] Lee, pp. 213-4.
[546] Friedrich & Brzezinski, pp. 15, 17.

instance in the Assyrian Empire, in Qin and in the Inca Empire. But for purely technical reasons totalitarian dictatorships are thus late phenomena, and the main examples, of course, are the Soviet Union, Nazi Germany and Communist China.

The modern dictatorships have thus, on the whole, been repressive ones. But are there also any non-repressive ones? A possible example is Turkey under the former professional military officer Mustafa Kemal (1881–1938). Kemal, who in his early career, among others, had participated in the massacre of 1,5 million Armenians in 1915–16[547], later, with the name Kemal Atatürk (father of the Turks), became the Turkish chief of state. Was this regime, it may be asked, a non-repressive military dictatorship? Under Atatürk's reign Turkey was secularized and modernized in various respects. Communications were developed, the finances of the state put in order, new laws of a western kind were introduced and the economy grew.[548] But in spite of all this there are remaining questions. One of these is how much of a dictator Atatürk really was. In 1923 he was democratically elected as president, but after that he managed, by partially non-democratic means, to remain in power until his death in 1938. Another question is about the citizens'/subjects' opinions about the reforms. Did they like them or not? Here I can only put these questions. Clear, however, is that Atatürk's Turkey is interesting in the discussion about dictatorships.

Other possible non-repressive, modern dictatorships are the dynastic Arabian kingdoms. At least some of these dictatorships have oil resources making it possible to satisfy much of their subjects' material needs. For a long time this has also seemed to be enough. But when the freedom issue became acute in the Arab spring in 2011 the oil country Bahrain disclosed itself as a repressive dictatorship.

The discussion may now be summarized. Practically all early dictatorships were dynastic, and among them there were repressive as well as non-repressive ones. There were however also exceptions and I have classified the Caliphate as a non-repressive party dictatorship. The late dictatorships have mainly been party or military dictatorships, and all of these have also—possibly excluding euphoric initial periods—been re-

---

[547] Judt, pp. 803-4; Lee, p. 364.
[548] Lee, pp. 337-40; Roberts, pp. 942-3.

pressive. Among the late dictatorships there are however also some dynastic ones. The issue about their repressiveness is still to some extent open—there may be repressive as well as non-repressive ones. These conclusions are summarized by means of the grey cells in figure 7 above. These cells are, according to the discussion here, empty.

SUMMARY

Dictatorship is the most common kind of state. Dictatorships have existed in all times, at all places, and they have been created, again and again, independently of each other. Their emergence is not difficult to explain. In a lot of cases the second invisible hand presented in chapter 3 has for instance operated. And therefore no prototype has been needed. The dictatorship can thus be considered the most natural type of state, though certainly not the best one.

At the end of the chapter the previous presentation is used for a systematic classification of dictatorships. The most important distinction is the one between dictatorships before and after the industrial revolution. Before that revolution there were very few states of other kinds at all, and the conditions, for the subjects, could, at least sometimes be as good, or perhaps even better, than in other states or in statelessness. There were, among all atrocious dictators, also some good ones, for instance Dinis of Portugal and Augustus of the Roman Empire. Or, for using the terminology adopted here, even if most dictatorships were repressive there were also some non-repressive ones.

After the industrial revolution things became however very different. The conditions within the dictatorships, for the subjects, were almost necessarily worse, or even much worse, than in the surrounding states of other kinds. All dictatorships tended to be repressive. And this made it increasingly important for the rulers, the dictators, to enclose the subjects, to hinder them from leaving the dictatorship. Before the industrial revolution this was hardly, for purely technical reasons, a problem— the subjects did not dispose of any means for the long travelling usually needed for getting outside the dictatorship. After the revolution the dictatorships could require effective fences such as the "iron curtain" symbolized by the Berlin Wall. At the same time the technical development of various media made it easier for the subjects to communicate with each other, but also for those in power to supervise them.

The mechanisms leading to the fall of dictatorships were also, and usually, other ones after than before the industrial revolution. Before the revolution the dictatorships were often continuously expanding since the dictators made themselves rich by conquering and plundering larger and larger areas. But those larger areas also entailed increasingly severe administrative problems which easily became uncontrollable. And so the dictatorships crumbled and thereby gave place either to new dictatorships, or to statelessness. But that mechanism gradually lost its importance after the industrial revolution, among others since expansion became increasingly difficult in a world in which larger and larger land areas were effectively defended by other states of other kinds.

Another difference between dictatorships before and after the industrial revolution relates to the problem of overthrowing those in power, or of creating a new dictatorship. Before the revolution, and since states at that time generally were much less consolidated, it was often sufficient just to murder the incumbent dictator. After the revolution much more of organization was required—either a party operating from below or professional soldiers operating from above. The results were party and military dictatorships.

And this indicates still a difference made important by the industrial revolution. Before it most dictatorships were dynastic, which means that the dictators following each other in a dictatorship, and when the more or less explicit rules were followed, came from the same family. The family model was by far the most common. After the industrial revolution dynastic dictatorships are of importance only in rich oil states.

7

DIRECT DEMOCRACIES

DIRECT DEMOCRACIES IN THE HISTORY OF THE WORLD

A direct democracy is a state in which all free citizens, or at least a large part of them, participate, directly, in the decision-making of the state. There is thus no assembly representing the citizens; the citizens themselves, rather, get together regularly in some public, open place for taking, there, the decisions considered essential for the community. For this to work there must obviously be some kind of rules for the wielding of power, at least implicit ones. Already the regular calling together of the meetings is an example of this.

It is now a long time since there were any states of this kind. The basic reason is that direct democracies, to be able to function, must be very small, and much smaller than a modern state for other reasons ought to be, or tends to be. Those coming together for the discussions and decision making clearly must not for purely practical reasons—or, to use a somewhat more technical term, for reasons of transaction costs (see the section "Transaction costs" in chapter 3)—be too many. Not even states as small as today's Andorra (population about 70 000), Iceland (about 200 000) and Luxembourg (about 450 000) could be ruled by common, citizen gatherings. Those direct democracies which have not disappeared by being attacked from the outside, but continued as states, have therefore been transformed into some other kind of state, usually to dictatorship. And in all such cases the transformations occurred long ago. On the Euro-Asian land-mass new direct-democracies have hardly emerged after the early Medieval Age. At other places, for instance in Central- or South-America, primitive direct democracies may possibly have existed somewhat later. Predecessors to the states of the Aztecs and the Incas may for instance have been of this kind.

Direct democracies thus share several properties—first, of course, the manner of decision-making, the defining property, but also that they all belong to history. But in spite of these common properties they have been of two clearly different types. The one type are the states, or in this case perhaps rather societies or states in-being, which in their early stages have gone through a direct democratic phase. A simple tribal society may thus, after some initial development and growth, enter a direct democratic phase, and then, after having grown still more, turn into a dictatorship, ruled by for instance a strong leader. How many direct democracies of this kind there have been is impossible to say since the traces may be extinguished in many cases. Obviously there have however been several ones. A number of Germanic tribes were for instance organized like this, and about them I will write more in the next section. But most probably there have been more instances than these. The Sumerian city-states may, for instance, at a very early stage, and prior to the dictatorships I wrote about in chapters 2 and 6, have been direct democracies.[549] And the same seems to be the case for the very first phase of what was to become the Roman Republic. Some kind of direct democracy seems to have preceded the kingdom which, in its turn, preceded the Republic.[550]

The other type of direct democracy is represented by Athens during its Golden Age. If the direct democracies of the first group emerged as transitional phases in primitive societies and were characterized by simple and hardly institutionalized rules, all of this was different in Athens. First of all Athens was so far from being primitive as, at that time, was at all possible—the city-state, rather, was the most advanced culture of its own time, and, indeed, one of the most influential cultures of all times. Furthermore, the direct democracy did not appear at an early stage, but only after a long period of oligarchy now and dictatorship then, and as a result of decisions taken by dictators. But even if Athens is the most prominent of direct democracies of this type, it is not the only one. Some other Greek city-states had similar constitutions.[551] But they were not many in any case, and probably there have not been any other direct democracies of this type than Athens' contemporary Greek ones.

In the ensuing sections I will describe the two types of direct democracy after each other and thereby let the first type be represented by the Germanic ones and deal with them first. Certainly they are later than the

---

[549] Jacobsen (1980a), p. 76; Roux, pp. 107-8.
[550] Finer (1997a), p. 393.
[551] Hansen, p. 112.

Greek ones but since they are less complicated it is nevertheless better to start with them.

THE GERMANIC DIRECT DEMOCRACIES

During a long period Germanic tribes from the east migrated towards the areas which constitute todays' Europe. Among those tribes were Alamanni, Angels, Burgundians, Franks, Goths, Jutes, Lombards, Saxons, Swedes, Vandals and so forth, and the migration reached its climax around the year 400. At least some of these tribes founded direct democracies in various places, for instance in the Swiss Alp valleys, within the areas of today's Sweden, Norway and Denmark, and in other places as well.[552] The embryo of the Carolingian Empire may for instance have been a Frankish direct democracy. And the same may be true even for other great states with, eventually, longer lives than Charlemagne's state. Various Germanic tribes were, in fact, destined to take over—long after the period of direct democracy—large parts of Europe. In northern Europe the Germanic languages are—as we know—dominant today. But for the moment it is the direct democracy period which interests us.

In the section "Modifications of the basic model" in chapter 3 I wrote that the forms for decision making in an initially small tribal society may develop in different directions when the community grows. The alternatives were dictatorship, oligarchy and direct democracy. For the Germanic tribes, or at least some of them, the alternative realized thus was the direct democracy.

The most important institution in these democracies was an institution called the "Thing", and among those there were different kinds depending on the size of the area they governed.[553] The biggest one, sometimes called the Land thing, governed the whole area of the state at issue, but beneath it there could also be regional things. Sometimes, however, if, for instance, the whole state expanded, the land things could also grow, and, if so, the power of the king and the great land owners could also increase at the expense of the power of the common citizens. Processes like these brought the communities towards feudalism, and in the Nordic areas what were to become the future Nordic countries began

---

[552] Palmer, Colton & Kramer (2007a), p. 22.
[553] Herlitz, pp. 3, 12.

to take form. In Sweden this transformation occurred during the reigns of the kings Birger Jarl (dead 1266), Magnus III of Sweden (Magnus Barnlock, dead 1290) and Magnus IV of Sweden (1316–74).[554] But here we are interested in the time before this transformation; the time when the Things were still there and also had some real power.

The things were important and surrounded by an impressive ceremonial.[555] They were assembled quite often—there is information about meetings each or every second week, which seems unlikely, but often it still seems to have been. The summoning was done by means of a so called fiery cross, a piece of wood which could have the message imprinted on its outside or, perhaps, be more elaborated as a small container carrying a written message in its interior. The rules for its handling were detailed. A person having received a fiery cross was thus obliged to continue spreading the message by delivering it to some other appropriate person; the destruction of a fiery cross was furthermore criminal and punished in due order. Those getting together at the things, and who were allowed to speak, and to take part in the decisions, were the grown up free men. They were also those bearing arms, that is the war-prepared part of the population. Beside these men there were, in the grown up population, obviously also the women, and, in addition to that, a great number of slaves or serfs without any rights whatsoever.

The right to speak was thus free and general for those participating in the things, and the same was true for the right to take part in the decisions, but still there was a kind of gradation. In the middle of the open place for the thing there was a stage on which, a bit above the ground, particularly important persons had their places. Perhaps there was a leader or chief, if such one existed, and perhaps there was some sort of war council, and there could also be representatives of families being big land-owners or being especially successful or highly esteemed for some other reason. There could furthermore be someone entitled "law-speaker", often recruited from one of the families mentioned. All of these persons were, among others, supposed to initiate discussions on various subjects, and to conduct and lead the deliberations. And obviously the

---

[554] Kent, pp. 16-28.
[555] Ross, pp. 9-15.

opinions of those considered particularly knowledgeable, experienced or prudent were revered especially.

The things handled many types of issues—questions related to war and peace were for instance, in all likelihood, almost ever present. Taxes to be taken were also decided about by the things. The things also issued new laws, interpreted existing law, and took decisions about sentences. These latter, which for a modern human being may seem utterly cruel, were often carried out immediately. And the sentences were often also, again for a modern observer, arbitrary since they were founded on different kinds of experiments which were thought to give information about the opinions of unearthly powers and thereby about guilt in the case at issue. This is what is called trial by ordeal.[556] Conflicts between two individuals could for instance be settled in a kind of ritualistic duel, the winner of which was considered innocent.

A very particular and interesting society with a background in the Germanic direct democracies was medieval Iceland. This society was formed when Iceland, at the end of the ninth century, began being populated, mainly by emigration from Norway. It was however hardly a democracy and, in fact, hardly even a state. But it was absolutely not an anarchy either. Actually it does not fit properly into any of the four categories of states I am working with. Still, and in spite of the fact that it was not a state, it might perhaps have been possible to discuss it in the next chapter about oligarchies—that would not have been completely unreasonable. Rather, I have however chosen to treat it in chapter 11, the one about statelessness.

THE ATHENIAN DIRECT DEMOCRACY

RISE AND FALL

The Germanic direct democracies thus appeared at an early stage in the development of the tribes concerned. In Athens it was not so—there the direct democracy was not founded until quite late, and then as a successor to other, earlier constitutional arrangements.

Athens was a city-state, the Greek word for which is "polis", which is the origin of our word "politics". Most of the Greek city-states began as kingdoms, that is dictatorships, or oligarchies, and so far nothing is

---

[556] Palmer, Colton & Kramer (2007a), p. 22.

difficult to explain. In all cases small groups of individuals were involved, for instance large land-owners, or sometimes, perhaps, a single individual having inherited or seized power. Perhaps the two constitutional forms also, in some cases, could interchange—sometime kingdom, sometime oligarchy. Possibly, in some cases and periodically, the king and the land-owners could also cooperate, which, if so, was not strange either since the king was dependent on the land-owners' militarily important horses.[557]

But later on the dictators became dominating, and this change was a direct consequence of the development of a new technique of violence. The infantry—and then I am referring to the so called hoplites about which I wrote in chapter 4—became increasingly important and therefore the great land-owners less crucial.[558] The field was left open for individuals with fitting capabilities to seize power, and that also happened.[559] The new power holders were called tyrants and the city-states, consequently, tyrannies. After this the tyrannies, in their turn, could however develop in various ways.[560] The city-state which here, in this chapter, above all is interesting is Athens, and I therefore concentrate on that one. Even if there were more Greek direct democracies Athens was not only the biggest and by far the most important, but probably also the first one.[561] And it was created by tyrants.

The tyrants active during the transitional phase were Solon (from about 640 to 558), Peisistratus (from about 610 to 528) and Cleisthenes (from about 570 to 507). The first one, Solon, introduced a new constitution including considerable elements of direct democracy. The second one abolished these reforms but was nevertheless of great importance for Athens' future—among other things he conquered the island of Salamis just outside the city of Athens and thereby laid the ground for the great naval power which the city-state was to become.[562] The third one finally, Cleisthenes, introduced a direct democracy which was different from, and more far-reaching, than Solon's. This direct democracy, with only brief interruptions, was then to survive until Athens, together with the rest of

---

[557] Roberts, p. 175.
[558] Finer (1997a), p. 329; Roberts, p. 179.
[559] Lane Fox, p. 89.
[560] Finer (1997a), p. 320; Lane Fox, pp. 58-68.
[561] Lane Fox, pp. 96-7.
[562] Encyclopædia Britannica Online, title word "Peisistratus".

the Greek peninsula, was conquered by Philip of Macedonia 170 years later.

Before describing the Athenian direct democracy in a somewhat more detailed fashion a few more words should be said about its rise and fall, and then in particular about the basic mechanisms. For the rise, as already emphasized, the growing, new kind of infantry, the hoplites, was of crucial importance. Since the military weight of the city-state now had shifted from the land-owners to the infantry soldiers the latter could claim political influence. Since they were much more numerous than the land-owners they could however not shape and put forward articulated demands about changes wanted. The logic of collective action made this impossible. At most they could, in one way or another, express general discontent, or, perhaps, suggest very general claims. We do not know that much about this however and may therefore just assume that they showed some kind of discontent, and then, after that, consider the whole issue from the point of view of the dictator or tyrant.

In the same way as hitherto I assume that the dictator follows his own self-interest. Using violence against those dissatisfied in the way so often done, and so often to be done, to suppress the rebelliousness was however hardly possible in this case since it was the very apparatus of violence which harbored the discontent. The alternative, rather, was to yield in some way which could be favorable even for the dictator. It is easy to interpret first Solon's, and then Cleisthenes', reactions in this way. Facing a large public meeting Cleisthenes presented, orally, a constitutional proposal which was utterly detailed, and which, plausibly, satisfied his own interests as well as those of the infantry soldiers.[563] If this interpretation is correct the mechanism which was described in the section "A fundamental mechanism of change" in chapter 3 was active. The Athenian direct democracy saw the light of the day.

THE CONSTITUTION

Those participating in Athens' direct democracy were the free men, altogether about 40 000 individuals. These men were the citizens. The citizenship was thus formalized or institutionalized and also inherited. There was a clear dividing line between citizens and non-citizens. In

---

[563] Lane Fox, pp. 92-3.

addition to the free men and their families the Athenian population consisted of free foreign inhabitants and of slaves—the latter at least as many
as all the other ones together, but probably many more. The citizens thus
constituted only a small part of the total population—perhaps around ten
per cent—but among them there were no differences. One citizen was as
good as the next.

The most important decision-making organ was the *assembly* or the
ecclesia. The meetings, around some ten or twenty per year, took place in
an open market place, the so called Agora, and all citizens so wishing
could participate. On the average about 6000 persons were present, all
having full freedom of speech. The voting usually was performed by show
of hands and the majority rule was used for decisions. The assembly dealt
with all important issues such as those about war and peace, appointments of military commanders, granting of new citizenships, issues about
taxes, legislation and decisions about sentences—there was no sharp
distinction between legislative and judicial power. Furthermore, among
the issues taken up, were expulsions from the city state of unwanted
persons, so called *ostracism*. This was an institution which Cleisthenes
had introduced and considered especially important—the purpose was to
get rid of aspiring tyrants at an early stage. For some particularly important decisions there was a rule of quorum—at least 6000 participants had
to be present.[564]

All important decisions were thus taken by the assembly, but still
its power was circumscribed by two mechanisms. The one was that the
assembly did not determine its own agenda, the other that the assembly's
decisions could be examined and declared invalid by a court.

The assembly did thus not decide about its own agenda—this was
rather done by the so called *council* or *boulé*.[565] Therefore, and even if all
citizens were entitled to take initiatives, nothing could be dealt with in
the assembly without having first been prepared in the council. And the
council, even if much smaller than the assembly, was anyway hardly
small—it had 500 members—and the rules for appointing these members
were quite elaborate and carefully thought through. First Athens was
divided into ten regions, so called *phylae*, and each of these should have

---

[564] Manin, p. 21; Roberts, p. 181.
[565] Manin, p. 17.

the same number of council members.566 The idea was to avoid formation of fractions or conflicts between citizen groups of various kinds, for instance peoples from the city, from the coast and from the inland. So the phylae were formed so that each of them contained a densely populated part, a coastal part and an inland part. And the council members were selected, for one-year terms, by means of lottery. To be electable an age above 30 years was however required, and furthermore the lottery was applied only to persons freely declaring themselves candidates, which far from all did.567 Being a member of the council was not only demanding and badly paid, but also entailed risks—what was considered careless or incompetent exercise of duty could afterwards be sentenced in court. So therefore only relatively well-off persons, engaged in the tasks, presented themselves as candidates. There was thus, prior to the lottery, a very considerable selection.

This selection was however, at least to some extent, counteracted by another rule according to which a single person not could belong to the council more than two years altogether. This was one of several manifestations of a principle of rotation which was important in Athenian politics.568 The participation in the affairs of the state should, within certain limits, be as widespread as possible. The rotation principle was therefore used also in other circumstances. The current administration, or the daily direction, of the work of the council rotated for instance among the phylae in such a way that each of them performed these tasks during one tenth of the year, and the organization of the work of the assembly was similarly distributed.

The members of the council were thus selected by lot, but this method was not used for all politicians or functionaries. *Magistrates*, to use the Greek term, which were considered particularly important, or requiring specialist competence, were thus elected.569 This was the case not only for military commanders, but also for technicians leading the construction of water-supply installations, ship-building, the building of fortifications, and so forth. Even functionaries with important tasks related to festivals, competitions and games of various kinds, and similar

---

566 Finer (1997a), p. 344; Roberts, p. 182.
567 Manin, p. 13.
568 Manin, pp. 28-32.
569 Finer (1997a), pp. 348-50; Manin, p. 14.

matters, were elected. All of these elections were for one-year terms but those elected could, in contrast to those selected by lottery, be reelected any number of times. The elections were done by the assembly.

I wrote above that the assembly's decisions could be declared invalid by a court and also that the members of the council could be sentenced by a court for being careless or incompetent. The courts here mentioned dealt mainly with "political cases", and even if there also were organs handling ordinary criminal cases and the like, the political courts were nevertheless very important and also, as it seems, more developed and institutionally complex.[570] They were also very big even if the size varied depending on the character of the particular case handled. The smallest variety had 501 judges. The decisions, according to the majority rule, were not taken by show of hands but by a secret procedure. The recruitment of the judges was very special. Every year, in a first step, a group of 6000 willing men above 30 years of age was selected by lottery. Then, for each session or case, the required number of judges was selected from this group, again by lottery.[571] [572]

COMMENT

Well, that is how it looked, the Athenian direct democracy, painted with a broad brush. It was in many ways a most remarkable creation. In its main features it was worked out and thereafter implemented by one single individual, the tyrant Cleisthenes. Thereafter it looked about the same during all the time it was functioning, from 508 to 338, that is for 170 years, and worked well, as it seems, throughout this period. When Athens fell the reason was hardly inner weakness—it rather fell together with rest of the Greek world when attacked by Philip of Macedonia. Then it is of course also true that Athens, being a direct democracy with a necessarily limited size, would have become ungovernable if it had expanded and become bigger. But this is another matter, it was not the cause of the actual fall. What above all characterized Cleisthenes' creation, besides its obvious democratic traits, was the frequent use of lotteries for selec-

---

[570] Manin, p. 19.

[571] Manin, p. 23.

[572] It may seem strange that the figure 6000 has appeared above in three different contexts. This, however, is no miswriting—it is in accordance with the sources quoted.

ting functionaries of various kinds, the important principle of rotation, and the habitual use of court procedures for remediation when judged necessary. Institutions like these, as far as is known, had hardly existed before, they were something new in the history of the world. It is not far-fetched to consider them as predecessors to systems for separation of powers in later ages (checks and balances).

But how did all of this really work? Mogens Herman Hansen, a prominent expert on Athenian democracy, has emphasized one aspect. He underlines the extensive and widely spread civic activities and writes as follows:[573]

> "[T]o our way of thinking it must have been deadly boring; that the Athenians went through it year after year for centuries shows that their attitude to this sort of routine must have been different from ours. They evidently enjoyed participation in their political institutions as a value in itself."

Perhaps it was like that even if the centuries Hansen talks about seem somewhat exaggerated—but 170 years is also a long time. It may however be asked if the rules really were literally adhered to all the time. We have for instance seen that there were no time limits for the magistrates elected—they could be reelected any number of times. During a substantial part of Athens period of greatness—the Golden Age which I described in chapter 2—the general Pericles, being reelected in this way, held his position for more than 20 years. His power and influence were enormous, and in the history books he is described not only as a statesman but also, almost, as a dictator.[574] So, we may ask, did the Athenians prefer electing a strong president to dealing, themselves, continuously with all kinds of political issues? Even if the question is difficult to answer, it may nevertheless, and most reasonably, be put.

Another issue is about freedom. In chapter 2 I wrote that Plato criticized the Athenian direct democracy and rather recommended a system such as Sparta's. But Plato's criticism was also caused by the verdict against his teacher Socrates. A court—in that case having 501 members—with a very narrow majority sentenced Socrates to death because of his ideas. He was accused of having lead astray the youth. This does not

[573] The quotation from Hansen is taken from Lane Fox, p. 94.
[574] Finer (1997a), p. 346; Manin, p. 14; Roberts, p. 199.

testify to liberty and tolerance. But other things point in other directions. Most noticeable is perhaps the generous, widespread appreciation of the social criticism produced by the freely working, satirical and humoristic dramatist Aristophanes.[575]

THE CASE OF SWITZERLAND

An important hypothesis put forward in this book is that a direct democracy never has developed into a representative democracy—or, in other words, that a representative democracy never has emerged from a direct democracy. Switzerland is interesting in this context since it is, now and then, presented as a counter-example.

The background is that modern Switzerland, being a representative democracy, not only uses referendums more frequently than any other modern democracy, but also has had very substantial elements of direct democracy in its historical past. It may therefore seem straightforward to conclude that Switzerland falsifies the hypothesis mentioned. The original direct democracy was gradually transformed, one may perhaps argue, into a representative democracy, at the same time as considerable direct democracy constituents, in the form of referendums, remained in place. A quick glance at the historical circumstances will however prove this conclusion wrong.

As early as during the time of the Western Roman Empire, and later during the time of Charlemagne, there were small, local communities at different places within the area which was to become Switzerland. Still somewhat later this area, when it belonged to the loosely amalgamated Holy Roman Empire, acquired capital strategic importance. The trade between the southern and northern parts of Europe had gradually become more extensive and in about 1220 a bridge was built across the St Gotthard Pass for facilitating the important trade between the Rhineland and Italy. But that also opened a possibility for the Swiss to exercise power. If they just could unite, and liberate themselves from the Holy Roman Empire, they could control the traffic across the bridge and impose high tariffs. So, in 1291 the three forest communities Uri, Unterwalden and Schwyz—the latter of which was to give its name to the whole state later on—united and formed the Swiss Confederacy, to which

---

[575] Roberts, p. 209.

further communities were to join, for instance the cities Zurich in 1351 and Berne in 1353. And in this way, what was to become Switzerland, was created, and the country also grew and became a significant military power. In chapter 4 I described the Swiss contributions to what I called the infantry's second period of strength. This Swiss infantry was used to break away from Holy Romans, among others through the important victories at the battles of Morgarten 1315 and Sempach 1386.[576]

The early forest communities mentioned above were direct democracies of roughly the same kind as the Germanic direct democracies dealt with earlier in this chapter, or at least there were considerable similarities. When talking about early elements of direct democracy in Switzerland's history it is thus these communities, or cantons, which are alluded to. And by the way it is also probable that the gradually more efficient infantry of these cantons was one of the prerequisites for their direct democracy. Infantry and democracy, as we have seen, tend to go together.

Gradually things however changed. Switzerland grew and became a European Great Power—militarily as well as commercially—with a climax in the beginning of the sixteenth century.[577] Then followed a period characterized not only by reduced influence in the surrounding world but also by internal disintegration. Powerful families took over in the earlier direct democracies and the antagonism between different population groups also increased. The oligarchic elements, both in the individual cantons and in Switzerland as a whole, became increasingly dominant and the direct democracy tradition was thus broken.[578] And this, in fact, is enough for stating that our hypothesis is not falsified by the Swiss example. When the Swiss direct democracies fell they were not replaced by representative democracy but by oligarchy. To make this still more obvious we can however take a look also at the following development, the one finally leading to the representative democracy of modern Switzerland.

I start in 1798 when Switzerland was occupied by Napoleon Bonaparte. He introduced for the whole country, which was at that time weakened and de-democratized, a new, uniform constitution, and thereby created the so called Helvetic Republic. This was however never to gain

---

[576] Finer (1997b), pp. 957-8.
[577] Steinberg, p. 29.
[578] Steinberg, p. 30.

any importance and after the end of the Napoleonic wars followed first the Congress of Vienna in 1815 and then, in all of Europe, a period of general turbulence and revolutionary tendencies. Important years during this period, for Switzerland as well as for large parts of the rest of Europe, were 1830 and 1848. At the first of these, 1830, some Swiss cantons— inspired by the revolutionary processes in France and in America (about which more follows in chapter 9)—began introducing representative systems. And at the later occasion, 1848, the cantons together created the modern Swiss federal state. And this one was a representative democracy even if, at an early stage, it was supplemented with considerable direct democratic elements in the form of referendum processes. Federal, or national, referendum processes, in contrast to the cantonal ones, were however not introduced until 1874.

The Swiss representative democracy thus appeared—in the same way as a number of other representative democracies—as a result of inspiration from America and France. In connection with this, but after rather than before, important referendum processes were also added to the Swiss constitution. This, or at least its scope, was certainly unique to Switzerland, and in that sense in all likelihood also a consequence of the Swiss tradition. But nevertheless it was completely dependent on the prior introduction of representative democracy. If the processes in other places, which resulted from the impulses from America and France, not had taken place, then Switzerland, today, would not have had any representative democracy, and no direct democracy either. The earlier development of representative democracy in other parts of the world was therefore a necessary prerequisite not only for Swiss representative democracy, but also for the frequent use of referendums in Swiss politics. It was not the early tradition of direct democracy which led to the Swiss representative democracy.

SUMMARY

A direct democracy, as defined here, is a state in which all free citizens, or at least most of them, take part in the public decision making. There is no representative assembly, only the gathering of the citizens in some public place. Furthermore the procedures, such as the gatherings and the decisions, are regulated by respected rules.

It is now long since any states of this kind existed, one obvious reason being that they have to be quite small, and much smaller than states for other reasons should be or tend to be. These remote direct democracies have however, even though sharing a number of important properties, been of two quite different types. The first type—exemplified by the German direct democracies—developed out of more primitive tribal societies, and for those involved they were thus the very first states. The direct democracy followed immediately after the non-state tribal society. And this state therefore, even if a state, was also quite primitive. The other type—exemplified by some ancient Greek city states and in particular Athens—was quite different. Rather than being primitive they were developed high cultures following after dictatorships and/or oligarchies.

This also means that the mechanisms involved in creating these two types of direct democracies were quite different. As for the primitive first type the creation may well have been the result of discussions and agreements among those concerned. But in the Greek city-states the fundamental mechanism of change, described in chapter 3, was active. Unrest or agitation among the hoplite infantry soldiers had to be countered in some way and—in Athens—the dictator Cleisthenes thought out, presented and implemented a detailed and sophisticated constitution which was to last for 170 years, a period including Athens Golden Age.

After the descriptions of the Germanic direct democracies and the Athenian one the chapter ends with a section about Switzerland. The reason is that Switzerland sometimes is said to exemplify a transition from direct to representative democracy, and the purpose of the section is to show that this was not so. Direct and representative democracies are as different from each other as from other basic constitutional orders. There is no way in which a direct democracy smoothly can develop into a representative one.

8

OLIGARCHIES

OLIGARCHIES IN THE HISTORY OF THE WORLD

Oligarchies are state monopolies of violence which among other things, and above all, are characterized by being controlled by a rather small group of persons. It might for instance be a group of families having acquired influence by means of great land possessions, gainful commercial activities, or something else. The ruling group is thus smaller than in democracies in which, in principle, the whole people takes part in the decision-making, and bigger than in dictatorships in which, again in principle, a single individual controls what is going on.

The size of the ruling group—intermediate size if one so wants—is however not the only characteristic of the oligarchies. Had it been like that the border-lines to both direct democracies and dictatorships had been less sharp than in fact they are. In a direct democracy a smaller group may for instance take hold of the power at the expense of the rest of the people, and in such cases, if only the size of the ruling group mattered, one could talk about oligarchies. And in dictatorships the power may now and then become spread over larger groups as when the mandarins took over in China or the army in the Roman Empire. Even here one could talk about oligarchies if the number of those ruling was the only relevant characteristic. An oligarchy, as I use the term here, is however not only characterized by the size of the governing group. Important is also that there is a generally known, and on the whole, respected set of rules specifying the individuals belonging to the ruling group, the procedures for selecting these individuals, and the functions or particular tasks of these individuals. The existence of such a set of rules thus distinguishes the oligarchies from cases to which the borders otherwise would have been fuzzy, for instance direct democracies run off the rails or dictatorships similarly run off. Thus I will talk about oligarchies only when the small ruling group also is supported by an open, well-known and basically respected set of rules.[579]

States in which the ruling group has an intermediary size, but which are lacking established and respected rules are in fact quite common, and of more types than the transformed direct democracies or dictatorships just mentioned. Consider for instance today's Russia. The efforts undertaken after the fall of the Soviet Empire for introducing representative democracy have obviously failed, and the present situation is characterized by small group ruling without generally respected rules. And for this reason—the lack of rules strict enough—the situation is probably unstable. Within a rather short period of time—perhaps within the next ten years—considerable transformations are likely to take place. Perhaps towards democracy, or perhaps back towards party dictatorship. Something similar, as I argued in the section "Dictatorship and market economy" in chapter 5, may be presumed about today's China. More about this kind of phenomena follows in the Appendix.

The number of known oligarchies in the history of the world is not that great, and all of them—except, perhaps, a few Indian oligarchies around the year −500[580]—have appeared within what in Chapter 2 was called the main course. Furthermore they existed only during an intermediate period—the first ones appeared long after the first states, and they had all disappeared before the modern age. The first western oligarchy was probably Sparta, then came the Roman Republic, and then, much later, in Europe of the Medieval Age and the Renaissance, a number of oligarchic city-states such as Venice appeared. But many more than that there have probably not been. The pattern of existence is thus similar to that for the direct democracies, whereas the contrast to the patterns for dictatorships, as well as for representative democracies, is striking. The former, as we have seen, have been many, have existed during all the time we are dealing with and in all parts of the world, and have also dominated for a very long period. The latter, the representative democracies, appeared only late, but after that spread rapidly over large parts of the world.

But even if the oligarchies have been relatively few, and existed only during an intermediate period, they have nevertheless differed

---

[579] Perhaps it should be noted that this second element in the definition, the respected set of rules, is not always present. Sometimes, or perhaps even often, although not in this book, an oligarchy is simply defined as state governed just by a limited group of some kind.
[580] Finer (1997c), p. 1221.

considerably from each other. The property variation is, in fact, probably greater than for any other of the four types of states dealt with in this book—at least it is more difficult to generalize about the oligarchies. In this chapter I will therefore take up three individual cases, namely Sparta, the Roman Republic and Venice.

SPARTA

THE SPARTAN SOCIETY

Sparta, we remember from chapter 2, was for a long time and beside Athens, the most important of the Greek city states. In the case of Sparta the city-state label is however somewhat misleading. There was thus no main city corresponding to Athens, just four large villages fairly close to each other. And neither was there any defensive wall until at a very late stage, after the Great Power era we are interested in here.[581]

But there were also interesting similarities between Athens and Sparta. In both states the dictatorships—the tyrannies—were abandoned at the time when Greek infantry soldiers, the hoplites, began to be used on a larger scale and thereby showed their strength, that is about the year 600.[582] In both cases this abandonment was a reaction against the tyranny and even if the extent of the change differed in the two states, it nevertheless went in the same direction. Athens, as we have already seen, went all the way to direct democracy, whereas Sparta rather stopped as an oligarchy. In Sparta as well as in Athens the new constitutional orders—the oligarchy and the direct democracy respectively—were however in place and fully developed prior to the Persian wars, so important and crucial for both states. In these wars the two states, for once, were on the same side and triumphed.

Even if Sparta never became an empire it nevertheless developed into a local great power. It occupied successively larger areas on the Peloponnesian peninsula and became the territorially greatest Greek city-state. Thereby it acquired not only valuable land but also labor force since the people of the occupied areas were made slaves. And as a society Sparta was the diametrical opposite to Athens with its free and open discussions, its philosophical and artistic creativity, and its extensive

---

[581] Hansen, p. 87.
[582] Finer (1997a), p. 318.

naval foreign trade. In contrast to this Sparta was a pure land-state almost exclusively aiming at war-faring. It was virtually, in fact, a permanent military camp. Since Sparta was an oligarchy I follow the terminology introduced in chapter 3 and call the ordinary Spartans, the individuals most nearly "free", citizens. This may seem strange since they, as we will see, did not at all enjoy the same rights as the citizens in democratic Athens. But still they were much freer than the many slaves. And possibly they were also loyal to their society.

Sparta's male citizens were its soldiers. It was they who did the fighting, and their training began early. At the age of seven the training of the sons of the citizens' families began, and when they had reached the age of twelve they were taken away from the families and put into training camps characterized by a brutal, mechanical discipline. During two years, from the age of eighteen to twenty, they endured the hard education for becoming effective hoplite soldiers. But not even this made them full citizens. For this they also had to be successfully adopted by a so called *syssitia*, a group of about fifteen men. These groups, which were the smallest entities in the military organization, and in which the men lived to the age of thirty, were characterized by, among others, homosexuality, strange and rigorously upheld meal rituals and an extreme soldier culture. The existence of these groups meant that Sparta was constantly mobilized. Spartan boys/men were thus compelled to live outside family and home from the age of twelve to thirty, even if they were allowed to marry during that time.

To this it should be added that Sparta, according to all evidence, was a manifest class society. A land-owner aristocracy was quite influential and many of the common people, even if not slaves, could nevertheless, according to the standards of the age, be quite poor.

After the Persian wars Sparta and Athens again became enemies and Sparta, due to its successes in the Peloponnesian war (431–04), came to dominate the Greek world. Somewhat later Sparta however met a superior enemy, even this one a Greek city-state, namely Thebes. At the battle of Leuctra in 371 Sparta lost forever its Great Power status.

THE CONSTITUTION AROUND −500

Four different institutions or organs participated in the decision-making, namely two kings, a board consisting of five so called *ephors*, a council of old men, the *gerousia*, and an assembly comprising all grown up, male citizens.[583]

Sparta thus had two kings—unique in the whole history of the world as it seems—and even if they inherited their positions they came from two different families. So already here there was a separation of power element, a barrier against a return to tyranny, which certainly was intended. The kings' most important task was leading the army in field, which, of course, was of utmost importance in the warring state of Sparta.

Going then to the three other institutions—the board, the council and the assembly—there was, among them and in the handling of current, routine affairs, a hierarchical order. The board was at the top, below it the council, and below it the assembly. But still the assembly was superior in the sense that it, at least formally, appointed the members of the board and the council. Let us however start with the current, routine affairs.

The board, which consisted of five *ephors*, appointed for one-year terms, had the executive power. It mobilized the army, sent orders to the commanders in the field, handled judicial affairs, supervised the educational system and received ambassadors from other states. The board, finally, was the only instance competent to summon the council. This latter could thus not do anything without the board wishing so.

The council, or the elderly council, or the *gerousia*, consisted of 28 elected men. To be electable an age of sixty (!) was required and the one elected remained in his position for life. Furthermore the two kings sat in the council which may be somewhat surprising. In spite of being highest in the decision-making hierarchy in a sense, the kings did not take part in the board of the *ephors* but rather in the council or *gerousia*. Possibly this contributed to the great prestige enjoyed by latter. Among the tasks of the council were decisions about death sentences. Furthermore the council prepared in detail all issues to be handled by the assembly, among others legislative proposals.

And thereby we have reached the assembly which, we remember, consisted of all grown up, male citizens. At first this assembly, as already mentioned, had the important task of appointing all members of the board and the council. This power was however not altogether un-circumscribed. The voting procedures were in fact such that those already

---

[583] Finer (1997a), pp. 336-40.

having power—for instance because of coming from big, well-known and perhaps rich families—were favored from the very beginning. When electing new board- or council-members there was thus no show of hands but the members of the assembly, rather, expressed their views by approval shouting, applauds and the like, and the one who thereby got, or was considered having got, the most evident, audible support, was elected. Furthermore, and in addition to the task of electing members of the board and the council, the assembly also had the important assignment of saying yes or no to proposals from the council. Even this assignment was however severely circumscribed.[584] Thus there was no free discussion—basically only those directly addressed by some superior (a king, an *ephor* or a member of the *gerousia*) were allowed to speak. And in addition to this the assembly was not sure to have its way if it voted "wrongly", that is against the council's proposal. In such cases it occurred that the council implemented its proposal anyway.

COMMENT

By now it should be clear why Sparta, in contrast to Athens, is classified here as an oligarchy. The powers of Sparta's popular assembly were, in contrast to those of Athens', and as we have seen, most considerably limited. In Sparta there was no freedom of speech as in Athens. In Sparta decisions were not taken by show of hands as in Athens, but by methods which, in reality, deprived the assembly of much of its formal influence. Going then to the institutions above the assembly, the conclusions are similar. In Sparta there were, beside the kings, the board and the council, which both were small and hardly democratically elected, and therefore represented a very considerable concentration of power. The Athenian correspondence to these two organs, the many-headed council appointed by means of lottery, was obviously more democratic even if some questions may be raised about that as well. Finally Sparta was also lacking a correspondence to the general right of initiative existing in Athens. For all of these reasons it is thus obvious that Sparta was not a democracy, but obviously it was neither a dictatorship. Sparta and Athens had both, from an earlier tyranny, developed in the same direction, but not equally far. Athens had gone all the way to democracy. Sparta had not

---

[584] Finer (1997a), p. 340.

gone that far but the power had nonetheless become spread among a considerable number of individuals. Sparta had become an oligarchy.

Still the respect for the rules in Sparta may be discussed. Had the formal rules for the assembly been fully respected Sparta had, at least almost, been a direct democracy. It is therefore, mainly, the lack of respect of the rules for the assembly which has made me classify Sparta as an oligarchy. One may, I think, quite reasonably, and because of the lack of respect for the rules, consider the assembly as non-existing. And if so only the kings, the board and the counsel remain, that is small groups of decision-makers. The rules for these organs seem however, on the whole, to have been followed, and therefore it should be perfectly adequate to consider the state an oligarchy.

Our knowledge about how Sparta got its constitution is limited— we know much more about the creation of Athens' direct democracy than about the emergence of Sparta's oligarchy. In Athens Solon, and in particular Cleisthenes, played important roles, but for Sparta it is difficult to find a corresponding person. A certain Lycurgus is sometimes mentioned, it is true, but the existence of this man has become increasingly doubted. It seems however clear, as I have already written, that the hoplites were important in both cases. It also seems likely that the constitutions, in both cases and on the whole, were introduced in one step. The introductory process was not drawn out and gradual. For Athens this seems quite clear, and similarly for Sparta even if not equally clear. But why then—and in spite of these similarities—did the two states not develop equally far away from tyranny? About this one may only speculate. Perhaps the personal characteristics of the Athenians Solon and Cleisthenes were decisive for Athens. And perhaps the great land-owners were decisive for Sparta.

Anyhow there is nothing in Sparta's development which is difficult to explain, no more than in Athens'. Everything is compatible with the logic of collective action. Sparta's constitution may—just as a possibility—have been thought out and implemented by a small group of big land-owners. The families of the two kings may have been land-owners of that kind, and the land-owners may also have considered it expedient, or perhaps even necessary, to introduce the really quite power-less assembly as a concession to those actually fighting the wars, the hoplites. If so, the fundamental mechanism of change, described in chapter 3, was operating.

THE ROMAN REPUBLIC

THE EMERGENCE AND DEVELOPMENT OF THE CONSTITUTION

As I wrote in chapter 2 Rome was founded around −750 and, in −509, was converted to the oligarchy usually called the Roman Republic.[585] Before that the state was ruled by a king, a council of elders and an assembly of warriors.[586] The time for the Republic may be counted to −134, or possibly to −31, when the era of the Empire began. Since the period from −134 to −31 was turbulent and to a large extent characterized by civil war it is, however, in this context appropriate to set the end for the Republic at −134. But even so its life-time was long. Between −509 and −134 there are 375 years. And even if the territorial expansion was to continue after −134, it had nevertheless gone far already by that time. From the village at the mouth of the Tiber it had expanded so as to include all of the Mediterranean as a Roman internal sea—*Mare Nostrum* (our sea). The Republic was in fact an extreme war-waging state, almost like Sparta even if everything was not about war as in the Greek state. Albeit the victories and war-booties were necessary preconditions the Romans of the Republic have still enriched the world with a large treasury of fantastic sculptures, architecture, writings, and so forth.

Here, however, we are concerned with constitutional development. And a development it was, in fact—a successive, gradual development. It was not as in Athens, and probably also in Sparta, basically a one-step process. But still the fundamental reason was the same as in Athens and Sparta, namely the involvement of large parts of the population in war-waging brought about by the new infantry technique. In Athens and Sparta it was the hoplites, in the Roman Republic the legionaries. These people—so called *plebeians* and when not fighting usually farmers—demanded influence and power by means of various kinds of expressions of dissatisfaction, strikes, and so forth. And the propertied, the so called *patricians*, mostly big land owners, were forced to give in step by step.[587] The fundamental mechanism of change described in chapter 3 operated in a long row of small steps following after each other.

---

[585] The main source for the presentation here is Finer (1997a), pp. 385-441.
[586] Finer (1997a), p. 393.
[587] Finer (1997a), p. 396.

Here—in the same way as in Athens and in Sparta—there is thus nothing which is incompatible with the logic of collective action. The development of the constitution in small, gradual steps did however make it increasingly difficult to handle. Successively more veto-rules made it, for instance, more and more complicated to reach any decisions at all. But it did not stop there. Eventually a situation which, without much exaggeration, could be described as run by two competing constitutions, one for the *patricians* and one for the *plebeians*, was reached. At least it could be said the constitution had two main parts relatively independent of each other. And in at least some cases that made it possible to take decisions contradicting each other. There were for instance not only two, but three, popular assemblies having legislative powers. And even if the areas of these legislative powers varied somewhat between the assemblies, they also overlapped to some extent. The assemblies could therefore now and then, each assembly for itself, take valid, contradictory decisions about the same matter. Political processes could collide.[588]

Describing the whole constitutional development in a more detailed way would lead us too far astray. I therefore confine myself to portraying the constitution as it was in the year −134, that is just before the start of the civil war and the crumbling of the Republic.

THE CONSTITUTION IN THE YEAR −134

The constitution thus had two main parts, the *patricians'* and the *plebeians'*.[589] The two parts were similarly, though not identically, structured. In both the roles of various functionaries with precise, far-reaching capacities, the so called *magistrates*, were spelled out. In the patrician part of the constitution their number was however greater than in the plebeian part. In both parts of the constitution there was also a scope for popular influence by means of assemblies—but in the patrician part there were two assemblies, in the plebeian part only one. And then, in addition to these magistrates and assemblies, there was still a very important institution, namely the *Senate*. It would not be wrong to consider this Senate as belonging to the patrician part of the constitution, but it is also possible to consider it as an institution shared by the two parts. For

---

[588] Finer (1997a), pp. 397, 399.
[589] Finer (1997a), pp. 397-411.

reasons which will become clear below I have settled for the latter alternative.

Let us now start by looking a bit closer at the functionaries—the magistrates—in the patrician part of the constitution. First, they did not only have precise tasks, they were also ranked in a fixed order. I start by describing the functionaries in this order—the significance of the order will be dealt with later on.

Highest ranked were the *censors*, of whom there were two. The Republic was all the time a multi-layered class-society and the censors should, among others, register the citizens in classes depending on their private economies, grant new citizenships, and—when considered called for—expel citizens. These tasks made it possible for the censors to intervene in the political careers of all other ones, and thus made them powerful. The censors held their positions for one year and a half whereas all other magistrates, in contrast, were appointed for only one year.

Next in the ranking order came the two *consuls*. They were, above all, military commanders-in-chief and, since war was almost perpetual, they usually were away from Rome, and in one place each furthermore. There therefore had to be stand-ins for the consuls in Rome, and this was one of the tasks for the next category of magistrates, the so called praetors. The consuls, and in their absence the praetors, also were entitled to summon the senate and the two assemblies.

The *praetors*, altogether six, were however not only stand-ins for the consuls, they also had other important obligations, in particular judicial ones. They were thus not only entitled to sentence in some cases but could also interpret, and complement, existing law, and thereby came to influence considerably the development of the Roman law. Furthermore they shared among themselves the ultimate responsibility for the administration of the provinces of the Republic.

Next came the *quaestors*, altogether eight, who essentially had financial tasks. They received the taxes collected and supervised the expenses of the state. They were, one might say, the Republic's ministers of finance.

And so, at last, came the *aediles*. They were altogether four, but split up into two pairs of which only the one belonged to the patrician part of the constitution. The other pair rather belonged to the plebeian part. But both pairs had the same tasks. Above all they were responsible for order, safety and cleanliness in the city of Rome, and for supervising markets, including prices. And they were also responsible for the provision of public festival games for entertainment.

These, thus, were the magistrates and the order was, as I have already mentioned, of great importance. This, in turn, depended on the constitution's frequent use of vetoes, also mentioned. Higher ranked magistrates could namely veto the decisions of those lower ranked, and this rule was clearly consequential since even lower magistrates had important tasks. The only restriction was that the group of magistrates vetoing had to be unanimous itself. And this was so not only for the vetoes here discussed but for all decisions. For every group of magistrates it was therefore the case that it could act only when unanimous—within each group every individual magistrate had a veto right.

After this we get to the two popular assemblies which can be considered belonging to the patrician part of the constitution. At a quick glance both these assemblies could perhaps seem democratic since they consisted of all male citizens, but in reality it was not so. First, since the meetings were held in or just outside the city of Rome, only a small share of all those permitted were actually able to participate.[590] Furthermore, the decision-rules clearly favored the patricians. So the assemblies were not democratic. That there were two assemblies rather than one, in spite of both having the same members, also has an explanation. The background histories of the two assemblies were different, they met in different places, their authorities were different, and the voting rules were also somewhat different even if the patricians were favored in both cases.

The first assembly—*Comitia Centuriata*—was the oldest one and had a military background. As already mentioned it was summoned by the consuls or the praetors. It had its meetings at the Field of Mars (so called after Mars, the god of war) outside the city of Rome, the proceedings were opened by trumpet fanfares, and the participants stood upright ordered in accordance with their military units. This was also the assembly in which the patricians were most favored by the voting rules. The very important main task of the assembly was to appoint censors, consuls and praetors, that is the three highest ranked categories of magistrates.

---

[590] Lintott, pp. 42, 202-3.

The second assembly—*Comitia Tributa*—had, we remember, the same members as Comitia Centuriata, and was equally summoned by the consuls or the praetors. The organization was however not military—the participants were rather assorted into thirty-five groups with equal voting power. Each one of the groups represented a geographical area in Rome and/or in Rome's neighborhood. The similarities with the corresponding order, the *phylae*, in direct democratic Athens were thus striking. Even here the voting rules favored the patricians although not as much as in the Comitia Centuriata. Among others the assembly appointed the lower ranked magistrates, that is the *quaestors* and the two patrician *aediles*.

The assemblies did however have more tasks than those already mentioned even if the distribution of these tasks is unclear. Some sources indicate one distribution, other ones another. This is so, for instance, for legislative issues, issues about war and peace, and death sentences. But irrespective of these uncertainties it is manifestly clear that the participants did not have the right to initiate issues to be dealt with—they could just say yes or no to proposals presented to them—and neither did they have any right of speech. The assemblies' capacities were thus utterly circumscribed. Once the magistrates were elected, it was they who ruled. The magistrates' short terms in office, and thus the frequently re-occurring magistrate elections, could however be considered a kind of "democratic" safety valve. Another one was an often used tactic for escaping the speech forbidding rule. Debates were held before the formal opening of the meetings, and these debates were even considered so important that they, in fact, constituted a basis for Roman rhetoric.

The magistrates were thus the real power holders and political careers were often made by climbing from lower to higher ranked magistrate positions. For starting at the lower end of the scale an *aedile*—in particular if he was privately rich and prepared to pay for it himself—could arrange lavish festivals and thereby make himself popular and thus enhance his own promotion upwards the scale. For going then to the upper end of the scale, only those having been *consuls* could be elected *censors*. And the censors did not only have a purple stripe in the toga as all other magistrates, they were also buried in full purple attire.

This was thus the first main part of the constitution, but then there was also the plebeian main part. And it was basically structured in the same way as the first one, although somewhat simpler. There was thus only two kinds of magistrates—first the two *aediles* mentioned above, and so the very important *tribunes of the plebs*.

Altogether there were ten *tribunes of the plebs*, and they had far-reaching capacities. They could deliver sentences of various kinds, and they could veto practically all other decisions, even those taken within the patrician part of the constitution. Furthermore they enjoyed a considerable immunity. There were however also important restrictions, basically of two kinds. First they could exercise their power only within the city of Rome and, furthermore, like all other magistrates they had to be unanimous for their decisions to become valid. Each tribune could thus veto the decisions of the other ones. And therefore their great number was a factor of weakness rather than strength—the more numerous they were, the greater the likelihood that someone would veto.

The plebeian assembly—*Concilium Plebis*—was essentially composed in the same way as Comitia Tributa, the only difference being that the patricians were excluded. The assembly thus consisted entirely of plebeians and it was summoned and led by the tribunes. Among its tasks were the elections of the plebeian *aediles*, and the tribunes. And in addition to this, and as the other assemblies, it also had some legislative powers, which added to the collision risks already mentioned.

After this we have finally reached the important *Senate*. It had 300 members appointed for life by the censors—thus one more component in the power of the censors. Electable were only former magistrates, although not tribunes, and military commanders with war marks of distinction. More than any organ the Senate therefore represented broad, heavy-weighted experience and continuity, which is clear already from its very designation. The word "senate" means something like "the elderly counsel"—a term we met already when discussing Sparta—and which has the same radical as for instance the English word "senior". But in spite of its impressive experience the Senate—formally—had only advisory capacity. Furthermore the senators were allowed to speak only when asked to.

In spite of this the Senate was however destined to play a crucial role—it was, in fact, thanks to the Senate that the problems with constant vetoes, and collision risks and actual collisions, could be lived with as long as was indeed the case. For understanding this it is important to know that not only the consuls, and in their absence the praetors, could summon the Senate, but that even the tribunes had considerable capacities in the context. True, they could not themselves become senators, but they could summon the Senate, and not only that. They could participate in the meetings, initiate proposals at them, and even chair them. Furthermore, the rule that a senator could speak only when asked to was not as restrictive as it seemed. When, once, a senator had gotten the word he could namely continue talking about whatever he wanted. This is what made it possible for the senator and military commander Cato—victorious in the war against Hannibal—to end all his speeches by "furthermore I think Carthage must be destroyed".

In reality the Senate thus got an important and central position and this, in combination with other parties' prudence, was the main reason why the total constitution worked as long as it actually did. The Senate was summoned for giving, after appropriate discussions, its advice. This advice was then taken up by some other organ with adequate capacity and was turned into a real, valid decision. And like that it went on for a long, although finite, period. Finally the whole system collapsed in the way described in chapter 2. The reasons were altogether internal. The social unrest resulting from the extreme class-differences in the late Republic could, in the end, not be dealt with peacefully within the framework of the contradictory constitution. After the murder of Tiberius Gracchus the civil war leading to the fall of the Republic began.

VENICE

THE CONSTITUTION'S BACKGROUND

In chapter 2 I wrote about Venice's history and therefore I concentrate on the constitutional topics here. When first populated Venice became, we remember, a province within the Byzantine Empire, which then appointed a functionary for administering the province.[591] Then, after having liberated themselves, the Venetians turned this functionary into their own highest ruler, or *doge*, who was elected by a common, open, popular assembly, the so called *Arengo*. During an initial period there were thus democratic tendencies, and Venice could almost be considered a direct democracy. Gradually the doges did however succeed in shaking off this electoral dependency and the dignity began being inherited. Dynasties

---

[591] The main sources for the presentation here are Finer (1997b), pp. 985-1019 and Lane, pp. 103-17.

emerged and Venice almost became a dictatorship. Around the year 1000 this led to uprisings, a doge was murdered, and after that constitutional transformations followed. Functionaries having in particular the task of supervising the doge were appointed and the common Arengo was substituted for by another assembly which, in spite of being much smaller than the Arengo, was called the *Great Council*.

This was thus, in broad terms, the process leading up to the constitution, in some respects very complex, which will be described in the next section. In its essentials the process was completed around 1420, that is at about the beginning of the Renaissance. And this means—in accordance with what was said in chapters 2 and 5—that Venice had already made its pioneering contributions to the development of economic institutions when the constitution became ready. The Venice governed in accordance with the new constitution was another Venice than the early, epoch-making, commercial city-state. But this does not make the constitution less interesting. It had emerged out of the same milieu, or culture, as the economic institutions, and it was very special and very effective. The other Italian city-states, at the same time, were troubled by constant rebellions and drawn-out family feuds, but in Venice there was practically nothing of this. Most well-known among the families troubled by feuds and revolts were perhaps Albizzi and de' Medici in Florence. Venice's lack of problems like these depended, at least partially, on important differences between its constitution and those of the other city-states. After having got its basically final form around 1420 the constitution was to shape Venetian politics until 1797 when Napoleon Bonaparte conquered the city, that is for a good 350 years. But before turning to the final constitution it is important to say a few more words about the very process of its development. What, more exactly, were the mechanisms involved? And, most important, were they compatible with the logic of collective action?

At first it should be observed that the process, in one important respect, differs from a pattern we have already met several times, namely the pattern of a dictator reacting to rebellions by means of gradual concessions. First, the early rebellions or expressions of discontent did not come from armed entities, but from ordinary, non-armed human beings. Second, it was not the ruling, powerful doge that conceded and introduced changes after the rebellions and the doge murder. Rather it was other, influential Venetians who supplied him with supervisors. But even if this differs from a common pattern, it is hardly unreasonable. At the time at issue there were, in Venice, many rich and therefore powerful merchants, and some of these may very well have cooperated for endowing the doge with supervising functionaries. In the same way well-off Venetians may also have formed the Great Council which, in the beginning, was not all that great, and which replaced the *Arengo*. The groups acting may very well have been quite small and homogenous so that their members knew each other, and probably were so. And groups like that are perfectly able to act constructively even for complex purposes. It is all fully compatible with the logic of collective action.

THE CONSTITUTION AROUND *1420*

The institutions exercising power were placed on three main levels. At the lowest level was the Great Council having around 1500 members. These members were not elected—the decisive element, rather, was family connections. To the council belonged all male descendants to those who, at the end of the thirteenth century (why this time is important will be clarified below), had constituted the council. The council was thus closed. Apart from some exceptions during the very early days no other ones than the sons of the original members, and their sons and so on, could become members of the council. But even if the council was closed in this sense it nevertheless became bigger and bigger, in particular as the members were appointed for life. The council's most important task was to elect, among its own members, the functionaries at the next level, the level just above its own.

At this level, the intermediate level, there was the *Senate* with 260 members, and also an institution called the *Council of Ten*. The senate took decisions about legislation, but could not initiate such issues—the initiatives had to come from above. Furthermore the senate elected, from among its own members or possibly, but not often, from the Great Council, the functionaries at the third and highest level. The Council of Ten handled particularly urgent issues but in addition to that also had its own particular and very important tasks. The council was in fact a kind of political court, or even a secret police.

The background was that all the Italian city-states had problems with families, or groups of other kinds, emanating from the own state but living for one reason or another in exile. Groups like that could intervene

in the politics of their own state, possibly violently, and therefore constituted a constant threat. When the Council of Ten was created, around the
year 1300, its main, assigned task was to identify and defeat threats like
these. Gradually the council was however also given similar internal
tasks, which meant fighting assumed political threats. To a large extent
the council, which was given some sentencing capacity, acted in secret
and, gradually, acquired a reputation for great brutality and cruelty. Individuals suspected could, if they were not executed secretly, be imprisoned
in narrow cells in the underground storage of the Doge's Palace or in
horribly hot chambers immediately below its lead roof. The most well-
known of all of these prisoners was the frivolous adventurer Giacomo
Casanova (1725–98). But even if the competence of the council thus was
very far-reaching its activities were nevertheless, at least to a large extent, initiated from above, from the highest level.

There, at the highest level, were the so called *Collegio*, consisting of
26 persons, and the highest power-holder, the *Doge*, who chaired the
Collegio. Initiatives for new legislation had to come from this Collegio
even if the ensuing decisions, as already mentioned, had to be taken by
the Senate, or at least at the intermediate level—they could not be taken
by the Collegio itself. But even if the competence of the highest level thus
were confined to initiatives—at least as far as legislative issues were
concerned—the creators of the constitution had nevertheless found it
important to regulate matters there in more detail. The Collegio itself was
therefore partitioned into a number of smaller units—units which not
only should assist the doge in various ways, but also supervise him.

So those were the main traits of the constitution. That we are
dealing with an oligarchy is already evident. All functionaries were recruited, as we have seen, from a closed group of Venetian families. But
this oligarchy worked well and without those destructive family feuds so
frequent in the other Italian city-states. The reasons for this relative
peacefulness were of different kinds, but they were partly related to the
constitution and those are the ones interesting us here.

Of great importance, and perhaps most important, were the rules
for the composition of the Great Council. These rules, implemented by the
doge Pietro Gradenigo (1251–1311) in 1297, guaranteed, as we have
seen, that at least all families important or powerful at that time could feel
sure about being represented even in the future, and thereby at least
some reasons for conflicts between these families were eliminated. This

necessarily implied, however, that the Council became bigger and bigger. From some points of view this was possibly a disadvantage, but it could also be advantageous since it made formation of factions within the Council more difficult. The great potential problem obviously was that families which eventually grew big and important, and which from the beginning were outside the Council, could feel entitled to be included and to that end perhaps even use violence. That, however, appears not to have happened in practice.

Important was also that most of the positions in the decision-making organs mentioned above were held only for short periods, a year perhaps or even less, and that the possibilities for re-election were strictly limited or even excluded. In this way a relatively large share of those formally qualified to take part in the governing of the state also, actually, did take part. This was, in fact, a kind of rotation. No one, and above all no family, needed to feel excluded. The rules for the Council of Ten may serve as an example. The members were elected for one year terms and immediate re-election was not allowed. Furthermore one and the same family could not have more than one member in the Council. And the one presiding the Council, which was one of the members, held his position only for a month—then the chairmanship went to another member. The appointments for the Council of Ten were thus subject to principles of short terms and of rotation, and the same was true for most other organs. But even so there were exceptions from these principles. Thus senators could be re-elected, and that also happened again and again. The Senate therefore, in the same way as the Roman Senate, came to represent a lot of experience and prudence. Another exception was the Doge who was elected for life.

Thereby we have reached a third group of reasons for the peaceful conditions in Venice. Even if I have written that there were, at the highest level, instruments for controlling the doge, he was nevertheless, and in comparison with the corresponding functionaries in the other city-states, a rather efficient actor. In the other states, there was, instead of a single main person, a group called *Signoria*. The members of such a group could find it hard to cooperate and hence the leadership of the state could be less efficient. But Venice did not have this problem, which may have contributed to its peacefulness and wellbeing. The fact that Venice had only one leading person was, we remember, a Byzantine legacy, but that did not prevent the Venetians from developing the institution in their own very particular way. The procedure for electing a doge was utterly complex, but not without advantages. The method, essentially the same all the time, was used in all doge elections—quite a number—from 1298 to 1797.

I start by describing the procedure. Those participating, and those electable, were all the members of the Great Council. The purpose of the process was to appoint, at first, an appropriate *Electoral College*, that is a group of persons likely to nominate a really good doge candidate, preferably the best one. Then, when this candidate was nominated, the proposal was presented for the Great Council which normally accepted it. Once the nomination was achieved the real election was thus a pure formality. What is remarkable in the process is however the activities before these final steps, the series of preliminary steps taken for getting, finally, the ideal electoral college. This is how it was done:

Step 1: A first, provisional electoral college consisting of 30 individuals is selected from the Great Council by lot casting.

Step 2: Those 30 are reduced to 9 by lot casting.

Step 3: Those remaining 9, by electing new, additional members, turn themselves into a new provisional electoral college of 40 members.

Step 4: Those 40 are reduced to 12 by lot casting.

Step 5: Those 12, by electing new members, turn themselves into a new provisional electoral college of 25 members.

Step 6: Those 25 are reduced to 9 by lot casting.

Step 7: Those 9, by electing new members, turn themselves into a new provisional electoral college of 45 members.

Step 8: Those 45 are reduced to 11 by lot casting.

Step 9: Those 11, by electing new members, turn themselves into a new final electoral college of 41 members.

Step 10: This final electoral college nominates a doge candidate.

Step 11: The Great Council accepts the nomination and elects the nominated candidate to doge.

What happens is thus that a first provisional electoral college, appointed by means of lottery, is transformed again and again. Every second transformation consists in a reduction of the number of members of the college by means of lottery, and every second transformation in enlargements of the council by means of elections by those remaining. There is thus in this procedure a considerable element of lottery, but the purpose of this was never that the appointment of the doge should be left to chance. The purpose, on the contrary, was to find the person most suitable for the job and then, finally, elect that person. The lottery was therefore of a completely different kind, and had a completely different purpose, than that in, for instance, Athens' direct democracy. In Athens the idea was to spread the political activities, and, to the extent possible, make all those permitted take part in them—in principle all were considered equally competent. In Venice the purpose was rather to make it impossible for special interests, for instance strong and influential families, to interfere with the nomination process to their own advantage. By lot casting all tendencies towards factional coalition formations should continuously be eliminated. The purpose was to get rid of all special interests just in order to bring forward the best doge.

Probably this was also achieved. In a modern, mathematical and statistical analysis of the procedure, posted on the Internet by the IT-company Hewlett-Packard, the authors mention that the procedure may have contributed Venice's extraordinary stability and long life.[592] The reason why these authors became interested in the procedure, and scrutinized it thoroughly, was that similar methods may be of interest in situations where a large number of computers need to "elect" a lead computer to direct cooperative operations. Anyway, since the procedure was so complex and long-winded, the Venetians were obviously prepared to go very far in order to avoid family feuds and similar political struggles.

COMMENT

Venice was, in its own age, a very successful state. People lived well and even though inequalities were considerable even the poorest were better off than in most other places in Europe. Equality before the law was

---

[592] Mowbray, Miranda & Gollman, Dieter, *Electing the Doge of Venice: Analysis of a 13th Century Protocol.*

significant and also freedom of speech. Social unrest was, in particular when compared with the conditions in the other Italian city-states or the contemporary European kingdoms, almost non-existent. To a large extent all of this resulted from the Venetians' skill as merchants and sailors, even if there also were elements of chance or good luck. When, for instance, the rest of Europe and large parts of its population were hit by crop-failure this could rather turn into an advantage for Venice. The crop-failure could increase the demand for long-distance, sea transports of grains.

Of great importance was however also the very special constitution. This gave, as we have seen, ultimately *all* formal influence to the Great Council. Considered as a council this was certainly very large, but as a share of the population it was nevertheless quite small. Still non-members seemed to concur with the activities of the Council and the other organs and institutions. Conversely it seems as if those having positions in these various organs on the whole also felt solidarity with the outsiders, the common people. But how could it be like this? Which were the mechanisms leading to this result?

Probably the explanation is related to those very manifest barriers against all kinds of factions or small groups, whether family-related or of other kinds, which characterized the constitution. All kinds of partial, special-interest politics were intensively discouraged. Political parties of the kind present in all democratic countries today, and which are considered indispensable there, could not be have been founded in Venice, and much less have worked. Probably this total absence of political parties was a necessary complement to the allocation of all formal political power to a small, sharply defined minority group. If the one was there, the other had to be so too. Today, a constitution like this would obviously, and immediately, lead to grave conflicts. A small minority's holding of all power would never be accepted. But in Venice, prior to the era of the representative democracy, it was quite acceptable. And not only that, it worked well and the result was very good. The political scientist and historian Samuel Finer has characterized Venice—at least until the end of the seventeenth century—as the best governed state in the world.[593]

But the constitution not only functioned well. Probably it was also unique. I do not know of any other constitution such as Venice's, or even

---

[593] Finer (1997b), p. 1016.

similar to it in the central respects here described. Most probably several persons from Venice's leading families had contributed to this remarkable innovation, for an innovation it was. But if one individual should be singled out—a kind of correspondence to Athens' Cleisthenes—that should be the doge Pietro Gradenigo.

SUMMARY

An oligarchy is a state governed by a limited group of some kind, but this is not the only defining property. As the concept is used here the governing also follows some set of generally respected rules. The number of oligarchies in world history is quite small, most of them (or perhaps all) appeared in what in chapter 2 was described as the main course, and they existed only in an intermediary period in the history of states. But even if they have been few, they have been quite different. Therefore I have described, in some detail, three oligarchies, namely Sparta, the Roman Republic and Venice.

The fundamental mechanism of change, described in chapter 3, was involved in the creation of Sparta and the Roman Republic, although in Sparta it probably, and on the whole, was a one-step process, whereas in the Roman Republic the mechanism worked again and again, until finally the constitution became unworkable. In both cases however, the grumblings necessary for initiating the mechanism came from infantry soldiers, the hoplites and the legionaries respectively. In Venice the creational mechanism was however quite different. The very particular, and for a long time very well working, constitution was to a large extent the result of the thinking of one man, the doge Pietro Gradenigo.

Here in the summary it may now be interesting to compare the three oligarchies in some respects. If we start by looking at the highest level power was more divided in Sparta and the Roman Republic than in Venice. Sparta had two kings, The Roman Republic two censors, two consuls, and so forth, while Venice had only one doge. For certain the doge was completed and supervised in certain respects but the topmost leadership was still less split than in Sparta and in Rome.

Going then to the lowest level—the popular if one so wishes—there were important differences even there. In Sparta all male citizens could participate in the assembly, but their power was utterly circumscribed, formally as well as in reality. They had no formal right to speak, and their decisions were neglected if not in accordance with what was wanted by higher functionaries. In the Roman Republic the influence of the popular assemblies was reduced in other ways. First, only citizens living in the city of Rome or its immediate surroundings were able to participate at all; second, only one of the assemblies was genuinely popular; and third, the three assemblies could end up taking different and contradictory decisions. The real power was therefore held by the all but popular Senate. In Venice finally the lowest level was represented by the Great Council, which was completely closed and the members of which all came from well-off and successful families. At the same time the constitution however included a number of rules designed to make impossible all kinds of partial interest politics within this group. The very complicated, but again and again practiced procedure for electing a new dodge was thus, in all likelihood, designed for avoiding all faction building. In today's representative democracies political parties are essential or even necessary. In Venice, long before the appearance of these democracies, they had, on the contrary, to be avoided by all means.

9

THE BIRTH AND SPREAD OF THE
REPRESENTATIVE DEMOCRACY

INTRODUCTION

The representative democracy is a constitutional order in which, in its simplest form, an assembly whose members are chosen by the citizens, and therefore represent them, takes the decisions of the state. The representative assembly is the basic, defining characteristic. Sometimes the pattern may however be more complex without any departure from the basic principle, which is why I say "in its simplest form". There may, for instance, be two assemblies rather than one, and there not only may be, but usually also is, some kind of ministry or president, a so called executive. In cases like these it is often required that a decision, to become valid, should be taken, in the same words, by both assemblies and the executive. Regardless of all variations like these all decision-makers are however popularly elected and there is always at least one representative assembly. And it is this one—the representative assembly—which is the most important element in the definition. Without such an assembly it is impossible to talk about representative democracy.

The representative democracy appeared at a very late stage in the history of states. But it not only appeared late. In this chapter I will furthermore assert that it appeared quite accidentally—by a stroke of luck as one might say. It could equally well have been the case that this accident never occurred, and in that case we would have lived in a fundamentally different, and much worse, world than the one we are in fact living in. This thesis about an accidental occurrence may perhaps seem surprising, and for some perhaps even challenging. This, in turn, may be so since the thesis is hardly ever expressed and most people, therefore, do not have an opinion about it—they neither accept nor refute it. It simply does not belong within the realm of accepted knowledge, not even within political science for that matter. Since the thesis is not widely accepted it must obviously be rigorously substantiated and in this chapter I will try to do so, but not immediately. It is better, I think, to start by describing the very process which led to the emergence of representative democracy. Then, when we are acquainted with this process, it is much easier to argue both for its uniqueness and for its unlikeliness.

In the next and following sections I will thus describe a historical sequence of events which should be noted since I earlier, after the historical presentations in chapter 2, wrote that there should not be much more of that kind of exposition. But here I thus make an exception. I will engage in what I have earlier called sequential history, and my doing so is due exactly to the unlikeliness of representative democracy. The other kinds of states, and above all dictatorships, have, as we have seen, appeared in many places, at different times, and completely independent of each other, and their emergence may therefore be explained by means of ordinary social science reasoning in the way I have tried to do in the preceding chapters. With representative democracy it is different—it appeared only once, at one single occasion, by one single, particular sequence of events. The appearance was *path dependent*. This first sequence of events has been a necessary prerequisite for all representative democracies existing today. After this first sequence it was relatively easy to continue, essentially by copying. Before that, it was impossible.

THE BIRTH

THE FEUDAL ORIGIN

The development was, as we will see, gradual. It started during the chaotic and primitive conditions characterizing Europe after the fall of the Western Roman Empire. Out of this chaos emerged, gradually, feudalism. And then, much later, and without that ever being the intention, something having similarities with representative democracy began to appear. What was decisive was the emergence of the feudal assemblies of barons or knights, since it was they which, in due time, were to be converted to the assemblies of the representative democracies.[594] But even if this step was necessary it was not sufficient. It was also necessary that the feudal assemblies survived long enough, which usually was not the case.

---

[594] This crucial connection, the one between the feudal assemblies and the democratic representative assemblies is, as far as I have been able to find out, overlooked by Fukuyama.

That happened in fact, and because of a series of lucky coincidences, only in one country, namely England. And there, gradually, it also developed into something similar to the kind of assembly a democracy must have in order to be called representative. But let us start from the beginning.

The emergence of the feudal system depended on two cooperating circumstances. The first was the widespread return to self-sufficiency in Europe after the fall of the Roman Empire, and the concomitant widespread reduction of commerce and use of money. The other was the development of the technique of violence which had made the knight such an utterly effective weapon. But this weapon was also costly. The king wanting to acquire the weapon therefore had to pay a lot, but since money no longer was in use a special kind of bartering came into being. Those able to supply fully equipped knights, for instance big land-owners, did so in return for—that was the barter deal—being allowed, by the king, to handle their fiefs, including their inhabitants, just about as they wanted. This barter deal between a king, on the one side, and a number of land owners, or barons, on the other, was feudalism's basic element.

The bartering could in principle be initiated from both sides. A number of land-owners could unite and choose a common, superior ruler, a king, but it could also happen that a king, governing some larger area, distributed power to land-owners within the area so that they could control their regions themselves. In the first case a number of smaller units were thus integrated into a larger entity, and in the second case an initially larger unit was split into smaller parts. Both processes seem to have occurred even if the first one, the integration, seems to have been most common. Around the year 1000 a number of feudally ruled kingdoms or states appeared in this way in various places in Europe.

The next step in the development was that the king and the barons started meeting each other simultaneously. Again the initiative may in some cases have come from above, and in other ones from below. As for the first it is, for instance, easy to imagine that the king convened all the barons together in order to get more support for his policies, or, perhaps, simply for gaining time and making the discussions simpler. But it is also easy to imagine that the barons, by acting together, strived to put pressure on the king, or to control him in some way.

Additional mechanisms also contributed to the emergence of the meetings or assemblies. Above all the monetary economy began spreading again and thereby the conditions for acquiring weapons changed, even though the knight weapon had developed further and also become more expensive. If only the kings could get hold of money enough, they could buy the weapons they wanted rather than being constrained by the earlier barter deals.[595] But feudalism did not, as a result, come to an end. Rather it changed slowly step by step. One such step was that the barons, while keeping their former privileges, were asked to supply the king with money rather than weapons, or, at least, rather than only weapons. In England, in the twelfth century, the barons' duty was for instance changed from delivering weapons to delivering so called shield-money or scutage.[596] And the barons got this money by taxing their own subjects.

Then, related to this, something new and important occurred. Some kings, to be sure about their future incomes, required that the barons, in advance, committed themselves to the payments. Had the assembly taken a decision about taxation, unwilling tax-payers in the regions should thereafter not be able to obstruct that decision. The barons' commitments were thus made on behalf of their subjects, and thereby a formal relationship between barons and subjects was established. In the short run this new order perhaps increased the power of the king and the barons at the expense of the subjects, but if so only in the short run. In the long run it was different since what was introduced was a principle of representation which was eventually to favor the subjects. Even if the subjects, in the beginning, had no alternative but to say yes to the demands of their baron or chief, they were nevertheless asked. And thereby there was introduced, in the relationship between the baron and the king, an element of representation. The baron, to some extent, represented his subjects.[597]

In this way, during the thirteenth, fourteenth and fifteenth centuries, assemblies of barons were created in many places—for instance within the areas which are today England, France, Italy, Poland, Spain, Germany, Hungary and the Scandinavian countries. For giving just a few examples such an assembly was in England called *parliament*, in France *états généraux*, in Spain *cortes*, in Germany *Landtage* and in Sweden *riksdag*.[598] Then, accompanying the growth of the money economy, not

---

[595] North & Thomas, p. 40.
[596] Finer (1997b), pp. 1027-8; North & Thomas, pp. 65-6; Palmer, Colton & Kramer (2007a), p. 36.
[597] Finer (1997a), p. 19; Finer (1997b), p. 1027; Roberts, pp. 511-2.
[598] Palmer, Colton & Kramer (2007a), p. 36.

only the tasks of these assemblies changed, but also their composition. Taxes could be collected not only from, and by means of, barons but also from other groups. Apart from the original "noble-men" the priests, and the burghers of the cities, were interesting from this point of view, and in some countries such as Sweden, even the farmers were considered fitting objects for taxation.[599] But taxing these groups without also giving them places in the assembly could, for the king, seem hard, or improper, or perhaps even impossible. In many places the assemblies were therefore enlarged so that even these new groups became included. In Germany the expression *Landtage sind Geldtage* (representative assemblies are financial assemblies) was coined.[600]

In these assemblies there was thus an element of representation, but still an important question remains. How were the assembly members appointed? For a start, and in many places, the members were most probably appointed by the king.[601] But for being able to talk about representation in a real sense it is obviously required that the ordinary people themselves have some kind of influence, for instance by electing the members. The question therefore is when, and where, the first tendencies towards election appeared, and how these elections were carried through. About all of this it is difficult to find exact information, but it nevertheless seems likely that mixed procedures such that some members, sometimes, were elected from below, while other ones were appointed from above, were common for a long time.[602] It is also easy to imagine that elections became more common when the assemblies got more members than the original noble ones. Certainly elections were also introduced at different paces in different places. We do however know that some kind of election was present in England as early as in the beginning of the fifteenth century.[603]

Assemblies of the kind described thus appeared in quite a number of places in Europe, but after that the further processes differed. The basic reason was the delicacy of the balance between the king, on the one side,

---

[599] Finer (1997b), p. 1029; Herlitz, pp. 18-9.
[600] Finer (1997b), p. 1026.
[601] Herlitz, p. 18.
[602] Finer (1997b), p. 1035.
[603] Finer (1997b), p. 1030; Palmer, Colton & Kramer (2007a), p. 37; Rosenberg & Birdzell, p. 56.

and the assembly, on the other. The two levels had emerged from the corresponding levels in the feudal structure and they were, therefore, we remember, mutually dependent on each other. The balance could easily tip, either to the king's advantage, or to the advantage of the barons, and in the new situation with the more developed assemblies there was still a balance like this. The power could shift to the advantage of the king, or to that of the assembly, and both occurred. In some places where the kings became strong, they were not only able to consolidate their own positions, but could also expand their territories. In this way, in the fifteenth century, a number of absolute monarchies, that is dictatorships, appeared.[604] Examples are France and Spain. Sweden also developed in the same way, albeit somewhat later. In other places, such as in the areas of today's Italy and Germany, the processes however went in the opposite direction, towards splitting. Among others a number of smaller states, as for instance the city-states of the Renaissance, appeared. The unification of Italy and Germany, as we know, did not occur until the latter half of the nineteenth century, that is long after the consolidation of the French and Spanish monarchies. But, irrespective of the direction of the balance tipping, the assembly disappeared, and thereby a necessary prerequisite for representative democracy.

In England the balance did however not tip—the country took its own way. The constellation with a king and an assembly balancing each other remained, and out of this balance, what was to become a representative democracy, began growing.[605] England thereby got a unique and crucial role in the history of the world.

THE ENGLISH EVOLUTION

Why, then, did England get this key-role? Why did the delicate balance not tip there, in the one direction or the other? Of great importance was that England's population was small—and then not only much smaller in absolute figures than today, which goes without saying, but also much smaller in relation to the populations of the other great countries in Europe than in our days. From this followed that the representative organs became fewer, and less complex, than in other countries, and

---

[604] North & Thomas, pp. 86-7.
[605] Palmer, Colton & Kramer (2007a), p. 157; Roberts, p. 572.

thereby their power also became more consolidated and less dispersed. In contrast to the situation in several other countries, having both national and regional assemblies, there were thus only national ones.[606] And at the national level, where other countries often had assemblies for three or even four estates, England had only two chambers or houses, an upper and a lower one.[607]

This was thus the background. As for the particular, historical process I do not have to be detailed—the process is extensively depicted in innumerable history books and a few main points will therefore suffice here.[608] As early as 1215 the English king was thus forced to issue the so called Magna Carta in which the liberties and rights of the feudal barons were made precise and expressed. After having been threatened with violence by the barons the king found it best to present the declaration of rights.[609] The fundamental mechanism of change was working—grumblings in the ranks entailed concessions from above. Then the parliament developed further and as early as in the fifteenth century, perhaps even earlier, at least some of the members were appointed by some kind of election.

After this the parliament succeeded in surviving all the time until its final victory in the Glorious Revolution 1688 and the issuance in 1689 of a new declaration of rights, the Bill of Rights, which went considerably further than Magna Carta. That all of this should succeed was however far from self-evident. The road leading to the break-throughs in 1688 and -89 was far from plain. Already the Tudor kings, even though basically positive towards the parliament, and sometimes even encouraging it or seeking its support,[610] made some efforts to reduce its power. When the Tudors had been followed by the Stuarts in 1603 the situation was however radically changed. The Stuarts wished to rule without the parliament and during Charles I (1600–49) the conflict even led to civil war. But it started with Charles, dissatisfied with parliament, dissolving it in the hope of

---

[606] North & Thomas, p. 146-7; Palmer, Colton & Kramer (2007a), p. 37; Roberts, pp. 700-1.
[607] Palmer, Colton & Kramer (2007a), p. 158.
[608] The main sources for the presentation here are Finer (1997c), pp. 1335-58 and Palmer, Colton & Kramer (2007a), pp. 155-69.
[609] Rosenberg & Birdzell, p. 119.
[610] North & Thomas, p. 147.

getting a new one appointed. This new parliament, appointed by an election in 1640, did however get the same composition as the old one.[611] What happened is interesting in two ways. First, the king did not get his way. Second, here is a clear example of a parliament being appointed by means of election.

Thereafter the civil war broke out in 1642. On the one side were the royal family and its adherents, on the other side members and supporters of the parliament, and especially those who were most eager to defend it, namely the puritans. Among the latter a certain Oliver Cromwell (1599–1658) soon arose as a leader. The king's side lost the war, but the parliament also suffered. After having triumphed Cromwell discounted the parliament and rather made himself almost a dictator. He reduced the number of members of the parliament—from about 500 to about 50. This diminished parliament, the so called Rump Parliament, sentenced Charles I to death, after which he was executed in 1649. Cromwell then ruled England until his death 1658. After the parliamentary elections in 1640 there were no new ones until 1660, that is when Cromwell had been away from the stage for two years. The parliament elected in 1640, even though severely reduced, is therefore called the Long Parliament.

So, even if the parliament was both truncated and pacified during Cromwell's time, it nevertheless survived. And gradually it started acting on its own again. First on the agenda was the issue of succession—who was to become king after the execution of Charles I and the death of Cromwell? For a king—with limited powers for sure, but a king nevertheless—the parliament certainly wanted, or perhaps considered inevitable. But even so there were conflicts within the parliament about the issue and two parties—the Tories and the Whigs—were formed in the 1680-s. The parties did however succeed in uniting and a climax in their, and in the parliament's, power handling was reached when Mary Stuart, who was married to the Dutch prince William of Orange, was made Queen in 1688. This was the so called Glorious Revolution. The following year, 1689, William became king, William III, after having accepted the Bill of Rights presented for him by the parliament. According to this declaration no law could be abolished by the king, no taxes be taken and no standing army maintained, without the acceptance of the parliament, and no

---

[611] "The same men were returned." Palmer, Colton & Kramer (2007a), p. 159.

citizen, however poor, be kept arrested, and imprisoned, without a trial in due legal order.

Hereby the essential prerequisites for a representative democracy were in place. The parliament was there with its established competences, and with its members, being appointed by voting citizens. Furthermore two political parties, the Tories and the Whigs, had been created. Step by step, and without any backlashes, these institutions would eventually develop into a complete democracy, above all by the gradual transfer of the king's power to a leading parliamentary committee, and by the equally gradual extension of voting rights to more and more citizens. In addition to this the English, inspired by the Dutch and the medieval city-states, had also started introducing successively more advanced economic institutions.[612] But this was not all. In North America a process, which should prove to be of fundamental importance, had already got momentum. In England's American colonies the settlers not only introduced the institutions of their home country but also developed them further in their own way. This is the topic of the next section.

Before that I will however just add that two important works of social philosophy were published during the phase of English history at issue here. The one was Thomas Hobbes' Leviathan—already mentioned—which recommended a constitutional order with an absolute dictator-king. When the book was published, in 1651, Cromwell was about to triumph in the civil war, and to say that Cromwell, after that, came very close to Hobbes' ideal is no exaggeration. It is easy to imagine that Cromwell had served as a model for Leviathan. The other work was John Locke's "Two Treatises of Government," which was published in 1690, that is the year after the Bill of Rights, and which constituted an ardent defense of the balance of power just achieved. I will write more about these two works in chapter 12, the one about the role of ideas.

THE AMERICAN FOLLOW-UP

In the beginning North America was much less attractive for the European colonists than South and Central America.[613] But since Spain was the totally dominating naval power when the colonization began, the English

---

[612] North & Thomas, p. 146.
[613] Roberts, p. 649.

were pushed northwards and thereby became pioneers in North America. As early as in 1607 they founded a settlement in Virginia, and after that the migration continued for various reasons. North America proved economically more interesting than at first thought, but in addition to that some groups, in particular the puritans, were dissatisfied with the conditions in the home country and therefore wished to leave it. These groups were in different ways dependent on the parliament which the Stuarts, having gained power in 1603, ignored and obstructed more than preceding Tudor rulers. In 1620 a group of puritans on board the ship Mayflower landed at Cape Cod in the neighborhood of today's Boston. And the migration continued, gradually facilitated by the weakening of the Spanish naval dominance. In 1700, when the English civil war as well as the Glorious Revolution belonged to history, there were about half a million Englishmen in North America, and thirteen colonies had been founded.[614]

For a start these were indeed colonies but soon conflicts between them and the mother country materialized. One reason was the mother country's great demand for tax contributions from the colonies to finance the wars against France. Even if one of these wars took place in North America and was about the French colonies Louisiana and Canada, the biggest and most important was nonetheless the so called seven years' war in Europe, in which France was defeated in 1763. The North American settlers saw no reason why they should contribute financially to this European war. Another reason for conflict was the mother country's request that the settlers' fighting with the Indians, and thus also the westward expansion across the continent, should be halted. The conflicts gave rise to violent actions. In 1773 in Boston's harbor a group of settlers, disguised as Indians, captured an English ship's cargo of tea—a product for which the settlers were charged duty—and throw it into the sea. The mother country countered this operation—the Boston Tea Party—by withdrawing Massachusetts' constitution and closing Boston's harbor.

These conflicts led to the war, the American Revolutionary War, in which the colonies triumphed and liberated themselves from England. The war started in 1775, and in 1776 the colonies delivered their declaration of independence. That was however before the end of the war which,

---

[614] Finer (1997c), pp. 1394-1405; Palmer, Colton & Kramer (2007a), p. 155-6.

under the command of George Washington (1732–99), continued with varying success until final victory in 1783. A peace treaty was concluded and independence achieved. The colonies' victory was to some extent due to the assistance received from French troops, a contribution delivered as a revenge for France's losses in the earlier wars against England.

What is of interest here is above all the colonies' constitutional development. From the very beginning the settlers copied the English model, even if they also were to renovate it in important respects.[615] This was hardly strange since many of the first settlers were puritans, who, in the mother country, had defended the rights of the parliament. Already at an early stage representative assemblies were thus instituted in the individual colonies, and all members of these assemblies were elected by citizens. In the colonies there thus never was the kind of mixture between appointment from above and election from below, which characterized England's early assemblies. In the new country election from below was the only method used, from the very beginning, even if the right to vote was not universal but dependent on income. In some colonies it did however, as it seems, include more than 50 per cent of the adult, male population. In addition to the assemblies even councils and governors, corresponding to ministries and presidents, were introduced.[616] These institutions were of great importance since they were prototypes for the future American presidential executive. In the beginning the councils and governors did however have the tasks of handling the contacts with the mother country. The colonies, to be sure, were still colonies.

During and after the war the constitutional development continued. When the war was still going on the colonies were associated in a confederation of states—a military alliance if one so wishes. Shortly thereafter, in 1788, they created a common federal state, the United States of America or the USA. As a preliminary for the ratification of the constitution, and as an argumentation in its favor, a series of articles entitled "The Federalist" or "The Federalist Papers" was published 1787–88. Authors were James Madison (1751–1836), often called the father of the constitution, Alexander Hamilton (1755–1804), the initiator of the publication and eventually also the fourth president of the US, and John Jay (1745–

---

[615] Finer (1997b) pp. 1050-1; Finer (1997c), p. 1489; Roberts, p. 653.
[616] Finer (1997c), pp. 1400-5.

1829). The book in which the articles were soon to be published together is considered a master piece in the literature of politics and political science. When the constitution, among others thanks to "The Federalist", was in place, the war commander George Washington was elected the first president of the United States. Thereby the American Revolution, the label usually used for the revolutionary war and the creation of the union taken together, came to an end. This thus happened almost 200 years after the founding of the first settlement in Virginia.[617]

The US created in this manner was much closer to the fully developed democracy than England at the same time. England, for a long time, made a halt with the conditions prevailing after the Glorious Revolution and the Bill of Rights. In North America, in contrast, the further development was mindfully driven on by the migrants. The American federation, the US, was from the beginning, in 1788, almost a complete representative democracy. What was missing was the general right to vote, but that was to materialize in due course. And the constitutional continuity has been unbroken all the time from the beginning until today. For certain the American Civil War 1861–65 was a discontinuity in essential respects, but not constitutionally.

But even if there was a continuity like this the first major occurrences—from the landing at Cape Cod to the creation of the federation— were eagerly followed in the contemporary world. And more than that. The interest in these matters around Europe, and above all in France, was enormous. Which brings us to France.

THE FRENCH FOLLOW-UP

The French Revolution was dramatic and violent, and much more socially subversive than the American one.[618] The American Revolution, as we have seen, essentially consisted in the liberation from England and in the founding of a modern society in a country where, before that, no society at all had existed. In France, on the contrary, the revolution was preceded by an absolute monarchy which, during the reign of the dominating Louis XIV (1643–1715), had reached its climax of consolidation. This state and

---

[617] Roberts, pp. 720-9.
[618] The main sources for the presentation here are Finer (1997c) pp. 1517-33, Palmer, Colton & Kramer (2007a), pp. 349-70 and Roberts, pp. 729-39.

society was shaken in its fundamentals by the revolution, and a number of far-reaching, modernizing reforms were implemented as well. These changes became however soon, and to a considerable extent, annihilated. First came the so called reign of terror with Robespierre (1758–94) as a dictator in reality, even if not formally, and then, after another dictatorial period 1795–99, followed the dictatorship of Napoleon Bonaparte. But even if the events of the revolution thus did not become an overture to a successive, unbroken series of constitutional changes towards democracy as in England and the US, they nevertheless became of great importance in France, in Europe and in other parts of the world. Before getting into this the revolution itself, and its background, should however be described.

At the outbreak of the revolution in 1789, and mainly as a result of the defeat in the European seven years' war and the participation in the American Revolutionary War, the finances of the French state were in an utterly precarious condition. The weak French king Louis XVI, in great need of increased tax incomes, saw no other possibility than to summon the Estates-General, which had not met since 1614. Thereby a process of great constitutional importance was started, but the understanding of this requires some knowledge about the background. Two different causal complexes are of importance in the context.

The first one relates to the general situation in France which was characterized by a strong, largely spread, popular discontent. Basically this depended on the extreme inequality between the privileged, tax exempted aristocracy and the great, poor and harshly taxed main part of the population. To this were added acute problems due to failed harvests and rising food prices. Taken together all of this gave rise to grave social unrest. The number of vagrants on the countryside increased enormously, riots and rebellions succeeded each other over the whole country culminating in the storming of the fortress Bastille on the 14-th of July— the day which was to become the national commemoration day of France.

The second causal complex relates to the influences from North America. What happened there profoundly impressed people and was discussed all around Europe, but in France more than in other countries. To some extent this was due to French participation in the American Revolutionary War, and the close relations between France and what was to become, or at the time of the outbreak of the revolution just had become, the United States. The American Benjamin Franklin (1706–90), who had

had an important role in American politics, became, in 1776, the ambassador of the United States in Paris, and there the interest in what he most willingly was saying was enormous. Also the French Joseph du Motier de La Fayette (1757–1834), who as a military officer had taken part in the American war and become influenced by this, played a central role in the French Revolution. But not only front-rank individuals like these were important. Common French soldiers also returned from America and told their compatriots about their experiences and their lessons learned.

France was thus particularly receptive to the ideas from the new country in the west. But France was also the cultural center of Europe, and French was the language of the cultural elites around Europe. So even if it was in France, and in French, which much of the most important debate and discussion was conducted, the ideas also spread over large parts of the rest of Europe. Starting at about 1760 a great number of books about what happened in America, and many more journal articles, were published, and everywhere in saloons and clubs this was also the foremost subject of discussion. The prominent American expert on the French Revolution Robert Roswell Palmer (1909–2002) even talked about a "veritable intoxication with the *rêve américain* (American dream)."[619]

It could be added that the development here described started, in a way, even earlier, namely when Charles-Louis de Secondat Montesquieu (1689–1755) in 1748 published his great work "The Spirit of the Laws". The book was not only inspired by John Locke's works but also by the experiences of the conditions in England acquired by the young Montesquieu during a two-year visit there. This, for sure, is rather about the English evolution—the American development had obviously hardly started during the life-time of Montesquieu—but it was, nevertheless an important part of the ideas forming the background of the French Revolution.

This was thus how things were when the Estates-General got together in May 1789, and immediately a conflict about the decision rules arose. Earlier each of the estates—the clergy, the nobility and the third estate—had voted for itself, and for a proposal to become a decision it was required that it was supported by a majority of the estates. Now, however, the members of the third estate, which had as many members

---

[619] Finer (1997c), p. 1486.

as the two other estates together, required that a majority of the total number of individuals rather should be needed. The king not only conceded but also urged the clergymen and noblemen to agree and in that way a new assembly, the National Assembly, was created. Since the supporters of the revolution sat to the left, as seen from the position of the chairman, and their adversaries to the right, the political concepts of "left" and "right", which since then have survived, were coined.

The supporters of the revolution were in majority since some of the members of the clergy and nobility estates had converted to them, and decisions leading to far-reaching, radical social transformations began being taken in a quick pace. First, as early as in August 1789, came the "Declaration of the Rights of Man and of the Citizen". It had great similarities with the English Bill of Rights, about a hundred years older, but was nevertheless epoch-making since it, to such a large extent, dealt with the rights and the inviolability of the individual human being. It was therefore immediately considered sensational, and was printed, spread and discussed everywhere in Paris and in France, and was also translated to other languages for being spread far beyond the borders of France. During the next two years or so, during which the assembly still was active, additional important social transformations were decided upon, among others a number of privileges were abolished. The resulting constitutional order was also declared legally binding. Legislation was the prerogative of the National Assembly, and the king could, at most, delay its decisions, a so called suspensive veto. During this period the motto "Liberty, equality, fraternity (brotherhood)" was also coined.

The constitutional order achieved was however soon to be annihilated even if substantial parts of the social reforms survived. At first came the reign of terror and some years later the dictatorship of Napoleon Bonaparte. The importance of the French Revolution therefore was more due to the development and spread of liberal and democratic ideas to which it gave rise, than to real and remaining constitutional advances.

COMMENT TO THE BIRTH

THE UNIQUENESS

We have now seen how representative democracy was born. The most important and most distinctive institution of this kind of democracy, the representative assembly, had its origin in the feudal assemblies of barons which appeared in a number of European countries. In all places but one these assemblies were however short-lived. The exception is England where the assembly not only survived but also began developing towards democracy. When that process had come some way Englishmen started migrating to North America where they immediately gave their colonies constitutions with representative assemblies. When these colonies together, later on, formed the United States even this new nation got a representative constitution, which thereafter evolved successively without interruptions. Just after the United States had been created the French Revolution, which was destined to be of enormous importance for the spread of the ideas of liberalism and democracy, broke out. But even so it did not initiate any real and unbroken constitutional development in the way the earlier events in England and North America had done. The material reforms in France were annihilated after just a few years.

In the beginning of the 1790s constitutions, which were to evolve into complete democracies, had thus become solidly founded in England and the United States, and the ideas which these processes had brought about had been developed, made more precise and spread all over Europe by the French Revolution. That this sequence of events was unique is obvious. What happened in England until the end of the seventeenth century, and which was a precondition for all the rest, did not happen in any other place. The first crucial events occurred only in one place, in England. It was not the same as for instance with dictatorships, which appear completely independently of each other at many times and in many places.

THE UNLIKELIHOOD

The uniqueness is thus obvious, but how about the unlikelihood? This problem can be encapsulated from two sides by means of two basic questions. This is the first one:

- What could have stopped the process which actually led to representative democracy, what could have made that process take another course?

If it is easy to find reasonable answers to this question the contention about the unlikelihood of representative democracy is strengthened. The other question, which addresses the problem from the other side, is this one:

- Have there been any tendencies, or sequences of events, which almost have led to representative democracies, and which could have done so if only the conditions had been slightly different than the real ones?

Perhaps there have been tendencies like this, and perhaps they have even been numerous. If so representative democracies should have appeared at several places and independently of each other. What actually occurred, that this kind of democracy appeared in one place only, should therefore be unlikely, but in a way totally different from the one I am contending. It should be unlikely because what was likely was the appearance of representative democracies in several places, at several times, independently of each other.

I will start with the first question and with what happened in England. What could have been different and thus stopped the process there. It is easy to imagine several such possibilities. The Stuart kings' attacks on the parliament could have been more successful, in particular the attacks of Charles I. Cromwell could have lived longer than in fact he did, and if so he could have delayed or perhaps even stopped those crucial activities of the parliament, which it actually engaged in after his death. Or, arguing along another track, the representative institutions with their characteristic concentration of power—only two national chambers, among others—could have taken a different form than in fact they did. All of this and much else could have stopped the English evolution and if so, and if something similar had not happened in some other place, we would not have had any representative democracy at all today.

Turning then to North America, what would have happened if it had not been colonized by migrating Englishmen? For instance because transoceanic seafaring of the kind necessary had not begun to be used, or because the Spanish naval power had continued being prohibitively strong. If so the American follow-up of the English evolution, probably necessary for the further development of representative democracy, would never have taken place. In that case England would never have received any vitalizing impulses from North America and in that case the English parliament could very well have perished in the same way as did several other assemblies in other parts of Europe.

The answer to the first question thus is that the sequence of events which actually led to representative democracy could have been broken in several different ways. For me at least none of these ways appears particularly unreasonable or far-fetched.

Then we can turn to the other question, the one about the conditions for representative democracy in other places, and other circumstances, than those where the first representative democracy actually did appear. I start with feudal Europe. There, as already mentioned, representative assemblies appeared in a number of countries. But even if all of these, but the English one, vanished, or at least lost all significance, it could perhaps, in some case, have been different. Could for instance, in contrast to what actually happened, the French king's summoning of the Estates-General in 1789 have initiated a development towards representative democracy. Perhaps, but this was nonetheless unlikely. In spite of the inspiration of the English and North American events The National Assembly crumbled, as we know, during the reign of terror, and the likelihood that it should have done the same in the absence of the English and American events seems, if anything, much greater. A similar question may be asked about Sweden (for further details see the section "The spread and diversification" later in this chapter). Could something like the English evolution have occurred during the Age of Liberty, that is the time between the Carolean and Gustavian periods of absolute monarchy? But the answer is again the same. It did not happen, and the likelihood of its happening does not increase by thinking away the English and American events. Another country which possibly came close to being a representative democracy and in which an English scenario perhaps could have materialized was the Netherlands.[620] But, once again, it did not happen. But of course, in principle, some assembly, somewhere in Europe, could have evolved in the way the English one did. That did however not occur, and since the conditions everywhere were worse than in England, favored by, among others, its small population, the likelihood for such an evolution was evidently very low as well.

But how about feudal structures outside Europe? There have, we remember, existed institutions similar to those of the European feudalism in different places in the world and at different times. This was so in for instance the Persian Empire with its satrapies, and even China, for long

---

[620] Findlay & O'Rourke, pp. 175-6; Finer (1997b), p. 1051; North & Thomas, pp. 86-7; Palmer, Colton & Kramer (2007a), pp. 123-5, 149-55.

periods, almost had a feudal structure. And the same was true for Japan during the period from about 1300 to 1600. In all these cases assemblies similar to the European baron assemblies could, in principle, have emerged, whereby embryos for representative democracies would have been formed. But, as far as I have been able to find out, this did not happen anywhere. The regional power-holders never assembled—the dictator rather met them individually, the one after the other. In Japan the regional chiefs rather fought each other constantly. In all the cases mentioned the assembly, which could have been a link towards representative democracy, thus was lacking.

Now I leave the feudal structures and turn to some other institutions which easily may be conceived as possible preludes to a representative democracy, and then in particular to its representative assembly. A first candidate is the council of the Athenian direct democracy. This council, we remember, was supposed to have the same number of members from each phylae, and these phylaes had interesting similarities with modern constituencies—each phylae needed to include a piece of coastland, a piece of inland and a piece of the densely populated city-area. Here there thus was a kind of idea of representation. But there the similarities stop. The members of the council were thus not appointed by elections, but by lot casting, and the council, furthermore, did not have decision-making power. In spite of this the possibility of a gradual evolution of the council into a modern representative assembly should perhaps not be excluded. Had Athens not been conquered by Philip of Macedonia, and also grown bigger, it would perhaps have been quite natural to transfer, bit by bit, decision making rights from the assembly (ecclesia) to the council and at the same time introduce elections rather than lot casting. Such a scenario does not seem unreasonable, but it did not occur. A similar, but not equally probable, reasoning could be carried out for Sparta's council of elders (gerousia).

In the Roman Republic there were also interesting potentials, and I am thinking in particular about the tribunes and the Senate. The tribunes, to begin with, were elected by the ordinary people, the plebeians, and thus represented them. Furthermore their number was ten, and they could veto each other and thus had to be unanimous to take a decision. They thus constituted, one might say, a kind of very small assembly. A successive evolution from this "assembly" to the kind of assembly present in modern representative democracies is however, at least for me, hardly imaginable. It is, I think, not at all as plausible as for the Greek cases, and in particular the Athenian one.

The Senate, however, is another matter. It was much greater, and also much more diversified in it composition, than the small group of tribunes. And it consisted of individuals who actually were elected, even if they, at first, had been elected as magistrates of different kinds and, thereafter, appointed senators by the censors. The substitution of a more direct election for this procedure does not seem unreasonable. The other difference of importance between the Senate and a modern representative assembly was that the Senate only was advisory and thus lacked the right to take decisions. But a change of this is not only easy to imagine, in reality it was in fact implemented in the Republic. In reality the Senate was entitled to take decisions. Of all interesting potential institutions I know about, and disregarding the feudal assemblies in Europe, the Senate of the Roman Republic is the one coming closest to a modern representative assembly. Rather close, but still not going all the way, and with a similar reasoning, came the Venetian Senate.

The conclusion following from this reasoning is that the arrival of representative democracy, in fact, was utterly unlikely. The only sequence of events which actually led up to such a democracy could easily have been broken at different places, and if that had happened we would not have had any representative democracy today unless it emerged in some other context. And contexts like that have not been abundant. On the contrary, as I have tried to show, the contexts which possibly could have given rise to a representative democracy have been quite few.

Before finishing this historical reasoning I should however mention that there have, in fact, existed fully realized representative institutions at an early stage—already around the year 1200—within some religious associations. In particular the Cistercian and Dominican Orders, each one on its own, had decision making systems of this kind.[621] The transfer of a decision-making order like this to a whole state does however seem utterly unlikely. That point of view does however belong to the next section, the one about the logical reasons for the unlikelihood of representative democracy.

---

[621] Finer (1997b), pp. 1030-2.

COMPATIBILITY WITH THE LOGIC OF COLLECTIVE ACTION

Representative democracy is thus utterly unlikely, but why? How come that dictatorships have appeared all over the world, at many times and independently of each other, and that yet the pattern for representative democracies is so totally different? Basically this is not remarkable at all, but rather a consequence of the logic of collective action. According to this logic there should, in fact, not be any representative democracy any-where, which can easily be shown with a quite simple argument.

First, the representative democracy is not only a collective good but also a very abstract and institutionally complex one, which directly depends on the representative assembly. A constitutional order including such an assembly is much more complex than one without. And this means that a representative democracy never can become introduced in one step taken by a large, heterogeneous group of people such as the population of a normal nation or country. This is a direct consequence of the logic of collective action as presented above. The decisions rather must be taken by some individual person, or some very small group of persons, which, in turn, arguably means that they have to be taken from above. But the one or those few being able to act in this way could hardly be interested in doing so; the ones favored by representative democracy are rather the large masses. And an important, basic hypothesis in this book is that all individuals, when acting, are steered by their own inte-rests. The conclusion therefore is that there never should have appeared any representative democracy since those able to introduce it have no interest in it.

The conditions in the Cistercian and Dominican Orders illustrate this reasoning in an interesting way. There, in fact, small representative democracies of a sort were created, but the circumstances differed in important respects from those in states. First, the Orders were small, clearly demarcated, homogeneous collectives—they consisted exclusively of individuals having freely chosen to join them. There were therefore no obstacles to introducing representative democracy from above. Further-more the distance between "above" and "below" probably was very little in all respects, for instance with respect to interests. The "upper level" of the Orders, if there was such one at all, could therefore very well have contributed to the introduction of the representative decisional structure.

But states are not religious orders but much larger and more strati-fied and heterogeneous phenomena. And exactly for that reason, as I have explained, representative democracy cannot be introduced from below because of the logic of collective action. And its introduction from above is equally unreasonable—even if we assume the presence of a prototype from the world of the religious orders. Those in charge simply have no interest in the matter.

But now the representative democracy actually does exist, and ob-viously, therefore, something is wrong with the reasoning just presented. The basic fault is the assumption about a one-step introduction. Some-thing like that has never happened, and could not have happened. And nor could it happen in some few steps. But if the process is split into sufficiently many, sufficiently small steps, matters may change. If so each individual small step may be such that it enhances the interests of some small group of power-holders, and if so the logic of collective action is no obstacle. Under such conditions the final result may also become some-thing never intended from the beginning. By looking at some of the indivi-dual steps we will see that this is in fact what happened.

When the feudal assemblies were created this did not conflict with the logic of collective action. Those involved were few and they were interested in the measure since it decreased their transaction costs. When these assemblies began to be used for pecuniary taxation, and their mem-bers thereby began turning into representatives, the same holds true. And so is the case for the gradual shift of the appointment of these members from above to electing them from below. All of these measures may very well have been rational from the point of view of the power-holders at the top, and therefore also introduced by them. The English kings not only tolerated but sometimes even appreciated the parliament. The Tudor King Henry VIII (who ruled in 1509–47) thus held that a king was never stronger than when supported by his parliament.[622] And when the English settlers began founding their colonies in the New World nothing conflic-ted with the logic of collective action either. For sure they introduced re-presentative assemblies almost immediately, but the possibility of such assemblies did not have to be figured out, there nature was known from England, and the groups who founded them were furthermore small and

---

[622] Roberts, p. 581; Palmer, Colton & Kramer (2007a), p. 88.

homogenous. And, continuing forwards, when the third Estate, in revolutionary France, required new, specified decision-making rules, this was again perfectly compatible with the logic of collective action. They were summoned as an individual estate, and not that many, and therefore could formulate and present exact demands. Thereafter the king, in his own interest, implemented the demands from above.

Well, like that one may proceed with one particular step after another in the sequences of events at issue, and conclude that they, all through, are compatible with the logic of collective action. The measures undertaken by the few, those at the top, and which they often felt compelled to undertake, were in their own, immediate interest. But the resulting, total effect was an institutional revolution favoring the interests of the large masses of people. A long sequence of events resulted in something which, according to the logic of collective action, would have been impossible in a few jumps, and still less in a single one. The reasoning thus shows the reasons for the extreme unlikelihood of representative democracy. It clearly illustrates its path dependence.

After this we may now, in a more comprehensive manner, form an opinion about the importance of the English evolution up to Glorious Revolution, the American Revolution and the French Revolution. That representative democracy never would have materialized in the absence of the English evolution thus seems utterly likely, that evolution was a necessary condition for what followed. About the same may be said about the American Revolution. Had that revolution not taken place the bud of the English representative democracy had been much more vulnerable and perhaps even vanished at some point. The American follow-up was therefore of crucial importance. It resulted in fact in the first close approximation to a complete representative democracy, and therefore the American democracy would most probably have survived even if the English one had fallen for some reason. The importance of the French Revolution is however, according to my reasoning, significantly less and often exaggerated. Had it not occurred, but the English and American evolutions remained realities, the world today could very well have looked about as, in fact, it does. Without what happened in England and America the French Revolution on the contrary, if it had occurred at all, would have had a course totally different from the one it actually got. It would have become a revolt or an uprising of the same kind as so many other ones in the history of the world, triggered by hunger and social discontent, but without all the constitutional aspects so important in the case of the real revolution.

The thesis about the unlikelihood of representative democracy may in fact be underlined by still another argument. The first, and so far also the last, institutionally well developed direct democracies of the world were those in classic Greece. Among them the one in Athens, created in −508, is the most well-known. The main parts of what was to become the world's first institutionally well developed representative democracy, the United States, were outlined by "The Founding Fathers" almost 2300 years later. Had the representative democracy been likely, it would hardly have taken that long. This long time may furthermore be considered as a confirmation of the thesis that the difference between direct and representative democracy is much more a difference of kind than of degree. Representative democracy is, institutionally, something totally different and much more complex than direct democracy. That is the reason why, when it finally happened, it emerged, in a roundabout fashion, along a very particular and unlikely path.

THE SPREAD AND DIVERSIFICATION

THE COURSE

After the processes described in England, North America and France, representative democracy spread across the world. To get an idea about how this happened we may start by looking at an individual, early example, the earliest in fact, namely Sweden.

In Sweden there was, as already remarked, in the same way as in several other countries, at an early stage—at least since the fifteenth century—a kind of representative assembly with a feudal background called "Riksdag".[623] During some periods this assembly was more or less active, during other ones pacified and without significance. The latter was the case during the Carolean (1654–1718) period and the main part of the Gustavian period (1772–1809), both to a large extent characterized by dictatorial rule. In 1789, however, the king Gustav III had to summon the "Riksdag" because of economic problems. After the murder of Gustav III in 1792 he was succeeded by his son Gustav IV Adolf, who, however, during his first years was substituted for by a guardian. In 1796 he took

---

[623] Herlitz, pp. 13-5, 20.

over the power himself, but soon afterwards he had, he as well, to convene the "Riksdag" because of a financial crisis of the state. This happened in 1800. At the end of the Gustavian period the "Riksdag" thus regained some power while the king was correspondingly weakened.

Then, in 1809, came the great change.[624] That year the Gustavian period ended and the development towards representative democracy began. The dissatisfaction with the king, Gustav IV Adolf, was great and widespread and in a *coup d'état* in 1809 he was arrested and imprisoned by a group of civil servants and military officers. But this group was dependent on the estates. The *coup* required their support, but for that support the estates also required and forced through a new constitution which balanced the power between the new parliament, the "Riksdag of the Estates", and a king.[625] The distribution of power thus followed the principles favored by Locke and Montesquieu even if the French Revolution and the English and American examples also had provided inspiration. A certain Jean Baptist Bernadotte (1763–1844) was chosen king, and thereby became Karl XIV Johan. Then, in 1866, the "Riksdag of Estates" was substituted for by the bicameral "Riksdag", and voting rights were thereafter, gradually, made more and more common for becoming universal in 1919.[626] Furthermore the power of the king was step by step reduced and finally disappeared altogether. From a constitutional point of view, or with respect to power, the king and the king's family are since long null and void.

So this is, briefly, what happened in Sweden, and the pattern was similar in a long series of other countries. During the nineteenth and twentieth centuries representative constitutional orders spread over substantial parts of the world, and were also developed in the process, among others by stepwise advances leading ultimately to universal suffrage. If there was a difference between what happened in Sweden and the somewhat later corresponding processes in other countries it is that social unrest, the pressures from below, the demands of the masses were essentially greater in the later cases than in Sweden. In 1809, when the crucial step was taken in Sweden, the Napoleonic wars in Europe had not yet come to an end. Then, after the Congress of Vienna in 1815, in which

---

[624] Herlitz, p. 30.
[625] Herlitz, pp. 30-1.
[626] Herlitz, pp. 32, 37.

international problems after these wars were settled, there followed a turbulent period in Europe. The so called July Revolution in 1830 was important and still more so the so called February Revolution in 1848. In both cases the events started in France but rapidly spread to large parts of the rest of Europe. At this time, as mentioned in chapter 6, the spread was facilitated by new techniques and phenomena such as the telegraph, railways and daily newspapers. And, in addition to this, the ideas of democracy and liberalism were also stirred up by the social forces released by the sprouting of industrialization. Liberalism got company with socialism. "The Communist Manifesto" by Karl Marx and Friedrich Engels was published in exactly 1848. The masses revolted and representative constitutions were forced through.[627] Then, as a result of the peace negotiations after World War One, still more countries got representative constitutions.[628]

The spread was however accompanied by differentiation. The representative constitutions were structured somewhat differently. The first variation of this kind was introduced when the American Founding Fathers decided to introduce a president from the very beginning. This was of course most reasonable, not only since a king holding real power was incompatible with their general philosophy, but also since there was no family with royal traditions available. The result was a representative democracy with a president, and this structure was then to spread to, in particular, Latin America.[629]

In England there was however a king and the constitutional development therefore became another one. What was once the king's own, personal council—his so called "privy council"—gradually got closer and more frequent contacts with the parliament and thereby, almost imperceptibly, turned into becoming the most important committee of the parliament.[630] But this also meant that this committee in reality became the ministry, or the executive, of the country. Since this committee was part of the parliament it however seemed natural that it enjoyed, and even should enjoy, the confidence of the parliament. Its constitutional

[627] Finer (1997c), pp. 1567-1608; Palmer, Colton & Kramer (2007b), pp. 469-72, 483-8; Roberts. pp. 748-52.
[628] Lee, pp. 12-8.
[629] Roberts, p. 726.
[630] Cox

role therefore became another one than that of the American president. The result was parliamentarism rather than presidentialism. One may also say that presidentialism was characterized by separation of powers, whereas parliamentarism was characterized by fusion of powers—separation and fusion of the executive and the legislative powers respectively. The parliamentary form of representative democracy—or rather preliminary versions of that kind of democracy—then spread to, in particular, European countries. Since they were kingdoms this seemed natural. It might have been strange to elect a president if there already was a king, and the English parliamentarism also had emerged out of a kingdom.

The next step in the differentiation relates to the voting system, and the main distinction here is the one between majority elections in single-member constituencies and proportional elections in multi-member constituencies. Majority elections were used at an early stage in England and the United States, the pioneering countries of representative democracy, while proportional representation is a later phenomenon. Among the pioneers, but then as late as at the end of the nineteenth century, were Denmark and Belgium. A reason for the lateness of proportionalism may be its dependence on political parties, and there were hardly any such prior to the coming of representative constitutions. Rather they began to form after these early constitutions, and as a consequence of them. The majority election system was therefore well established in England and the United States when the proportional system started appearing, so it spread to the countries on the European continent, to the Scandinavian countries, and to those in Latin America. In particular it may be mentioned that all those representative democracies which were created after World War One got proportional systems.[631] The countries in the British Commonwealth, on the contrary, adopted the mother country's system. Australia and New Zealand thus used majority elections from the beginning, and the British colonies which achieved independence after World War Two also introduced majority elections. New Zealand however turned to proportionalism in 1996.

When representative democracy spread across the world it thus also developed in various directions, and thereby different kinds of representative systems emerged. I have just mentioned the distinctions bet-

---

[631] Lee, pp. 15-8.

ween presidentialism and parliamentarism, and between majoritarian and proportional election, and these distinctions may be used for distinguishing four main types of representative democracies. For today's world this gives the following result. One single country, the United States, has presidentialism combined with majoritarian elections; England and almost all countries within the British Commonwealth have parliamentarism combined with majoritarian elections; many European countries, particularly in Western Europe, have parliamentarism combined with proportional elections; and the Latin American countries have presidentialism combined with proportional elections. This four-fold classification is however not exhaustive since there also are some other types. There are for instance mixtures of presidentialism and parliamentarism, and an example of this, which has gained followers, is today's France. Among the followers are some of the newly established democracies within the area of the former Soviet empire. Variations of the electoral system may lead to other kinds of democracies than the four types mentioned. All of these possible variations do however not prevent us from treating the four types mentioned as main types or basic types. In the next chapter I will discuss the properties of these four types in various respects.

COMPATIBILITY WITH THE LOGIC OF COLLECTIVE ACTION

The spread of representative democracy is much easier to explain than its birth. After the complex birth procedure the system was known and clear prototypes—or at least prototypes of very obvious preliminary versions of the fully developed representative democracy—existed in the real world. So what remained was just the introduction, or implementation.

To explain this—the spread or the implementation—it is enough to refer to the fundamental mechanism of change described in chapter 3. At the lower, popular level there is social unrest, serious rebellions and the like, which those at the upper level, those having power, have to handle in one way or another. The method usually used so far in history—crushing the upheavals violently—was hardly available. Those expressing discontent and threatening to revolt were much too conscious about the existence of other and better alternatives. The only option at the power-holders' disposal was thus to concede step by step. And so they did, and all was perfectly compatible with the logic of collective action. In this way representative democracy spread across great parts of the world.

SUMMARY

The representative democracy appeared very late in the history of states. In this chapter it is argued that it might never have happened at all, and if so we would live in a world very different from, and much worse, than the one we are in fact living in. The basic reason for this unlikelihood is that a representative democracy—because of its inclusion of a representative assembly—is an abstract, and very complicated, collective good, and that such a good only can be implemented from above. But the power holders there have no interest in it. And all those who really would benefit from it—all those eventual citizens below—cannot introduce it because of the logic of collective action. But if so, how did it happen? How come that any representative democracy ever appeared?

The answer given is that the appearance was path dependent; that the emergence occurred in a number of small steps and that the fundamental mechanism of change described in chapter 3 was working in several of these steps. It started in feudal medieval Europe where there was no monetary system after the collapse of the Roman Empire and in which the heavily armed knight had become a formidable weapon. The embryo of the crucial institution—the representative assembly—was the kings meetings with their vassals. In one country, England, this order was comparatively stable and lasting, and it also came to include representative elements when the economy gradually became more monetized and taxing therefore became possible and interesting. This was the English evolution and from England emigrating puritans brought this constitutional order to North America and also developed it further. This development, here called the American follow-up, was then also followed by the French follow-up, usually called the French revolution. The importance of this last occurrence is however, according to the arguments presented here, often exaggerated. The English evolution and the American follow-up were much more important and crucial—without them we would in all likelihood not have had any representative democracy today. With them, but without the French Revolution, things might however possibly have been about as they are.

After the description of this path towards representative demo-cracy the arguments for its uniqueness, for its unlikelihood, and for its compatibility with the logic of collective action are presented in a rather detailed manner. It is also noted that after the fall of the antique Greek direct democracies more than 2000 years elapsed before the appearance of the representative democracy. This again testifies both to the unlikely-hood of the representative democracy and to the very great difference between direct and representative democracies.

When once the representative democracy thus was born the spread and diversification of it was however a different and, in a sense, easier matter. Essentially it was a process of copying. In contrast to the time before the birth, the nature of the representative, constitutional order was known, and large parts of the populations in various countries, as well as their rulers, knew what was at issue. This, though, was to a con-siderable a result of the French Revolution—its importance lay in the spread of democratic ideas. Conditions in Europe became turbulent as epitomized by the July revolution in 1830 and the February Revolution in 1848. The power holders had to react. The fundamental mechanism of change worked and more and more countries got representative constitu-tions.

At the same time these constitutions did however develop in somewhat different directions. Differentiation took place. A first impor-tant distinction was the one between presidentialism and parliament-arism, and a later the one between majority elections and proportional elections. In that way four main types of representative democracy em-erged. In the next chapter a theory about these four types is developed.

10

THE PROPERTIES OF REPRESENTATIVE DEMOCRACY

GENERAL PROPERTIES

DEFINING PROPERTIES

The most basic property of representative democracy is that there is always a group of decision-makers, an assembly, which represents the people. First the people elect the representatives who, thereafter, take the decisions. The representatives are much fewer than the citizens—typically the representatives may be counted in hundreds and the citizens in millions. To be fully developed it is however not sufficient that a democracy has an assembly of this kind. Further conditions must be fulfilled, and I divide these conditions into three groups.

The first group is related to the elections of the representatives. These elections must occur reasonably regularly, at reasonably short time intervals, and there must be an established and respected set of rules stipulating when and how elections are to be held. The representatives are thus elected only for distinct periods and at the regularly occurring elections they may perhaps become reelected, or perhaps replaced by others. In some democracies, and for some functionaries, there are however limits to the number of possible reelections. The president of the United States may for instance be reelected only once.

The next group of conditions is about the right to vote. This right should be universal among the adult citizens, which means that the rule one man/woman one vote should hold. Close to this rule is also the rule about vote secrecy—the citizen so desirous shall be able to keep his or her vote a secret without any difficulty. Furthermore the procedures for counting the votes must be such that manipulation is effectively excluded. The publicly declared results should be reliable.

The third group of conditions relate to opinion formation and are less formal than the former conditions, but certainly no less important. First there must be freedom of opinion. The citizens must have possibilities to form opinions freely and, at least within very wide limits, to express their opinions publicly and without reprisals. In the same way mass media of various kinds must enjoy freedom of expression. Furthermore—again at least within very wide limits—organizations advocating various ideas and opinions, for instance political parties, must be allowed to form freely. This, in turn, means that political debate, in particular at election times, practically always is characterized by competition between various constellations and ideologies and interests—at least there must not, under any circumstances, be any obstacles in the way of that kind of competition. The scrutinizing of the incumbents' manner of handling their tasks is a critically important element in public opinion formation, in particular during election campaigns.

ECONOMIC PROPERTIES

The representative democracy is—at least from the points of view of the overwhelming number of common people—by far the best kind of state yet to have appeared. This is so in part because of the freedom and tolerance which, in combination with a protective judicial system and equality before the law, characterize the democratic society. But this is not all. The representative democracy is also the only kind of constitutional order which is capable of harboring a fully developed, properly functioning market economy. It may also be said that the constitutional order represented by the representative democracy or its predecessors, as developed in particular in England and North America, could adopt all those market improving economic institutions which were invented in Venice and other city-states, and also did so. In this way there was established a combination which in a marvelous way could take advantage of all the creativity existing among individual human beings all around society. These individuals could, within the framework of the systems of rules outlined above, freely make inventions and found enterprises for exploiting them. The activities of the individuals were coordinated by the signals provided by free market pricing. In that way the total very great amount of knowledge, and inventiveness, spread among people, would ultimately benefit everybody. This potential for creativity and growth is well exemplified by Western nations from the industrial revolution onwards.

THE SIZE LIMITS—UPWARDS AND DOWNWARDS

The system with a representative assembly make the transaction costs associated with state decision making drastically lower than in a direct democracy, and a representative democracy may therefore be very large. India, the largest democracy in the world, has today more than 1200 million inhabitants. But there are also other factors which can put a limit on the size at much lower population figures. For the proper working of the democratic processes—and I am then talking about everything related to opinion formation, discussions and debates in various forums, decision making and information about decisions taken, and so forth—it is important that people can communicate with each other. A reasonably well spread common language is thus vitally important, and representative democracies therefore tend to be nation-states.[632]

This being so does however not only depend on the need for a common language. Sometimes important cultural differences go hand in hand with linguistic ones, and if so the cultural differences may constitute a problem even if people are able to talk with each other. An interesting example is Spain with separatist movements in both the comparatively poor and undeveloped Basque Country and the well-off and successful Catalonia. In both regions most inhabitants speak Spanish even if the original languages are different.[633] The present separatist ambitions are therefore to a large extent culturally inspired. Another interesting multi-language example is Belgium. The tensions between Flanders to the north, with the Dutch-related Flemish language, and the French-speaking Wallonia to the south, are sharp and dividing. And here the possibilities for communication are not as good as in Spain. Even if many Flemings are familiar with French, most Walloons do not speak Flemish.[634] The problems are acute, and in spite of the smallness of the country it could, as it seems, crack at just about any time. But there is also at least one exception, or counter-example, namely Switzerland. In spite of its regions dominated

---

[632] Here it may be appropriate to quote John Stuart Mill when he writes that "Free institutions are next to impossible in a country made up of different nationalities. Among a people without fellow-feeling, especially if the read and speak different languages, the united public opinion, necessary to the working of representative government, cannot exist. Mill, chapter 16.
[633] Judt, p. 701-2.
[634] Judt, p. 707-13.

by the German, French and Italian languages respectively, this democracy works very well. Perhaps a reason is that these regions, in spite of their different languages, have very similar cultures and cultural backgrounds. Another probable reason is however the country's federal constitution.

FEDERALISM

A federal state, or a federal union, consists of a number of smaller units, so called federated states or just states. There are thus two levels, a federal or national one, and a state level. The states are, within limits made precise in the federal constitution, free to do whatever they want. Among today's representative democracies Argentine, Australia, Austria, Brazil, Canada, Germany, India, Mexico, Switzerland, the United States and Venezuela and are federations—with reservations about the democratic status of at least Venezuela however.

These federations may be compared with feudal administrations— the similarities are obvious. In both there are a number of units at a lower level which, within precise limits, are free to act as they want, while, at the same time they are kept together by a central power and in some respects obliged to follow its directives. In the dictatorship chapter I also said that feudal structures usually appeared when dictators were forced into them—those dictators who from the very beginning freely opted for feudalism were few indeed.

The history of the democratic federations also displays regularities even if other ones than those of the feudal dictatorships. It thus seems as if most federations have emerged by amalgamation of smaller units—the future states—rather than by splitting previously larger units. When uniting the smaller units have kept some of their original power, but not all of it. Some power they freely transferred to the central authority, that is the new national level. The incentive for unification has in most cases, perhaps even in all of them, been of a power-political or military nature. This, as we have seen, was the case when for instance the United States, and Switzerland, were created. But why was a new state, a new national level, created in these cases? Why was not a military alliance between the states concerned enough? Irrespective of the particular motives in the individual cases it is obvious that the new state, with its taxing power, could control the resources necessary for military expenses. It was made impossible for the individual units—if any of them had such tendencies—

to act as "free riders". This may have been the great advantage of a federation compared to a military alliance.

Like that it has thus been when some federations were created, and perhaps it has even been like that very often. In his book "Federalism"—published in 1964—William Riker presented the very strong hypothesis that *all* federations created until that time had been brought about in the way described.[635] For military reasons a number of smaller units had formed a larger entity. After careful, empirical scrutinizing he found the hypothesis confirmed.[636]

Now a number of years have passed since 1964 but probably it is still true that most of today's federal representative democracies originally were created by the unification of a number of smaller units. Seldom, or perhaps never, was a federation created by the splitting of an originally larger unit. The process has usually been in the opposite direction, towards unification and consolidation. Continuing the logic here presumed one may also suspect that the federal level—in federations already created—is able to counter splitting tendencies, and thus often has an advantage. If so this may lead to a continuing strengthening of the federal level at the expense of the states. Or, in other words, competence is bit by bit transferred from the state level to the federal level.

But even if this is a tendency, it need not always be like that. In both Spain[637] and Belgium[638] constitutional changes favoring an emerging state level have been implemented recently. Diminishing the internal tensions has been the intention. Only the future can tell us about the success of the measures.

PEACEFULNESS

The so called democratic peace theory appears in different versions.[639] A weak version says that representative democracies never, or almost never, fight wars against each other. A stronger version says that representative democracies seldom or never start wars, not even against non-democratic countries. The weak version seems quite reasonable, but how

---

[635] Riker (1964), p. 13.
[636] Riker (1964), p. 48.
[637] Judt, pp. 520, 701-2.
[638] Judt, p. 464.
[639] See for instance Pinker.

about the strong one? What, one may ask, is meant by "start"? How, for instance, should United States' war in Iraq in 2003 be assessed?

To the extent that these theories or hypotheses are correct it should however not surprise the reader of this book. We have seen that the methods for becoming rich at the disposal of full blown democracies, by means of properly working markets, as a rule are superior to conquests and plundering. So already for this reason wars of conquest are less interesting for modern democracies than for dictatorships. To this should be added the risk that the market mechanisms already existing, and in particular those involved in foreign trade, will be destroyed by war. Democracies thus have much less to gain from war, and much more to lose, than other kinds of states.

THEORIES ABOUT DEMOCRATIC POLITICS

INTRODUCTION

In chapter 1 I mentioned William Riker's contention that political science got a piece of testable theory when Duncan Black presented the so called median voter theorem,[640] and that the discipline, before that, had been completely void of theory. That Riker ranked this theorem highly is obvious. At another occasion he described the theorem as "certainly the greatest step forward in political theory in this century".[641] And definitely it is an important theorem—a theorem which can be classified as belonging to general theories about democratic politics. In fact it may be considered as the one of two main theorems within this area. The other one—the theorem about minimal winning coalitions—has, interestingly enough, William Riker himself as its originator.[642]

When speaking about two main theorems I do not only mean that the two theorems are important, but also, and principally, that they represent radically different approaches. In the next section I will describe the nature of the difference. Already here it may however be said that the two theorems—as well as a lot of later theorizing about democratic politics inspired by them—share the property of being about voting and coalition formation, that is about just a limited part of the democratic processes

---

[640] Black (1948), and, more extensively, also Black (1958).
[641] Riker (1990), p. 178.
[642] Riker (1962).

and their consequences. But even if these theories are limited in this sense they are, in other respects, often quite unfocused. The aspects of democratic politics dealt with are mostly so general that they may be relevant for direct as well as for representative democracies. And in those cases when it is clearly stated that it is the representative democracy which is at issue, it is nevertheless, at least usually, unclear what kind of representative democracy is intended.

Now, these assertions about generality, and about lack of focusing, should not, on their own, be considered as criticism. Earlier I have for sure, on the contrary, argued that the good theory is characterized by being generalizing and abstracting. The general nature of the theories is therefore not necessarily a deficiency; it could be the other way round. Anyway quite a lot has happened since Riker made his declaration. In what follows I will give a short presentation of the more established theoretical approaches existing today.

THE TWO THEOREMS

The median voter theorem deals with the result of vote casting in assemblies of various kinds—from small committees to a nation's entire electorate. Starting with the latter case, an entire electorate, we may assume that each citizen has an opinion or a contention which may be described by a point on a scale, for instance a left-right scale. If so it is possible to describe the electorate in its entirety by means of a distributional curve over the scale such as in figure 8. When having that curve we also realize that the size of the area under the curve between two points of opinion, for instance M and F, is proportional to the number of citizens having opinions in that interval. We also see that the curve in this particular case happens to be tilted somewhat to the right—which means that the electorate has a slight right-wing tendency (about which more later on). My choosing of a left-right scale depends only on the fact that it is by far the most common scale in political science—in principle it could rather have been some other kind of scale. What is essential is the assumption that the citizens' opinions may be represented by points on the scale.

Now, if the number of members of an assembly is odd there is one person, the median person, or the median voter, who divides the assembly into two equally sized groups. The median voter has as many other voters on one side as on the other. In the figure the median voter, and the median voter's opinion, is represented by the position *M*. The assumption about an odd number of members is however interesting only for very small assemblies. When large assemblies, such as the electorate of an entire nation, are considered the position of the median position on the scale is, in practice, independent of whether the number of members is odd or even.

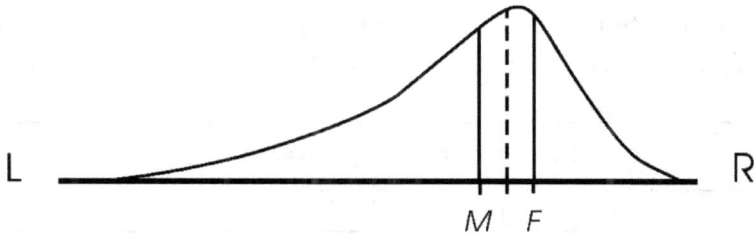

Figure 8: The median voter theorem

To arrive at the median voter theorem only a few additional simple and rather uncontroversial assumptions are now required. A first one is that the simple majority rule is used for taking decisions and another that all members of the assembly take part in the decisions. And so there is the so called *single peakedness condition*, which says that a member of the assembly evaluates a proposal lower the farther away from his or her own position on the scale it is (more about this condition follows in the section "Rank-order theories" below).

The median voter theorem now says that under the conditions stipulated the opinion of the median voter, *M*, will become the result of voting, the resulting decision. That this is so is easy to see. Suppose, for instance, that the proposal *F* is put against *M*. If so all people to the left of the mid-point between *M* and *F*, represented by the broken line, will vote on *M*, while all to the right of the mid-point will vote on *F*. That the former group is largest, and thus wins, is obvious since the point *M* divides the total assembly into two equally sized halves. But the point *F* has no special properties. The same kind of reasoning, as the one just conducted for *F*, may be conducted for any other point beside *M*. Thus *M* wins all imaginable votes.

Then we turn to the theorem about minimal, winning coalitions. In figure 9 a situation which may be used for clarifying the theorem is described. Assume that there are, in the context of an election, five electoral groups, E_1 - E_5, and that these groups are equally sized, which means that each of them constitutes 20 percent of the total electorate. Assume furthermore that five proposals, P_1 - P_5, are put forward, for instance by five political parties, in the election campaign. The proposal P_1 says that each of the groups E_2 - E_5 shall be taxed by 25 units each—it may for instance be monetary units of some kind—and that these means should be transferred to the people in group E_1. The proposals P_2 - P_5 are analogously constructed. Each of them favors its particular electoral group. It is all through a matter of pure transfers, dictated by pure self interests.

	E_1	E_2	E_3	E_4	E_5
P_1	+100	−25	−25	−25	−25
P_2	−25	+100	−25	−25	−25
P_3	−25	−25	+100	−25	−25
P_4	−25	−25	−25	+100	−25
P_5	−25	−25	−25	−25	+100
Result	+50	+50	+50	−75	−75

Figure 9: The theorem about minimal, winning coalitions

Let us now assume that the simple majority rule is used and that all voters vote for the proposal which, in a narrow sense, favors themselves—all members of E_1 thus vote for P_1, and so forth. If so, obviously, no proposal, taken for itself, is able to win—every single proposal will only get 20 percent of the votes. If, however, the proposing parties start negotiating with each other, things may change. Let us for instance assume that the three first parties join in a coalition and turn their three proposals into one single, common proposal. This common proposal will then get 60 percent of votes and thus win. The result is shown in the bottom-line of the table—altogether 150 units will be transferred from the groups E_4 - E_5 to the groups E_1 - E_3.

Now, if we rather had considered a smaller coalition, one consisting of only two parties, it obviously could not win since it would get only 40 percent of the votes. A bigger coalition, for instance one of four parties, obviously would win, but the yields, for each of the winners, would be smaller than in the three-party coalition. The coalition which will form will therefore be a minimal, winning coalition. And this is exactly what the theorem says—elections of the kind considered result in minimal, winning coalitions.

Then, of course, there is a remaining problem—since there are several possible three-party coalitions one may most reasonably wonder which one will actually form. This problem I will however ignore here. One may furthermore consider the example in figure 9 extreme—even if it is true, someone may say, that self-interests are important, politics nevertheless is never all that callous. Perhaps that is so, but I have made the example extreme in order to underline the contrast between the two kinds of theories I am talking about. And having said that I will now compare them.

The median voter theorem belongs to a group of theory approaches which we may call rank-order oriented. Rank orders of political alternatives are essential. Voters, or politicians, think, without the reasons being made precise within the theory, that a certain proposal, or a certain policy, is best, then another one, and after that still another one, and so forth. What is at issue, and is ranked, could, from a purely theoretical point of view, have been the candidates in a beauty contest as readily as political proposals. The reasons for the opinions formed, or for the ranking, are not in any way included in the model. The ranking is not in any way, within the framework of the theory, related to any consequences for the voter him- or herself. Possibly there are no consequences at all.

The theorem of minimal, winning coalitions is different in all these respects—it belongs to a group of theoretical approaches which we may call incentive oriented. A description of the direct consequences for the actors is a central and necessary element in the theory—the actors are steered by their incentives as being determined by the clearly formulated outcomes or consequences. The theory, or model, is unthinkable without a description of these consequences.

The two theorems are thus basically different, and for that reason it is interesting to use them as starting points when describing other cases of theorizing about democratic politics. In the next section I will take up theorizing of a purely rank-order character, in the section after that theorizing in which the actors are altogether steered by their incentives, and then, in still a third section, models in which both approaches are used together.

Before that it is however proper to add a few words about William Riker's contention about the importance of the median voter theorem. I have already mentioned that Riker's opinion about a prior lack of empirically testable theory disclosed, mildly speaking, some disregard for history. A number of important political philosophers in the historical past seemed totally forgotten. But in addition to that some social scientists in Duncan Black's own time, and before him, had reached results in accordance with the median voter theorem. But still there was the important difference that these results were verbally formulated and therefore lacked the formal stringency of Black's presentation in 1948.

Among these contemporary, or almost contemporary, predecessors were the lawyer and president of the Harvard University, A. L. Lowell, who presented his result around the year 1900, the economist Harold Hotelling 1929, the political scientist Elmer Eric Schattschneider 1942 and the political scientist V. O. Key 1942.[643] Moreover the political scientist Maurice Duverger should be mentioned in the context. His formulation of the result was not published, that is true, until 1951, that is a few years after Black's presentation, but in all likelihood he was unaware of Black's result and thus formulated the theorem on his own.[644] All of this taken together suggests that the theorem, so to speak, was in the air. Still Duncan Black's contribution of giving the theorem a formally strict formulation was greater than one at first, perhaps, is inclined to realize. It required namely the discovery, and the exact expression, of the single peakedness condition.

RANK-ORDER THEORIES

The median voter theorem is thus based on the idea that individuals, for instance voters, rank political alternatives. Within this general world of ideas there are more results than the theorem about the median voter, and some of them are much older. Among the pioneers were two Frenchmen, active during the French Revolution, namely the naval engineer Jean-Charles de Borda (1733–99) and the mathematician Antoine de Condorcet (1743–94). They were interested in various methods for electing

---

[643] Hotelling; Key, p. 220; Schattschneider, p. 85. The information about Lowell is given by Schattschneider, p. 85.
[644] Duverger, p. 387-8.

members of a society or in an assembly—for instance in the French Academy of Sciences or in the Estates-General.

For presenting the problem involved I will start with the situation depicted in figure 10. For the membership to be assigned there are three candidates, A, B and C, and those electing are altogether 101. As shown in the table those electing are however ranking the candidates differently. Now, the problem is how to proceed for making the election as reasonable and just as possible. That was the issue engaging Borda and Condorcet.

Number	1:st place	2:nd place	3:rd place
50	A	B	C
49	B	C	A
2	C	A	B

Figure 10: The problem of rank-ordering

Let us begin by assuming that each of those electing only mentions—for instance by means of a voting paper—his or her favorite candidate. If so A gets 50 votes, B 49 votes and C 2 votes, and A consequently wins. But such a voting method both Borda and Condorcet found unsatisfactory. It was not enough, they contended, only to take into account the favorite candidates of those voting. One should rather, and reasonably, consider the total rank-orders of those electing—one should thus also allow for whom they ranked second and third. This information, they argued, was also of relevance. But even if Borda and Condorcet agreed so far they still recommended different ways of honoring this extra information.

Borda advised a method using ranking numbers. A first place gave the number 3, a second place the number 2 and a third place the number 1. The figures are then added for the candidates so that each of them gets a total number of points. In the situation at issue the result will be the following:

A gets $(50 \times 3) + (2 \times 2) + (49 \times 1) = 203$ points.

B gets $(49 \times 3) + (50 \times 2) + (2 \times 1) = 249$ points.

C gets $(2 \times 3) + (49 \times 2) + (50 \times 1) = 154$ points.

The result thus becomes different than with the first method. The candidate B wins, not the candidate A.

Condorcet's idea about how the total rank-orders should be respected was different than Borda's. According to Condorcet the final winner should rather be selected by putting the candidates against each other pair-wise. So let us test this method by applying it on the situation in the table.

If A is put against B, A will get 52 votes (50+2 electors think that A is better than B) and B will get 49 votes (49 electors think that B is better than A). The electorate, in its entirety, thus favors A to B. But this does not finish the procedure. We also have to put B against C and with the same reasoning as earlier we then find that 99 electors think that B is better than C, and only 2 think that C is better than B. So far the electors have thus found that A is better than B, and that B is better than C. But still we have not put C against A, which also has to be done. And then we find, with the same kind of reasoning, that 51 electors think that C is better than A, and only 50 that A is better than C. The collective electorate has thus ended in an illogicality, a contradiction or a circle. It holds that A is better than B, that B is better than C, and that C is better than A. The method does not give any result at all. There is, as it is usually put, no Condorcet-winner.

Now, things do not always turn out that awkwardly, but sometimes they may do so, and Condorcet was well aware of the problem. His proposal was that the pair showing the least majority should by disregarded and only the remaining ones taken into account. In our example this means that the confrontation between C and A, in which C wins by just a single vote, is left out. Doing so gives the victory to A. The reasonableness of this suggested solution may be discussed, but I will not continue along that line but rather take up some other problems in the context.

At first it should then be said that the difference between Borda and Condorcet is of considerable methodological interest. Condorcet only pays attention to the electors' ranking of the candidates. If, for instance, some elector thinks that A is much better than B, and that B is just a little bit better than C, Condorcet does not take into account the "distances" which the elector in this way sees to exist between the candidates. The only thing important for Condorcet is that the elector prefers A to B, and B to C—period. Borda, on the contrary, with his counting of "points", implicitly introduces a kind of distances, although in a rather unrefined way.

If we still stick to the elector thinking that A is better than B, and B better than C, the points thus imply that C is twice as long away from A as B. Distances, yes, but not the distances our elector has in mind. Borda and Condorcet are thus both inadequate, but each one in his own way. They constitute extremes of a kind, and modern so called utility theory, in its different appearances, lies between them. I will however not discuss this theory here.

I will only say that the curve in figure 5 above, as well as those in the figures 7, 8 and 9 below, have their problems. Consider for instance the hump in figure 5. If the distances along the scale had no meaning, as with Condorcet, the part of the scale under the hump could without any problems be elongated—it could be drawn out as a rubber band. If so the order between all points on the scale should remain the same. The hump would however sink, and if the scale was drawn out long enough it would rather become a valley. The curves in the figures mentioned thus require, for keeping their significance in different respects, a utility theory which is not too close to Condorcet's.

Then comes the question why Condorcet's method sometimes does not given any solution at all. Why is this so? This and related questions have been dealt with extensively by several theoreticians in modern times, and some of the results may be mentioned here. Very generally it may then at first be said that the impossibility of appointing a Condorcet winner in the example above was due to the fact that, in that example, the single peakedness condition was not fulfilled. But for making this understandable the meaning of this condition must now be clarified. As I said above the condition requires that each individual evaluates proposals lower the farther away from the individual's own position they are. In that formulation there is thus implied an idea about a scale that is common for all individuals, in the case at issue a left-right scale. And just this, that the scale has to be common, is an important part of the single peakedness condition. So let us keep this in mind while taking a look at the situation in table 3.

We may for instance imagine that the scale looks as in figure 11, that is in such a way that A comes first, then B and finally C. A thinkable, but not necessary, interpretation is that A is left-position, B an intermediate position, and C a right-position. Anyway we now see the electoral group with 50 members fulfills the single peakedness condition—it puts the highest value on A and then follows B and C in due order. And the group with 49 members also fits the pattern—it ranks *B* first, and the alternatives on both sides of *B*, that is *A* and *C*, are ranked lower than *B*. But the last group, the one with only two members, breaks the pattern. This group ranks *C* highest but then, when moving leftwards along the scale, comes *B* which the group ranks lowest, and after that *A* which the group ranks higher than *B*. Thus the alternatives are not valued successively lower the farther away from the group's favored position on the scale we get. Thus the single peakedness condition is not fulfilled.

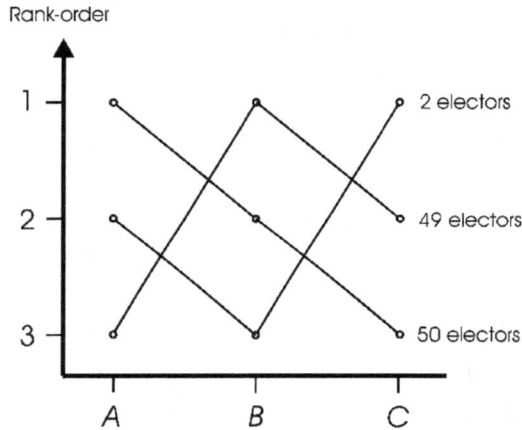

Figure 11: The single peakedness condition not fulfilled

Now someone perhaps objects that this may depend on my constructing the scale in a particular way, namely so that *A*, *B* and *C* follow each other in order. But I could have chosen some other scale as for instance *BCA*, or *BAC*, or some other one of the altogether not that many existing possibilities. But whichever scale is chosen the result will be that the single peakedness condition is not fulfilled. Or, in other words: It is not possible to find a scale such that each group's valuations of the alternatives become lower the further away from the group's own position we get.

The Condorcet problem and similar problems have been treated in detail in an extensive literature. The most advanced result in this category of theorizing is the so called Arrow's theorem, having Kenneth Arrow (born in 1921), economist and pupil to the formerly mentioned Harold Hotelling, as its originator. He thought about a group of individuals facing the problem of ranking a number of alternatives, that is arriving at a decision about a ranking order common for the whole group. He started by assuming that each of the individuals had a ranking order of the alternatives of its own. The problem was to find a decision rule leading from the individual ranking orders to a common one. Arrow formulated a number of seemingly very reasonable, or even innocuous, requirements for possible decision rules. Then, and that is the very theorem, he proved that no decision rule fulfilling these requirements existed—such a rule was a logical impossibility. Arrow's result thus was an impossibility result.[645] There was, in the general case, not even any rule by which a best alternative could be singled out.

Even here the single peakedness condition is crucial. Arrow assumed that the individuals' rank-orders of the alternatives could take any possible form, which meant that the single peakedness condition did not have to be fulfilled. If, however, the single peakedness condition is added—which perhaps is reasonable—it becomes possible to find a decision rule, namely the common majority rule, which satisfies all of Arrow's requirements and which leads to a common decision. Perhaps this could be a consolation. Perhaps the single peakedness condition really is fulfilled in many realistic cases.

But irrespective of this I find it difficult to find that the theorizing about rank-orders which I have given a glimpse of is of much scientific interest, whether positively of normatively. The theorizing appears too much as logical exercises for their own sake. About this the opinions may however, perhaps, differ. But in any case the rank-order theories must be mentioned in a book like this one. And the presentation has not come to an end here. I will return to the topic in the section "Combined theories" below.

INCENTIVE ORIENTED THEORIES

Before that we should however take a look at those theoretical approaches which—in the same way as the theorem of minimal, winning coalitions—are incentive oriented. But first it should then be said that there is not to my knowledge that much theorizing of this kind. When incentive-steered action appears it is usually in models also containing rank-order components, and in those cases we are thus dealing with combined

---

[645] For further information see for instance Arrow.

theories of the kind treated in the next section. Still there is at least one example, but even if the incentive-steering is basic it differs most considerably from the theorem about minimal, winning coalitions. That theorem was about the behavior of political actors within a given institutional structure. It was positive, or descriptive.

The work I will now take up, namely "The Calculus of Consent" by James Buchanan and Gordon Tullock, is of a wholly different character.[646] It discusses how democratic institutions in some basic respects may be structured, and how they ought to be structured. An important point of departure is the question why the citizens in a democracy accept majority decisions, and thereby, as a consequence, also accept ending up in a minority now and then, and thus being overruled by a majority. Behind this question lies the contention about unanimity as an ideal, and here Buchanan and Tullock continue an older tradition with, among others, Knut Wicksell (1851–1926) and Vilfredo Pareto (1848–1923) as front-rank personages. The so called Pareto-criteria is a formalized expression of the idea that all individuals should be respected, that no one should be favored at the expense of somebody else. And what is sometimes called the Wicksell criteria, which is in fact a requirement for unanimity, was presented a few years prior to the Pareto-criteria, and is quite similar. Long before Wicksell and Pareto the principle was however expressed by the Romans who said that what affects all, should be approved by all (Quod omnes tangit, ab omnibus approbetur).[647]

In practice the striving for unanimity however meets with great and basically insurmountable problems, and is therefore destined to fail. In any reasonably large assembly it would be necessary to negotiate and negotiate, and to negotiate again, practically eternally. And still there would always remain some ones who obstructed, requiring concessions favoring themselves for supporting the common decision in the making.[648] But if unanimity is impossible to achieve, how far should one depart from

---

[646] Buchanan & Tullock.

[647] Finer (1997b), p. 1030.

[648] A well-known example is the Polish parliamentary body, or Diet, during the years 1652–1791, which has given rise to the expression "Polish Parliament". There a unanimity rule resulted in chaos and made it impossible to make any decisions at all. See for instance Palmer, Colton & Kramer (2007a), p. 195 and Roberts, pp. 612-3.

it? To some kind of qualified majority? Or all the way to a simple majority? Or should one always depart equally much, or should that perhaps be dependent on the kind of issue under consideration, or on something else? These are the kind of problems treated by Buchanan and Tullock.

For presenting their basic reasoning I will use figure 12, which depicts some matters relevant for a decision making assembly. The reasoning is so abstract that we may, for the moment, leave undecided whether it is a representative assembly or a popular meeting in some kind of very small direct democracy. What is important is that it is not a very small group, for instance a board or committee of some kind.

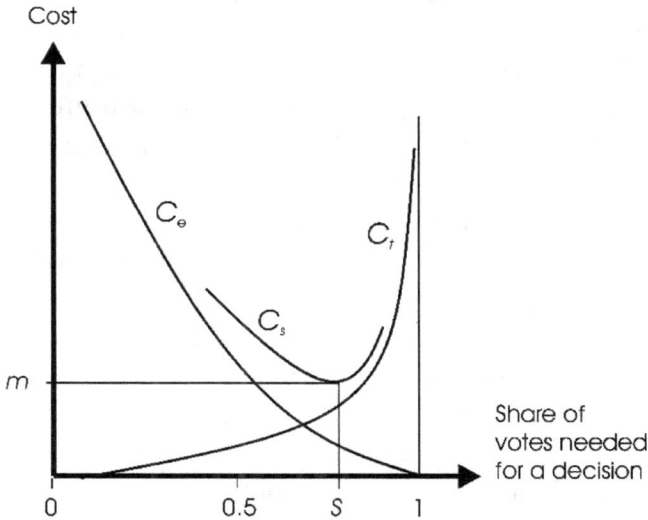

Figure 12: Decision making according to Buchanan and Tullock

In the figure there are two axes. Along the horizontal axis the majority required for a decision is indicated. At the middle of the axis the figure 0.5, which stands for simple majority, is marked, and furthest to the right the figure 1 standing for unanimity. Between 0.5 and 1 there are qualified majorities of various sizes.

Along the perpendicular axis two kinds of costs related to the decision making are indicated. The first one are the costs of the decision making itself in the assembly. These are transaction costs of exactly the kind treated in chapter 3. In the figure they are labeled C_t and, as we see, they rise when the majority required for a decision increases—when approaching unanimity the curve escalates steeply. This seems quite natural, not only since unanimity requires that more individuals agree with each other, but also since the possibilities for the single individual who wants to obstruct and thereby gain favors for him- or herself become greater the fewer those are who are able to replace that member in the decision making constellation.

The other kind of costs, called by Buchanan and Tullock external costs, are labeled C_e in the figure. They consist of all those disadvantages afflicting the individuals in the losing minority because the decision taken was against their wishes. According to Buchanan and Tullock these cost are at first dependent on the decision rule—the larger the qualified majority required is, the lower are these costs. But they are, secondly, also dependent on the character of the issue decided about. For some issues—perhaps such ones where the only problem is to reach a common practical solution, for instance regarding the design of traffic signs—it may not be that important for the individual if he or she ends up in the majority or the minority, what is important is to reach a decision. For such issues the descending curve in the figure will therefore get a low position fairly close to the horizontal axis. For other issues it may however be more embarrassing to belong to the losing minority, and for such issues the descending curve will get a higher position than in the figure, or perhaps even much higher.

And this leads to the conclusion. Buchanan and Tullock first add the costs C_t and C_e and thereby get a sum of the costs, labeled C_s, which is specific for every kind of issue. A curve of this kind is drawn in the figure, and that particular curve has a minimum indicated m. The conclusion then is that the qualified majority fitting, or even optimal, for every kind of issue is the place of this minimum. For the kind of issue assumed in the figure the optimal qualified majority, or the optimal share of votes to be required, thus is s.

This, we see, gives us a kind of more precise answer to the question we started from, namely why people sometimes accept belonging to losing minorities and thus being overruled by majorities. The answer is that the disadvantages thereby endured are fully compensated for by the advantages of avoiding meetings, discussions and negotiations in absurdum. But the answer is more precise than that. It also means that the more issues are of such a character that it is important not to be overruled, the more important it is to devote time and negotiation efforts for getting them solved. In the model of Buchanan and Tullock this is achieved by making the required, qualified majority, that is s, larger.

This is Buchanan's and Tullock's basic reasoning in its broad outlines, even if it also contains parts which I have omitted here. They thus make a distinction, which they consider fundamentally important, between the decisions by which a constitution is created and the decisions which, thereafter, are taken within the framework of, or with the help of, this very constitution. Buchanan's and Tullock's way of thinking is thus in some respects richer and more nuanced than in the presentation above. On the other side it is however also easy to point to some formal deficiencies or shortcomings in their argument. It is, for instance, by no means obvious that there is a curve for external costs of the very simple and regular kind as the one Buchanan and Tullock use. But even so their reasoning is characterized by a considerable measure of originality and a basic strength which decidedly deserves to be taken into account.

What I am in particular thinking about is the interest for the situation of the losing minority, the predicament of which is characterized by means of the concept of external costs, and the conflict between these costs and the costs of reaching decisions, that is the transaction costs. A case treated by Buchanan and Tullock, with which we are already acquainted, is the relationship between direct and representative democracy. In the latter one the transaction costs are much lower than in the former one, but in this very case it is therefore by no means sure that the external costs are higher—they may very well be as low in a representative democracy as in a direct one. Buchanan and Tullock also raise the issue whether the legislature in a representative democracy should have one or two chambers—Sweden, as an example, had two chambers in an earlier period but switched to one chamber in 1971. Buchanan's and Tullock's main argument—briefly formulated—is that two chambers entail higher transaction costs and therefore are justified only if the external costs decrease at least correspondingly. They also conduct similar kinds of discussions for different ways of dividing a country into constituencies. Furthermore they contend, most reasonably, that there is a great difference between being a constant loser and being a loser only now and then.

At last, and to complete the presentation of examples, Buchanan and Tullock also take up the important question of what should be decided in public decisions and what should be decided in private ones. This issue thus concerns, using our earlier terminology, the size of the public domain. Their answer—again in all brevity—is that the public domain may be made bigger, and ought to be made so, in small, homogenous countries than in large, heterogeneous ones. The reason is that the transaction costs always can be made lower in the former kind of countries than in the latter ones, and that therefore the minimum value of the sum for the two kinds of costs occurs at a relatively larger domain in the earlier than in the latter. This result is not only interesting in itself, it is also interesting since it is so totally at odds with the most common answer to the question put, namely that the public authorities shall engage in those matters which cannot be handled by markets, in correcting market failures.

Buchanan's and Tullock's reasoning is thus purely incentive oriented, but it is nevertheless, as I have already remarked, to a large extent of another character than Riker's theorem about minimal, winning coalitions. There is however an important common point. Riker shows how the majority will act in order to take as much as possible from the minority, and Buchanan and Tullock are interested in making this problem of the minority, by means of suitable institutions and decision rules, as small as possible.

COMBINED THEORIES

Among theories combining rank-order and incentive components the earliest, and still the most well-known, is probably the one presented by the economist Anthony Downs in 1957 in the book "An Economic Theory of Democracy". I will start by describing the approach in a simple version in order to comment on it, thereafter, in various respects. The starting point is a distribution of the electorate along an axis—for instance a left-right axis of the kind I introduced when describing the median voter theorem. A possible distribution of the voters is presented in figure 13. In the figure, furthermore, three political parties with their positions are indicated. It may for instance be the positions adopted in an election campaign.

After this it is now possible to tell wherein the combination of different approaches consists, and I start with the voters. Downs introduced them by writing "that each citizen casts his vote for the party he believes will provide him with more benefits than any other."[649] Here the self-in-

---

[649] Downs (1957), p. 36.

terest is thus extreme and, as we will see in the following, that is also what Downs intends. But how can the voters vote in this way within the framework of Downs' model? The only thing they can do is to choose some point on the model's left-right scale, and this is enough for triggering doubts. Compare for instance with the redistribution proposals discussed in connection with the presentation of the minimal, winning coalition theorem above, and depicted in figure 9. Downs' voters, it easy to imagine, would eagerly have voted for proposals like that if they had been able to, but such proposals cannot be captured by a simple scale.

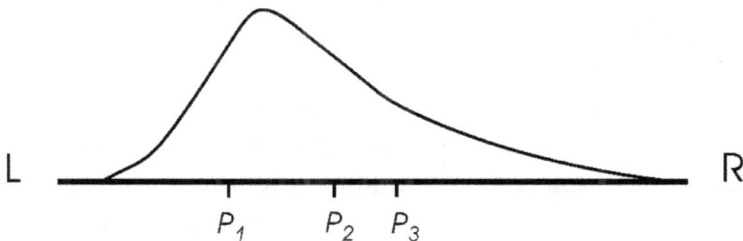

Figure 13: A left leaning electorate according to Downs

But let us nevertheless see how Downs, in more detail, conceives his scale. It indicates, he says, the share of society's total economy which should be private. The extreme left-position thus means that 0 percent should be in private hands, and the extreme right-position that 100 percent should be in such hands. The points in between indicate that a certain, numerically precise share should be in private hands (which one of the many shares with the same size is however left open) and the rest be run by the state. This is thus how Downs conceives his scale, and obviously a scale like that can be a part of a simple model. But it seems equally obvious that the voters' positions on such a scale are only vaguely related to their own, narrow self-interests. The voters own, private incentives hardly provide any guidance at all for the selection of a point on the scale. In spite of Downs' declared ambitions it is therefore much more reasonable to characterize this part of his model as rank-order based than as incentive oriented. This part of the model belongs to the same conceptual world as the median voter theorem.

With the politicians everything is however totally different. They not only have incentives—these incentives are also blatantly abrasive. Downs describes the politicians like this:[650]

"We assume that they act solely in order to attain the income, prestige, and power which come from being in office. The politicians in
our model never seek office as a means of carrying out particular
policies; their only goal is to reap the rewards of holding office *per
se*. They treat policies purely as means to the attainment of their
private ends, which they can reach only by being elected."

The politicians thus strive for being elected and therefore, according to
Downs, they are also vote-maximizing. The purpose is however not to
change and improve society, but only private gains.

Obviously we have here, within the one and same model, a sharp
contrast between the two most important categories of actors. On the one
side we have the voters who, in spite of Downs' ambitions to the contrary,
hardly have any interests or incentives at all. On the other side we have
the politicians with pure, narrow self-interests. Is it reasonable, one may
ask, to treat these two groups so differently—they are, after all, rather
close to each other. Even politicians are voters, and many voters, even if
not politicians, are still party members. For this reason, but even for purely methodological reasons, it is, I think, perfectly in order to remain skeptical towards a theoretical approach which, within itself, harbors such a
flagrant contrast, or almost contradiction. For the sake of fairness and
clarity it should however be added that Downs himself never describes
his theory as combined. That description is mine, following from the arguments presented here, and I have no idea about whether Downs would
agree or not.

Why did Downs make the assumptions about incentives which, in
fact, he did? When asking this I include both the assumptions about the
voters and those about the politicians since Downs meant that even the
former were steered by their self-interests. The answer to the question
has its background in Downs being an economist. He was, in fact, a pupil
to Arrow, who, in turn, was a pupil to Hotelling. And Downs had read
Joseph Schumpeter's book "Capitalism, Socialism and Democracy", which
was published in 1942. In that book Schumpeter brought to mind Adam
Smith's distinction between the incentives for an activity, and the results
of the activity. Smith, we remember, held that it was the self-interests of
the butcher, brewer and baker which made us confident about our dinner,

---

650 Downs (1957), p. 28.

not their benevolence. And Schumpeter, arguing that this idea had a much wider of area of application than markets, extended it to politics. He wrote as follows:[651]

> "Similarly, the social meaning or function of parliamentary activity is no doubt to turn out legislation and, in part, administrative measures. But in order to understand how democratic politics serve this social end, we must start from the competitive struggle for power and office and realize that the social function is fulfilled, as it were, incidentally—in the same sense as production is incidental to the making of profits."

This was Downs' point of departure. Even if Schumpeter stated that there was a connection of the kind described—that politics in relevant aspects worked in the same way as markets—one could not be all that sure. So Downs set for himself the task of investigating whether Schumpeter was right. It was for that reason that he made his assumption about voters' and politicians' self-interests. Is it possible—that is the question which Downs asked and which is the main question in his entire book—to deduce from that assumption results which confirm Schumpeter's contention? Do the assumed, particular forms of maximizing of the voters and the politicians lead to results which, from a general point of view, were as good and beneficial as the results of the market actors' profit maximization?

So this is why Downs made his assumption about the incentives of the voters and the politicians, but he hardly succeeded in showing that Schumpeter was right, and hardly either that he was wrong. Downs' reasoning about these issues is complicated, or sometimes even obscure, without leading to any distinct results. And this is hardly surprising. The very great difference between the almost completely incentive-free voters and the politicians with sharply chiseled out incentives is not the only weakness of the reasoning. There are more problems. In particular there are no well described institutions or institutional structures. The whole political process takes place in an institutional vacuum. In spite of several indications that Downs has a parliamentary system in mind rather than a

---

[651] Schumpeter (1942), p. 282.

presidential one (more about this distinction in the next main section) he never says so.

Concerning the question about the factors determining the number of parties he thus essentially, and consciously, disregards the distinction between proportional elections in multi-member constituencies and majority elections in single-member constituencies (again see next section). Rather he uses his basic model, without any institutional assumptions, with its distribution of the electorate for explaining the number of parties. In a situation such as the one depicted in figure 14 one we will thus probably get two parties, whereas the situation in figure 15 probably results in four parties.

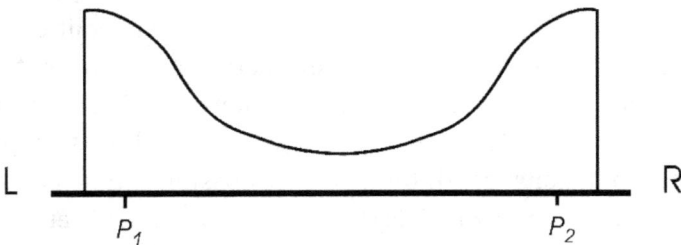

Figure 14: A polarized electorate according to Downs

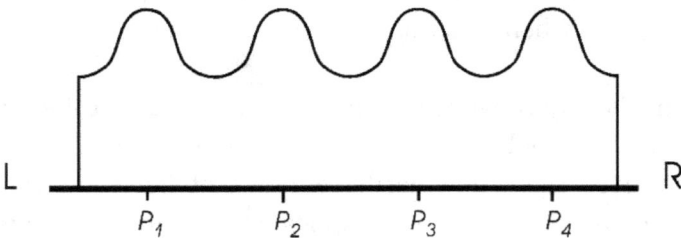

Figure 15: A multi-party-favoring electorate according to Downs

It may be added that Downs' parties are homogenous, they lack inner structure. The individuals in the party leaderships and the party members all think in the same way. Finally it should however also be said that the absences mentioned not necessarily represent failures—I have certainly myself, again and again, emphasized the prudence of starting with the simple in order to introduce the complications later on. What I am saying is just that the simplicity is too great to lead to conclusions of the kind intended. It is, within the framework of Downs' model, impossible to decide whether Schumpeter's contention that the results would be good, or even optimal, when the political actors maximize their private interests, is correct.

THE SPATIAL MODEL

But even if Downs failed in demonstrating any generally beneficial effects of the assumed self-interests in politics, his book has nevertheless been of great importance. Most important is perhaps that his concentrated description of the political struggle by means of a scale over which the electorate is distributed, and on which the parties take positions, has become widely adopted. One usually talks about the *spatial model*, and certainly this model, in some respects, is quite effective. Looking at the figures above it is for instance easy to characterize the society in figure 5 as being skewed to the right, the one in figure 7 as being skewed to the left, and the one in figure 8 as being polarized. Departing from distributions like these it is also easy to discuss party strategies, which Downs himself to a large extent did. What happens if, for instance, this or that party moves from one specified point to another? How will the voters react? How will the other parties react? Will any new parties be created?

The model may also be developed. If, in some contexts, it seems too simple, for instance because of containing only one scale, more may be added. To the left-right scale may for instance be added an environmental scale. Additions like that result in what is usually called multi-dimensional spatial models. That models of this kind—one- as well as multi-dimensional ones—have become popular and extensively used is obvious. A clear sign of this is the book "Analytical Politics" which was published in 1997, that is exactly four decades after Downs' book. The authors— Melvin J. Hinich and Michael C. Munger—most properly mention Harold Hotelling, Duncan Black and Anthony Downs as the pioneers of the spatial theory for voting and for competition between parties. Furthermore, and more generally, they write:[652]

> "Spatial theory is the only theory that provides an integrated model of voter choice, party platforms, and the quality of outcomes. For a complete model, formal spatial theory is the only game in town."

---

[652] Hinich & Munger (1997), p. 6.

With all respect for the pioneers of the theory this is a flagrant exaggeration. There are important political phenomena which could not be captured by the spatial model, irrespective of its having one or more scales. Take for instance a situation in which pure, interest-driven transfers between groups of voters are proposed, that is a situation like the one in figure 9 above. Even if the setting there is extreme and barefaced it is obvious that situations having elements like that are common in politics, and the models used must therefore be capable of including them. But a spatial model can never be used in that way. However many the scales there is no way of placing the voters and parties in figure 9 on them.

The limitations of the spatial model may be demonstrated in other ways as well. Even if the model allows for several scales the one-dimensional version—and then in the traditional left-right form—is by far the most common. And within the framework of such a model it is, in fact, impossible to explain a phenomenon as common as a coalition executive. To show this—which actually may be seen as a little theorem—we may turn to figure 16, which depicts an assumed party configuration in a parliament. In the parliament there are six party-groups and the figure shows both their positions on the left-right scale and their sizes as measured by the numbers of their members.

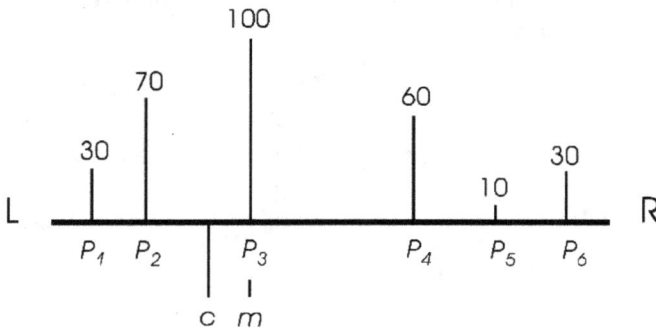

Figure 16: The impossibility of a spatial coalition explanation

Let us start by imaging that no coalition executive at all has been formed, which means that all propositions presented for the parliament will be voted upon directly. The results will then, according to the median voter theorem, become the ones marked by the median position m. But the very purpose of a coalition executive is just to forestall this—the intention of the parties forming a coalition is to bring the decisions closer to their own positions. So let us therefore, as an example, assume that the parties P_1 - P_3 form a coalition executive and at the same time determine that the policy of this executive should be c rather than m. This is obviously perfectly possible. The three parties together have a safe majority and therefore, all the time, can take decisions in accordance with c. There is a problem, however, namely that the position c, for the party P_3, is worse than m, and therefore P_3 will never accept the coalition agreement. The reasoning may be repeated for other coalitions, for instance coalitions in the middle or at the right, and the result will always be the same. Since the coalition should constitute a majority there will always be some party in it preferring the median policy to the proposed coalition policy. Consequently it is impossible to explain the emergence of a coalition executive within the framework of a one-dimensional spatial model.

If, however, one introduces interests as well—and thus assumes that elements such as those in the earlier figure 9 constitute parts of politics—it becomes quite easy. Examples will be given in the following main section, the one about democracies of different kinds. After having said this it is tempting to quote once again the work of Hinich and Munger mentioned above, which is full of complicated, formal arguments and mathematical calculations. They thus do not abstain from considerable complications but still write that "[t]he process of coalition government formation is complex and beyond the scope of this book."[653] Perhaps the reason is their promotion of the spatial model to "the only game in town."

SUMMARY

I have now very briefly presented the most important, and most well-known, theories about democratic politics. They are all interesting, and in all of them there are valuable results. It is for instance useful to know that the majority rule sometimes does not yield any decisions at all—sometimes there is no Condorcet winner. The spatial model with its distribution of the voters over a scale—or perhaps several scales—also captures elements which sometimes are important in political situations. That political parties often strive for positions in the middle, and that the median voter theorem therefore contains much truth, is also obvious. But even so,

---

[653] Hinich & Munger (1997), p. 111.

this is not enough. The rank-order approaches do not suffice, and perhaps they are not even the most important.

In other social sciences—and in particular in economics—the incentive oriented theories dominate completely, and certainly they must be given an important place in political science as well. Theories which do not explicitly model politics as a result of human ambition can hardly become successful. In Riker's theorem about minimal, winning coalitions this ambition is obvious. In Buchanan's and Tullock's theory the incentives are important as well, although in another manner. Where Riker focuses on the strategic options for forming a majority for taking as much as possible from the minority, Buchanan and Tullock rather concentrate on this losing minority's problems. How can these problems be limited without increasing the transaction costs associated with the decision making too much? This is Buchanan's and Tullock's basic question.

I thus contend that incentives always must be of crucial importance in theories about democratic politics—and, for that matter, about other kinds of politics as well—and for this kind of theories Riker, Buchanan and Tullock have made important pioneering contributions. A remaining deficiency, however, is that the institutions of the democratic processes still remain too peripheral. In chapter 3 I wrote that incentives, according to the modern institutional theory, to a large extent are formed by institutions. Different institutions give rise to different incentives. This underlines the importance of including the institutions fully in the theorizing. In the next section I will present an attempt towards that end.

A THEORY ABOUT DEMOCRACIES OF DIFFERENT KINDS

THE THEORY'S MAIN CHARACTERISTICS

I will start by presenting briefly the broad outlines of the theory in order to become more detailed in the sections that follow. The theory is based on two main ideas. The first one is that the number of political parties, and important properties of these parties, to a large extent are determined by the constitution. One may also say that the political actors get different characteristics in different constitutional settings. The other main idea is that these properties of the parties or the party-systems, or the different actor constellations, in turn, affect the political processes and their results. Different constitutions thus result in different kinds of politics, and political results, but in order to gain insight into these matters we have to consider first the parties. We have to use the parties with their properties as a kind of intermediate variable. Different constitutions produce different actor constellations, and different actor constellations produce different kinds of politics.

When speaking about different kinds of constitutions I have in particular two characteristics in mind. The first one is the method used for electing the members of the representative assembly, or the legislature, and here I make a distinction between majority elections in single-member constituencies and proportional elections in multi-member constituencies. The second one is the method used for appointing the government or the executive, and here I distinguish between presidentialism and parliamentarism. To make this latter distinction clearer it should be said that with presidentialism the executive, and then foremost the president, is chosen in different popular elections than those for the legislature—and thus the executive and the legislature may get diverging political inclinations. In a parliamentary system, on the contrary, only the legislature is chosen directly by the people. Then, and after that, the legislature appoints the executive, and therefore the majority of the legislature and the executive normally will have corresponding political inclinations. I thus, in summary, distinguish between two methods for electing the members of the legislature and two methods for appointing the executive. By combining these distinctions we get the four main types of constitutions shown in figure 17.

The figure also shows, schematically, the actor constellations in the four cases. Here I will only describe these constellations briefly; the explanations for their being as they are follow later on. In countries with proportional elections and parliamentarism we thus get several parties which are highly disciplined. The discipline is in fact so strong that the parties, in some respects, may be considered as homogenous actors, and therefore they are marked with unbroken circles in the figure. These countries are mainly present in Western Europe. In countries with majority elections and parliamentarism we get a small number of parties—perhaps only two—with a lower degree of discipline than in the former case, and hence the broken circles. To this group belong Great Britain and the countries in the British Commonwealth, with the exception of New Zealand. In countries with proportional elections and presidentialism there easily appear quite a number of parties, which may be more or less disciplined. Furthermore the president, marked by the uppermost small circle, is an independent actor apart from the parties. These countries are, on the whole, those in Latin America. At last we have the countries, or rather *the* country, namely the US, with majority elections and presidentialism. There the party discipline in the Congress is so low that it seems reasonable to consider the individual members, rather than the parties, as the real actors. Hence the many small dots in the figure.

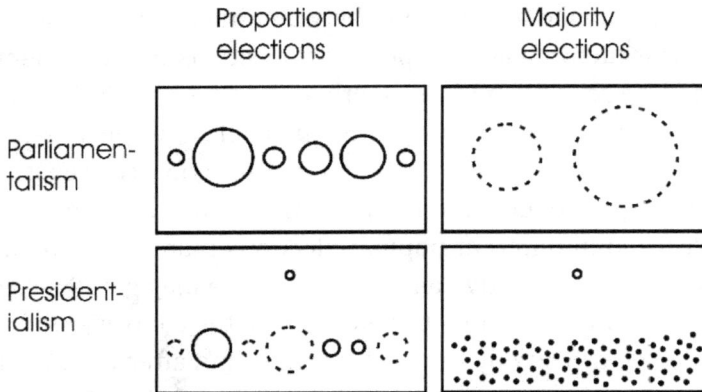

Figure 17: Four main types of democratic constitutions

The circles and the dots in figure 11 are thus the actors in politics, and obviously the actor constellations are very different in the four cases. Since politics consists in the actors' interaction with each other—cooperating with or countering each other—the political processes will therefore also become different in the four cases, and thereby, most likely, also their results.

I thus work with four main constitutional types, but this structure, it has to be added, is not exhaustive even if it captures many of today's democracies. There are also constitutions of other kinds. The four main types discerned here may however, I think, be considered as basic types, and therefore be taken as a point of departure for theorizing about democratic politics. It is, to repeat, prudent to start with the simple in order to introduce complications later on, and when that proves necessary.

I also want to say that the theory presented here lays claim to being a real, logically constructed theory. Departing from a number of basic assumptions about the nature of the incentives in the four constitutional settings, and about how the actors are steered by these incentives, conclusions are drawn about the nature, and the content, of the political processes. These conclusions thus are, or at least pretend to be, just conclusions. They should be the result of logical reasoning departing from the earlier assumptions and intermediary conclusions. In relation to reality the conclusions are thus hypotheses, that is statements which may be tested empirically and thereby be proved true or false. But even if the theory thus pretends to be logically constructed, there are also, in the following, some empirical examples. These are however intended only as illustrations for making the reasoning more tangible. They are not there for supporting the logic—it must stand by itself. Neither are they there for providing empirical support or evidence—for that they are much too few.

THE ACTORS AND THE INSTITUTIONS FORMING THEM

The incentives of those active in politics are to a large extent formed by the constitution, and in particular the effects on the political parties are important. I will therefore start by saying something about parties in general in order to turn, after that, to being more specific about their nature.

In a democratic country there are always political parties, that is organizations created especially for making policies. The parties usually have some sort of political program. All citizens can, if so they wish, become members of some party. The individuals who are candidates for various functions in elections usually belong to some party, and voting therefore, at least to some extent, normally means voting for a party. The candidates elected will then, in their different functions, take the political decisions. In the parties with their political ideas or programs therefore all the activities of the voters, of the members, and of those having been elected to different functions are integrated. This integration is the parties' important and overriding task.

But even if there always are parties their existence could not be taken for granted. Parties are big organizations and such things, as we saw in chapter 3, do not automatically appear even though they may benefit a large number of persons. If the costs for those taking the initiative are too large the logic of collective action may be an obstacle. For political parties, in particular, that obstacle may however, at least sometimes, be smaller than for other kinds of organizations. Thus some political parties first appeared among the members of a representative assembly—that, as we have seen, was the case with the left and right parties in the Estates-

General of the French Revolution, and the Whigs and the Tories in the English Parliament. In these cases the groups involved were small and the organizational work required therefore comparatively limited. The processes have been similar in several other cases, and when the parliamentary parties have been in place it has not been difficult to enlarge them into bigger, canvassing organizations. But there are also parties which have been created at the grass root level and after that made their way into legislatures and executives. Even in such cases the problems may however be smaller than for organizations in general. In parties the initiators may benefit more from their contribution than the members in general. If the party is successful the initiators are thus often those who reach high positions, and power positions, first. But all of this does not preclude that the creation of parties sometimes also may meet with the same kind of obstacles as the creation of organizations in general. It may very well be the case that parties, which many voters would support if they existed, are never in fact created.

But still there are quite a lot of parties, and these parties, as well as the party structure at large, thus look different in different constitutional environments. So the question is how this shaping of the parties and the party systems works. To answer that question four hypotheses are important.

The first hypothesis says that majority elections in single-member constituencies reduce the number of parties. This is the well-known regularity which after the French political scientist Maurice Duverger (born 1917) usually is called Duverger's law.[654] In spite of seeming almost self-evidently true this law is however not generally accepted within political science.[655] One of the reasons may be that the law often is presented in a stronger version saying that majority elections reduce the number of parties to two, and that this often is not the case, or perhaps even never, is not difficult to see. To deny the presence of a reducing mechanism because of this is however to throw out the baby with the bath water, which becomes obvious if one takes a more detailed look at the circumstances.

---

[654] Duverger, p. 217.
[655] Bealey, title-word "electoral systems".

It is thus important to distinguish between the constituency level and the national level, since it is at the former that the reducing mechanism works. In the constituency the party, or the candidate, getting most votes, or getting a so called relative majority, wins. In the long run this rule, most reasonably, should entail that only parties or candidates considering themselves as possible winners remain, and that other parties withdraw, or perhaps never get created. At the national level things are however different. If the country not is too large, and in particular if it is homogenous enough in cultural and ethnical respects, the same parties may very well dominate all over the country. The few parties competing with each other in the constituencies are the same from the one constituency to the other across the nation. Today's Great Britain with its main three parties is a good example. If, however, the country is large and heterogeneous things may turn out differently. Certainly the individual constituencies may still display the same pattern with a small number of parties competing with each other. But these parties may be different ones from constituency to constituency across the regions of the country. The result thus is quite a number of parties in spite of the use of majority elections in the constituencies. Even in a large and heterogeneous country this splitting may however to some extent be counteracted. Economics of scale may for instance play a role—the more constituencies a party competes in, the less it probably costs, at the margin, to compete in yet another constituency. But still the number of parties will in all likelihood increase with the size and heterogeneity of the country. India is an example. But even in India the fundamental reducing mechanism works at the constituency level—denying that seems hardly possible. The soft version of Duverger's law, the one saying that majority elections in single-member constituencies reduce the number of parties, apparently holds.

The second hypothesis says that parliamentarism, in particular when combined with proportional elections, gives the party leaderships strong *incentives* for creating unity, and above all voting discipline within their groups in the legislature. Of the four hypotheses presented here this one seems to be the less discussed in the literature, and I have not seen any systematic discussion of it anywhere. I have only found a few, very general endorsements[656] and one, again very general, denial[657]. These conten-

---

[656] Hinich & Munger (1994), p. 134; Laver & Shepsle, p. 301; Lipset, p. 199;

tions are in fact so general that they rather apply to the final result—disciplined parties—than to, specifically, the incentives. But here, as I have emphasized, it is the incentives we are interested in. The discussion about the means belongs to the third hypothesis below.

My reason for the hypothesis about strong incentives is the importance, in a parliamentary system, for a party to belong to the executive, and the discipline as an almost necessary condition for the fulfillment of this aim. That or those parties which form the executive in a parliamentary system hold the power, the other ones are outside. It is by belonging to the executive that a party is able to satisfy its voters' interests of various kinds. But the executive cannot be an executive without a reliable support from the legislature—it has to enjoy so called parliamentary confidence. If it is required that the legislative majority explicitly expresses its confidence one usually talks about positive parliamentarism. If, on the contrary, it is enough that no majority has expressed any dissatisfaction one talks about negative parliamentarism.

But irrespective of the kind of parliamentarism confidence must firstly be expressed by a party's own members in the parliament, and consequently they must not fail in discipline. In parliamentary systems with proportional elections one more aspect is however important. Since the executive in such a system normally consists of several parties its formation must be preceded by coalition negotiations in which the main ingredients of its future politics are laid down. In these negotiations the party leaderships must be confident that their people in the legislature, when voting later on, will support the agreements reached. A party not able to act like this will quickly become considered untrustworthy and excluded from all future coalition negotiations—it will never be admitted into any executive.

The third hypothesis says that proportional elections put effective *means of discipline* in the hands of the party leaderships. This mechanism thus is about means rather than about incentives. That the party leaderships actually dispose of strong means of discipline in a proportional system is sometimes mentioned in the literature, but again this happens quite seldom and the discussion is somewhat scanty. Furthermore, the ar-

---

Powell, p. 60.
657 Sartori, p. 95.

gument most often advanced in favor of the idea is debatable. What is usually said is that the party leaderships determine the lists of candidates, and therefore also have the power of excluding candidates who have lacked in discipline.[658] But the same argument could, in principle, be applied to majority elections as well—even in such a system the party leaderships may be of importance for the nomination of candidates even if there are no lists.

The real reason rather seems to be that the individual candidates in a proportional system, to the extent that they take part in election campaigning at all, work largely for the whole party, and comparatively little for their own success, whereas the candidates in a majority system to a much larger extent work for their own cause. Or, in other words, the candidates in a proportional system largely produce a collective good, whereas those in a majority system concentrate on producing an individual good. And this makes the candidates in a proportional system comparatively defenseless—if their party leaderships want to get rid of them they have no electoral support of their own to mobilize. Such support, however, is enjoyed by the candidates in a majority system. Ultimately, and if necessary, the candidate in such a system can even get along without the support of any party at all. Parties are not necessary components of a majority system—it may, in principle, work without parties. Since a vote for a party in a majoritarian system always means a vote for a particular person, it is, in principle, possible to vote for that person directly. A proportional system can however not work without parties. The voters must vote for parties in order to make it possible to determine the number of members in the legislature belonging to each party. Exactly that is the very meaning of proportionality.

The fourth hypothesis, finally, says that parliamentarism, contrary to presidentialism, puts strong means of discipline in the hands of the leaderships of the party or parties belonging to the executive. This mechanism, which is mostly discussed with reference to British politics,[659] is based on the fact that the executive, when facing a defeat in the parliament, may threaten to dissolve the parliament and announce a new election. The idea is that the risk of not being reelected may force obstructing

---

[658] See for instance Duverger, p. 183 and Shugart & Carey, p. 173.
[659] See in particular Cox, pp. 80-7 but also, for instance, Duverger p. 404 and Shugart & Carey, p. 173.

parliamentarians to toe the party line. It must however be underlined that this mechanism, at most, explains the discipline of the party, or parties, in the executive, not of those in the opposition.

THE ACTOR CONSTELLATIONS IN THE FOUR CASES

After this account for the significance of the properties of the constitutions I will now return to the actor constellations in figure 11 in order to be more specific about their background and characteristics.

Starting with the combination *parliamentarism and proportionalism* we get in that case quite a number of parties—in the figure I have drawn six of them, but there may easily be more than that, and perhaps also fewer. The reason for the relatively great number is that the reducing mechanism—working in a majority system according to Duverger's law—is absent. The lack of such a mechanism also makes the formation of new parties comparatively easy. Even with rather weak electoral support a party may make its way into the legislature and, eventually, grow larger and larger. The threshold for newcomers is low.

Naturally the sizes of the parties differ, which in the figure is shown by the varying sizes of the circles. The parties are also strongly disciplined, which is why the circles are unbroken. In this manner I want to show that the parties, in their external activities and on the whole, can be considered as individual, homogenous actors. The discipline is caused by the party leaderships' strong incentives for establishing such an order, and their possession of means for the purpose. But this discipline and uniformity is only an outward feature, that is something exhibited in relation to other parties, to the electorate and to lobbyists. In their inner life the parties are of course not homogenous. They have inner discussions and inner power struggles. But this is of less importance in this theory. Here our main interest is in the outward activities.

In spite of their inner lives the parties are thus characterized by a high degree of discipline and concord, and this probably also entails a considerable stability over time. A short-lived party is probably not able to build the unity necessary for its political activities. But this then also leads to possibilities for developing coherent, elaborated party programs. Disciplined parties of the kind here discussed therefore probably have well integrated programs, and these programs may be basically ideological (and thus perhaps possible to place on a left-right scale), or mainly interest oriented (by for instance representing agricultural interests). Obviously there may also be different mixtures of ideological and interest-oriented parts. The low threshold for new parties also opens the door for ideological extremism.

Finally it should be said that the distinction between legislature and executive is of less interest in parliamentary systems, and that is the reason why no such separation is shown in the figure. The important distinction in these systems rather is the one between those governing and those in opposition. Some of the parties—with positions in the legislature as well as in the executive—belong to the former group. Other parties—with positions only in the legislature—belong to the latter group.

We move on now to the combination *parliamentarism and majority elections*. According to Duverger's law there are fewer parties here than in the former constellation. In the extreme case there may be just two parties as in the figure. These parties are disciplined but not as disciplined as in the former constellation, and the circles indicating the parties are thus drawn with broken lines.

The less rigid, although palpable, party discipline has several causes. First, in this constellation as well as in the former one, the party leaderships have incentives to enforce discipline, although not equally strong. That there are any incentives at all depends on the executive's need for support from the legislature, if that support disappears the executive also disappears. That the incentives nevertheless are weaker than in the former case depends on the fact that the majorities here usually are safer than in the proportional election case. The sizes of the two parties in the figure are, as we see, quite different, and this is no coincidence. In a country with majority elections the seat difference in the legislature is usually much greater than the vote difference in the electorate. The result in the electorate is amplified in the legislature.

A more exact expression of this matter is given by the so called cube-rule.[660] Suppose that there are two parties and that these in an election, in the whole nation, get V_1 and V_2 votes respectively. The number of seats which the two parties then get in the legislature may be labeled S_1 and S_2. The cube-rule now says that

$$(S_1 / S_2) = (V_1 / V_2)^3,$$

---

[660] Bealey, title-word "cube rule".

which means that the big party in the electorate becomes, proportionally, much bigger in the legislature, and the small party correspondingly much smaller. On the whole the cube-rule has proved valid in Great Britain.

The incentives thus are not as strong as in the proportional election case, and the same holds true for the means. But they are not non-existent. Even if a candidate in a constituency, in principle, can act alone without the support of any party, that may still prove difficult. Adherence to a supporting party is always important, and a threat of withdrawn support therefore a means of discipline. And in addition to this the incumbent party may threaten new elections and thereby tame at least some of its more obstinate parliamentary members.

The upshot thus is that the parties are disciplined even if not as disciplined as in the case with proportional elections. From this follows, in the same way as in the constellation with parliamentarism and proportional elections, that the parties have a considerable stability over time, and that they develop coherent, elaborated party programs. Still there is an important difference. Since the parties here are few and big the ideological content of their party programs will probably become quite prominent and the interest component correspondingly smaller. Agricultural parties thus often tend to promote interests intensively, but such parties are mostly also small, and for small parties there is no space in a majority election system. The same is the case for small, ideologically extreme parties.

Next we get to the combination of presidentialism and proportional elections. Here, as I have already said, it is first important to distinguish between the president and the executive, on the one side, and the legislature on the other—entities being appointed in different popular elections. In the legislature the proportional elections, and thus the lack of a reducing mechanism, may result in quite a lot of parties. The question about discipline is however open. It is true that the party leaderships, because of proportionalism, dispose of considerable means of discipline, but still it is difficult to say anything in general about the incentives. Obviously there are not the same incentives as in a parliamentary system, but there may be others. For a party leadership wishing to conduct a policy of obstruction and blocking—about which more below—a disciplined group in the legislature may for instance be an important asset. Incentives for discipline are thus not necessarily missing and therefore there may be disciplined as well as undisciplined parties in the legislature. In the figure some circles are thus drawn with unbroken lines and other ones with broken lines.

At last we get to the combination of *presidentialism and majority elections* and, as I have already said, there is only one country, namely the US, with a constitution of this kind. First then the president, in the same way as in the preceding case and for the same reason, is indicated with a separate symbol in the figure. Considering then the legislature the majority elections should result in a small number of parties, and since we now know that we are talking about the US we can also say that so it is. The Democrats and the Republicans, the two great parties, dominate completely. Furthermore, following our previous reasoning, the discipline of these two parties ought to be low since both incentives and means are missing. So that is my reason for having a large number of dots, standing for the individual members of the Congress, rather than circles for parties in the figure.

I wrote above that disciplined parties probably also have considerable stability over time and therefore also are able to develop coherent and elaborated party programs. The parties in the US do not have any stability like this and therefore they should also lack party programs of this kind. And so it is. At most there are general declarations, or so called platforms, which are adopted at the regularly recurring party congresses and which, with respect to content, may differ considerably over time.

THE SIGNIFICANCE OF PARTY DISCIPLINE

The incentives emerging in different constitutional environments thus result in different kinds of actors and different actor constellations. But these results do not necessarily favor good politics. What the incentives bring about is one thing, what is required for the working of good politics is another.

Above all the executive must enjoy a certain stability. In all our constitutional environments a small, unified leadership of some kind is required. The work in the legislature has to be led, and even in other situations such as in the contexts of external threats, nature-catastrophes, and so forth, a small, strong leadership is needed. A well functioning state without a leadership of this kind is hard to imagine, and has probably never existed. In our four cases this leadership is the task of the executive.

Using this idea as a point of departure we can start with the parliamentary systems. In these the executive is chosen by the legislature, and for the sake of the necessary stability it is important that those having once made that choice, at least on the whole, stand by it. They must not waver or change positions unpredictably, for if so the executive is undermined. A parliamentary system therefore requires stable, well disciplined parties. About this all political scientists agree. In this case the incentives thus lead in the proper direction. The incentives, and the means, resulting in unified, homogeneous parties favor the functioning of the system as well.

The recent introduction of open lists in Sweden, making it possible for voters to support specifically individual candidates, is from this point of view interesting. Since this may give some members of the legislature a stronger personal base, and thus make them somewhat less dependent of their party, it may also lead to some loosening of party discipline. Since the majority behind the executive in this kind of system often is quite narrow—see next section—this may be a problem. It is surprising how little this has been discussed in connection with the introduction of open lists.

Going then to the presidential systems the executive consisting of the president and the government appointed by him or her is always there. This is so since the president, appointed in separate popular elections, is independent of the composition of the legislature. These matters are however important even from another point of view. For a decision to become valid it is often required that it is supported not only by a majority of the legislature but also by the president. But since the legislature and the president are appointed in separate elections, and therefore may have different political inclinations, this means—as we will see in the next section—that the process may come to a deadlock. And this is a problem, in particular, if the parties are disciplined. If a parliamentary system requires disciplined parties it is the other way round with presidential systems. In such a system the discipline rather threatens its proper functioning. This has been stated by some political scientists—for instance Giovanni Sartori—although not at all as frequently and as emphatically as concerning the need for discipline in parliamentary systems.[661]

---

[661] Sartori, p. 94.

In this respect the political processes in the United States should thus work well since the party discipline there, according to our reasoning, is expected to be low. In fact this expectation is on the whole, and over long periods fulfilled, but this is also due to another factor which is not constitutionally conditioned. This is that the party leaders in the US are not able to control the nomination of candidates. Rather the candidates, for example the ones for the two houses of the Congress, the House of Representatives and the Senate, are nominated in so called primaries preceding the real elections. This system was introduced by the parties themselves—or rather by their grassroots—as a reaction against the party leaders' earlier self-serving of power.

Even if primaries have been used in some states since long the great change started in 1968 when the Democratic Party nominated Hubert Humphrey as its presidential candidate. Humphrey, who then lost to Richard Nixon, had not competed in any primaries and the opposition within the party argued that the nomination was a betrayal of the opinions expressed by the Democratic primary voters. Changes were proposed by a committee appointed for the purpose, and thereby a process of change towards today's system, with nominations actually decided by means of primaries, began.[662]

THE ACTORS' INTERACTION, LOBBYING AND ELECTION CAMPAIGNS

Politics is a multi-facetted phenomenon taking place in different arenas and in different manners. Here I will deal with three kinds of activities which are particularly interesting, and pose a central question for each one of them. The first activity takes place within the formal institutions, that is the executive and the legislature. The main question here is about the actors within these institutions. How do they interact with each other, and which are the results? The second activity is the actors' interaction with the lobbyists. What does this interaction look like, and what are the likely outcomes? The third activity is the competition for votes. What do the political actors do in order to get into the executive and the legislature, which strategies do they use? In what follows I will try to answer these questions in separate sections for each of the four constitutional

---

[662] Beck, pp. 218-21; King, pp. 65-6; Wattenberg, pp. 75-6.

contexts, but before that it is necessary to make the questions somewhat more precise.

The first question, the one about the institutional actors' interactions with each other, may be divided into the following two questions:

- How do the actors act in order to form *decisive* constellations?

- How do the actors act in order to form *blocking* constellations?

The distinction here made between decisive and blocking constellations may be clarified with a simple example. Suppose that we have a presidential system with two houses in the legislature and that, for a decision to become valid, it is required that it gets the support of the president and of the majorities in both houses. This formation—the president plus the two majorities—is then a decisive constellation. It is able to enforce a decision. But this also means that it is comparatively easy to hinder the decision, to block it. Obviously the president can do that alone, or a majority in either house. These blocking constellations are thus essentially smaller than the decisive ones. One may also say that, in the situation assumed, it is much more difficult to change the *status quo*, which only a decisive constellation can do, than to keep the *status quo* unchanged, which is in the hands of a blocking constellation. But even if it is like that in the situation assumed, it need not be so. If we rather consider a parliamentary system with only one chamber in the legislature—such as for example the Swedish—decisive and blocking constellations have the same size. A simple majority in the legislature can change the *status quo*, and such a majority can also keep the *status quo* unchanged.

The next question is about the activities of the so called lobbyists and here a distinction between *legal power* and *influential power* should be made. Those having positions in the executive or the legislature have legal power, which means that their decisions are followed. If they decide, according to the rules, about a certain matter, it will be so. This, of course, takes for granted that the decision-making institutions are so generally respected that their decisions, at least on the whole, are implemented. But this is another matter. Here, in this context, we can assume that this kind of respect is there, and then the legal power about which I am talking is also there.

And it is precisely because the actors in the executive and the legislature hold this legal power that other actors, outside this cluster, try to influence them. Such other actors are often called lobbyists even if the term often is given a narrower sense than in this book. In Sweden the big, central trade-union organizations are for instance obvious lobbyists in the sense of the term used here, since they try to achieve their goals by, among others, influencing the legal power holders. Still, for some reason, they are usually not called lobbyists. Here, however, I call these organizations, as well as other organizations and individuals, trying to influence the legal power holders, lobbyists. And to the extent that they are successful they dispose of influential power.

But what is then the source of influential power? Lobbyists or lobby organizations are sometimes called pressure groups. This terminology is, following the incentive oriented philosophy adopted here, hardly recommendable. One gets the impression that the lobbyist, almost by using some kind of physical force, moves the legal power holder, against its (or his or her) will, from one position to another. But that, of course, is not what happens. The reasonable approach rather is to consider the whole matter as a negotiation between the lobbyist and the legal power holder in which they both give and take. The lobbyist may for instance tell the legal power holder that if you support this or that decision, favoring our members, we will try making them vote for you in the next election. This is thus one possible kind of agreement, even if there obviously are other ones as well. What is important, however, is that the interaction of the legal actor and the lobbyist is looked upon as a negotiation. If the negotiation is fulfilled it leads to some kind of agreement—possibly unexpressed or implicit—but an agreement nevertheless which both sides consider beneficial. Thus it is a mutually beneficial agreement.

The third activity is the campaigning for votes. How do those wanting to become members of the executive or the legislature act—the incumbents wanting to be reelected as well as challengers wanting to replace them? For the discussion of this issue it is important to characterize the relationships between the voters and those elected, and a distinction important in that context is the one between *instruction* and *delegation*.

Instruction means that the campaigning candidate (or party), if elected (or if getting strong enough), also is given a task to fulfill. It may for instance be the case that the candidate, while campaigning, presents various proposals for political measures and also says that he or she, if elected, will try to get the measures implemented. If then a voter, who favors those measures, supports the candidate with his or her vote, that voter most probably expects the measures to be implemented, or at least hopes for that. A sequence of events like that may be described as a negotiation. Candidates promise to do their best for the implementation of the proposals, and the voter contributes by supporting the candidate. In this sense the two parts have interacted and agreed upon a kind of implicit contract. Even if the proposals were initially presented by the candidate they may, after the voter's action, also be looked upon as an instruction from the voter to the candidate elected. The voter instructs the candidate to fulfill what he or she, in the campaign, has promised to fulfill. Or, to put it in terms of the modern so called principal-agent theory, the voter is the *principal* and the candidate is the *agent*.[663]

A candidate may however, when campaigning, use other methods than proposing specific political measures. The candidate may for instance try to sell him- or herself, emphasize his or her own good qualities in various respects, point to its own impressive past performances, and so forth, and in that way try to inspire confidence among the voters. In that kind of campaign an instruction relationship between the voter and the politician is hardly created. The voter does not instruct the candidate but rather, and because of the confidence felt, leaves the candidate free to decide him- or herself about how to handle those issues that come up. The voter delegates the decision-making to the one elected. The relationship between the voter and the elected may thus be characterized as delegation.

With this the presentation of the necessary preliminaries has come to an end and we can start formulating hypotheses about politics in the four constitutional contexts in a coherent manner.

COUNTRIES WITH PARLIAMENTARISM AND PROPORTIONAL ELECTIONS

The political main actors in these countries, according to the hypotheses presented above, are a number of well disciplined political parties. The first question then is about the interacting of these actors—what do they do in order to form decisive or blocking constellations? Initially it may then be stated that the system not only requires a reasonably stable executive, but also that there are strong incentives for the parties really to create such an executive. The parties succeeding in gaining the govern-

---

[663] See for instance Milgrom & Roberts.

mental power are not only able to satisfy their voters' desires of various kinds, the party leaderships are also favored considerably. They probably get essentially higher incomes than those in opposition, and they become prominent and celebrated in a totally different manner than the opposition politicians.

From this follows that the interaction between the actors essentially occurs in relation to elections and is about the government issue. To some extent the negotiations may start before the election, even if they obviously cannot be concluded until the final electoral result is known. And almost always the negotiations are about coalitions since, in this kind of system, it is very rare that a single party alone gets the majority necessary for forming a stable government. Normally we thus get coalition negotiations aiming at the formulation of a governmental program for a long period ahead, possibly for the whole mandate period. If so, what happens during the mandate period when the various issues are put on the agenda, one after the other, is, basically, just a formal implementation of decisions which, in reality, had been taken when the coalition government was formed.

But a certain amount of negotiating during the mandate period should not be excluded. Above all such negotiations may become necessary if the original negotiations, in spite of the participants' efforts, had failed in reaching a majority government. If so the government formed, during the mandate period, may have to deal with various supporting parties. Even so the ones negotiating are however disciplined parties.

I have already written that the parties in this constitutional setting probably have detailed political programs, and that these programs may have ideological as well as interest-based elements. And this is of great importance for the subject matter of the coalition negotiations. On the whole it is much easier to negotiate about, and make compromises about, interests than ideologies. Concerning interests agreements may easily take the following very simple form: "If you, and your party, support the interests of our voters, then we, and our party, will support the interests of your voters." Concerning ideologies it is much more difficult, there are no simple compromises. Parties which are strongly ideological, or whose ideologies are very distant from each other, will therefore find it difficult or impossible to cooperate in a government. For this reason most parties' programs probably have considerable interest components, and possibly several, or perhaps all, parties avoid very strong or pregnant ideological program elements. Probably there are also parties which are almost completely interest oriented.

Parties of this latter kind are often able to secure for themselves a key role in the coalition negotiations. Since they do not carry any ideological load they can join and support any other parties in exchange for having their interests honored. Let us for instance assume that there are two coalitions about to be formed—we may call them the left- and the right- coalition respectively—and that neither of them, so far, has succeeded in reaching a majority. Let us also assume that there is a small interest oriented party which, by its cooperation, could turn either one of the two coalitions into a majority coalition. Such a party is then able to negotiate with both constellations—each in turn, forth and back—and withhold its final choice until it draws the conclusion that there are no more concessions to its interests to be achieved in the governmental program that will result.

Interests are thus likely to be of great importance in the coalition negotiations, and small purely interest-oriented parties can require and obtain important favors. But irrespective of the appearance of parties like this the negotiations should, normally, result in minimal, winning coalitions. The politics' strong interest component points in this direction. And this, by the way, underlines still more the strong arguments in favor of strong party discipline—from the point of view of the parties as well as system. The discipline obviously becomes particularly important when the governing coalition's marginal is narrow.

Closely related to the parties' discipline, their stability over time, and their relatively extensive and detailed party programs, is the nature of political careers—these are always, or almost always, party careers. Those reaching high positions in this kind of political system do so by advancing upwards within a party. It does not occur, or is at least quite rare, that individuals, who have not been active in a party, are brought into the business and immediately placed in high positions. Those reaching the top must be trained, tested and found loyal and reliable.

After this we get to the lobbyists and their efforts in trying to influence the holders of legal power. What do they do? Since the relatively few, well consolidated parties are the legal power holders, the lobbyists turn to them. Or, to be more exact, they address directly the party leaderships since these are strong and the parties disciplined. The participants in the discussions, or negotiations, are the leaders of one of the small number of political parties, on the one side, and some organization, perhaps some central trade organization, on the other. This means that the total number of contacts in the lobby activities is quite small, that the activities usually take place in closed rooms, and that they, therefore, in their outer manifestations, are barely visible.

This, however, does not mean that the lobbying is ineffective. Taking into account the great role of interests in this constitutional context, the conditions for the lobbyists should be quite favorable. In exchange for support for its interests the lobbyist can encourage its members to vote for the political party concerned. The lobbying thus is, in summary, hardly visible, quite cheap for the lobbyists since the number of contacts with the legal power holders required are few, but probably very effective.

An interesting example of lobbying—in this case in Sweden—is given by the former prime minister Göran Persson in his book "The one in debt is not free".[664] He describes the negotiations which the Social Democratic government formed in 1994 carried on with the Center Party and the Federation of Swedish Farmers (LRF). The background was a Social Democratic proposal about "taxes on farm buildings, taxes on the farmers' lands, taxes on tractor fuel, and so forth." "There was," writes Persson, "not much which we should not tax." In order to ward off these outcomes Bo Dockered, by then the president of RLF and the lobbyist in the context, contacted Göran Persson, at that time minister of finance, and an agreement was reached. The proposals about taxes were withdrawn and in addition to that the value added tax on food was lowered from 21 to 12 percent. In exchange the Center Party, close to LRF, supported important parts of the Social Democratic politics in general. "The agreement cost us quite a lot of money," writes Persson and continuous: "That was the price we had to pay for a wide-ranging agreement, which was to hold all through the process of sanitizing the budget."[665]

Then, at last, there is the third question, the one about the struggle for voters. I have already written that the parties probably have well

---

[664] Persson, pp. 74-9, my translation.
[665] Another interesting example is the close collaboration in Japan between the Liberal Democratic Party and the interest organization Japan Agriculture. According to the article "Farming in Japan—Field work" in The Economist, April 13th, 2013, Japan Agriculture is Japan's the most powerful lobby organization.

integrated party programs and that the positions of the party leaderships are well consolidated. From this it follows that the ideas presented to the voters are those of the parties—it is the parties which campaign. Certainly individual candidates for positions in the legislature may take part in the campaigning, but if so they primarily make use of their party's messages, not their own. And these messages are, probably, to a large extent taken from the party programs, and they may contain ideological as well as interest components. The latter are important and for some parties they may dominate completely.

With this kind of campaigning the relation between the voters and the politicians will take the form of instruction. To the extent that the parties with their candidates become elected to positions in the legal power institutions, this is in order for them to implement the proposals they have campaigned on. When taking power they carry with them their voters' instructions. For interest issues this is particularly evident. In the campaign a party may for instance have addressed some delineated, well defined group of voters—say university students—and promised to introduce improvements for this group if gaining power. The hope of course is to get the students' votes, and to the extent the party succeeds with this the instruction also becomes pertinent. The party has promised, the voters have gone along, and the party therefore should deliver—or at least do its best to do so.

After this we get to the other constitutional types and I will then focus in particular on what seems to be important differences in relation to the case with parliamentarism and proportional elections just treated.

COUNTRIES WITH PARLIAMENTARISM AND MAJORITY ELECTIONS

Here there is a mechanism reducing the number of parties—in the extreme case to only two. In Great Britain there are for instance three major parties but for long periods two of these—Labour and Tories—have been so dominant that either of them, alone, has been able to form a government.[666] The third party—the Liberals—has normally had to

---

[666] The party forming the majority government has in some cases, and due to the mechanism captured by the cube rule, had a remarkably weak electoral support. Thus, the governments formed after the elections in 1974 (two elections) and 2005 were supported by 37 %, 39 % and 35,2 % of the voters respectively. And, the highest share of the votes a party ever got during the same period was 50 %,

remain an outsider, even if it did join the government after the 2010 election. In reality, and for long periods, those competing for power have been the two main parties. In this section I will confine myself to a two-party constellation like that. It is that constellation which, above all, is interesting as a contrast to the constitutional context discussed in the previous section.

Most important in this case is that there is no interaction at all between any main actors. There are just two main actors of which one, in parliament, usually is considerably larger than the other, and therefore can form a government alone. After winning an election it becomes the governing party. Thus there are no coalition negotiations. And this is of outmost importance since it was by means of such negotiations that the interest issues were brought to the fore-front in the proportional context.

From this follows the hypothesis that politics, in this particular system, may be quite ideological. Above I have, we remember, been skeptical about the frequent use of the spatial model in political science and argued that the understanding of politics also requires the introduction of interests in a way not permitted by that model. But perhaps my criticism of the spatial model goes too far for the very constitutional context at issue here. In this case the essentials of politics, at least sometimes, may possibly be captured quite well by a one-dimensional spatial model with two parties competing with each other somewhere in the neighborhood of the median.

A further consequence of the absence of coalition negotiations is that the opposition may find it quite natural to form a shadow cabinet. This is so since the opposition is whole and unified—it does not contain small parties which, in a somewhat different parliamentary situation, may make deals with the government. Shadow cabinets are also, as a rule, formed in Great Britain. Another consequence of the absence of coalition negotiations is that the governmental program does not have to be settled on from the beginning. The incumbents can, with their party program as a point of departure, bit by bit prepare and raise various issues during the mandate period. There is thus probably more real decision making during the course of the mandate period than in the previous case.

---

which happened in 1955.

But even if there are no coalition negotiations, and even if there is no need for discussions about a total governmental program when the government is formed, this system is still parliamentary with the resulting incentives for, and requirements of, coherence and stability over time. The parties will therefore, in the same way as in the proportional case, have coherent, elaborated party programs. And, again in the same way as in the former context, political careers are most probably party careers.

Coalition negotiations between parties are thus rare, but that does not preclude that other kinds of negotiations may become necessary. Even if the governing party usually is considerably larger than the second party it is still the case that the Members of Parliament are less disciplined than in the case with proportional elections. Even the big party may therefore, now and then, have to engage in negotiations with obstinate, individual parliamentary members in order to secure its majority. In particular this may perhaps be so for issues emerging during the period between elections, and which are thus not covered in any governmental program.

The lobbying is in this case probably somewhat less concentrated, and also somewhat less effective, than in the previous case. If so one reason could be that the lobbyists not only address the party leaderships but also to some extent, and due to the lower discipline, individual parliamentarians, and another that politics in its entirety is less interest oriented than in the proportional case. An indication about the nature of these matters is given by the relation between the Trade Union Congress and the Labour party. The former once created the Labour party, but since then the party has, to a large extent, liberated itself from the trade union movement. "Unions are being kept at arms' length in the modern Labour party", writes the prominent expert on British politics Dennis Kavanagh.[667] Things seem to be quite different than in Sweden with its very close collaboration, to a large extent within common institutions, between the two branches of the labor movement, the political branch and that of the unions.

The issue about the fight for votes I have already touched on. It is of course, in the same way as in the proportional case, to a considerable extent carried out at the national level, but to this is added, in this case,

---

[667] Kavanagh, p. 157.

the intensive campaigning in the individual constituencies in which the candidates struggle for their own destinies. The relation between voters and elected therefore should include more of delegation than in the previous case.

Let me finish this section with a comment on Margaret Thatcher's accomplishments as British prime minister during the years 1979–90. She was authoritative, charismatic and ideological and she carried through very important, fundamental changes in the British society, changes which one may like or dislike.[668] The changes were however, by and large, accepted by Labour—New Labour as led by Tony Blair—when that party eventually gained power. What is interesting here is that Thatcher—irrespective of all evaluations—could achieve what in fact she did. My hypothesis is that she, in spite of all her remarkable personal qualities, never could have done the same in a parliamentary system with proportional elections. In such a system she would immediately have become occupied by coalition negotiations and therefore the scope for more fundamental changes would also have disappeared. With majority elections it is not so.

COUNTRIES WITH PRESIDENTIALISM AND PROPORTIONAL ELECTIONS

In the countries with presidentialism something new, having to do exactly with the president, is added. If we, for the sake of comparison, return to the countries with parliamentarism and proportional elections there was in them, most likely, no main actor, no party, supported by a majority of the electorate, and in that sense coming close to representing a general interest. All parties were probably smaller than that, and the breadth needed for governing was thus not a result of any election, but rather achieved by means of coalition negotiations. The case with parliamentarism and majority elections was however, in this respect, somewhat different. There the reigning party and its leadership were treated as though backed by a majority of the electorate.

Still further in this direction go the countries with presidentialism—but only with respect to the president. The presidential election is usually, after more or less elaborate nomination processes of various kinds, a competition between two individuals, and these two meet each

---

[668] Judt, pp. 539-47.

other in something which, in practice, may be considered as one single, big national constituency. In that situation it may be natural for the candidates to disregard somewhat their own party affiliation, and the associated perhaps rather narrow party programs, in order to appeal to larger groups of voters. The candidates become more generally oriented and will also try to avoid, perhaps, offending particular groups of voters. In French politics this tendency of the president candidates—and thereby probably also of the president—to move from the party program to a more general program is called the Élysée-effect.[669] This effect should first of all be present in countries with proportional elections, that is the kind of countries which are the subject of this section. This is so since the parties there probably are more numerous, and thus also smaller, than in the case of majority elections. And therefore their programs are also addressed to smaller and more clearly delineated voter groups.

The president thus is one of the main actors but then there are also the actors in the legislature. Since we know that the kind of constitution we are dealing with here—presidentialism with proportional elections— is used above all in Latin America, we may turn directly to the circumstances there. Several of the states there are, as noticed above, federal states and thus have, already for that reason, two chambers or houses in the legislature. And some of the other states, even if not federal, still have two houses in the legislature. This being so we may make our area of interest still more precise. The countries we are dealing with are not only characterized by presidentialism and proportional elections, but also by having two houses in the legislature.

This has the important consequence that the difference between decisive and blocking constellations often is big. The president alone, or a majority in just one of the houses, may block a decision and thus fix matters at the *status quo*. For changing the *status quo* the endorsement of the president and of both house majorities may, on the contrary, be required. And decision rules like this in fact hold for many kinds of issues. So these are the conditions under which the actors, with their varying ambitions, interact with each other.

Of course it may happen that most actors agree and that therefore decisive constellations easily are formed. In such cases the system ob-

---

[669] Charlot & Charlot, pp. 133-41.

viously works properly. And the same is case if a proposal does not pass, for instance because of failing to get a majority in one of the houses, and if all actors have voted according to their convictions. Even in such a case it is easy to argue that everything is in order. The intention of those who wrote the constitution may very well have been that a change of the *status quo* should require wide support, and if such support is not there it is thus perfectly in order that the decision is not taken. Assuming, again, that everybody votes according to his or her convictions.

What creates problems is however the scope for tactical voting, or even blackmail, given by the system. The system, it is easy to see, makes it possible for small groups to block proposals which, in fact, they approve of, just in order to get something completely different such as favors of some kind. This possibility is thus built into the system, but the conditions for making use of it are much better for a disciplined party than for a non-disciplined one. Here there thus is a strong incentive for the party leaderships for really creating the discipline made possible by proportionalism. The hypothesis is that many parties take advantage of this option.

Concerning blocking with a purpose of blackmail it should at last just be added that it has, reasonably, to be directed towards someone having capacity to deliver. The one being able to deliver is the president and blocking activities are therefore, in all likelihood, initiated by some group in the legislature and aimed at the president. A blocking president seeking some kind of concession from some legislative group seems much less likely.

Here my discussion about the first question, the one about the main actors' interaction with each other, is completed. As for the two other questions, those about lobbyism and about the struggle for votes, I find it difficult to draw any precise conclusions. Much seem to depend on the degree to which the parties are disciplined. Rather I will turn to the great and important theme about the Latin American dictatorships—a theme which I left in chapter 6 arguing that it rather belonged here.

The Latin-American dictatorship-democracy-pattern, if so it may be called, is utterly special and there is hardly anything similar in any other part of the world. What is special are the shifts between democracy and dictatorship—back and forth. Now and then the democratic process is brought to a halt—often by the creation of a military dictatorship—only, after a while, to be reestablished again. But we have also seen that presidentialism and disciplined parties function badly together—the risks for blocking and blackmail is too great. The political process easily gets gridlocked. My hypothesis is that these two phenomena are related to each other. An at least partially contributing cause of the recurring dictatorial periods is that the democratic process does not work, and cannot work. The combination of presidentialism with proportional elections is destructive, in particular when combined with two-house legislatures.

THE COUNTRY WITH PRESIDENTIALISM AND MAJORITY ELECTIONS

This country is the US, but what follows is still not a description of that country. In the same way as hitherto it has claims to following logically from earlier assumptions and conclusions. The examples are still presented just as concretizing illustrations. The statements made about politics are hypotheses. If they seem correct that is good for the theory. If they on the contrary seem wrong, or obviously are wrong, the theory fails somewhere and has to be corrected.

Let us then, in the same way as in the preceding sections, start by looking at the actors' interactions with each other. The point of departure is that we have a president and two chambers or houses—in this case represented by the House of Representatives and the Senate—and that a proposal, to become a decision, requires support from the president and the majorities of both houses. Decisive constellations are thus, as in the previous case, much bigger than blocking ones.

Going beyond this, politics in this system will be very different. The reason is the very low party discipline, so low in fact that not only the president, but also the individual senators and members of the House of Representatives, can be considered as separate actors. And this pattern is a consequence not only of the constitution but also, as mentioned above, of the primaries. There are thus many more actors than in any of the other constitutional systems and this means, for pure transaction cost reasons, that the formation of permanent coalitions is difficult. But it is not only difficult, neither is it important for the actors in the same way as in a parliamentary system, and neither of importance for the functioning of the system, but rather the opposite.

A memento, however, is the formation of disciplined groups such as the Tea Party caucus in the Congress. This is a new phenomenon which certainly should be dealt with here. Since the groups at issue are considerably smaller than party groups in the Congress, and even may be bipartisan, their existence do not contradict the main conclusions about parties arrived at here. In spite of the caucuses the parties, as it seems, have the properties derived later on in this section. But even so, and since the groups may be well organized and disciplined, they hamper the functioning of the system. As I have already said presidentialism and party discipline go badly together and the same holds true for presidentialism and disciplined caucuses. What we are witnessing in the US today seems to be black mail politics and grid locking of a kind usually characterizing Latin American politics.

But even if all actors in the Congress consequently not are individuals, there are still quite a number of independent actors. A first consequence of this is that the formulation and sanctioning of policies is not a batch-process as in above all in parliamentary systems with proportional elections, in which, as we have seen, the policies to a large extent were fixed when the government formed. Here the policy formulation is rather a continuous process, moving along step by step as the decisions, taken by the president and the Congress, follow each other in succession. Another consequence is that members of the Congress, when voting on issue after issue, to a large extent follow their own, personal opinions, which leads to constellations of various sizes and compositions. The majorities may very well be larger, or even much larger, than the minimal winning ones. And the majorities may also include individuals from both parties in patterns varying from decision to decision.[670] To the extent that there are any negotiations at all these probably occur when a decisive constellation, or a blocking one, almost is about to materialize. In such cases the state of affairs obviously can be changed by only a few members shifting side, and efforts to persuade those ambivalent individuals are therefore probably made. In such activities some persons, for instance the president, the chairmen of the relevant committees or the leaders of the party groups in the houses, may be especially active.

Then we get to the lobbying. Even here the lobbyists naturally address the main political actors, but these are now much more numerous than in the preceding cases. Certainly there are some key persons such as for instance the chairmen of the congressional committees but still the lobbyists have, in principle, to turn to one congress member after

---

[670] This general pattern is supported by for instance Mayhew.

the other to try to achieve the desired decisive or blocking constellation. The lobbying therefore becomes spread out and visible, and also very costly for the lobbyists. This does however not mean that it is particularly effective, rather the opposite. Obviously it is also much easier to aim at blocking constellations than decisive ones. An example is the National Rifle Association which has hitherto successfully worked for the presservation of the very old US weapon laws. A change of the *status quo* has so far, with a few exceptions, been hindered.

It is often held that lobbyism is particularly conspicuous in the US and that it influences politics there more than in almost all other countries. According to the hypothesis presented here this is an optical delusion. The American lobbyism is certainly spread out and easily visible—ever-present at Capitol Hill—and also expensive for the lobbyists. But it is hardly effective. Its effectiveness is, in all likelihood, not anywhere near that of the lobbying of, for instance, the great organizations in Sweden.

To these general conclusions about the US lobbying must however be added a few words about the procedure called *earmarking*, a procedure used especially for achieving majorities for budgetary proposals. What happens is that a senator, or a member of the House of Representatives, when negotiating with the relevant committee chairman promises to support the general proposal in exchange for the earmarking of a small share of the total sum for a project favored by the congressman, for instance in his or her own district. The procedure has, according to numerous observers, resulted in many strange activities—for instance the building of bridges leading to nowhere. But the earmarking also facilitates the activities of the lobbyists most noticeably. If a lobbyist strives to get a particular project, which may be financed through earmarking, undertaken, it obviously suffices to find one suitable congressman—there is no need to build a whole coalition. In exchange the lobbyist can, as usual, give for example a campaign contribution or canvass for votes for the congressman.

The existence of earmarking thus, to some extent, changes the conclusions about lobbying presented above. It should however also be added that the earmarking in no way is constitutionally supported, and therefore does not really belong to the issues discussed here. The possibility of earmarking emerged during the 1970's but since then strong forces have also been mobilized for eliminating them, and in 2010 they were prohibited.[671]

And so finally the struggle for votes. To draw conclusions about that I think it helps first to consider the contrast offered by countries with parliamentarism and proportional elections. In those countries, as I have argued, the parties campaign with detailed programs and the relation between voters and politicians is largely characterized by instruction. In that system this was expedient, basically because the possibilities for the campaigning parties to get their proposals implemented were quite good. The winning coalition was, in principle, supported by more than half the electorate, and each of the parties in that coalition could count upon having at least some of its proposals implemented.

In the system discussed here all of this is completely different. Certainly the candidates may formulate some very general phrases about their political opinions in order to inform the voters about their general inclinations, and perhaps for profiling. But precise proposals, intended to be implemented, are hardly used in campaigning. No one, not even a chosen president, can count upon being able to actually implement policies proposed while campaigning. Even the president will, in many cases, have to engage in negotiations with a Congress in which majorities do not necessarily belong to the president's party, and for which the opinions of the individual members anyway are unknown. Under such conditions it is probably imprudent, and perhaps even somewhat ridiculous, to campaign by making detailed proposals for various kinds of measures. The possibilities for getting them implemented are much too remote. Better then to try to sell oneself as an individual, to inspire confidence, to try to be looked upon as one who in future situations, whatever they are, will act wisely and with sound judgment. According to the reasoning followed here, the campaigning thus, on the whole, will look like that. From this it follows that the relation between the voters and those elected, again on the whole, will be characterized by delegation rather than by instruction. And if all of this applies to presidential candidates, it applies still more to the individuals aiming for positions in the Congress. Their possibilities, after being elected, for getting campaign proposals implemented are, if anything, still less than the president's.

---

[671] The article "Dr No Retires" in The Economist, January 25th, 2014.

The political careers here also differ from those in systems with more disciplined parties. In principle it should be possible for individuals with relevant experiences, other than political or party-political activities, to get directly from the outside into politics and into high positions. Political careers, which are not party-careers, should be perfectly possible. American politics also displays several examples of this. The war hero and general Dwight Eisenhower moved directly from the military to become president. But not only that—both parties sought him and he finally settled for the Republicans. The movie star Ronald Reagan was for certain politically active early on, but not on a full time basis. Furthermore he shifted from the Democrats to the Republicans in 1964, and became the governor of California only two years later. And in 1980 he was elected president of the US. Hardly a party career either. The general Colin Powell never made a political career but could very well have done so. When he had retired from the military in 1993 both Democrats and Republicans tried to make him their presidential candidate in the 1996 election. A party career was not required for reaching the highest position, and a party affiliation could be arranged by either party when and if the one approached declared himself interested.

THREATS AGAINST REPRESENTATIVE DEMOCRACIES

Representative democracies can of course fall, and many have fallen, in several different ways. They may be attacked from outside, and they may be undermined from inside by anti-democratic parties working within, and by, the system. The taking of power by the Nazis in Germany in the 1930's is an example. Karl Popper's well known book "The Open Society and its Enemies" is about threats of this kind.[672] Democracies may however also fall because they, in more general ways, prove unable to function. I have already mentioned the very special Latin American democracies which now and then have been turned into military dictatorships. More examples of a similar kind could be mentioned. Some of the democracies created through the peace process after World War One soon became dictatorships, and in some cases at least the reason was functional failures. In his book "The Future of Freedom", published in 2003, the author Fareed Zakaria contends that a democracy, in order to function,

---

[672] Popper (1945a) och (1945b).

has to be established within a society which already disposes of an, in other respects, for instance administratively and legally, reasonably well developed institutional basis.[673] If such a basis is missing the conditions for the survival of a democracy are bad. Zakaria exemplifies with other and later attempts to create democracies than those after World War One, but perhaps his reasoning is valid even for them. There is however also another factor which possibly may have played a role. All of those democracies created during the twentieth century, which have fallen, have, as far as I know, had proportional election systems. This may have amplified and increased the significance of internal conflicts present already from the beginning in the countries concerned.

Quite a number of representative democracies have thus fallen, and some of the mechanisms possibly at work in these cases have been suggested above. Representative democracies could however also, it is easy to imagine, fall in other ways, namely because of slow processes, operating over extended periods of time, which finally make them unable to function. So far nothing like that has happened in any representative democracy, but the threats are there and have been discussed by some authors. Ludwig von Mises contended that market interventions of the state tended to lead to further interventions and that the public sector, or domain, thereby became larger and larger until the democracy stopped working altogether.[674] Mancur Olson held that the market economy, due to the activities of the gradually increasing number of organizations, successively worked worse and worse, or, as he expressed it, became increasingly "sclerotic".[675] That processes like these, if they exist, may lead to the fall of a representative democracy is not an unreasonable idea. Above we have also seen how interest politics may become more prominent in some constitutional systems than in others. According to the hypotheses presented here politics emphasizes interests most in countries with parliamentarism and proportional elections, and least in countries—or rather the country—with presidentialism and majority elections. If this is correct the public sectors, or domains, should grow more rapidly in the former countries than in the latter. If it is also the case that this growth is difficult to control—or perhaps even unavoidable because of being built

---

[673] Zakaria
[674] von Mises, pp. 858-61.
[675] Olson (1982), p. 74.

into the system—this clearly is a threat.[676] The growth of the public sector or domain may thus lead to the fall of a representative democracy. So far this has however not occurred. So far it is just a hypothesis about a possibility.

SUMMARY

This chapter has three main parts. The first one deals with the general properties of representative democracies, the second presents some important theories about democratic politics, and the third presents a theory of my own about democracies of different kinds.

The most important property of a representative democracy is the presence of a representative assembly of some kind—it is that assembly which makes the democracy representative. Other important institutional or formal characteristics, as presented in the chapter's first part, are respected rules about regular elections, about universal right to vote, about vote secrecy and about manipulation-free vote counting. But even some less formal characteristics such as freedom to form opinions, and to express them, are of crucial importance. Apart from these defining characteristics some other important ones are also mentioned. Thus, the representative democracy is the only constitutional order capable of harboring a fully developed market economy. And, according to the democratic peace theory, representative democracies do not fight wars against each other.

The second part of the chapter starts by presenting two main theorems, the median voter theorem and the theorem about minimal, winning coalitions. It is argued that they represent two major, and different, approaches towards theorizing about democratic politics. The first theorem is rank-order oriented and the second one incentive oriented. After this presentation some other theoretical approaches are described and related to the two theorems. It is argued that theories about politics—like economic theory for instance—have to be incentive oriented. And this leads to a critique of the rank-order oriented spatial model so common in political science. It is for instance, as shown, impossible to explain a phenomenon as common as a coalition executive within the framework of a one-dimensional spatial model.

---

[676] Moberg

The theoretical approaches presented in the second part of the chapter—even if interesting in a lot of ways—are to a large extent silent about institutions. Since it has been repeatedly argued in this book that incentives are formed by institutions this obviously is a shortcoming. In the theory about democracies of different kinds, developed in the third part of the chapter, institutions are however included.

By making first a distinction between parliamentarism and presidentialism, and another one between proportional and majority elections, four main types of democracies are singled out. Parliamentarism combined with proportional elections is common in continental, Western Europe, parliamentarism combined with majority elections characterizes the United Kingdom and most countries in the British Commonwealth, presidentialism combined with proportional elections is frequent in particular in Latin America, and presidentialism combined with majority elections, finally, prevails in only one country, the US.

Then, as an intermediary step, the legal actors and actor constellations, in the four settings are derived. What makes this possible is that the incentives related to party structures are quite different in the four cases. After this, finally, it is possible to derive results about political processes and results. Three basic questions are put for each of the democracy types. First, how do the legal actors interact with each other in order to form decisive or blocking constellations? Second, what do lobbyists do in order to influence the legal actors—and which are the results? And third, what do political actors, incumbents as well as aspiring ones, do in order to become elected?

Here are some of the results—hypothetical since we are all the time dealing with a theory—of this questioning. Interest politics is most common or frequent in countries with parliamentarism and proportional elections. In countries with parliamentarism and majority elections the number of main actors is small, perhaps no more than two, and if so there will not be any coalition negotiations and a shadow cabinet may also be formed. Presidentialism and proportional elections work badly together and therefore the legislative process in countries with this combination is often gridlocked. This, by the way, may also explain the many military coups in Latin America. Presidentialism combined with majority elections finally—and then we are speaking about the US—leads to a very special kind of politics. The composition of legislative majorities and minorities may vary from vote to vote, and the winning majorities may very well be considerably larger than minimal winning. And lobbying—contrary to a commonly held opinion—is much less effective than in countries with parliamentarism and proportional elections. It is however much more spread and visible, and also much more expensive, for the lobbyists.

Again, and finally, it should perhaps be emphasized that all of these results are hypotheses. They are not descriptions of reality but rather pretend to be logical derivations from basic assumptions. If they are corroborated that is good for the theory, if not the theory has to be changed.

11

STATELESSNESS

INTRODUCTION

Hitherto, in this book, I have talked about statelessness only in very general terms. Statelessness has just been the conditions prevailing when there is no state at all, that is no dictatorship, no direct democracy, no oligarchy, no representative democracy, and no state in between these main types. There are however good reasons for making the stateless condition more clear, to introduce relevant nuances and distinctions. All stateless conditions are not similar. For a start there are thus conditions characterized by a general lack of structures, of institutions. This, of course, is quite common, and most stateless conditions are probably of this character. Among them it is however important, I believe, to distinguish between the statelessness prevailing before the creation of any state at all—which is thus a kind of virginal condition—and the statelessness appearing after the collapse of a former state. The former condition need not be particularly anarchistic or chaotic. The latter may be atrocious and horribly brutal. In addition to these unstructured, stateless conditions there have also been those with developed and sophisticated institutional structures, even if that particular element which makes a state a state, namely a monopoly of violence, has been missing. An interesting example—possibly the only one—is medieval Iceland. The following sections deal with these different kinds of statelessness.

STATELESSNESS PRIOR TO THE CREATION OF STATES

In chapter 2 I wrote, using the world in a meaning quite different from the common one, that the world was only gradually nationalized. When the first states were created most human beings hence lived outside states, and like that it continued for a long time even if the share of humanity living like this successively became smaller and smaller. Here one may thus talk about a kind of virginal condition, and the question is what it was like. Thomas Hobbes' opinion, as expressed in Leviathan, was that in the state of nature there is no property, no justice or injustice, there is only war and "force, and fraud, are in war the two cardinal virtues."[677]

Perhaps it was like that, but perhaps not necessarily. In many cases it may also have been otherwise. During the time of the early states the number of human beings on earth was much smaller than today and the average population density therefore also smaller. Many people lived in tribes—sometimes settled, sometimes nomadic—and were perhaps led by some chief or some elderly council. Tribes like this could perhaps live quite well and without conflicts, whether internal or with their outer world, but still be too simply or primitively organized to be considered states. This kind of statelessness was therefore not necessarily all that chaotic or dominated by internal violence.

But it should also be said that our knowledge about these early conditions is limited. And not only that. For several areas it is also not known when the first states were established, and therefore neither when the first transitions from statelessness to states occurred. I have for instance not mentioned any state in western South America prior to the Inca state, but there were predecessors. As early as about –10 000 people moved into these areas and archeological finds bear witness to societies of some complexity.[678] Here it thus seems unclear when the passage from statelessness to states occurred. And the fact that the very distinction between statelessness and state almost necessarily lacks precision, does not decrease this indistinctness. Furthermore, when states emerge this often happens gradually. Within the Persian Empire, to mention just one example, there were, in the early stages, considerable areas outside the main densely populated areas, and the main communication roads, not reached by the monopoly of violence.[679]

It is thus difficult to form an opinion about the type of statelessness that, in their areas respectively, preceded the first states. But this does not make the distinction between this kind of statelessness, and the one following after the collapse of a prior state, less important. The arguments that are possible, or in some cases perhaps even reasonable, regarding the relatively peaceful and perhaps even idyllic character of virginal statelessness are in all likelihood never valid for the post-state stateless-

---

[677] Hobbes
[678] Conrad, p. 350.
[679] Finer (1997a), p. 307.

ness. That kind of statelessness is rather, and generally, a most horrible condition.

STATELESSNESS AFTER STATE COLLAPSES

INTRODUCTION

Even if the world gradually has become more and more nationalized, this process has not been continuous. States created have again and again, for one reason or another, collapsed, and after that, in many cases, been followed not by new states but by stateless conditions. Some of the intervals in figure 1 in chapter 2—for instance between the Egyptian kingdoms[680] or the Chinese dynasties—are of this kind. But this kind of statelessness is not limited to remote times. Even in modern times, and in today's world, it is a common phenomenon. The roving and stationary war lords described in chapter 3, and used as a point of departure for the theory presented there, were for instance active in the statelessness characterizing China between the First and the Second World Wars.[681] That this kind of statelessness can be so much more atrocious than the virginal one is a consequence of its following after a collapsed monopoly of violence. The means of violence are there, but the use of them is no longer monopolized. All can use them against all, or at least many against many. Hobbes' description of statelessness seems in fact to fit this condition much better than the "state of nature" he pointed to, and, we remember, he actually wrote his book influenced by an ongoing civil war in England.

The fragmenting of the original monopoly of violence may however be more or less far-reaching. In cases with just a few fragments—two, or three or anyway not more than a handful—one usually talks about civil war rather than about statelessness. In the civil war leading to the break-up of the Roman Empire a number of generals with their almost private armies confronted each other. In the American Civil War (1861–65) there was a northern and a southern side. In the Spanish Civil War (1936–39) there was a military, revolutionary side, the Falangists, and a governmental side, the Republicans, which, in turn, was divided to some extent. In all of these cases, after the civil wars, new states with the same borderlines as the old ones were created. But even so the constitution

---

[680] Mieroop, p. 27.
[681] More examples are given in the Appendix.

could be changed. In the Roman case there was a shift from the oligarchy of the Republic to the dictatorship of the Empire, and in Spain from representative democracy to dictatorship. In the US the constitution however survived. The country was a representative democracy before the war and continued being so after.

But the fragmenting of an earlier state may proceed further than in the cases mentioned and if so one hardly talks about civil war, but rather about statelessness. Conditions characterized by such far-reaching dissolution are also more than numerous in the history of the world. One example is the period after the fall of the Western Roman Empire in the area of modern Western Europe which is often called the Dark Ages, starting about the year 700.[682] Another one is Germany during the Thirty Years' War (1618–48).

This war was not preceded by a state collapse but rather by the progressive weakening of an already, from the very beginning, feeble and loosely connected state, namely the Holy Roman Empire. Simultaneously with this weakening the conflicts within the area also grew. Some of those conflicts were religious, but not all. There were also manifest conflicts between the central power, striving for control, and the many regional states fighting for their independence. The war started as a civil war, but in due course the Great Powers of the age, among them France and Sweden, intervened. What took place on German soil for thirty years was everybody's war against everybody. Individual generals, with their own small, private armies, fought now against one enemy, then against another, all the time hoping to be able to form their own duchies. It was an armed anarchy and the destruction was ghastly. It all ended with the Peace of Westphalia, resulting from comprehensive international cooperation. The Great Powers played their full parts, and the Holy Empire became still smaller and weaker.[683]

This happened in Europe and more examples, European[684] as well as non-European ones, could easily be mentioned. The Mayas and the Toltecs in Central America had created states, or at least societies similar to states, before the Aztecs, but the transition to the Aztec state was not continuous or without pain. The two centuries preceding the creation of

[682] Palmer, Colton & Kramer (2007a), p. 23.
[683] Morris, p. 454; Palmer, Colton & Kramer (2007a), pp. 135-43, 175, 191.
[684] See for instance North & Thomas, p. 82.

the Aztec state around 1400 were characterized by war and chaos in the area.[685] And, taking a totally different part of the world, India, after the collapse of the Mughal Empire in the beginning of the eighteenth century, was for a long time plagued by an anarchy having great similarities with the Thirty Years' War in Europe.[686]

But violence related to state dissolution is not only a historical phenomenon. Rather, and on the contrary, it seems to have become more common in recent times. In the introductory first chapter I mentioned Somalia, but, as will be seen in the Appendix, there are more examples. Here, in this chapter, I will however give somewhat more detailed accounts of two other cases in the recent past, namely Liberia and Yugoslavia.

LIBERIA

During the 1950's Liberia in West Africa became one of the most prosperous countries in Africa.[687] The economy grew rapidly—during the decade GNP increased by an average 11.5 percent per year. The infrastructure was expanded in a fast pace and the same was the case for public welfare politics. But in spite of these positive developments, and the possibilities they gave rise to, all was to change. In 1989 a civil war broke out and thereafter, with somewhat of an interruption in 1996–99, conditions became increasingly chaotic. Small groups of soldiers, sometimes only local gangs, ravaged everywhere. Child soldiers with automatic carbines (AK-47, Kalashnikov) took part in the fighting. What possibly had started as a civil war, according to the term as made precise above, soon turned into a stateless condition. About 250 000 human beings were killed and around a million were forced to leave their homes and belongings. Considering that the total population was not greater than about three millions these figures are extremely high.[688] To bring a halt to the

---

[685] Diehl, p. 336.

[686] Palmer, Colton & Kramer (2007a), pp. 291-3.

[687] The main source for this section is Moran, but I have also to some extent used some later sources available at the Internet.

[688] Moran, pp. 22, 105, 120. Moran's data are however in several cases valid only for the period up till 1997. Some of the figures here are therefore somewhat higher than Moran's since even the period 1997–2003 has been taken into account.

chaos an international intervention, which did not materialize until 2003, was required. But what were the reasons for what happened up till then? How could a once so successful country break down so quickly and completely?

Liberia is because of its particular relations to the US unique. During the US age of slavery it happened that some slaves became free, and there were also some people of African descent who never had become slaves. Some white citizens considered these individuals threatening and they were therefore moved back to Africa, to the country which eventually became Liberia. The state was founded in 1847 and got a constitution similar to that of the US. An earlier American president, James Monroe (1758–1831), a great slave owner himself, worked intensively for the creation of the new state and its capital, Monrovia, was named after him.

The Liberian president with the longest service in office is William Tubman. He was born in 1895, became president in 1944, and then remained in this position until his death in 1971. It was during Tubman's reign that the remarkable economic expansion occurred. Foreign investments increased greatly. The country got, because of generous rules for ship registration, the world's largest mercantile fleet. Its rubber industry was the largest in the world, its iron export the world's third largest, the extraction and export of diamonds was considerable, and so was the industry dealing with tropical wood.

Tubman as well as all presidents before him belonged to the very small part of the population descending from the original immigrants from America. And one of the big problems of Liberia was the tension between this minority and the dominating native population, which, in turn, consisted of several tribes in conflict with each other. The country was thus split, but still ruled all the time by the very small "American" element in the population. And within that element there was, in spite of the constitution's similarity with that of the US, only one political party, the "True Whig Party". In spite of his background Tubman tried however to attenuate the tensions between the "Americans" and the native inhabitants. But at the same time the democracy, already quite defective, became still more circumvented. Tubman became more and more of a dictator—in particular after an attempt to murder him in 1955.

Tubman was succeeded by William Tolbert, a man having the same background and ambitions as Tubman, but less aptitude for the task. At the same time Liberia, depending on its exports, was hit by economic problems because of a weakened world economy, and so the scene was set for changes. In a military coup in 1980 the young Samuel Doe (1951–90) with some military training seized power. Tolbert and most members of his ministry were executed. For the first time Liberia was led by a person belonging to the native part of the population. But Doe favored his own tribe at the expense of the others and the dissatisfaction with him grew. After a rigged election in 1985 the opposition against him grew still greater and one of his former collaborators, Charles Taylor, acted.[689]

Taylor, born in 1948, was to become a key person in Liberia during the long and chaotic period from 1989 to 2003. Before that he had lived a varied life not only in Liberia but also in the US and in Muammar Gadaffi's Libya. Turning Liberia's great natural resources into his own private fortune seems to have been his ambition.[690] Now, when this is written in 2014, he has been detained in The Hague since 2006 accused of war crimes and crimes against humanity, and, in April 2012, in a first trial, found guilty and sentenced for some of the crimes. In September 2013 the sentence was confirmed and then Taylor was transferred to a British maximum-security prison.

After Doe's rigged election Taylor started by acquiring a guerilla soldier training in Libya. Then he created the opposition movement NPFL (National Patriotic Front of Liberia), brought together a minor group of armed sympathizers in the Ivory Coast, bordering on Liberia, and, from there, crossed the border into the Liberian province Nimba. The people there, feeling oppressed by Doe, immediately sided with Taylor, thereby initiating the conflict. The Liberian Army AFL (Armed Forces of Liberia) commanded by Doe retaliated by means of extensive attacks against the civilian population, burned entire villages and applied, in general, a kind of scorched earth policy. But even so the army was not successful. Doe was captured, tortured and executed.

In spite of its considerable achievements NPFL was however split. A splinter organization, INPFL (Independent National Patriotic Front of Liberia), was created. This one focused with some success on occupying the capital Monrovia, while the former organization, NPFL, rather tried to control the countryside. During the course of the fighting NPFL was fur-

---

[689] Moran, pp. 77, 97-8.
[690] Moran, pp. 35, 138.

ther split, as well as AFL. Completely new warring groups, labeled with their own abbreviations, were created. The warring groups became successively more numerous and the fighting turned into an armed chaos, an armed anarchy. Prior to the international intervention in 2003 Charles Taylor controlled only a third of the country.

But even if this chaos, by and large, prevailed from 1989 to 2003 there was, as already mentioned, nevertheless a certain, relative calmness by the end of the 1990's. This was partly due to an international intervention. During this period an election, in which Charles Taylor won overwhelmingly, was held. Taking into account the enormous devastation brought about by Taylor this was strange, but international observers still held that the election was properly conducted. Perhaps Taylor's private ownership of important TV and radio companies, and of newspapers, was an explanation.[691] Anyway the fighting soon began again after the election, and peace was not established until 2003.

The end of the fighting resulted from an international intervention—by African as well as non-African states. Also important was a female resistance movement—Women of Liberia Mass Action for Peace—based on non-violence. All of this will however be put to one side here—not because it is not important, but because it is not directly related to the problems of statelessness. I will only add that Liberia's president today is Ellen Johnson-Sirleaf (born in 1938), elected in open and free elections in 2005 and reelected in 2011.

YUGOSLAVIA

The country which somewhat later was to get the name of Yugoslavia was founded after World War One, in the context of the Treaty of Versailles.[692] It was created by enlarging Serbia, which was an independent state before the war, with parts of the former Austro-Hungarian Monarchy, which had gone under in the war. At first the new country was named the "Kingdom of Serbs, Croats and Slovenes" which gives an indication of its heterogeneity. The country started as a representative democracy. In 1928 the king, Alexander I, however made himself dictator. In 1929 he introduced the name Yugoslavia (the land of the southern Slaves), and in

---

[691] Moran, pp. 105-6.
[692] The main source for this section is Judt, pp. 665-85.

1934 he was murdered by a Macedonian with Croatian support. After the murder some liberalization took place and new elections were held in 1935.[693] But after that World War Two soon started and the country was attacked by Italy and Germany. The attack was ultimately successfully fended off, but it also, in spite of being repelled, triggered an intensive civil war. On the side of the attacking Axis powers was, among others, the Croatian organization Ustaša. On the other side was the final victor Josip Broz, later on Marshal Tito, with his Partisans.[694]

The dictatorship built by Tito after the war was in some respects an ordinary, hard dictatorship. A secret police and military were used to trace and crush nationalistic aspirations threatening the unity of the state. Croatian rebellions were for instance squeezed out in this way at the beginning of the 1970's. But in other respects the dictatorship was re-markable and, in fact, relatively liberal. Thus Tito broke with the Soviet Union in 1948, and thereby also left the Soviet power sphere. In this way Yugoslavia became the leader of the continually expanding group of neut-ral states. The economy also developed in another direction than the Soviet one, and in due course even got some market economy elements. Enterprises were to some extent run by those employed, by the workers. In chapter 5, we remember, I wrote about "The idea about a demand steered unmixed state economy", and something like that was in fact im-plemented in Yugoslavia.[695] Furthermore the country was given the struc-ture of a federation with a number of smaller republics which, in fact, really seemed to enjoy a certain amount of independence. This was a way of providing a limited, although controlled, political space for nationalist elements. The economies of the republics were, at least to some extent, free in relation to the central power. The leaders of the republics also served, in order and following a rotation principle, as subordinate presi-dents, just below the dictator. All of this made Yugoslavia, at least on the surface, a pleasant and attractive country. Many Western people went there for their vacations and Dubrovnik was a highly regarded holiday site.

This state was however eventually to be turned into a horrible stateless condition. Understanding this statelessness may be facilitated by

---

[693] Lee, pp. 323-8.
[694] Judt, pp. 34-5.
[695] Nove, pp. 299-303.

beginning with the situation that followed it. Seven new states—the ones shown in table 4—were created within the area. This division has its roots far back in history. Among others it coincides well, even to the borderlines, with the republics introduced by Tito, who by the way was a Croat. The only essential difference was that Tito's Yugoslavia had only six republics since Kosovo and Serbia there constituted one republic together. The area covered by the present seven states also coincides well with territory of Yugoslavia between the World Wars.

Table 2: The states following former Yugoslavia

Country	Capital	Population, millions	Language	Religion
Slovenia	Ljubljana	2.0	Slovene	Catholicism
Croatia	Zagreb	4.5	Croatian	Catholicism
Bosnia–Herzegovina	Sarajevo	3.9	Bosnian, Serbian, Croatian	Islam (ca 50%), Orthodox, Catholicism
Serbia	Belgrade	7.5	Serbian	Orthodox
Montenegro	Podgorica	0.6	Serbian	Orthodox, Islam
Kosovo	Pristina	2.1	Albanian, Serbian	Islam, Orthodox
Macedonia	Skopje	2.0	Macedonian, Albanian	Orthodox, Islam

In addition to capitals and populations the table also gives some further information about the seven states. Starting with the languages it should first be noted that Croatian, Serbian and Bosnian are very close to each other and one therefore often talks about a single language, Serbo-Croatian. Within the area there are thus only four main languages, namely Serbo-Croatian, Slovene, Albanian and Macedonian. But still there are also some minor languages such as for instance Hungarian.

Besides the language differences there are also important cultural ones, both in general and more specifically concerning religion. In particular the culture of the north-western states Slovenia and Croatia is to a large extent "western" and these states are also far more economically developed than the others. In Slovenia and Croatia Catholicism is also strong. The other states, and in particular Serbia, Montenegro, Kosovo and Macedonia, with a historical past within first Byzantium and then the Ottoman Empire, are more "eastern" oriented. In these states orthodox churches and Islam are the dominating religions. In Bosnia-Herzegovina both linguistic and religious patterns are utterly mixed. Some such mixture certainly characterizes the other states as well, but not at all to the same extent. Finally it is important to note that Serbia, the state having the largest population, during the fourteenth century was a Great Power within the area. Many Serbs and Serbian leaders have therefore, well into modern time, entertained a Great Serbia dream, and perhaps some still do. In that context some places in Kosovo, among others, are of great symbolic importance for Serbia.[696]

This, very briefly recapitulated, is the general background. If we now return to Tito's Yugoslavia, the following, in very broad outline, is what happened. First Tito died in 1980 whereby the dictatorship was weakened. Thereafter, during the 1980's, Yugoslavia was hit by severe economic problems, to some extent caused by economic setbacks in western countries, but also by inadequate reactions to these setbacks. At the end of the 1980's Yugoslavia therefore fell prey to hyper-inflation. Added to all of this then came the collapse of the Soviet Empire in 1989, leading to fundamental changes in all of Eastern Europe.[697]

The fragmentation of Yugoslavia however started even before this collapse. In June 1989 the Serbian communist leader Slobodan Milošević (1941–2006), in front of a million-person auditorium, made a strongly demagogic speech celebrating the 600-th anniversary of an important battle in Kosovo in 1389.[698] Then, in November 1989, the Berlin Wall fell, and after that one thing followed the other. After referendums or general elections some of Yugoslavia's republics declared themselves independent in 1991. First out were Slovenia and Croatia and then followed Bosnia-Herzegovina. This however triggered revolts by the Serbian minorities in these states and Serbia, led by Milošević supported these minorities militarily. The fact that the earlier Yugoslavian national army (NJA) to a large extent was Serb-controlled, and that this structure remained, faci-

[696] Roberts, pp. 1143-5, 1150-1.
[697] Judt, p. 671.
[698] Judt, p. 673.

litated this support. The fighting became lengthy—in particular in Bosnia-Herzegovina, where ethnical cleansing also went further than in any other place. In Srebrenica several thousand Bosnian Muslims were murdered in 1995.[699] And in this way the fighting then went on in large parts of earlier Yugoslavia. Ethnical cleansing was carried out in several places and the Serbians were not the only ones culpable. But they were worse than any of the others.[700] And not only sizeable military units were operating but also smaller entities such as criminal gangs of various kinds.[701] International organizations—among them the EU and the UN—tried to bring the fighting to an end, but without success. The course of events did not change until 1999 when NATO, using much more direct methods than previously, intervened and stopped Serbia's until then successful campaign to drive the Albanians out of Kosovo. Thereby it became possible, in due time, to establish peace and create the seven new states. But prior to that hundreds of thousands of human beings had been killed, tortured or raped, and millions had been forced to flee.[702]

COMMENT

I have now tried to say something about the kind of statelessness which follows after the collapse of previous states. A first conclusion is that conditions of this kind are quite common and have been so all through the history of the world. Usually they are also horrible. And this is a sufficient reason for studying them more carefully. They are obvious objects of study for political science. In this context there is also reason for underlining the obvious fact that there are interesting intermediary situations between the established state and the stateless condition. The disintegration of a state may be more or less comprehensive.

Turning then to the two cases described above, Liberia and Yugoslavia, there are similarities as well as differences. An important similarity is that both, before the transformation to statelessness, were fairly well developed and prosperous societies. Their leaders, Tubman and Tito respectively, could both, as it seems, be described as rather decent dicta-

---

[699] 7400 according to Judt (picture text in the last collection of photos in the book). See also Judt, p. 814 and Roberts, p. 1151.
[700] Judt, p. 675.
[701] Finlan, p. 19.
[702] Judt, p. 665.

tors. But this did not help. When the disintegration had started both states broke down rapidly in spite of their relative initial prosperity. For
states missing that kind of prosperity the odds are possibly still worse.
Even if the statelessness now (2014) characterizing Somalia was preceded by a consolidated state, that state was still not as developed and economically successful as for instance Liberia or Yugoslavia.

Another important similarity between Liberia and Yugoslavia is
that both, even when they were well consolidated, harbored within themselves very intense and severe ethnical and cultural divergences. Perhaps
it may therefore be argued that it was these divergences rather the statelessness which led to great problems when the state disappeared. And if
so—and if one really wishes to stress that line of argument—the problem
was not the statelessness as such but rather the ethnic and cultural divisions. Perhaps the statelessness would not have been a problem if only
the divisions had been less far-reaching and intensive, and perhaps that
kind of argumentation has some validity. But against this it could first be
argued that a strong state is particularly important in exactly those cases
where a serious split, irrespective of the reasons, really is there. And, furthermore, there are in fact hardly any examples of population groups,
however ethnically and culturally homogenous, leading a good life without the protection of a state—at least not in the modern, industrialized
world. Even in the absence of ethnic and cultural divisions a state thus
seems necessary. In the historical past there are however examples of
successful statelessness. Medieval Iceland, which is the subject of the next
section, is a particularly interesting case.

Before turning to that it should however just be added that there
are also interesting differences between Liberia and Yugoslavia. Most
important is perhaps that Liberia, after the period of statelessness, again
became a state with the same territory as the old one, while Yugoslavia
was divided into seven new states.

MEDIEVAL ICELAND

The statelessness in medieval Iceland was virginal since there had not
been any state there before, but it was not therefore institutionally minimal. On the contrary there was a sophisticated legal system, a kind of well
developed civil law system.[703] The society came into existence by emigra-

tion from Norway during the ninth century when Iceland, for all practical purposes, was uninhabited. The main reason was the increasingly high taxation in Norway instituted by the king Harald Fairhar (circa 850 to circa 930). Here we thus have a case of successful exit from a dictatorship.

The emigrants, from a Viking country, disposed in the beginning of big, sea-worthy ships, but they could not renew their fleet since Iceland's woods were small and soon spent. In due course they therefore rather became dependent on driftwood which could be used only for small boats. The island was however large—with about the same area as Newfoundland—and the first emigrants, settling in different places around the island therefore had plenty of land. From having been sailors they gradually turned to becoming farmers and cattle breeders. But the Icelanders were not only enclosed on their island, they were also remote. And therefore—in the same way as the ancient Egyptians—they were not threatened by external enemies. There was no need for building a defense, or for exhibiting a united front. And, having fled from Harald Fairhair, they did not want a new king.

These were thus the basic conditions for the original Icelanders. The societal problems which could emerge were internal conflicts among themselves, for instance about ownership of land. These problems the Icelanders solved in their very own way, and thereby the utterly special medieval, Icelandic society was created.

In this society there was no central state power, and thus neither any monopoly of violence of the kind normally characterizing a state. So this is my reason for dealing with Iceland in this chapter about statelessness. And since there was no state there was no criminal law. Anyone having some kind of dispute with his neighbor could for instance, without any penalty, murder this neighbor—at least without any penalty executed by "society". But this did not, of course, prevent the relatives of the murdered from intervening and murder the murderer or someone close to the murderer. Blood feuds of this kind were not uncommon, but in the long run naturally quite unpleasant. Therefore a civil law developed, a law which those in dispute could use if so they wanted, and this law gradually became more sophisticated and more complicated.

---

[703] This section is almost entirely based on Byock.

I will return to this civil law, but to begin at the beginning the first Icelanders created local "things" around the island. These things, finally around 40 of them, had however, in spite of being local, no sharp, geographical boundaries. They rather consisted of a strong individual, a chief, and a number of free settlers being his associates. In reality these things therefore were kinds of associations in which the chair-man and the members were mutually dependent on each other. The chair-man, or the chief, benefitted from the members, or the settlers, since they made him stronger, and the members benefitted from the chair-man since they, by being kept together by him, did not have to act alone. But this likening of the things to associations also implies that all settlers, if so they wanted, were free to remain totally outside, and some of them did so—perhaps mostly those living very remotely. The association comparison also entails that the settlers, again if they wanted, could shift their membership from one thing to another, and this also happened. And this explains the things' lack of sharp, geographic borderlines—members of different things could live mixed with each other, and also did so to some extent.

But still, and on the whole, the members of the same association, or thing, lived fairly close to each other, and the associations, or things, also met regularly a few times a year. In addition to these local things there also was—from 930—an Althing, common to all the things on the whole island. The Althing met in the summer when, at these northern latitudes, there was daylight all the day and night around, and it eventually developed into a great, national, social festival. The chiefs of the local things went there and were often also accompanied by many of their own free settlers—their association members. But even if the Althing was a popular festival, it was not a democratic institution. Its foremost agency—the legislative or law council, of which only chiefs from the local things could be members—instituted new laws. And the laws instituted were always civil, never criminal. Neither was there any central power holder—a king, or a president, or anything like that. The closest to anything like this was the law-speaker, who should know all existing law by heart and, when asked to do so, read the passages requested. Courts of law were also founded.

After this we may now return to the civil law system. Even if blood feuds and the like not were illegal, they were nevertheless troublesome. The Icelanders therefore developed a culture in which reasoning between conflicting parties, and arrival at settlements, became more and more common. In those contexts the things under their chiefs played important roles. An individual being party to some conflict could start by contacting his chief. If the other party, or parties, to the conflict belonged to the same thing the chief could perhaps settle it directly by using his authority, and by perhaps also referring to some relevant passage in the law. If the other party to the conflict rather belonged to another thing, the chief could contact the chief of this other thing in order to get a solution. Procedures like these, settlements without the use of any court, became gradually more common. But even so, the parties could still fail to reach an agreement in this way and if so they could turn to a court, either locally or at the Althing. Both procedures, private settlements and court settlements, also resulted in a growing number of decided cases, or precedents, and thereby in a more and more developed and extensive civil law.[704]

Well, in its broad outlines, that is what medieval Iceland looked like. There was no state but in spite of that there was no war of all against all as in Hobbes' Leviathan. On the contrary a considerable degree of order was upheld. In the local things, similar to associations, the chiefs and the ordinary settlers were important for each other in a way somewhat resembling the relationships between the war lords and their subjects in China between the two World Wars (see chapter 3). And when other issues than legal ones became urgent—for instance relating to the creation of new infrastructure—the chiefs concerned could discuss the matters with each other and agree on common solutions; since the chiefs were few the logic of collective action did not raise any obstacles. Finally, and since there were no external enemies, a need for a common, central national leadership was never felt. And it all worked quite well.

SUMMARY

This chapter starts with a distinction between statelessness before the creation of states and statelessness after state collapses. About the former, also called virginal statelessness, not much is known, among others since it now long since any conditions like that existed. It is how-

---

[704] An interesting and penetrating analysis of this legal system can be found in Friedman, pp. 263-7. While mentioning Friedman's book I cannot resist the temptation to quote its wonderful opening sentence. It goes like this: "If there were only one man in the world, he would have a lot of problems, but none of them would be legal ones."

ever conceivable that this kind of stateless sometimes could have been quite tolerable.

The statelessness after a state collapse is however almost certainly a most horrible condition. The reason is that all the means of violence of the prior state are there, but no longer monopolized. This kind of conditions have appeared again and again as long as there have been states, from the very first ones into our own time. Several of the intervals in figure 1 in chapter 2, for instance between the Egyptian kingdoms or the Chinese dynasties, were at least to some extent of this kind. A much later example is Germany during the Thirty Years' War. And in the present world there are a number of cases mentioned in the section "Failed states" in the Appendix.

After a general description, and in order to make matters more precise, two recent examples are described in more detail. The one is Liberia and the other Yugoslavia.

The chapter finishes with a description of a very peculiar kind of statelessness, namely that of medieval Iceland. There was no state there, but still it was a highly organized society. Successively an increasingly detailed and sophisticated civil law was developed and applied. A prerequisite for this very strange, and possibly unique, order was the state's complete lack of external enemies. So that reason, otherwise almost omnipresent, for acquiring state controlled means of violence was absent.

12

THE ROLE OF IDEAS

IDEALIST AND MATERIALIST CONCEPTIONS OF HISTORY

Now, when this book is approaching its end, the reader perhaps thinks that I have written very little, and perhaps much too little, about religion and religious ideas, and even about other ideas, for instance philosophical ones. Other presentations of similar subjects usually include quite extensive accounts of ideas of various kinds and also give them important explanatory roles. The economist John Maynard Keynes (1883–1946) once expressed this idea about ideas in a very pregnant way. In his great work "The General Theory of Employment, Interest and Money" he wrote:[705]

> "The ideas of economists and political philosophers, both when they are right and when they are wrong, are more powerful than is commonly understood. Indeed the world is ruled by little else. Practical men, who believe themselves to be quite exempt from any intellectual influences, are usually the slaves of some defunct economist. Madmen in authority, who hear voices in the air, are distilling their frenzy from some academic scribbler of a few years back. I am sure that the power of vested interests is vastly exaggerated compared with the gradual encroachment of ideas."

The role of ideas as important causes of change is thus emphatically underlined, and this view is often called *the idealist conception of history*. Opposed to this there is however a completely different view called *the materialist conception of history*, of which the most prominent advocates are Karl Marx and Friedrich Engels. Engels, for instance, wrote that:[706]

> "The materialist conception of history starts from the principle that production, and with production the exchange of its products, is the

---

[705] The quotation is taken from Heilbronner, p. 14.
[706] Even this quotation is from Heilbronner, p. 144.

basis of every social order; that in every society that has appeared in history the distribution of the products, and with it the division of society into classes or estates, is determined by what is produced and how it is produced, and how the product is exchanged. According to this conception, the ultimate causes of all social changes and political revolutions are to be sought, not in the minds of men, in their increasing insight into eternal truth and justice, but in changes in the mode of production and exchange; they are to be sought not in the philosophy but in the economics of the epoch concerned."

Here the whole view is thus turned around. It is not, as with the idealist conception, the ideas which form the material conditions, but rather the material conditions which give rise to the ideas.

Now it may of course be argued that both positions are extreme. Could not the truth be somewhere in between? Could it not be the case that ideas in some contexts are important, and that material conditions in other situations are what matters? So it could be, and certainly also is. But before continuing along that track I think it is important to realize that there are many kinds of ideas, and that therefore it is important to distinguish between ideas and ideas. Thus Isaac Newton developed ideas within physics and mathematics and obviously these ideas, as well as lots of other ideas developed within the sciences, have been of utmost importance. They have, among other things, been of crucial importance for the improvement of the material living conditions of human beings. Denying this is just impossible. Human thinking is of fundamental importance and has been so all through man's history.[707] That the steppe people who long ago developed the spoked wheel were thinking, and that this thinking was enormously consequential, goes without saying. The wheel did not appear by itself, prior to thinking. But having said that we may look in somewhat more detail at the ideas which are of particular importance here in this book.

I then think especially about two kinds of ideas. The one is ideas about the structuring of state institutions, or rather about constitutional matters. Obviously there are many such ideas, and often they are concerned with the nature of the good state. The question is how these ideas emerged. What came first, the states or the ideas about them? The other

---

[707] For an extreme development and articulation of this position see Deutsch.

kind of ideas are the religious ones. How did they emerge, and what is their relevance for the topics discussed in this book?

CONSTITUTIONAL IDEAS

SUPPORT FOR THE MATERIALIST CONCEPTION

Some of the constitutional ideas presented in this book have emerged in ways which lend support to the materialist conception, whereas other ones, rather, lend support to the idealist approach. I start with the former, and the most important example there is the emergence of representative democracy and the philosophical ideas developed in that context. Above all the philosophers Thomas Hobbes (1588–1679) and John Locke (1632–1704) are interesting, and I will start with Hobbes.

In his work Leviathan, published in 1651, Hobbes endorsed autocracy or dictatorship. At that time England had been plagued by civil war since 1642 and Cromwell was well on the way of making himself dictator. Against this background it is easy to think of Hobbes' ideas as an interpretation of the reality surrounding him. If so the civil war was the chaotic state of nature described in his book, and Cromwell the unifying power which, in the same way as the Old Testament sea monster Leviathan, could bring peace and order. Continuing then with John Locke his great work "Two Treatises of Government" was published in 1689, or barely forty years after Hobbes' Leviathan. But in spite of this very short time much had happened in England. The civil war had come to an end, Cromwell had died, and the Glorious Revolution in 1688 had taken place. After Cromwell's dictatorship an order in which the king and the parliament shared power had followed, and Locke's great contribution consisted in his analysis and interpretation of this system, in his vital defense of it, and in his pushing for further development in the same direction. This, of course, was a very important contribution. But still it was the case, on the whole, that reality came first and the ideas followed suit. Also Locke interpreted the reality in which he lived. To really stress the argument one could even guess that Locke, if he had lived at Hobbes' time, would have written as Hobbes, and that Hobbes, conversely, would have written as Locke if he had lived in Locke's time. The thought does not seem unreasonable.

Locke's contribution was thus important since he influenced the development of ideas which followed the institutional development.

When once the original institutions, due to circumstantial mechanisms, had emerged, the analysis of these institutions, and the ideas resulting from this analysis, were of great importance for the further development of the institutions. An important part of this continued process was Montesquieu's great work "The Spirit of the Laws", which was published in 1748, and in which the doctrine of separation of powers was elaborately presented and defended. The work was inspired not only by Locke, but also by the impressions the author had received while visiting England in his youth. And, taking a step still further forward in time, the US constitution was obviously a result of intensive and extensive thinking. Those who thought, and thereafter created the constitution, were The Founding Fathers, and among them above all James Madison. But while stating that it is also important to note that these men knew about the English evolution and had read their Locke. Their contribution, however important, therefore essentially consisted in modifications of the English system which, in turn, was not a result of thinking, but rather something which, step by step, had emerged as a result of circumstances.

Representative democracy thus emerged as a result of a series of lucky coincidences, but at an early stage this development was interpreted by philosophers and the resulting ideas were of great importance for the further development of the institutions. And this is not the only process of this kind—a process in which reality comes first and the ideas follow suit. When Plato wrote his great work "The Republic" the Athenian direct democracy had existed for a long time as well as the Spartan oligarchy, and Athens, in its conflict with Sparta, had become the weaker state. And that was the situation in which Plato formed his anti-democratic ideas. He contended that Sparta's constitutional order was better than that of Athens. Plato interpreted the prevailing situation. Going then to another of the great political scientists, Niccolò Machiavelli, we will find a similar pattern. Machiavelli thought highly of the powerful kings and their kingdoms and criticized the small city-states of his own time, which not only fought each other but also regularly used the mercenaries which he so strongly disapproved of. This was, again, a retrospective interpretation of an already existing, real situation. If we then take one more long step forwards in time, and also abandon constitutional matters in order to turn to economic and other more general social conditions, the market economy was well developed when Adam Smith published his epoch-making work "The Wealth of Nations" in 1776. He described, analyzed and interpreted the reality in which he lived. And to end with the front-rank personage of the materialist conception, Karl Marx himself, the same holds true. His great works were inspired by the society of early liberalism and capitalism, in the midst of which he lived.

SUPPORT FOR THE IDEALIST CONCEPTION

But even if reality in many cases has preceded the development of ideas, there are also interesting examples of the opposite—when ideas have come first and thus created the real, material conditions. Solon and Cleisthenes in Athens really seem to have worked out first, in their minds, the functioning of a direct democracy and implemented it thereafter. Certainly it is also true that this was a result of demands of one kind or another from the warring hoplites and that, therefore, it did not come about in isolation. But still it was, in all likelihood, Solon and Cleisthenes who figured out how the soldiers' demands could be satisfied, not the soldiers themselves. In the same way Venice's very interesting and complex constitution seems, to a large extent, to have been devised first and implemented thereafter. The main architect of this constitution was most probably the doge Pietro Gradenigo.

In these cases it is however also important to note that those having had the ideas—Solon, Cleisthenes and Gradenigo and their likes—first and foremost have been power-holders. And it hardly could have been otherwise since a constitution, because of the logic of collective action, must be implemented from above. So even if these power-holders thought very carefully, they were no philosophers. Under no circumstances have they made themselves known as philosophers, and they were even less "academic scribblers" of the kind Keynes wrote about. On the whole I therefore believe that those individuals who really are considered philosophers, and who have philosophized about the properties of the good state, lend more support to the materialist conception of history than to idealist the one. These philosophers have in their thinking, as a rule, started from and analyzed a reality already present.

RELIGIOUS IDEAS

INTRODUCTION

Religious ideas are of a different kind than those about constitutions and state institutions, and certainly they have been important with respect to the issues discussed in this book. Among others many conflicts and wars have religious conflicts as their background or cause. Conflicts followed for instance the splitting of the big religions into gradually more numerous sub-varieties. The original Christianity was first split when the so called orthodox churches within Byzantium were created in opposition to, or as an alternative to, the Christendom in the Western Roman Empire. The latter was then in due course transformed into Catholicism which, in turn, gave rise to protests and thereby to various Protestant churches. The original Muslim movement was also split, in that case into two branches, the Shiites and the Sunnis. Between all of these religious strands conflicts have been frequent and severe and often led to wars. And these religious wars have sometimes been wars between states, sometimes civil wars.

Most interesting here are the latter—the civil wars—since they are related to the religion's relevance for the order or disorder within the individual state. And this aspect is, of course, of utmost importance for the political power-holders. In some cases these may have considered religious ideas as a threat, but in other cases they may rather have considered them a benefit. In some cases both may perhaps have existed simultaneously—some particular religion may have been a benefit, while other competitors rather were threats. Irrespective of whether the religious ideas were considered as benefits or threats the states concerned were however *dependent* on these ideas. And there have been many states like that in the history of the world. Besides all of these states there are however also—and mostly rather late in history—those that have been and are *independent* of religious ideas.

STATES DEPENDENT ON RELIGIOUS IDEAS

Many states in the history of the world have had—and a number of today's states also have—a religion which is closely linked with the state power itself, which is in fact a part of this power. Typical examples are the ancient Egyptian kingdoms. In them, we remember, the pharaohs were considered intermediaries to the gods, or sometimes even as gods themselves. States like that have been numerous in history. To use a distinction with which the reader is familiar by now, it seems likely that the religion in these states came from above, and, to the extent that it spread among ordinary people, also was implemented from above. It need however not always have been like that. A state religion may emerge in other ways.

Religious ideas may thus also grow from below, and have done so several times. In the beginning an individual—perhaps someone eventually becoming known as a religious founder—may develop a faith or a doctrine, a religion, adopt acolytes, and thereby spread the message in increasingly wider circles. Doctrines like this may threaten the power-holders, or at least be considered threatening by them, and these power-holders may then react in various ways. What is most straight-forward is perhaps just to try to crush the adherents to the religion at issue. Christianity in the early Roman Empire is an obvious example. The power-holders considered the more and more numerous Christians—at least in the beginning—as a great problem, and the Christians were therefore persecuted for a long time with extreme harshness. Another example comes from China where the Confucians, in Qin, were treated with enormous brutality.

In both cases the state did however change its attitude towards those formerly persecuted. In the Roman Empire Christendom, starting with the emperor Constantine the Great, was elevated to a state religion. The reason, according to legend, was Constantine's experience of a divine vision, but it is difficult to believe that this was the only reason. Not even a dictator has that much power. It rather seems proper to interpret the promotion of the religion as the adaption of the power to public opinion realities, as a necessary opportunistic measure. The religion was turned from being a threat to the state to being its instrument of power. The religion got, in principle, the same function as in for instance ancient Egypt. And in China something similar also happened. Long after Qin, and in particular during Song in the beginning of the eleventh century, Confucianism was raised to the position of a state religion.[708] Or perhaps rather state ideology, since Confucianism was more of a moral code than a real religion.

In these cases an originally small religion or movement has thus grown, in due course become considered as threatening, and finally became adopted by the state as a constituent of this state itself. But this does not necessarily mean that the ideas as such have been of much impor-

---

[708] Finer (1997a), pp. 28-30, 514-5.

tance. The very great stability of the Chinese societies over a long period testifies, in particular, to such a limited role of the ideas. During two thousand years the structure of this society was about the same, before as well as after the elevation of Confucianism to state ideology. A reasonable interpretation of the elevation—and here I argue in the same way as in the Roman case—is that it was an opportunistic, political, measure undertaken by the power-holders. When those having the ideas no longer were persecuted, but rather were turned into a kind of honorary subjects, the central power's conditions for maintaining the established order improved considerably. It is, in the context, easy to bring to mind Karl Marx's saying about religion as "opium of the masses".

Islam is interesting among other things because of its special history of emergence, by its growing simultaneously from above and from below. The adherents to this religion were never a small, suppressed minority, but on the contrary immediately successful when following the founder of the religion, and the skilful military commander, Muhammad. After him a number of states having Islam as state religion were created. First out was the Caliphate, then came the Ottoman Empire, and thereafter a long series of states, for instance the Arab states of our own time. That we are dealing with state religions here is made clear already by the fact that the religious and political leaders are very close to each other, or sometimes even the same. Characteristic for these states is also that the laws or the law—the so called Sharia law—is taken directly from the original religious documents.

States with an established state religion of the kind described can hardly be anything but dictatorships. It is obviously difficult to combine lack of religious freedom with freedom in other areas, for instance concerning the establishment of enterprises, of organizations, and so forth. The arguments here are just about the same as the ones for the incompatibility of dictatorship and market economy. As far as I have been able to find out this is also in accordance with reality. I have not found, in the history of the world, any state with an established state religion which has not also been a dictatorship. In today's world there is no other state religion than Islam, and the states having Islam as the state religion are all dictatorships.

But even if states with a state religion are dictatorships, these dictatorships do not, as far as I have been able to find out, differ in any fundamental ways from other dictatorships. The classification of dictatorships which I suggested in chapter 6 is, I contend, valid also for states with a state religion. Among the states existing today Saudi Arabia may for instance be classified as a more or less repressive dynastic dictatorship and Iran as a repressive party dictatorship. In the latter case the Muslim movement has great similarities with a political party, and is in fact also organized in that way. The party Hezbollah—the party of God—participated actively in the Iranian revolution in 1979. And that Libya, with its Sharia law, and until the break-down in 2011, was a repressive military dictatorship goes without saying. States with a state religion do thus, as I see it, fit well into the irreligious classification introduced in chapter 6. Religious state ideologies do not, regarding their functions in the state, differ in any interesting ways from other state ideologies, such as for instance communist or fascist ones. Rather, and in these respects, the similarities are striking, even if the content of the ideologies otherwise, and obviously, may be very different. In this sense religious ideas are therefore of limited interest in the science of the state.

States with a state religion are thus clearly dictatorships, but the reverse, on the contrary, is not necessarily true. A dictatorship seems to be able to tolerate a certain amount religious liberty—the dictator may himself to some extent stipulate where the limiting borders should be drawn. Thus there was, we remember, a certain religious liberty in the Mughal Empire. And nevertheless, and in other respects, the Great Mughals did not lack despotic qualities. But this relative liberty still appears to be an exception. By and large, as it seems, dictatorships lack religious liberty.

STATES INDEPENDENT OF RELIGIOUS IDEAS

I have argued above that a representative democracy is the only kind of state which can harbor a fully developed market economy. In the same way, and with the same arguments, a representative democracy is the only kind of state which is able to deliver an almost complete freedom of religion. The only exception from this rule, in the same way as for enterprises and organizations, is that religious activities directly aiming at attacking or undermining the state cannot be tolerated. The religion must not compete with the state's monopoly of violence. But apart from this religious liberty prevails, and usually this liberty is also, in democratic countries, protected by law. The result is that human beings with different religious beliefs live peacefully together. And the religious practices are private concerns. They do not affect the structuring and functioning of the institutions of the state. The state is in that sense independent of religious ideas. There is no state religion, and there cannot be. Even here, and in this sense, the religious ideas are thus of limited significance.

But this does not make states—and the science of the state—less interesting.

SUMMARY

The chapter starts with the observation that ideas have a much less prominent role in this book than in many other texts about similar matters. Various philosophers are, for instance, usually treated quite extensively. But not so in this book—and why? That is the topic for the chapter.

Ideas can be of very different kinds and the ones singled out as particular interesting here are constitutional ideas and religious ones. About them, and their roles, two very different opinions exist. The one is called the idealist conception of history and the other the materialist conception. The first one basically says that ideas come first and that they, when they have appeared, transform the material world. The second says the opposite, that changes in the material world come first, and that these changes give rise to ideas.

Now, all through this book material matters, and among them in particular means of violence, have been in the forefront. Again and again the fundamental mechanism of change as described in chapter 3 has been used for explaining constitutional alterations. Discontent and rebelliousness among Greek hoplites and Roman legionaries led to the Greek direct democracies and to the Roman Republic. And the emergence, and spread, of representative democracy is similarly, although not identically, explained. Among others the feudal assemblies of knights were of crucial importance. These are just some examples but they all lend support to the materialist conception of history. Material changes come first and then ideas. Philosophers interpret the real world they are living in rather than forming it. Hobbes interpreted his contemporary world and so did Locke, and the same holds true for a lot of other ones known as philosophers. But even so there are exceptions. The ones I mention are the Greek tyrant Cleisthenes and the Venetian doge Gradenigo. They thought out, and implemented, completely new institutions. Their ideas formed reality. But in spite of that they are not recognized as philosophers.

Going then to religious ideas they are certainly important. There have been a lot of religious wars between states and a lot of religious conflicts within states. Since this book is about states and their properties it is the latter kind of conflicts which are of real interest. And for discussing them I make a distinction between states dependent on religious ideas, and those not dependent on such ideas. Those dependent have a state religion, for instance Islam, and no other religions are permitted. But for these states the religiousness of the ideas is not of particular importance. Even if there are enormous differences between religious ideas of various kinds and for instance communist ideas or fascist ideas, their role in the state is quite similar. In all cases, a state which is dependent on any kind of such ideas prohibits all other ideas. In all cases we are dealing with dictatorships.

States independent of religious ideas can, on the contrary, easily tolerate a lot of different religions as well as several different political ideologies. They all have their adherents and antagonists and compete with each other. I have earlier contended that the representative democracy is the only kind of state which can harbor a fully developed market economy. In the same way, and for the same reasons, the representative democracy is the only kind of state which can deliver freedom of religion.

APPENDIX:

THE STATES IN THE PRESENT WORLD

INTRODUCTION

In the present world almost all land areas are covered by, or claimed by, some state, or lie, in a stateless condition, within an area of some failed state (more about that in the section "Failed states" below). The exception is an unclaimed sector in the Antarctica. What above has been called the nationalization of the world has thus almost reached an end. There are also more states in the world than in at least the rather recent past. Following the decolonization after the Second World War a great number of new states emerged, and the same happened after the collapse of the Soviet empire in the 1990th.

Thus, in the present world, there are 195 states.[709] As seen in table 3 (quasi-logarithmic) the size of their populations differ most considerably. The two largest states are China and India with 1361 and 1241 million inhabitants respectively. Then, in the great interval between 512 and 1024 there is no state at all. The third nation, the only one in the next interval, is the US with 318 million inhabitants. Going then to the smallest states (sometimes called microstates)—the 39 ones with populations less than a million—they are to a large extent, though not exclusively, island states in the southern Pacific and in the Caribbean Sea. Since islands can be small, and have non-expandable territories, this seems quite natural.

Obviously it is an important task to classify these contemporary states in some interesting way. At first it should then be said that among them there are no direct democracies, and no oligarchies, in the senses defined earlier in this book. The states are—apart from the failed ones—representative democracies, or dictatorships, or something in between. These intermediate states are quite a large number and they are also very interesting. The ways in which they differ from democracies, and from dictatorships, and from each other, may vary in several ways, and an

---

[709] The main sources for this Appendix are articles in The Economist, reports from Freedom House posted on the Internet, and Wikipedia.

analysis of these matters should be a first rate priority within the political
science discipline.

Table 3: The populations of the present world states

Population in millions	Number of states
0-1	39
1-2	11
2-4	19
4-8	27
8-16	33
16-32	26
32-64	19
64-128	12
128-256	6
256-512	1
512-1024	0
1024-2048	2

Here, following the mode all through the book, I will take an institutional approach. And among institutions a very important one, as we
have seen, is the assembly of representative democracies. Now, when
looking at the contemporary states, one finds that all of them except one,
namely Saudi Arabia, have some kind of assembly at the national level,
more or less representative for sure, but at least superficially similar to
the ones in real representative democracies. This being so it seems possible to start the analysis with an examination of these assemblies. I will
do so and thereby use the scheme presented in figure 18 which will be explained step by step as the reasoning goes on. Already here it should however be noted that the classification to be undertaken concerns only the
present situation and its rather immediate past. Longer term history is
not taken into account. Thus, and for instance, Chile will be considered a
democracy in spite of the former Pinochet dictatorship.

Dictator-ships	Non-dictatorships						
	Exact rules					Not exact rules	
	Rules followed			Rules not followed		States	Failed states
	All elected	Some appoin-ted	Party restric-tions	States	Failed states		
Table 4	Table 5	Table 6	Table 7	Table 8		Table 9	

Figure 18: A classification scheme for the present world states

DICTATORSHIPS

I will start the classification in the non-democratic end. At first we have Saudi Arabia with no national assembly at all. Then there are a number of states with assemblies which are totally void of decision-making power (so called rubber-stamp assemblies), or which have no members elected in a democratic way, or both. These states are listed in table 4.

Table 4: The present dictatorships (the numbers indicate populations in millions)

Azerbaijan, 9	North Korea, 25
Belarus, 9	Oman, 3
Brunei, <1	Qatar, 2
China, 1361	Saudi Arabia, 30
Cuba, 11	Swaziland, 1
Egypt, 86	Thailand, 66
Guinea Bissau, 2	United Arab Emirates, 8
Laos, 7	Vietnam, 90

Now, in order to make things a bit more clear I will shortly describe the nature of the assemblies here. Actually they fall into three groups.

In the first group are the sultanate Brunei and the Arab states Oman, Qatar and the United Arab Emirates. All of them are thus, in the same way as Saudi Arabia, Muslim states. In these states all political parties are forbidden, or all assembly members are appointed from above, or the assembly, according to the constitutional rules, has only advisory capacity, or there is some combination of these characteristics.

In the second group are China, Cuba, Laos, North Korea and Vietnam. These are communist states in which the communist party is the only party permitted and in which all important decisions are taken within the party organs such as the Politburo and the Central Committee. The assembly, the composition of which is furthermore effectively controlled from above, is thus totally lacking power.

In the third group, finally, are Azerbaijan, Belarus, Egypt (after the coup of Abdel Fattah al-Sisi), Guinea Bissau, Swaziland and Thailand (after the military coup in May 2014). On the surface these countries have some similarities with real representative democracies. They are not, for instance, ruled according to one particular faith or ideology as the states in the former two groups. But still the executive, or rather the dictator, has robbed the assembly of all real influence. An example is Alyaksandr Lukashenka in Belarus.

The states in table 4 are, as I see it, the dictatorships of the present world. And, applying my classification of dictatorships in chapter 6, the ones in the first group, the Muslim states, are dynastic dictatorships and those in the second group, the communist ones, party dictatorships. The third group is however more heterogeneous. Azerbaijan could be considered a party dictatorship, Guinea Bissau a military dictatorship and Swaziland a dynastic dictatorship. Belarus is less clear even if the dictatorship has emerged from party politics. So, from that point of view, it could be considered a party dictatorship. And the two new dictatorships, Egypt and Thailand, are clearly military dictatorships.

Summarizing there are, according to this account, 16 dictatorships in the world with a total population of 1710 millions. In the final section of this Appendix, entitled "Discussion", these states will be treated as a separate group.

DEMOCRACIES AND QUASI-DEMOCRACIES

After having looked at 16 dictatorships 179 states remain, the non-dictatorships according to figure 18. A main characteristic of these states, as they are presented here, is that they have some kind of assembly, that this assembly has some real influence, and that at least some its members are democratically elected from below. For clarity it should be noted that if some members of the national assembly are elected by some kind of local assembly, that is also considered democratic as long as the local assembly at issue is democratically elected. The number of houses in the assembly—one or two—will however be of less importance in what follows. Irrespective of this number I will therefore, whenever further details not are required, just talk about the assembly.

But even if there is an assembly with some real power, and some of its members are democratically elected, there is a lot of room for important variations, and this leads to the next distinction in figure 18, the one about rules. The rules I am thinking about (already mentioned in different places in chapter 10) are about the regularity of elections, about the electing and appointing of members of the assembly, about the right to vote, and about the formation of political parties. The distinction is between states having reasonably exact rules of these kinds and states not having that.

The existence of rules does however not necessarily mean that they are followed. They may be more or less disregarded or violated, and this leads to still a distinction as seen in the figure, namely the distinction between states following the rules and those not doing so. Continuing then with the states which actually follow their rules it may be expedient to divide them further. This could certainly be made in different ways but I have settled for a division into three groups. The first group includes the states in which all assembly members are elected democratically and in which the formation of political parties is free. These states are presented in table 5.

In the next group of states some assembly members are appointed from above. This, for instance, holds for the members of the House of Lords in the United Kingdom. The states with constitutions like that are presented in table 6. Most of the states in the table are former British colonies which now belong to the British Commonwealth. Or, to be more specific, this is the case for all the states except Bhutan and Ireland. In Bhutan the king appoints five members of the upper house and in Ireland some members of the upper house are appointed by the prime minister and the rest elected by various interest groups. Since the undemocratic appointments in these cases concern only the upper house it may be noted that an upper house, at least in some cases, have less power than the lower house.

Table 5: States following formal democratic rules without restrictions (the numbers indicate populations in millions)

Andorra, <1	Hungary, 10	Paraguay, 7
Argentina, 40	Iceland, <1	Peru, 30
Australia, 23	India, 1241	Philippines, 99
Austria, 9	Indonesia, 250	Poland, 39
Belgium, 11	Italy, 60	Portugal, 10
Belize, <1	Japan, 127	Romania, 20
Benin, 10	Kiribati, <1	Saint Kitts
Bolivia, 10	Kosovo, 2	and Nevis, <1
Bosnia and	Latvia, 2	Samoa, <1
Herzegovina, 4	Liberia, 4	San Marino, <1
Botswana, 2	Liechtenstein, <1	Senegal, 14
Brazil, 201	Luxembourg, <1	Serbia, 7
Burkina Faso, 17	Macedonia, 2	Seychelles, <1
Cape Verde, <1	Malawi, 16	Sierra Leone, 6
Chile, 17	Malta, <1	Slovakia, 5
Comoros, <1	Marshall	Slovenia, 2
Costa Rica, 5	Islands, <1	Solomon
Croatia, 4	Mauritius, 1	Islands, <1
Cyprus, <1	Mexico, 118	South Africa, 53
Czech Republic, 11	Moldova, 4	South Korea, 50
Denmark, 6	Monaco, <1	Spain, 47
Ecuador, 16	Mongolia, 3	Suriname, <1
El Salvador, 6	Montenegro, <1	Sweden, 10
Estonia, 1	Namibia, 2	Switzerland, 8
Federated States of	Nauru, <1	São Tomé
Micronesia, <1	Netherlands, 17	and Príncipe, <1
Finland, 5	New Zealand, 5	Taiwan, 23
France, 66	Niger, 17	Timor-Leste, 1
Georgia, 4	Norway, 5	Tunisia, 11
Germany, 81	Palau, <1	Turkey, 77
Ghana, 25	Panama, 3	Tuvalu, <1
Greece, 11	Papua New	United States, 318
Guyana, <1	Guinea, 7	Uruguay, 3
		Vanuatu, <1

In the third group of states the formation of parties is not completely free—some parties, or kinds of parties, are prohibited. Only parties which are extreme in one way or another may however be prohibited, and the prohibition rules must also be reasonably exact. If this is not so, the state at issue will be classified somewhere else. The states fulfilling the requirements are presented in table 7.

Table 6: State following formal democratic rules, but with some assembly members appointed from above (the numbers indicate populations in millions)

Antigua and Barbuda, <1	Ireland, 5
Bahamas, <1	Lesotho, 2
Barbados, <1	Saint Lucia, <1
Bhutan, <1	Saint Vincent and the Grenadines, <1
Canada, 35	Tonga, <1
Dominica, <1	Trinidad and Tobago, 1
Grenada, <1	United Kingdom, 64

Table 7: States following formal democratic rules, but with some restrictions on party formation (the numbers indicate populations in millions)

Israel, 8
Lithuania, 3
Tanzania, 45

In Israel parties which deny Israel's Jewish character, which oppose the democratic system, and which incite racism are prohibited. In Lithuania the Communist party is prohibited, and in Tanzania parties which are formed on religious, ethnic or regional bases are prohibited as well as parties opposing the union between Zanzibar and the mainland. It should however also be noted that Germany is a border case here. There parties which do not adhere to the democratic foundations of the German state can be abolished by the constitutional court.

The tables 5, 6 and 7 include, I contend, all democracies in the world, but still there are also states in those tables which cannot be considered democracies, the quasi-democracies. This is so since the criteria used are necessary but not sufficient conditions for democracy. Or, to be more specific, there are basically two reasons why the states can fail as democracies.

First I have only dealt with institutional matters in a rather narrow sense. And therefore some of the states in the tables may very well be characterized by corruption and/or by limited mass media freedom to such an extent that they cannot be considered democracies. The only thing important for the classification so far is the methods used, in a rather limited sense, for selecting the members of the assembly. The reason for this restriction is however not, which should be emphasized, that corruption and other inadequacies are considered unimportant. On the contrary they are of course utterly important. The reason for the restriction is rather an ambition to start with purely institutional properties in order to, hopefully, make it possible to arrive at hypotheses about correlations between these properties and other less institutional characters later on. In that way, I think, it will be easier to achieve a theoretical understanding of the causal mechanisms behind state structures than if all factors were included from the beginning.

Second, even when considering institutional matters I have been somewhat limited—I have only taken into account the rules for forming the assembly. Non-democratic traits may however be introduced by other rules, or by breaking of other rules, and for this reason I consider the following states in the lists as quasi-democratic.

Andorra is considered quasi-democratic because of the (although mostly symbolic) influence of France and Spain in its governmental affairs. Burkina Faso is categorized similarly because of manipulation of the latest presidential election. And Lichtenstein and Monaco are considered quasi-democratic because of the not negligible power of the monarch. In Monaco France also has some influence.

Now, taking away these four states (from the tables 5, 6 and 7) leaves us with altogether 106 states with a total population of 3467 millions. In the final section of this Appendix these 106 states will be treated as a separate group. And the same is the case for the four exceptions with a total population of 17 millions.

NON-DEMOCRATIC STATES OF TWO KINDS

THE FIRST KIND

After this we get to the states not even fulfilling our necessary conditions for democracy. There are two kinds of states like this. First, and still following the presentation in figure 18, there are the states which have the same kind of rather exact rules as those in the tables 5, 6 and 7 but in which these rules, in one way or another, are disregarded or violated.[710] These are the states presented in table 8. The table includes altogether 46 states but four of these, namely the Central African Republic, the Ivory Coast, Sudan and Ukraine, will later on be classified as failed states, and therefore just the remaining 42 are taken into account here. Altogether they have a population of 1275 millions, and they will be treated as a separate group in the final "Discussion" section.

Table 8: States violating their formally democratic rules (the numbers indicate populations in millions)

Albania, 3	Ethiopia, 87	Republic of the
Angola, 21	Fiji, <1	Congo, 4
Armenia, 3	Gabon, 2	Russia, 144
Bangladesh, 153	Guatemala, 15	Rwanda, 11
Bulgaria, 7	Guinea, 11	Singapore, 5
Burundi, 10	Haiti, 10	Sri Lanka, 20
Cameroon, 20	Honduras, 9	Sudan, 38
Central African	Ivory Coast, 23	Tajikistan, 8
Republic, 5	Jamaica, 3	Togo, 6
Chad, 13	Kenya, 44	Turkmenistan, 5
Colombia, 47	Kyrgyzstan, 6	Uganda, 35
Democratic Republic	Madagascar, 21	Ukraine, 45
of the Congo, 68	Malaysia, 30	Uzbekistan, 30
Djibouti, <1	Maldives, <1	Venezuela, 29
Dominican	Mauritania, 3	Zambia, 15
Republic, 9	Nicaragua, 6	
Equatorial	Nigeria, 174	
Guinea, 2	Pakistan, 186	

THE SECOND KIND

The second kind of non-democratic states differ still more from those in the tables 5, 6 and 7. As shown in figure 18 they do not have any exact rules at all, at least no such rules as those characterizing the states in the tables 5, 6 and 7. If they have any rules they are of some other character.

---

[710] A flagrant violation is the slaughtering, or ethnical cleansing in fact, in Rwanda in 1994. At least 800 000 Tutsis were killed by militants from the majority Hutu people.

And the rules they have may also be disregarded, in some cases flagrantly so. These states are presented in table 9.

Table 9: States with other kinds of rules, followed or violated (the numbers indicate populations in millions)

Afghanistan, 26	Kazakhstan, 17
Algeria, 39	Kuwait, 3
Bahrain, 1	Lebanon, 5
Cambodia, 15	Mali, 15
Eritrea, 6	Morocco, 33
Gambia, 2	Mozambique, 24
Iran, 77	Myanmar, 53
Iraq, 34	Nepal, 26
Jordan, 7	Yemen, 25
	Zimbabwe, 13

Here, in somewhat more detail, are the reasons for considering the states being of this kind. In Afghanistan political parties could be denied registration on vague, or, according to one source, even "flimsy", grounds. In Algeria political parties must be approved by the executive before being able to operate legally. In Bahrain no political parties at all are allowed. In Cambodia representatives of opposition political parties are harassed, sometimes jailed, on unclear grounds—in practice there is thus a restriction on the formation of parties without "exact" rules. In Eritrea, although the constitution aims at "political pluralism", there is only one legal party (the state, therefore, should perhaps be considered a dictatorship). In Gambia, and in Iran, the situation is similar to the one in Cambodia—in practice there is a restriction on party formation but without exact rules. And the same holds true for Iraq even if there is also an exact rule, namely the banning of the Baath party. In Jordan there are restrictions on the formation of political parties but they are vague and inexact and the same is the case in Kazakhstan. In Kuwait political parties are banned altogether. Lebanon has a very particular constitution distributing power between the countries main religious groups. Mali is now in a transitional phase in the aftermath of a military coup in 2012. In Morocco various religious parties are harassed and banned for non-precise reasons. In Mozambique religious and ethnic parties are similarly banned. In Myanmar the formation of parties is subject to unclear restrictions. Nepal, after having had a constitution banning ethnical parties, is now in a transitional phase with an interim constitution. In Yemen elections have been upheld for so long that it is impossible to put the state into table 8. In Zimbabwe, finally, manipulation of election days in various ways has been so systematic and serious that a classification in table 8 hardly is possible, and the outright killing of hundreds of human beings in the opposition strongly underlines this assessment. This is much more than a simple violation of rules.

Even in this group of states, the ones in table 9, there are however some states which I consider failed, namely Afghanistan, Iraq, Lebanon, Mali, Nepal and Yemen. When they are taken away a group of 13 states with a total population of 290 millions remains. These will be treated as a separate group in the final "Discussion" section.

FAILED STATES

The failed states are characterized either by statelessness as described in chapter 11, or plagued by severe civil war, or by a lack of control of considerable parts of their own territory. They are thus failed in the sense that they do not enjoy, or exercise, a monopoly of violence. The present states which can, as I see it, be considered failed in this sense are listed in table 10. A first comment is that most of these states—though not all—were, as already remarked, preliminarily listed in the tables 8 and 9. The reason for this was their constitutional properties. But still they have failed and so they are put into table 10. Some of the states in table 10 have however not appeared in any table before, namely Libya, Somalia, South Sudan and Syria. The reason is that they hardly have any constitutions at all.

Table 10: Failed states (the numbers indicate populations in millions)

Afghanistan, 26	Mali, 15
Central African Republic, 5	Nepal, 26
	Somalia, 10
Iraq, 34	South Sudan, 11
Ivory Coast, 23	Sudan, 38
Lebanon, 5	Syria, 22
Libya, 6	Ukraine, 45
	Yemen, 25

Here are, in more detail but still briefly put, the reasons for considering the states failed. In Afghanistan large areas in the southern part of the country are controlled by Taliban warriors. In the Central African Republic a horrible civil war is going on. In Iraq the Shia government has lost control not only over Kurdish areas but also over considerable Sunni parts of the country. And in addition to this the Islamic State (ISIS) has also penetrated some areas. In the Ivory Coast the government in the Christian southern part of the country has only limited control over the Muslim northern part. In Lebanon the government fails in controlling the powerful Shia militia Hezbollah. In Libya no central government has been established after the Arab Spring and the death of Gadaffi. In Mali the government has lost control over the vast northern part of the country where Tuareg rebels and al-Qaeda terrorists are ravaging. Nepal is severely divided between a China-oriented north and an India-oriented south. Somalia has since long been plagued by severe internal conflicts and civil war. South Sudan, the latest new state in the world, is engaged in severe conflicts with Sudan and has not yet succeeded in establishing a government of its own. The government of Sudan lacks control over important border areas, among others, but not only, Darfur. In Syria a horrible civil war in the aftermath of the Arab spring is going on, and ISIS has also intervened. In Ukraine the government has lost control over some eastern parts of the country including Crimea. Yemen is, among others, severely plagued by al-Qaeda jihadists.

DISCUSSION

Table 11 presents the states in the groups resulting from the discussion so far. The groups are ordered according to their degree of democracy. First come the "Democracies and quasi-democracies". Then come the intermediary groups in what I consider as their "democratic" order, and after them dictatorships. And so, finally, after these real states come the failed ones.

At first it should be noted that the classification is preliminary, just a start. In the preceding text I have already pointed at some borderline cases and certainly there may be more such ones. One reason for this is that the criteria used for the classification, as presented in figure 18, also are preliminary and certainly could be made more precise in further investigations. But even so it should be emphasized that the criteria used here, even in this preliminary version, are institutional. This is important and makes the classification procedure used here another one than those common in various kinds of democracy- or transparency-indexes. These latter ones are usually more "sociological" (based for instance on expert interviews). That may certainly be good from some points of view, but equally certainly the institutional approach also has its advantages. Basically, I think, that this approach is necessary for being able to arrive, finally, at real explanations rather than correlations. So even if the criteria used here can and should be developed further in future studies I think it is important that their institutional character remains.

Table 11: A classification of the present states in the world

Group	Number of states	Total population, millions
Democracies and quasi-democracies	106	3 467
First intermediary group	4	17
Second intermediary group	42	1 275
Third intermediary group	13	290
Dictatorships	16	1 710
Failed states	14	291
Sum	195	7 050

Table 11 is thus preliminary but even so it can be used for formulating a number of interesting political science tasks or problems. A first one, which in fact concerns the whole table, is about the almost omnipresence of assemblies—only Saudi Arabia is excluded. Why have they been created in all those states which are not democracies? Which have the intentions of those having created them been?

Turning then to the group named "Democracies and quasi-democracies" it certainly should be further divided. A main point is that corruption and/or restrictions on mass media in some of these states are so widespread that they must be called quasi-democracies. Another that young democracies may be more unstable and vulnerable than more established ones, and that the new ones therefore deserve particular interest. In a further analysis some of these states should rather be put in some intermediary group. Many of the states in the group are however full, well working democracies. But since these are dealt with in chapter 10, and in particular in the section "A theory about democracies of different kinds", I leave them here.

Going then to the intermediary groups the really interesting ones are the second and the third. The states in the first of these groups are, with the possible exception of Burkina Faso, small and hardly of general interest. But it may also be the case that Burkina Faso, in a more subtle or appropriate classification, should be put to the second intermediary group.

These intermediary groups, the second and the third, include many states and a large part of the world population, and are of utmost political science interest. Since institutions in this book are considered important for the forming of incentives, I will start in that end. Obviously not only the incentives of those at the top are influenced but also the incentives of ordinary citizens or subjects. Thus, when some kind of pseudo-democratic institutional order prevails, as in these intermediate states, various kinds of protest movements, or rebellions, may very well be more severe, and include greater masses, than in more authoritarian states. Two kinds of conflicts are, I think, particularly important here.

First we have conflicts, which may be continuous, outdrawn and long-lasting, between those at the top and the many below. The former ones strive for a more authoritarian order, the latter ones for a more democratic order. And thus the fundamental mechanism of change (described in chapter 3) may operate even if perhaps very slowly. The other kind of conflict, which also seems to be quite common, is between various population groups—either between various tribes, as in particular in Africa, or between different religious groups. And these two kinds of conflicts can, in some states, obviously be present simultaneously. A description of these patterns should be a first rate political science priority.

Breaking of rules, or perhaps lack of precise rules, are also common characteristics for the states at issue here. But even so the means used for rule-breaking and manipulation may be of different kinds such as vote-rigging, vote-buying, and in particular vote-buying in collaboration with criminal gangs (Jamaica), inadequate registering of voters, harassment of opponents, use of private armies (the Philippines), "oathing" to vote only for their own tribe (Kenya), and so forth. Describing these methods in more detail, and classifying them, is also an important political science task.

But even if the second and third intermediate groups have some common properties they also seem to differ in some interesting ways. A hypothesis thus is that the authors of the constitutions in many of the states in the second intermediary group (table 8) may have had some kind of democratic ambition, whereas for the states in third group (table 9) that is much less likely. It is also interesting to look at the failed states with some kind of constitutional structure. All of these states were classified either in table 8 or table 9. Those from table 9 are however clearly more numerous, and this is so in spite of the fact that the number of states in table 9 is considerably smaller than the number in table 8. This certainly makes the third intermediary group still more interesting.

About the dictatorships I will not say anything here since they are extensively dealt with in chapter 6. I will rather finish with the issue of corruption, and that of lack of freedom of mass media. These phenomena may be present always and everywhere, but still the frequency may vary. The hypothesis here is that the frequency is lowest among the states in the first group (those at the democratic end), then successively higher in the states in the intermediary groups, and, finally, highest in the dictatorships. A problem however is that when we move along the groups of states in the direction indicated—from democracies to dictatorships—it becomes increasingly difficult to define corruption. What is corrupt? From whose point of view is it corrupt?

SUMMARY AND CONCLUSION

I think it is fair to say that political science so far has concentrated on democracy and democracies even if it is true that the interest for systematic studies of dictatorships has increased in later years. But then there are also the large number of states, in which a considerable part of the contemporary world's population lives, which are neither democracies nor dictatorships but something in between. These intermediary states, and their institutions, merit, I contend, much more systematic interest from political scientists. And then I am not talking about studies focusing on individual countries or areas, but about comparative and, to the extent possible, generalizing social science. In this Appendix I have tried to indicate some possible ways for pursuing such studies.

REFERENCES

Acemoglu, Daron & Robinson, James A. (2012), *Why Nations Fail—The Origins of Power, Prosperity, and Poverty*. Random House, Inc., New York.

Alesina, Alberto & Spolaore, Enrico (2003), *The Size of Nations*. The MIT Press, Cambridge, Massachusetts.

Anthony, David W. (2007), *The Horse, The Wheel and Language—How Bronze-Age Riders from the Eurasian Steppes Shaped the Modern World*. Princeton University Press, Princeton.

Arrow, Kenneth J. (1951), *Social Choice and Individual Values*. Yale University Press, New Haven, London.

Bard, Kathryn A. (2000), *The Emergence of the Egyptian State*, in Shaw, Ian (ed.) *The Oxford History of Ancient Egypt*. Oxford University Press, Oxford, New York.

Basham, A. L. (1980), *Early Imperial India*, in Cotterell, Arthur (ed.), *The Penguin Encyclopedia of Ancient Civilizations*. Penguin Books.

Bealey, Frank (1999), *The Blackwell Dictionary of Political Science*. Blackwell Publishers, Oxford.

Beck, Paul Allen (1997), *Party Politics in America*. Longman, New York.

Benson, Bruce L. (1990), *The Enterprise of Law—Justice Without the State*. Pacific Research Institute for Public Policy, San Francisco.

Bernal, Ignacio (1980), *The Olmecs*, in Cotterell, Arthur (ed.) *The Penguin Encyclopedia of Ancient Civilizations*. Penguin Books.

Bertman, Stephen (2003), *Handbook to Life in Ancient Mesopotamia*. Oxford University Press, Oxford.

Black, Duncan (1948), *On the Rationale of Group Decision Making*. Journal of Political Economy, February 1948.

Black, Duncan (1958), *The Theory of Committees and Elections*. Cambridge University Press, Cambridge.

Bloch, Marc (1962), *Feudal Society—The Growth of Ties of Dependence*. Routledge.

Bogdanor, Vernon (ed.) (1991), *The Blackwell Encyclopedia of Political Science*. Blackwell, Oxford.

Brewer, Douglas J. & Teeter, Emily (2007), *Egypt and the Egyptians*. Cambridge University Press, Cambridge.

Browning, Robert (1980), *The Later Roman Empire*, in Cotterell, Arthur (ed.), *The Penguin Encyclopedia of Ancient Civilizations*. Penguin Books.

Buchanan, James M. & Tullock, Gordon (1962), *The Calculus of Consent*. The University of Michigan Press.

Buchanan, James M. (1965), *An Economic Theory of Clubs*. Economica, February 1965.

Burrow, T. (1980), *The Aryan Invasion of India*, in Cotterell, Arthur (ed.), *The Penguin Encyclopedia of Ancient Civilizations*. Penguin Books.

Byock, Jesse L. (2001), *Viking Age Iceland*. Penguin Books, London.

Charlot, Jean & Charlot, Monica (1992), *France*, in Butler, David & Ranney, Austin (ed), *Electioneering—A Comparative Study of Continuity and Change*. Oxford University Press, Oxford.

Chrissanthos, Stefan G. (2008), *Warfare in the Ancient World—From the Bronze Age to the Fall of Rome*. Praeger, Westport, Connecticut, London.

Coase, Ronald H. (1937), *The Nature of the Firm*. Economica, Volume 4.

Coase, Ronald H. (1960), *The Problem of Social Cost*. Journal of Law and Economics, Volume 3.

Conrad, Geoffrey W. (1980), *The Incas*, in Cotterell, Arthur (ed.), *The Penguin Encyclopedia of Ancient Civilizations*. Penguin Books.

Cotterell, Arthur (1980a), *The Indus Civilization*, in Cotterell, Arthur (ed.), *The Penguin Encyclopedia of Ancient Civilizations*. Penguin Books.

Cotterell, Arthur (1980b), *Shang*, in Cotterell, Arthur (ed.), *The Penguin Encyclopedia of Ancient Civilizations*. Penguin Books.

Cotterell, Arthur (1980c), *Chou*, in Cotterell, Arthur (ed.), *The Penguin Encyclopedia of Ancient Civilizations*. Penguin Books.

Cotterell, Arthur (1980d), *Imperial Unification*, in Cotterell, Arthur (ed.), *The Penguin Encyclopedia of Ancient Civilizations*. Penguin Books.

Cotterell, Arthur (1980e), *The Crisis of the Early Empire*, in Cotterell, Arthur (ed.), *The Penguin Encyclopedia of Ancient Civilizations*. Penguin Books.

Coward, Barry (2003), *The Stuart Age—England 1603-1714*. Pearson—Longman, London.

Cox, Gary W. (1987), *The Efficient Secret—The Cabinet and the Development of Political Parties in Victorian England*. Cambridge University Press, Cambridge.

Derry, T. K. & Williams, Trevor I. (1960), *A Short History of Technology—From the Earliest Times to A.D. 1900*. Dover Publications, Inc., New York.

Deutsch, David (2011), The Beginning of Infinity—Explanations that Transform the World. Viking, New York.

Diehl, Richard A. (1980), *The Toltecs*, in Cotterell, Arthur (ed.) *The Penguin Encyclopedia of Ancient Civilizations*. Penguin Books.

Disney, A. R. (2009), *A History of Portugal and the Portuguese Empire—Volume One*. Cambridge University Press, Cambridge.

Downs, Anthony (1957), *An Economic Theory of Democracy*. Harper Collins, New York.

Downs, Anthony (1967), *Inside Bureaucracy*. Harper Collins, New York.

Duverger, Maurice (1964), *Political Parties: Their Organization and Activity in the Modern State*. Wiley, New York.

Eraly, Abraham (2007), *The Mughal World—India's Tainted Paradise*. Phoenix, London.

Fairbank, John King & Goldman, Merle (2006), *China—A New History*. The Belknap Press of Harvard University Press, Cambridge, Massachusetts, London.

Findlay, Ronald & O'Rourke, Kevin H. (2007), *Power and Plenty—Trade, War and the World Economy in the Second Millennium*. Princeton University Press, Princeton, Oxford.

Finer, Samuel E. (1997a), *The History of Government—Volume I, Ancient Monarchies and Empires*. Oxford University Press, Oxford, New York. (Includes the pages 1-610 of the complete work.)

Finer, Samuel E. (1997b), *The History of Government—Volume II, The Intermediate Ages.* Oxford University Press, Oxford, New York. (Includes the pages 611-1061 of the complete work.)

Finer, Samuel E. (1997c), *The History of Government—Volume III, Empires, Monarchies and the Modern State.* Oxford University Press, Oxford, New York. (Includes the pages 1062-1701 of the complete work.)

Finlan, Alastair (2004), *The Collapse of Yugoslavia 1991–1999.* Osprey Publishing.

Friedrich, Carl J. & Brzezinski, Zbigniew K. (1965), *Totalitarian Dictatorship and Autocracy.* Praeger Publishers, New York.

Friedman, David D. (2000), *Law's Order—What Economics has to do with Law and why it Matters.* Princeton University Press, Princeton.

Fukuyama, Francis (2012), *The Origins of Political Order—From Prehuman Times to the French Revolution.* Profile Books, London.

Gascoigne, Bamber (1971), *A Brief History of the Great Moghuls.* Robinson, London.

Gascoigne, Bamber (2003), *A Brief History of the Dynasties of China.* Robinson, London.

Grayson, A.K. (1980a), *Babylonia,* in Cotterell, Arthur (ed.) *The Penguin Encyclopedia of Ancient Civilizations.* Penguin Books.

Grayson, A.K. (1980b), *Assyria,* in Cotterell, Arthur (ed.) *The Penguin Encyclopedia of Ancient Civilizations.* Penguin Books.

Hansen, Mogens Herman (2006), *Polis—An Introduction to the Ancient Greek City-State.* Oxford University Press, Oxford.

Hayek, Friedrich A. (1944), *The Road to Serfdom.* George Routledge & Sons Ltd., London.

Hayek, Friedrich A. (1967), *The Dilemma of Specialization,* in Hayek, *Studies in Philosophy, Politics and Economics.* University of Chicago Press, Chicago.

Heilbronner, Robert L. (1953), *The Worldly Philosophers—The Lives, Times and Ideas of Great Economic Thinkers.* Simon & Schuster, New York.

Herlitz, Nils (1939), *Sweden: A Modern Democracy on Ancient Foundations.* The University of Minnesota Press, Minneapolis.

Herrin, Judith (2008), *Byzantium—The Surprising Life of a Medieval Empire.* Penguin Books, London.

Hicks, John (1969), *A Theory of Economic History.* Oxford University Press.

Hinich, Melvin J. & Munger, Michael C. (1994), *Ideology and the Theory of Political Choice.* The University of Michigan Press, Ann Arbor.

Hinich, Melvin J. & Munger, Michael C. (1997), *Analytical Politics.* Cambridge University Press, Cambridge.

Hirschman, Albert O. (1970), *Exit, Voice and Loyalty—Responses to Decline in Firms, Organizations, and States.* Harvard University Press, Cambridge, Massachusetts.

Hirschman, Albert O. (1995), A *Propensity to Self-Subversion.* Harvard University Press, Cambridge, Massachusetts.

Hobbes, Thomas (1651), *Leviathan.*

Horodowich, Elizabeth (2009), *A Brief History of Venice—A New History of the City and Its People.* Constable & Robinson, London.

Hotelling, Harold (1929), *Stability and Competition.* The Economic Journal, Volume XXXIX.

Jacobsen, Thorkild (1980a), *Sumer,* in Cotterell, Arthur (ed.) *The Penguin Encyclopedia of Ancient Civilizations.* Penguin Books.

Jacobsen, Thorkild (1980b), *Akkad,* in Cotterell, Arthur (ed.) *The Penguin Encyclopedia of Ancient Civilizations.* Penguin Books.

Judt, Tony (2005), *Postwar—A History of Europe since 1945.* Vintage, London.

Kavanagh, Dennis (1996), *British Politics—Continuities and Change.* Oxford University Press, Oxford.

Kent, Neil (2008), *A Concise History of Sweden.* Cambridge University Press, Cambridge.

Key, V. O. (1964), *Politics, Parties and Pressure Groups.* Thomas Y. Crowell Company, New York.

King, Anthony (1997), *Running Scared—Why America's Politicians Campaign Too Much and Govern Too Little*. Free Press, New York.

Kriwaczek, Paul (2010), *Babylon—Mesopotamia and the Birth of Civilization*. Atlantic Books, London.

Lane, Frederic C. (1973), *Venice—A Maritime Republic*. The John Hopkins University Press, Baltimore.

Lane Fox, Robin (2006), *The Classical World—An Epic History of Greece and Rome*. Penguin Books, London.

Lange, Oskar & Taylor, Fred M. (1964), *On the Economic Theory of Socialism—edited and with an introduction by Benjamin E. Lippincott*. McGraw-Hill, New York.

Laver, Michael & Shepsle, Kenneth A. (1994), *Cabinet government in theoretical perspective*, in Laver, Michael & Shepsle, Kenneth A. (ed.) *Cabinet Ministers and Parliamentary Government*. Cambridge University Press, Cambridge.

Lee, Stephen J. (2008), *European Dictatorships, 1945-1945*. Routledge, London, New York.

Leick, Gwendolyn (2001), *Mesopotamia—The Invention of the City*. Penguin Books, London.

Liebeschuetz, Wolfgang (1980), *The Early Roman Empire*, in Cotterell, Arthur (ed.) *The Penguin Encyclopedia of Ancient Civilizations*. Penguin Books.

Lintott, Andrew (1999), *The Constitution of the Roman Republic*. Oxford University Press, Oxford.

Lipset, Seymour Martin (1990), *Continental Divide—The Values and institutions of the United States and Canada*. Routledge, New York.

Macdougall, Doug (2004), *Frozen Earth—The Once and Future Story of Ice Ages*. University of California Press, Berkeley, Los Angeles, London.

Machiavelli, Niccolò (2005), *The Prince*. Oxford World's Classics, Oxford University Press, Oxford.

Manin, Bernard (1997), *The Principles of Representative Government*. Cambridge University Press, Cambridge.

Matthews, John (1988), *Roman Life and Society*, in Boardman, John & Griffin, Jasper & Murray, Oswyn (ed.) *The Oxford History of the Roman World.* Oxford University Press, Oxford.

Mayhew, David R. (1991), *Divided We Govern—Party Control, Lawmaking and Investigations, 1946–1990.* Yale University Press, New Haven.

Mieroop, Mark Van De (2011), *A History of Ancient Egypt.* Wiley-Blackwell.

Mill, John Stuart (1861), Representative Government. Available at Internet.

Millgrom, Paul & Roberts, John (1992), *Economics, Organization and Management.* Prentice-Hall International.

von Mises (1963), *Human Action—A Treatise on Economics.* Fox & Wilkies, San Francisco.

Mitchell, William C. (1984), *Schumpeter and Public Choice, Part I—Precursor to Public Choice?.* Public Choice, Volume 42.

Moberg, Erik (1998), *The Expanding Public Sector—a Threat to Democracy?*, in Eliasson, Gunnar & Karlson, Nils (ed.) *The limits of Government—On Policy Competence and Economic Growth, Papers from the Sixth Conference of the International Joseph A Schumpeter Society in Stockholm.* City University Press, Stockholm.

Moran, Mary H. (2006), *Liberia—The Violence of Democracy.* University of Pennsylvania Press, Philadelphia.

Morris, Ian (2010), *Why the West Rules—For Now, The patterns of history and what they reveal about the future.* Profile Books, London.

Morton, W. Scott & Lewis, Charlton M. (2005), *China—Its History and Culture.* McGraw-Hill, New York.

Nicholson, H. B. (1980), *The Aztecs*, in Cotterell, Arthur (ed.) *The Penguin Encyclopedia of Ancient Civilizations.* Penguin Books.

North, Douglass C. & Thomas, Robert Paul (1973), *The Rise of the Western World.* Cambridge University Press, Cambridge.

North, Douglass C., Wallis, John Joseph & Weingast, Barry R (2009), *Violence and Social Orders—A Conceptual Framework for Interpreting Recorded Human History*. Cambridge University Press, Cambridge.

Nove, Alec (1978), *The Soviet Economic System*. George Allen & Unwin, London.

Ogilvie, R. M. (1980a), *Rome before the Republic*, in Cotterell, Arthur (ed.) *The Penguin Encyclopedia of Ancient Civilizations*. Penguin Books.

Ogilvie, R. M. (1980b), *Republican Rome*, in Cotterell, Arthur (ed.) *The Penguin Encyclopedia of Ancient Civilizations*. Penguin Books.

Olson, Mancur (1965), *The Logic of Collective Action—Public Goods and the Theory of Groups*. Harvard University Press, Cambridge, Massachusetts, London.

Olson, Mancur (1982), *The Rise and Decline of Nations—Economic Growth, Stagflation and Social Rigidities*. Yale University Press, New Haven, London.

Olson, Mancur (2000), *Power and Prosperity—Outgrowing Communist and Capitalist Dictatorships*. Basic Books, New York.

Oppenheimer, Stephen (2003), *Out of Eden—The Peopling of the World*. Constable & Robinson, London.

Palmer, R. R., Colton, Joel & Kramer, Lloyd (2007a), *A History of the Modern World—To 1815*. McGraw-Hill, New York.

Palmer, R. R., Colton, Joel & Kramer, Lloyd (2007b), *A History of the Modern World—Since 1815*. McGraw-Hill, New York.

Persson, Göran (1997), *Den som är satt i skuld är icke fri—Min berättelse om hur Sverige återfick sunda statsfinanser*. Atlas.

Pinker, Steven (2011), *The Better Angels of Our Nature—Why Violence has Declined*. Viking, Penguin Books, London.

Plimer, Ian (2009), *Heaven and Earth—Global Warming: the Missing Science*. Quartet Books, London.

Popper, Karl. R. (1945a), *The Open Society and its Enemies—Volume 1 Plato*. Routledge & Kegan Paul.

Popper, Karl. R. (1945b), *The Open Society and its Enemies—Volume 2 Hegel & Marx*. Routledge & Kegan Paul.

Powell, G. Bingham, Jr. (2000), *Elections as Instruments of Democracy— Majoritarian and Proportional Visions*. Yale University Press, New Haven, London.

Riker, William H. (1962), *The Theory of Political Coalitions*. Yale University Press.

Riker, William H. (1964), *Federalism—Origin, Operation, Significance*. Little, Brown and Company, Boston, Toronto.

Riker, William H. (1983), *Political Theory and the Art of Heresthetics*, in Finifter, Ada W. (ed.), *Political Science: The State of the Discipline*. The American Political Science Association, Washington, D.C.

Riker, William H. (1990), *Political science and rational choice*, in Alt, James E. & Shepsle, Kenneth A. (ed.) *Perspective on positive Political Economy*. Cambridge University Press, Cambridge.

Roberts, J. M. (2007), *The New Penguin History of the World*. Penguin Books.

Rollason, David (2012), *Early Medieval Europe 300–1050—The Birth of the Western Society*. Pearson.

Rosenberg, Nathan & Birdzell, L. E. Jr. (1986), *How the West Grew Rich— The Economic Transformation of the Industrial World*. Basic Books.

Ross, Alf (1952), *Why Democracy?*. Harvard University Press. Cambridge, Massachusetts.

Roux, Georges (1992), *Ancient Iraq*. Penguin Books, London.

Samuelson, Paul A. (1954), The Pure Theory of Public Expenditure. Review of Economics and Statistics, Volume 36.

Samuelson, Paul A. (1955), *Diagrammatic Exposition of a Theory of Public Expenditure*. Review of Economics and Statistics, Volume 36.

Santley, Robert S. (1980), *Teotihuacán*, in Cotterell, Arthur (ed.) *The Penguin Encyclopedia of Ancient Civilizations*. Penguin Books.

Saraiva, José Hermano (1997), *Portugal: a companion history*. Carcanet Press Limited, Manchester.

Sartori, Giovanni (1994), *Comparative Constitutional Engineering—An Inquiry into Structures, Incentives and Outcomes*. MacMillan, Hampshire.

Savory, R. M. (1976), *Law and traditional society*, in Savory R. M. (ed.) *Introduction to Islamic Civilization*. Cambridge University Press, Cambridge.

Schattschneider, Elmer Eric (1942), *Party Government*. Rinehart, New York.

Schumpeter, Joseph A. (1942), *Capitalism, Socialism and Democracy*. Harper Torchbooks, New York.

Schumpeter, Joseph A. (1954), *History of Economic Analysis*. Oxford University Press, New York.

Shugart, Matthew Soberg & Carey, John M. (1992), *Presidents and Assemblies—Constitutional Design and Electoral Dynamics*. Cambridge University Press, Cambridge.

Smith, Adam (1979), *The Wealth of Nations*. Pelican Classics, Harmondsworth, Middlesex.

Spruyt, Hendrik (1994), *The Sovereign State and Its Competitors—An Analysis of Systems Change*. Princeton University Press, Princeton.

Steinberg, Jonathan (1996), *Why Switzerland?*. Cambridge University Press, Cambridge.

Stockton, David (1988), *The Founding of the Empire, in Boardman*, John & Griffin, Jasper & Murray, Oswyn (ed.) *The Oxford History of the Roman World*. Oxford University Press, Oxford.

Thapar, Romila (1966), *A History of India—volume one*. Penguin Books, London.

Tiebout, Charles M. (1956), *A Pure Theory of Local Expenditures*. Journal of Political Economy, October 1956.

Truman, David (1951), *The Governmental Process—Political Interests and Public Opinion*. Alfred A. Knopf, New York.

Tullock, Gordon (1965), *The Politics of Bureaucracy*. University Press of America, New York.

Walters, Collin (1980a), *Ancient Egypt*, in Cotterell, Arthur (ed.) *The Penguin Encyclopedia of Ancient Civilizations*. Penguin Books.

Walters, Collin (1980b), *Early Roman Egypt*, in Cotterell, Arthur (ed.) *The Penguin Encyclopedia of Ancient Civilizations*. Penguin Books.

Watson, Francis (1979), *A Concise History of India*. Thames and Hudson, London.

Wattenberg, Martin P. (1998), *The Decline of American Political Parties, 1952–1996*. Harvard University Press, Cambridge, Massachusetts.

Weber, Max (1946), *Essays in Sociology*. Oxford University Press, New York.

Weinberg, Steven (1993), *Dreams of a Final Theory—The Search for the Fundamental Laws of Nature*. Vintage, London.

Weinberg, Steven (2001), *Facing Up—Science and Its Cultural Adversaries*. Harvard University Press, Cambridge, Massachusetts.

Wiesehöfer, Josef (2001), *Ancient Persia—from 550 BC to 650 AD*. I.B. Tauris Publishers, London, New York.

Wilkinson, Toby (2010), *The Rise and Fall of Ancient Egypt—The History of a Civilization from 3000BC to Cleopatra*. Bloomsbury.

Willetts, R. F. (1980), *The Graeco-Roman City*, in Cotterell, Arthur (ed.) *The Penguin Encyclopedia of Ancient Civilizations*. Penguin Books.

Willey, Gordon R. (1980), *The Maya*, in Cotterell, Arthur (ed.) *The Penguin Encyclopedia of Ancient Civilizations*. Penguin Books.

Wintrobe, Ronald (1998), *The Political Economy of Dictatorship*. Cambridge University Press, Cambridge.

Young, T. Cuyler Jr. (1980), *Persia*, in Cotterell, Arthur (ed.) *The Penguin Encyclopedia of Ancient Civilizations*. Penguin Books.

Zakaria, Fareed (2003), *The Future of Freedom—Liberal Democracy at Home and Abroad*. W. W. Norton & Company, New York, London.

NAME INDEX

www.ingramcontent.com/pod-product-compliance
Lightning Source LLC
Chambersburg PA
CBHW072104270326
41931CB00010B/1460